Palgrave Macmillan Studies in Banking and Financial Institutions

Series Editor
Philip Molyneux, Bangor University, Bangor, UK

The Palgrave Macmillan Studies in Banking and Financial Institutions series is international in orientation and includes studies of banking systems in particular countries or regions as well as contemporary themes such as Islamic Banking, Financial Exclusion, Mergers and Acquisitions, Risk Management, and IT in Banking. The books focus on research and practice and include up to date and innovative studies that cover issues which impact banking systems globally.

Marcelo J. Sheppard Gelsi

Corporate Structure and Banking Resolution

Analysing the Case of Financial Conglomerates

palgrave
macmillan

Marcelo J. Sheppard Gelsi
Universidad de Montevideo
Montevideo, Uruguay

ISSN 2523-336X ISSN 2523-3378 (electronic)
Palgrave Macmillan Studies in Banking and Financial Institutions
ISBN 978-3-031-59947-7 ISBN 978-3-031-59948-4 (eBook)
https://doi.org/10.1007/978-3-031-59948-4

Cover illustration: Alexander Spatari getty images

This Palgrave Macmillan imprint is published by the registered company Springer Nature Switzerland AG
The registered company address is: Gewerbestrasse 11, 6330 Cham, Switzerland

Paper in this product is recyclable.

Foreword by Professor Rosa M. Lastra

When I first met Marcelo J. Sheppard Gelsi as an LLM student at Queen Mary University of London and we started our conversations in the area of financial law and regulation, I quickly realized that I was in the presence of a very fine student; Marcelo Sheppard was already an established scholar in the University of Montevideo in Uruguay before coming London. His unique range of talents: a formidable intellectual capacity, a vast knowledge of the subject, a rigorous analytical mind, an ethos for hard work, managerial skills and a keen spirit to improve himself and always find an answer in the face of any difficulty, were in ample evidence during his PhD studies. Indeed, notwithstanding COVID and the related crises, Marcelo Sheppard under my supervision and that of my colleague and friend, Professor Rodrigo Olivares-Caminal, completed in time his dissertation (no small feat given the challenges of the pandemic) and deservingly sees today his PhD thesis being published by Springer.

The book provides a multi-jurisdictional legal analysis of the regulation of bank-based financial conglomerates. Though clearly anchored in the law, Marcelo Sheppard feels at ease when navigating through history, philosophy, politics and economics. This methodological approach together with the substantive analysis of the subject matter—the examination of the regulatory and corporate structure of a particular type of financial conglomerates, those that have a strong international presence and are bank-based—explains why the book is a distinct contribution to the literature on bank regulation, resolution and governance and why it is destined to become an essential reference for academics, practitioners and policy-makers and for all those that have an interest in financial regulation, business organization and cross-border resolution.

The book draws upon a tripartite classification of financial conglomerates (commercial, structural and regulatory) with emphasis on the 'structural models'. The comparative analysis of the German model of complete integration, the US bank holding company model and the idiosyncratic British model are one of the salient features of the novelty of his study. The book also examines the 'types of capitalism' associated with each model, and in particular how the bank-based financial conglomerates have influenced industry developments in Germany, UK, US and the EU.

Among the many insights of the study, let me highlight the following. The book correctly argues that while there are benefits in universal banking, regulators need to be aware that concentrating financial functions under the same "roof" creates the danger of developing "mammoth entities" which may be potentially difficult to manage, supervise and resolve. This is important also in the light of the consolidation that has taken place following the global financial crisis (and the more recent crisis with Credit Suisse) given that "mammoth entities" are so significant, or so big or so complex, that their potential resolution could lead a to tax-funded bail-out or rescue package. Issues of structure, competition and resolution matter for the future of our financial system.

The book considers the absence of universally accepted definition of what constitutes a financial conglomerate (given differences in terminology across jurisdictions and the lack of harmonization in this area) and, by assessing the cross-sectoral and cross-border dimensions, it provides an updated and comprehensive conceptual framework to address these gaps. Furthermore, the analysis of the "systemic risk lens" introduced in the aftermath of the Global Financial Crisis (GFC) gives a new dimension to the relatively new category (or categories) of SIFIs: systemically important financial institutions.

In the light of the developments in the area of resolution post-GFC, the book also offers elements to understand which strategy is best in planning for and an in implementing resolution, depending upon the level of centralization or decentralization (single point of entry versus multiple point of entry), the retail or wholesale nature of the business, the reliance on branches or subsidiaries and the universal or territorial approach to insolvency.

In addition to his brilliance and ability, Marcelo Sheppard has succeeded as a wonderful family man, bringing up four children with his wife and running a happy home while achieving high accolades in his academic and professional career.

December 2023

Professor Rosa M. Lastra
Sir John Lubbock Chair
in Banking Law
Centre for Commercial Law
Studies
Queen Mary University
of London
London, UK

Foreword by Professor Rodrigo Olivares-Caminal

After the collapse of Lehman Brothers and what is now known as the Great Financial Crisis, the world focused on how to prevent and reduce the severity of future banking crises, ensuring that the taxpayer does not have to bear the price. In doing so, part of the focus has been on international banking groups, especially those with a strong international component and operating across more than one financial industry (i.e. banking, insurance and/or securities), to make sure that they are "resolvable". This is why Dr. Sheppard's book is so important and topical and is the latest contribution to the analysis of bank-based financial conglomerates.

Insolvency law in general and bank resolution law in particular is a powerful driver of commercial law but also financial law more specifically due to the sensitiveness and proneness to runs. It is up to the legislator (or the policymaker when this function has been delegated) to decide how to protect assets, preserve essential functions and eventually how to distribute the pool of assets. Due to our globalized reality, we need to accept that there is no single legislator (or policymaker), so problems can and do occur in cases where international banking groups operate across borders. Moreover, history shows that there is an interrelationship between corporate insolvencies, banking group resolutions and sovereign debt crises, so the analysis of bank-based financial conglomerates is essential to prevent exacerbating the problems if and when they occur.

As discussed in this book, banks are special because they operate on a fractional reserve system. As such, their fragility is exacerbated and just a rumour can cause a bank run. That is why there is an array of tools in place to prevent a banking crisis and eventually—if the unavoidable cannot be avoided—deal with them in the most efficient manner reducing the spread of risk, maintaining essential functions running and minimizing economic costs. The bank resolution framework that was promoted after the Great Financial Crisis tried to provide new tools, putting the onus on prevention and a swifter resolution moving from bailing out to bailing in. It remains to be seen whether these mechanisms will be efficient in another major crisis like the one of 2007-09 and how it addresses asymmetry issues leaving space—unfortunately—for opportunism and inefficient resolutions.

This book has a practical approach with a corporate focus, analysing the three main models of bank-based financial conglomerates (i.e. the German universal approach, the British bank conglomerate model, and the American holding company structure). It is very interesting to revisit Herrig and Santomero's classification of the 1990s and to see how it is still effective and can be followed to analyse the resolution strategies of bank-based financial conglomerates. This book also looks at the motivations and historical foundations to better understand the corporate structures adopted today in each of the models and, the ensuing regulations of each of the jurisdictions of these. Moreover, it looks at how these corporate structures have defined their governance. Finally, it also addresses at how the adopted model by the bank-based financial conglomerates can condition, among other factors, the resolution strategy. I would like to particularly highlight how the historical foundations of each model analysed in this book serve as an explanation to better understand how things have evolved in the way that they did and why nowadays there are these divergent models and rules. The outcome greatly enriches the result.

It was a pleasure to have worked with Dr. Sheppard in the past as co-director of his thesis jointly with my friend and colleague Prof. Rosa Lastra. This work is in part the result of his research and a great contribution to the legal practice. A book on such an important topic could have great relevance in the next crisis. Hopefully the crisis will not happen, but the book will still be of great relevance.

December 2023

Professor Rodrigo
Olivares-Caminal
Centre for Commercial Law
Studies
Queen Mary University
of London
London, UK

Preface

Our actions often carry a significant autobiographical aspect, and this book is no exception. 26 December 2002 was my first day of work at one of the leading law firms in my country. It was quite unusual to be hired on a day after Christmas in the southern hemisphere, when most people take holidays in January. What was happening was that Uruguay was suffering one of the worst banking crises in its history after Argentina's debacle in 2001.

On that day, I was entrusted in a working group tasked with defending three of the world's largest banking groups, along with several of their directors who concurrently held positions in a local bank that collapsed amid a significant bank run. It was within this complex scenario that my interest in banking groups and financial conglomerates begin. The distinct corporate structures of each of those banking groups significantly influenced their governance, centralization, business operations, and, notably, their resolution mechanisms in the face of insolvency.

This book, which I present to you, evolves from this "biographical" interest, digging further into the topic. I sought to scrutinize the principal corporate forms within three archetype jurisdictions. Each model explored in this work is filled with unique historical, legal, and philosophical foundations. While not aiming for exhaustive coverage, this book will show the influences of each of these variables in shaping Bank Based Financial Conglomerates (BBFCs). Finally, the book explores the resolution of

BBFCs and proposes a possible resolution strategy for each of the models according to four factors integral to insolvency law.

This book tries to go beyond theory by analysing case studies based on publicly available information. Therefore, the book will look at the structures and annual reports of BBFCs such as Barclays, Deutsche Bank, Citi, Credit Agricole and Santander.

This book is about financial regulation, bank insolvency and resolution regimes with a specific focus on BBFC. The Great Financial Crisis (GFC) has emphasized the two main problems of BBFCs, its cross-sectoral and cross-border issues. While there are several books that focus on the regulation of banks, insurance companies and securities firms, this book will be the first analysis of BBFC from a structural, commercial and resolution standpoint, analysing not only three major jurisdictions but three different BBFC models.

The main objectives of the book are:

a) Finding a working definition of Financial Conglomerate from an epistemological and regulatory perspective.
b) Describing the different financial conglomerate models across the US, the UK and Germany.
c) Determining the historical and philosophical foundations of universal banking in Europe, holding company model in the US and British model in the UK.
d) Providing the reader with an explanation of how BBFC influenced industry developments in the US, Germany and the UK and the type of capitalism involved in each jurisdiction.
e) Assessing which banking resolution strategy best fits each model across jurisdictions.

The contribution of this book to the literature on banks and conglomerates is threefold.

It is the first systematic effort to analyse bank-based financial conglomerates from a structural perspective after the inception of systemic risk regulations following the collapse of Lehman Brothers.

It analyses the legal frameworks of three jurisdictions to shed light on the conceptual characterization and its regulatory framework. Further, it answers what intellectual forces affected the BBFC and how they influenced the industry.

It shows how the traditional structural classification has proven resilient since it was key to design and structure the resolution strategies in each jurisdiction.

While financial conglomerates may be oriented to any of the three finance activities, banking, securities and insurance, this book has chosen to analyse the bank-based financial conglomerates because of the relevance that banks have in vast jurisdictions and because of the risks and challenges that they pose to financial stability.

Montevideo, Uruguay Marcelo J. Sheppard Gelsi

Acknowledgements

There is a Spanish saying, "*Es de bien nacidos ser agradecidos*" which can be loosely translated into English as it is only right and proper to be grateful. As I complete this book, first of all I would like to express my gratitude to my mentors Professors Rosa M. Lastra and Rodrigo Olivares-Caminal for their guidance and support.

Special thanks to Professor and former Rector of Universidad de Montevideo Juan Manuel Gutiérrez Carrau and to Professor Luisa Peirano, who inspired me to engage in this project. I am indebted to Dr. Daniele D'Alvia for his guidance in this process.

Finally, I am extremely thankful to Sofia, my wife, who was my strength along the way and who, with her caring advice and love made this project alive and healthy. Thank you to our loving children, for the time you gave me, and for your understanding. Special thanks to my parents and the rest of my family, who were there for me at all times.

About This Book

This book seeks to provide a coherent conceptual framework for the regulation of bank-based financial conglomerates considering different models across jurisdictions.

This book examines the regulatory and corporate structure of a particular type of financial conglomerates, those that have a strong international presence and are banking focused (i.e. bank-based financial conglomerates or BBFCs). The book draws upon a tripartite classification of financial conglomerates (commercial, structural and regulatory) to focus on the types under the structural classification. These are the Complet Integration (or German model), the "Bank-parent, non bank subsidiaries" model (or British model), the holding company model (or US model). The book further examines the types of capitalism involved in each model, how BBFC have influenced the industry and the legal regulation of BBFCs in its prototypical jurisdiction (Germany, UK and US). Developments in the EU are also considered.

The book purports that the definition of financial conglomerate is contentious because of its cross-sectoral and cross-border dimensions. The same concept may have different meanings analysed through different lenses. The "systemic risk lens" introduced after the Global Financial Crisis (GFC) has created new categories of SIFIs.

It also examines how the corporate structure of each model influences the resolution strategy: Single Point of Entry or Multiple Point of Entry.

Based upon a four-factor analytic framework used in resolution planning (centralized or decentralized type of structure; retail or wholesale business; subsidiary or branch-based structure and universal or territorial approach to resolution) the book proposes a resolution strategy for each of the different models.

List of Cases

(continued)

(continued)

List of Legislation

(continued)

(continued)

Second Banking Directive 89/646/EEC, OJ 386 30/12/1989.	74, 120
Spanish Ley 10/2014	26
French Code Monetaire et Financier	26
Brazil law No. 4595/64	26
Argentine Law No. 21.526	26
Bank Holding Company Act of 1956, 12 U.S.C. (BHCA)	130, 153, 154, 156, 159, 160, 161, 172, 176, 177. 184, 206, 221
Uruguay Decreto 614/992	25
Directive 2014/59/EU of the European Parliament and of the Council of 15 May 2014 establishing a framework for the recovery and resolution of credit institutions and investment firms and amending Council Directive 82/891/EEC, and Directives 2001/24/EC, 2002/47/EC, 2004/25/EC, 2005/56/EC, 2007/36/EC, 2011/35/EU, 2012/30/EU and 2013/36/EU, and Regulations (EU) No 1093/2010 and (EU) No 648/2012, of the European Parliament and of the Council Text with EEA relevance (BRRD)	28, 188, 199, 200, 230dfa
Dodd-Frank Wall Street Reform and Consumer Protection Act, Pub. L. No. 111-203, § 929-Z, 124 Stat. 1376, 1871 (2010) (codified at 15 U.S.C. § 78o) [Bluebook R. 12.4]. ("DFA")	34, 35, 38, 51, 52, 133, 161, 167, 171, 174, 175, 178, 187, 206, 212, 214, 221, 223, 241
The Banking Act 2009 (Banking group Companies) Order 2014	37, 125
Spanish Commercial Code- Código de Comercio (Spain)	37
German Financial Conglomerate Supervision Act—FKAG	37
Directive 2000/12/EC of the European Parliament and of the Council of March 20, 2000 relating to the taking up and pursuit of the business of credit institutions, O.J. Eur. Comm. No. L 126/1 (2000) as amended ("Banking Directive")	25, 38, 105, 114

(continued)

(continued)

Directive 2013/36/EU of the European Parliament and of the Council of 26 June 2013 on access to the activity of credit institutions and the prudential supervision of credit institutions and investment firms, amending Directive 2002/87/EC and repealing Directives 2006/48/EC and 2006/49/EC ("CRD").	35, 62
Consolidated text: Directive 2013/36/EU of the European Parliament and of the Council of 26 June 2013 on access to the activity of credit institutions and the prudential supervision of credit institutions, amending Directive 2002/87/EC and repealing Directives 2006/48/EC and 2006/49/EC (CRD V)	
Investment Service Directive 93/22/EEC of 10 May 1993	74
Glass-Steagal Act. Act of June 16, 1933, 48 Stat. 162 (GSA)	76, 77, 80, 87, 89, 112, 129, 130, 132, 143, 152, 157, 176
Single supervisory mechanism—Council Regulation (EU) No 1024/2013 (SSM)	35, 39, 52, 91, 214
German Cooperative Act	97, 99
UK Banking Act 1979	104, 113, 218
UK Banking Coordination (Second Council Directive) regulations	114
EU Own Funds Directive, 89/229/EEC, OJ L 124, 5/5/1989	114
EU Solvency Ratio Directive, 89/647/EEC, OJ 386, 30/12/1989	114
Regulation (EU) No 575/2013 of the European Parliament and of the Council of 26 June 2013 on prudential requirements for credit institutions and investment firms and amending Regulation (EU) No 648/2012. (CRR)	90, 91, 93, 116, 159
UK Credit Unions Act 1979	119, 120
UK Co-operative and Community Benefit Societies Act 2014	119, 125
The Credit Unions (Northern Ireland) Order 1985	119
MiFID European Parliament and Council Directive on markets in financial instruments (No. 2004/39/EC).	123
Financial Services (Banking Reform) Act 2013	125, 192-193

(continued)

(continued)

The Financial Services and Markets Act 2000 (Ring-fenced Bodies and Core Activities) Order 2014	36, 125
The Financial Services and Markets Act 2000 (Regulated Activities) Order 2001 (SI 2001/544) (RAO).	115
Financial Services and Markets Act 2000 (FSMA) as amended	26, 118, 122, 125
Financial Institutions Supervisory Act of 1966 (P.L. 89-695, 80 STAT. 1028)	130
International Banking Act of 1978 (P.L. 95-369, 92 STAT. 607)	130, 172, 173
Financial Institutions Regulatory and Interest Rate Control Act of 1978 (P.L. 95-630, 92 STAT. 3641	130
Depository Institutions Deregulation and Monetary Control Act of 1980 (P.L. 96-221, 94 STAT. 132)	130, 131, 165
Garn-St Germain Depository Institutions Act of 1982 (P.L. 97-320, 96 STAT. 1469)	131, 165
Competitive Equality Banking Act of 1987 (P.L. 100-86, 101 STAT. 552 (CEBA)	131, 159, 172, 260
Financial Institutions Reform, Recovery, and Enforcement Act (FIRREA) P.L. 101-73, 103 STAT. 183)	131, 206
Federal Deposit Insurance Corporation Improvement Act of 1991 (FDICIA, Pub.L. 102–242)	131, 166, 167
Riegle-Neal Interstate Banking and Branching Efficiency Act of 1994, Pub. L. No. 103-328, H.R. 3841, 103rd Cong.	131, 132, 145
Gramm Leach-Bliley Financial Services Modernization Act of 1999, (GBLA) (Pub.L. 106–102)	129, 132, 155, 163
Sarbanes-Oxley Act of 2002 (P.L. 107-204).	132
McFadden Act of 1927 (Public Law 69-639, 69th Congress, H.R. 2)	144, 153, 160, 177
Douglas Amendment (1986)12 U.S.C. §1842(d).	144
The Sherman Antitrust Act of 1890 (26 Stat. 209)	147
The Trust Indenture Act of 1939 (TIA), Pub.L. 76–253)	152
The 1940 Investment Company Act (15 U.S.C. §§ 80a-1–80a-64.)	152

(continued)

(continued)

Contents

Abbreviations

ABCUL	Association of British Credit Unions
AICU	Association of Independent Credit Unions
AIF	Alternative Investment Fund
AIG	American International Group
BaFin	German Federal Financial Supervisory Authority (Bundesanstalt fürFinanzdienstleistungsaufsicht).
BBFC	Bank-Based Financial Conglomerates
BHC	Banking Holding Company
BHCA	Banking Holding Company Act
BVR	National Association of German Cooperative Banks
CALD	Council of Australian Law Deans
CBCA	Cross Border Cooperation Agreements
CCC	Competition and Credit control
Citi	Citigroup
CRD	Capital Requirements Directive
CRR	Capital Requirements Regulation
CSE	Consolidated Supervised Entity
CUSO	Credit Union Service Organization
DB	Deutsche Bank
DFA	Dodd Frank Act
D-INBI	Domestically Important non-bank institutions
DSGV	German Savings Bank Association Deutscher Sparkassen-und Giroverband
D-SIBs	Domestically Systemic Important Banks
D-SIIs	Domestically Important Insurers
EEA	European Economic Area

EFSF	European Financial Stability Facility
ESM	European Stability Mechanism
EU	European Union
FC	Financial Conglomerate
FCA	Financial Conduct Authority
FDIA	Federal Deposit Insurance Act
FDIC	Federal Deposit Insurance Corporation
FHC	Financial Holding Companies
FHLBB	Federal Home Loan Bank System
FICOD	Financial Conglomerates Directive
FIR	Financial Intermediation Ratio
FMU	Financial Market Utilities
FRB	Federal Reserve Board
FSA	Financial Services Authority
FSB	Financial Stability Board
FSLIC	Federal Savings & Loan Insurance Corporation
FSMA	Financial Services and Markets Act
FSOC	Financial Stability Oversight Council
GAAP	General Accepted Accounting Principles
GATS	General Agreement on Trade in Services
GDP	Gross Domestic Product
GFC	Great Financial Crisis
GFCI 24	Global Financial Centres Index
GSA	Glass Stegall Act
G-SIBs	Globally Systemically Important Banks
G-SIIs	Globally Systemic Important Insurance Firms
HK	Hong Kong
HSBC	The Hong Kong and Shanghai Banking Corporation
IAIS	International Association of Insurance Supervisors
ICFC	Industrial and Commercial Finance Corporation
ILC	Industrial Loan Companies and Industrial Banks
ILCU	UK the Irish League of Credit Unions
IPO	Initial Public Offering
IPU	Intermediate EU Parent Undertaking
ISDA	International Swaps and Derivatives Association
LLC	Limited Liability Company
MiFID	Markets in Financial Instruments Directive
MPOE	Multiple Point of Entry
NAIC	National Association of Insurance Commissioners
NBA	National Banking Acts
NBNI G-SIFI	Non-Bank, Non-Insurance Systemic Importance Financial Institutions
NCUA	National Credit Union Administration

NCUSIF	National Credit Union Share Insurance Fund
NOW	Negotiable order of withdrawal account
NYBA	New York Banking Act
OCC	Office of the Comptroller of the Currency
OECD	The Organization for Economic Co-Operation and Development
OLA	Orderly Liquidation Authority
OLF	Orderly Liquidation Fund
OTS	Office of the Thrift Supervision
PRA	Prudential Regulation Authority
SCOTUS	Supreme Court of the United States of America
SEC	Securities and Exchange Commission
SIBHC	Supervised Investment Bank Holding
SIFI	Systemically Important Financial Institution
SLCU	Scottish League of Credit Unions
SLHC	Savings and Loans Holding Company
SPOE	Single Point of Entry
TBTF	Too Big to Fail
THC	Thrift Holding Companies
TLAC	Total Loss Absorbing Capacity
UFCU	Ulster Federation of Credit Unions
UK	United Kingdom
UNICTRAL	United Nations Commission on International Trade Law
US	United States
WTO	World Trade Organization
WWI	World War I
WWII	World War II

List of Figures

List of Tables

CHAPTER 1

Introduction

Financial Regulation is thus the authorities' attempt to achieve the maximum efficiency of the financial sector while averting the risk of its transmitting potentially uncontrollable shocks to the real economy.

T. Padoa-Schioppa Conference on Financial Conglomerates, March 1988, Commission of the European Communities

1.1 The Aim of the Book

This book provides a comparative analysis of BBFC after the Great Financial Crisis (GFC), where the systemic risk lens was incorporated. The FC doctrine has developed mainly in Europe before the FICOD[1] and gained force again after the GFC, but there is no systemic or comparative analysis of BBFC after the crisis. The aim of this book is to fill the gap in the FC doctrine focusing on three aspects of BBFC: (i) capital structure (i.e. capitalism), (ii) legal regulatory framework and (iii) impact on resolution.

This book selected a structural classification of FC and identified three different models of FC based on traditional structures: the German model, the UK model and the US or Holding model. This book's objective is to answer three research questions: (1) How BBFC influenced the industry, what were its philosophical foundations, and what type of

[1] FICOD

M. J. Sheppard Gelsi, *Corporate Structure and Banking Resolution*, Palgrave Macmillan Studies in Banking and Financial Institutions, https://doi.org/10.1007/978-3-031-59948-4_1

capitalism has evolved in the chosen jurisdictions—that are traditionally identified with each model—Germany, the UK and the US; (2) what is the legal regulatory framework in each of the three selected jurisdictions; (3) which are the most appropriate resolution strategies to selected SIFIs based on each of these jurisdictions.

The contribution of this book to the dialogue of FC is threefold. First, it is the first systematic effort to analyse BBFC from a structural perspective after the inception of systemic risk regulations post-GFC. Second, it analyses the legal regulation of three jurisdictions to shed light on the conceptual definition of the BBFC. Further, it answers what intellectual forces affected the BBFC and how they influenced the industry. Third, it shows how the traditional structural classification has proven resilient since it was key to design and structure the SIFI resolution strategies in each jurisdiction. Further research on how BBFC have influenced the industry and types of capitalism in other jurisdictions, mainly Latin America, Eastern Europe, the Middle East, Asia and Oceania may follow.

While FCs may be oriented to any of the three finance activities, banking, securities and insurance, this book has chosen to analyse the BBFC because of the relevance of banking in vast jurisdictions and because of the risks and challenges it poses to financial stability. Evidence from the investigation provides material for further research into aspects of securities or insurance-based FC.

The "Conceptual Framework Chapter" (Chapter 2) will function as a toolbox and will examine the building blocks that will be used along the rest of the book. Because of this, this introductory chapter only deals with the aim of the book and its structure.

1.2 Structure of the Book

This chapter provides an overview of what this book and it answers what the research has achieved, why it is important to advancing the agenda on FCs after the GFC, and describes its contribution to the field. As chapter two deals with a conceptual chapter, it only responds to the mentioned problems and do not introduce the building blocks that will build the different chapters of the book.

Chapter 2 focuses on the conceptual framework of FCs. It discusses what a bank is and why they are special. It draws a triple classification of financial institutions: a commercial classification, a structural classification and a regulatory classification. The commercial classification comprises banking groups, FCs and mixed conglomerates. The structural classification relies on the legal and operational separation of FC and distinguishes between the German model, the British model and the US model. Finally, the regulatory classification relies on categories of systemic importance and distinguishes G-SIBs, G-SIIs and NBNI G-SIFIs. After introducing each model, the German model, the UK model and the US model, the book legally compares the regulation of BBFC in the jurisdictions where the models historically apply, Germany, the UK and the US.

Chapter 3 focuses on the first element of the Structural classification and examines the German model of BBFC. This chapter deals with the definition of universal banking and its historical and philosophical foundations. It analyses how the BBFCs influenced the industry in Germany and its implications in a bank-based type of capitalism. As universal banking is one of the most important types of BBFCs this book examines the benefits and costs of universal banking. In order to compare how the BBFCs are legally regulated in Germany, Sect. 3.1.6 analyses the German banking system and the three pillar structure. It argues that while there are benefits in universal banking, regulators need to be aware that concentrating the three financial functions under the same "roof" may create the peril of developing "mammoth entities" which may be potentially difficult to manage, supervise and resolve.

Chapter 4 outlines the British model which has been historically present in the UK. This chapter examines the British system, its specialized system and self-regulated industry. It also explains the ties between banks and finance in the UK and the City of London as a driving force in finance that shaped the entire British economy. As in Chapter 2, Chapter 3 examines the structure of the UK banking system, analysing what a bank is, the big four clearing banks, foreign banks and overseas banking. It also establishes the distinction between credit unions, building societies and investment banks. As the UK was one of the first to implement ring-fencing, it details this process. It is argued that ring-fencing regulations aim was to end universal banking. While this might have been a theoretical aspiration, UK did not mandate a complete separation and therefore universal banks in a broad sense continue to exist in Britain today.

Chapter 5 considers the US model. It introduces the historical and philosophical foundations of the US banking system and federalism, i.e. the "nerve" that sustained the whole structure. The US system developed a unique "unit bank" system underpinned by restrictive laws on branching. This chapter analyses the benefits and costs of unit banking. A following section concentrates on the US and the evolution of capital markets and explains how US banks could not finance the industry because of a mismatch between big firms and small unit banks. In order to answer the comparative legal research question, this book examines the US banking system, commercial banks, thrifts and credit unions. Finally, it surveys the different legal structures allowed for a BBFCs in the US. This book argues the genesis dilemma of the emergence of BBFCs (a "chicken and egg situation") is present in the American financial regulation and finally, it warns from the "Icarus effect" on financial regulation in the US. The current chapter will be longer than Chapters 3 and 4 because the US is more complex than the UK and Germany, being a federal state with regulations at various levels and a deeper history and evolution of corporate forms than in the other selected jurisdictions.

Taking into account findings in Chapters 2, 3, 4 and 5, Chapter 6 concentrates on the resolution of BBFCs. Once it has analysed the corporate structure that prevails in each one of the selected jurisdictions, the philosophical and historical foundations of each model, and the type of capitalism involved in each jurisdiction, based on four selected indicators this book analysed a multiple case study in order to assess which resolution strategy best fits three SIFIs: DB (Germany), Barclays (UK) and Citigroup (US). The first indicator relies on how FCs structure themselves, through branches or subsidiaries. The second indicator shows the degree of centralization of FCs, centralized or decentralized. The third indicator concentrates on the business model, retail or wholesale. The fourth indicator indicates the territorial or universal approach to resolution. It also analyses the costs and benefits of SPOE and MPOE resolution to finally answer the last research question: which resolution strategy best fits each model, analysing a representative SIFI of each jurisdiction.

Chapter 7 sets out the concluding remarks which include the findings resulting from the comparison of the different models in Chapters 3, 4 and 5, the resolution strategies proposed in Chapter 6.

CHAPTER 2

Conceptual Framework

The concept of FC is difficult to define.[1] Firstly, because the concept has been transferred from the commercial to the financial law literature. In addition, different regulatory and legislative bodies have referred to similar concepts in different ways. Secondly, because the same concept has been described from different perspectives, i.e. the commercial, structural and regulatory. Thirdly, because the nature of FCs is evolving and the risks of different financial activities differ from each other. Fourth, because by their very nature, FCs tend to expand geographically and into new markets.

The aim of this chapter is to establish a concept of "financial conglomerates" by examining their different classifications, thus shedding light on a common conceptual framework that help the conversation on FCs in the future.

The first section analyses what a bank is, and why they are special. This book will mainly examine BBFCs, since the banking sector is most

[1] A definition is "an exact statement or description of the nature, scope, or meaning of something". Oxford Dictionary online, https://en.oxforddictionaries.com/definition/definition. Accessed 20 January 2018. When the defined object changes over time, the time variable needs to be taken into account. As Schweitzer contends "constant change has always been the hallmark of free-enterprise economy. Paul Schweitzer "Banks and Banking—A Review of a definition", *Banking L.J*, Vol. 6, No. 7 (1977), 94.

M. J. Sheppard Gelsi, *Corporate Structure and Banking Resolution*, Palgrave Macmillan Studies in Banking and Financial Institutions, https://doi.org/10.1007/978-3-031-59948-4_2

prone to affect financial stability and is the main source of financing for a vast zone of the world. The second section examines three different classifications of groups of financial institutions relying on the commercial activity they perform ("Commercial classification"), on the legal and operational separateness ("Structural classification") and on categories of systemic importance ("Regulatory classification"). This analysis follows below.

2.1 What Is a Bank?

The first question is to define what a bank is. According to Effros there are two approaches; the first one is to include a "list of activities" and the second consists of a "formula approach".[2] The list of activities may include: "receiving deposits, discounting bills and notes, lending money, conducting safe deposit functions, buying and selling currencies, effecting transfers between accounts and collecting and clearing negotiable instruments".[3] The second approach is based on a formula which relies on "the irreducible concept of accepting deposits and making loans".[4] Often, the legislative solution adopted in a jurisdiction combines the two approaches: a bank or credit institution is an entity which receives deposits and grants loans and does other activities.

List Approach

Historically, this first approach was adopted by the SCOTUS in the Austen v. United States Bank of New York Case: "a bank, (…) is an institution usually incorporated with power to issue its promissory notes (…); or to receive the money of others on general deposit to form a joint fund that shall be used by the institution for its own benefit, for one or more of the purposes of making temporary loans and discounts.; of dealing in notes, foreign and domestic bills of exchange, coin, bullion, credits and the remission of money; or with both these powers, and with the privileges in addition to these basic powers, of receiving special deposits and

[2] Robert Effros "Central Bank in the Age off Standardization" Manuscript (Effros, 1999). See also Robert Effros *Current Legal Issues Affecting Central Banks*, Vol. I (IMF 1992), 9.

[3] Ibid.

[4] See Effros "Central Bank", 2.

making collections for the holders of negotiable paper, if the institution sees fit to engage in such business".[5]

The *list approach* was applied in the US by the United States NBA: "All National Associations…shall have power…to carry on the business of banking: by discounting and negotiation promissory notes, drafts, bills of exchange, and other devices of debt; by receiving deposits, by buying and selling exchange, coin, bullion, by loaning money on personal security, and by obtaining, issuing, and circulating notes according to the provisions of this chapter".[6]

Germany also followed this list approach when enacting the German Banking Act in 1998. For the German Act, banking business comprises: (1) the acceptance of funds from others as deposits […]; (2) the granting of money loans and acceptance credits (credit business); (3) discount business; (4) principal broking services; (5) safe custody business; […] (8) guarantee business; (9) bill collection business; (10) underwriting business; and, (11) "acting in the capacity of a central counterpart".[7]

This same approach has been taken by the European Union in Annex I to the "Bank Consolidation Directive" (2006/48/EC), recital 14. The EU has changed its approach from the formula approach to the list of activities approach, since in the First and the Second Banking Directive the former was adopted.[8]

It can be observed, nevertheless, in the EU the first two activities of the mentioned Annex are accepting deposits and lending, which resembles the second approach.

The *list approach* disadvantage is that the list has to be updated regularly because the purpose and activities of banks have changed over time. In order to address this disadvantage different solutions have been proposed: (1) periodical legislation update; (2) broad interpretations of the nature of the activities; and (3) procedures to delegate the authority/power to administrative authorities to make such changes.[9]

[5] *2 Auten v. United States National Bank of New York, 174 U.S. 125, 141–42 (1899).*

[6] 12 U.S.C. § 24 (7).

[7] Banking Act Section 1, http://www.gesetze-im-internet.de/kredwg/. Accessed 2 May 2023.

[8] See First Banking Directive article 1.

[9] See Effros "Central Bank", 2.

Formula Approach

Before the UK adopted a statutory definition of a Bank, "the most prominent was the definition developed by Diplock LJ in the 1966 case of United Dominions Trust v. Kirkwood". "Common to all modern definitions and essential to the carrying on of the business of banking is that the banker should accept from his customers' loans of money on deposit, that is to say, loans for an indefinite period upon running account, repayable as to the whole or any part thereof upon demand by the customer".[10]

This formula can be found in the legislation of different countries such as the UK,[11] Spain,[12] France,[13] among others.[14]

The US, since the enactment of the Bank Holding Company Act (BHC) in 1956, takes the *formula approach* "For purposes of this chapter—(1) In general—Except as provided in paragraph (2), the term "bank" means any of the following: /…)—(i) *accepts demand deposits or deposits that the depositor may withdraw by check or similar means for payment to third parties or others; and (ii) is engaged in the business of making commercial loans*" [Emphasis added].[15]

In 1962 SCOTUS defined a commercial bank in United States v. Philadelphia National Bank: "Commercial banks are unique among financial institutions in that they alone are permitted by law to accept demand deposits. This distinctive power gives commercial banking a key role in the national economy. For banks do not merely deal in, but are actually

[10] Heidi Schooner and Michael Taylor *Global Bank Regulation: Principles and Policies* (Elsevier 2010), 2.

[11] UK Financial Services and Markets Act 2000, Schedule 6.

[12] See Spanish Ley 10/2014.

[13] See French Code Monetaire et Financier article L311-2, https://www.legifrance.gouv.fr/affichCode.do;jsessionid=9E64E5C022EFB33D9EB4FD9807BB2EE1.tplgfr41s_1?idSectionTA=LEGISCTA000006170352&cidTexte=LEGITEXT000006072026&dateTexte=20171101. Accessed 20 January 2023.

[14] Brazil, Argentina, Paraguay and Uruguay legislation tend to refer to a slightly different formula, that of those entities that engage themselves in "financial intermediation". See Brazil law No. 4595/64, article 17, https://www.planalto.gov.br/ccivil_03/leis/l4595.htm. Accessed 20 January 2023. See Argentine law No. 21526 article 1, http://www.bcra.gob.ar/Pdfs/SistemasFinancierosYdePagos/MarcoLegalCompleto.pdf. Last modified 20 January 2023.

[15] BCHA. par. 1841.

a source of, money and credit; when a bank makes a loan by crediting the borrower's demand deposit account, it augments the Nation's credit supply. Furthermore, the power to accept demand deposits makes banks the intermediaries in most financial transactions (since transfers of substantial moneys are almost always by check rather than by cash) and, concomitantly, the repositories of very substantial individual and corporate funds".[16]

The two components of the *formula approach* determined the name of the institutions on both sides of the Atlantic. While in the US the generic name for banks is "Depositary Institution", in Europe the chosen name is "Credit Institution".[17]

Even though the formula approach focuses on the main function of lending and deposit taking it might be restrictive. Taking into account the fast-paced change of finance technology and innovation, some of the activities of banks might fall outside the formula.

A Third Approach

A third approach would be to address the formula approach with a sufficient range of discretion to include the necessary changes of the banking activity. A resulting possible definition would be that a bank is an institution that engages in "financial intermediation" where the characterization of the peculiarities of what financial intermediation is would be transferred to the remit of the Financial Authority.[18] The room for manoeuvre in this field is important due to the fast-changing nature of banking business.

As Keynes observes: "Perhaps the most difficult question is how much to decide by rule and how much to leave to discretion".[19] While this is not easy, a static implementation of both the list and the formula approach might not be sufficient in an ever-evolving area being challenged by technology.

[16] *United States v. Philadelphia National Bank et al., 374 U.S. 321, 397 (1963).*

[17] Rosa Lastra *Central Banking and Bank Regulation* (LSE, 1996), 73.

[18] See article 1, Decreto 614/992 of Uruguay.

[19] John Maynard Keynes *Proposals for an International Currency (Clearing) Union*, 1941. http://la.utexas.edu/users/hcleaver/368/368keynesoncutable.pdf. Accessed 30 March 2023.

2.2 Are Banks Special?

For centuries, banks have assumed special functions in the economy. Mainly because of this, governments and Central Banks have treated banks in special ways. This section will examine if the features that made banks special in the past remain true today, particularly after the GFC.

Banks are special in various ways. Banks as financial intermediaries have the following basic functions: (1) transformation of short-term liabilities (generally in small amounts by depositors) into long-term credits[20]; (2) provision to bank customers of means of payment being themselves payment intermediaries[21]; (3) transmission by Central Banks of monetary policy[22]; (4) screening of potential borrowers, monitoring their activity and enforcing repayments[23]; (5) being subject to regulation and supervision, and having access to central bank facilities.[24]

After the GFC[25] the financial authorities focused on the role of "critical functions" in order to design the relevant framework of resolution of failing banks. In this sense, according to the Financial Stability Board (FSB), the critical functions are "activities performed for third parties where failure would lead to the disruption of services that are vital for the functioning of the real economy and for financial stability due to the banking group size or market share, external and internal interconnectedness, complexity and cross border activities".[26] This definition recognizes

[20] Thorsten Beck, Diane Coyle, Mathias Dewatripont, Xavier Freixas and Paul Seabright "Bailing Out of the Banks: Reconciling Stability and Competition—An Analysis of State-Supported Schemes for Financial Institutions", CERP (2010), 9; Thomas Padoa Scioppa, "The Transformation of the European Financial System", ECB (2002), 7; Lastra, "International Financial", 141.

[21] Beck et al. "Bailing Out of the Banks", 9 and Lastra "International Financial", 141.

[22] Edward W. Kelley Jr "Are Banks Still Special?", Federal Reserve (1997), https://www.federalreserve.gov/boarddocs/speeches/1997/19970129.htm. Accessed 20 January 2023; E. Gerald Corrigan "Are Banks Special?" Federal Reserve of Minneapolis (1982), https://www.minneapolisfed.org/article/1983/are-banks-special. Accessed 20 January 2023. Thomas Huertas, "Are Banks Still Special?" LSE (2017), 1.

[23] Beck et al. "Bailing Out of the Banks", 9.

[24] Corrigan "Are Banks Still Special?", 3; Huertas, "Are Banks Still Special?", 1.

[25] GFC is an acronym used to define the financial crisis originated in the USA in July 2007 with the credit crunch. See Lastra and Wood "The Crisis of 2007–09", 531–550.

[26] FSB *Recovery and Resolution Planning for Systemically Important Financial Institutions: Guidance on identification of Critical Functions and Critical Shared services*", FSB, 16 July 2013.

the relevance of banking activities to the economy and is a demonstration of their special nature.[27] Indeed, the "critical function" literature is an extension of the old "list approach" banking definition, which is in fact functional. The continuity of the critical functions of a failing bank is an "objective of resolution" and stresses the specialty of banks as authorities aim to ensure the bank activities (or critical functions) are performed in a resolution circumstance.[28]

Maturity Mismatch, the "Mary Poppins Effect" and Transaction Accounts

In the first place the bank's special balance sheet structure produces a "maturity mismatch" between depositors—who can claim their credit at any time—and long-term loans—generally not liquid—that make the banks vulnerable to runs.[29] In a seminal work in 1983, Diamond and Dybvig concluded that in the event of a panic even those depositors who would have preferred to maintain their deposits in the bank in other safer circumstances would require to withdraw their funds, and that the economic consequences of the run would be further reaching than in other areas of business since "even 'healthy' banks can fail, causing the recall of loans and the termination of productive investment".[30]

Friedman and Schwarz conclude their work on the Great Contraction referring to this phenomenon: "it happens that a liquidity crisis in a fractional reserve banking system is precisely the kind of event that can trigger – and often has triggered – a chain reaction. And economic collapse often has the characteristic of a cumulative process (...). Because no great strength would be required to hold back the rock that starts

[27] According to Rosa Lastra, Rodrigo Olivares Caminal and Costanza Russo, "The Provision of Critical Functions at Global, National and Regional Level-Is there a need for further legal/regulatory clarification if liquidation is the default option for failing banks?" European Parliament (2017): "in the banking sector, the most important critical functions are deposit taking, lending and loan servicing, and payments (clearing and settlement)".

[28] Bank Recovery and Resolution (BRRD)—Directive 2014/59/EU.

[29] Padoa Scioppa "The Transformation of the European Financial", 8; See Lastra, "International Financial", 141; Eva Hupkes "Form Follows Function- A New Architecture for Regulating and Resolving Global Financial Institutions", European Business Organization Law Review (2009), 372.

[30] Douglas W. Diamond and Philip Dybvig "Bank Runs, Deposit Insurance, and Liquidity", *Journal of Political Economy*, Vol. 91, No. 3 (June 1983), 402.

a landslide, it does not follow that the landslide will not be of major proportions".[31] Although the liquidity crisis might be a common cause of triggering the bank run, because of the nature of the fractional reserve banking system, a bank run can be initiated even if the bank is solvent[32] by a psychological lack of confidence[33] or "Mary Poppins"[34] effect.

This specific mix of features of banks makes them vulnerable to runs "with a potential systemic impact and very important externalities to the economy".[35]

In the second place, banks issue transaction accounts in which

> they incur liabilities payable on demand at par and are readily transferable by the owner to third parties. The owner of a transaction account can demand and receive currency in the face amount deposited in the account; write a check in the full amount of the account; or perhaps most importantly the owner of the account can transfer the full amount of the account to a third party almost instantaneously by wire transfer. The liquidity, mobility, and acceptability of bank issued transaction accounts permit our diverse economic and financial system to work with the relative ease and efficiency to which we are accustomed.[36]

The transaction account issuance is one of the key elements that distinguish banks from other types of financial and non-financial institutions.[37]

Not only are banks special, but also bank failures are special "since they create externalities (contagion to other healthy institutions; under a fractional reserve system a bank will be unable at any time to honour

[31] Milton Friedman and Anna Schwartz *The Great Contraction 1929–1933* (Princeton University Press 1965), 123.

[32] Padoa Scioppa "The Transformation of the European Financial", 8.

[33] Lastra "International Financial", 192.

[34] The "Mary Poppins Effect" refers to the scene of the Disney film where the son of the main character initiates a bank run when he shouted to the bank manager that he wanted his money back. The run against the bank was triggered by a psychological fear that the bank would not comply with its obligations and was not related with the safety and soundness of the bank.

[35] Xavier Vives "Competition and Stability in Banking", IESE Business School, University of Navarre, Working Paper WP 852 (2010), 44.

[36] Corrigan "Are Banks Special?", 1.

[37] Ibid.

the convertibility guarantee) and affect the stability and integrity of the payment system. They often become a matter of public interest".[38]

Payment System

As Huertas explains it, traditionally, non-banks rely their money on banks, while at the same time banks have access to accounts at the central bank. Households and institutions "use banks to access the payment system. Banks lend to non-banks and provide the economy at large with liquidity back-stop".[39]

The Committee on Payments and Settlement Payments (CPMI) affirms that one essential element of the financial system is to provide a safe and efficient payment and securities settlement system. "Payment systems...are a major channel by which shocks can be transmitted across domestic and international financial systems and markets. Robust payment systems are, therefore, a key requirement in maintaining and promoting financial stability".[40]

Bank failures are also special since they determine the integrity of the payment system. Ordinary people rely on banks to pay their bills and a sudden interruption of the chain of payments would imply serious social problems. In this regard, banks "perform a quasi-utility function" similar to the electricity or gas access functions.[41]

The payments and clearing systems exhibit "utility-like" features and characteristics of "natural monopoly".[42] The economic literature has examined the reasons for regulating the banking industry. The most relevant reasons are the existence of market failure and deficiencies, the negative spillovers into society (such as the costs of bank runs), the existence of information asymmetries and the persistence of natural

[38] Lastra "Northern Rock and Banking", 141.

[39] Huertas "Are Banks Still Special?", 2.

[40] Committee on Payments and Securities Settlement (2001, January 2001). Core Principles for Systemically Important Payment Systems. BIS (2001), https://www.bis.org/cpmi/publ/d34e.pdf. Accessed 20 January 2023.

[41] Charles Goodhart "If Banks Should Act as Utilities, Why Not Treat Them as Such?" (Vox 2011), https://voxeu.org/article/if-banks-should-act-utilities-why-not-treat-them-such. Accessed 12 March 2023.

[42] Bruce Summers "Clearing and Payments Systems: The Role of the Central Bank", Federal Reserve Bulletin (1991), 86.

monopolies. In the particular case of the payment system, it has been considered a public good, especially after the GFC.[43]

Monetary Policy Transmission Mechanism

Because of the bank special balance sheet and fractional reserve system, banks have been used by central banks as the "transmission belt" for "money and credit creation". As Corrigan puts it,

> the required reserves of the banking system have often been described as the fulcrum upon which the monetary authority operates monetary policy. The reserves in the banking system also serve the complementary purpose of providing the working balances which permit our highly efficient financial markets to function and to effect the orderly end-of-day settlement of the hundreds of billions of dollars of transactions that occur over the course of each business day.[44]

Historically, the central banks have used banks through a policy rate that is: a. the rate that central banks lend to banks, or b. the rate "at which banks can borrow central bank money in the market". Monetary policy has traditionally conducted open market operations with banks, or "varying the amount that they lend directly to banks". When central banks vary the banks reserves, they change the ability of banks to lend, with direct impact on other economic variables such as employment and inflation.[45]

[43] Lastra "International Financial", 114. See Charles Goodhart *Money, Information and Uncertainty* (MacMillan, London 1989), 202–203.

[44] Corrigan "Are Banks Special?", 2. For a different vision see Benjamin. Friedman and Kenneth. N. Kuttner "Implementation of Monetary Policy: How Do Central Banks Set Interest Rates?" NBER Working Paper No. 16165 July 2010, JEL No. E43, E52, E58: "Central banks no longer set the short-term interest rates that they use for monetary policy purposes by manipulating the supply of banking system reserves, as in conventional economics textbooks; today this process involves little or no variation in the supply of central bank liabilities".

[45] Huertas "Are Banks Still Special?", 3; Tobias Adrian, and Hyun Shin "Financial Intermediaries, Financial Instability and Monetary Policy." Proceedings of the Federal Reserve Bank of Kansas City Conference at Jackson Hole (2008), 287–334; Mervyn King "Twenty Years of Inflation Targeting. Stamp Memorial Lecture London School of Economics" (9 October 2012), http://www.bis.org/review/r121010f.pdf. Accessed 12 March 2023.

Monitor Function

Several scholars argue that banks are special since they solve "information asymmetries". Theoretical models developed by Diamond, Tamakrishnan and Thakor, and Fama stress the special "monitoring functions of banks", the "comparative advantage" of banks against other financial institutions, as the "enhanced incentives (relative to public debt holders), in monitoring debt contracts".[46]

Fama argues that banks have a low-cost financial information history of the client, who is usually at the same time borrower and depositor, which gives bank a "comparative advantage" in making and monitoring "repeated short-term inside loans".[47]

While this function is still important for banks, as Huertas correctly states, other financial institutions, especially Private Equity firms, monitor companies in which they invest or to which they lend.[48]

Provision of Central Bank Facilities, Regulation and Supervision

Since banks provide essential functions to the economy, financial stability[49] has relied on the stability of the banking sector, especially on the safety and soundness of systemically important institutions.[50] Mainly because of this, banks have access to central bank lending facilities and are subject to supervision and regulation.[51]

As Corrigan states, "banks and bank regulators have long since recognized the importance of banks acting in ways that preserve public confidence in banks' capacity to meet their deposit obligations, thereby

[46] Amar Gande and Anthony Saunders "Are Banks Still Special When There Is a Secondary Market for Loans? *Journal of Finance*, Vol. 67 (2012), 1649–1684; Douglas W. Diamond, "Financial Intermediation and Delegated Monitoring", Review of Economic Studies, Vol. 51 (1984), 393–414. Ram T. S. Ramakrishnan and Anjan V. Thakor, "Information Reliability and a Theory of Financial Intermediation", *Review of Economic Studies* (1984), 51, 415–432; Eugene Fama "What's Different About Banks?" *Journal of Monetary Economics*, Vol. 15 (1985), 29–39.

[47] Fama "What's Different", 38.

[48] Huertas "Are Banks Still Special?", 2.

[49] John Fell and Garry Schinasi "Assessing Financial Stability: Exploring the Boundaries of Analysis", *National Institute Economic Review*, No. 192 (April 2005), 102.

[50] Huertas "Are Banks Still Special?", 1.

[51] Ibid.

minimizing the likelihood of large, sudden drains of bank deposits. Deposit insurance and direct access to the lender of last resort are uniquely available to banks to reinforce that public confidence. Indeed, deposit insurance and access to the lender of last resort constitute a public safety net under the deposit taking function of banks. The presence of this public safety net reflects a long-standing consensus that banking functions are essential to a healthy economy".[52]

Huertas has argued that after the GFC, the traditional features of banks that made them special have weakened, making them "less special". In the first place, after the crisis, the bank monetary policy mechanism weakened since a second core element of monetary policy has emerged in the form of quantitative easing[53] and "eligibility easing", which reduced the need for central bank lending facilities.[54] Secondly, the payment systems are becoming "more robust", meaning that they are able to continue to operate even if a bank is resolved or liquidated. Central banks have implemented real-time gross settlement basis payments, which might in the future permit any institution to gain access to it.[55] Thirdly, macroprudential supervision has a broad scope encompassing many different financial institutions and not only banks.[56]

Another important challenge to banks would be the establishment, in the future, of digital currencies by the central banks. This would also make banks less special.[57] The first implication of the distributed ledger technology would be that every individual would be able to have a bank account in the central bank. This might have some advantages in comparison with the traditional bank account. As Broadbent argues "Shifting deposits to the central bank, and away from the leveraged commercial

[52] Corrigan "Are Banks Special?", 3.

[53] Lastra "Northern Rock and Banking", 42.

[54] Huertas "Are Banks Still Special?", 6, "During the crisis, however, central banks supplemented QE with EE (eligibility easing). They expanded the collateral eligible to support normal central bank liquidity facilities and they extended the range of counterparties eligible to access normal central bank liquidity facilities".

[55] Ibid.

[56] Lastra "International Financial", 114; House of the Lords, European Union Committee "The Future of EU Financial Regulation and Supervision, https://publications.parliament.uk/pa/ld200809/ldselect/ldeucom/106/106i.pdf. Accessed 20 January 2023.

[57] Huertas "Are Banks Still Special?", 12.

banking sector, has two important implications. On the one hand, it would probably make them safer. Currently, retail deposits are backed mainly by illiquid loans, assets that can't be sold on open markets; if we all tried simultaneously to close our accounts, banks wouldn't have the liquid resources to meet the demand. The central bank, by contrast, holds only liquid assets on its balance sheet. The central bank can't run out of cash and therefore can't suffer a 'run'".[58]

In summary, as Huertas recognizes, banks would be as special as central banks would like them to be.[59] As long as the system is based in the basic functions discussed above, banks will remain special and regulation and supervision would still be indispensable for the economy to work as we know it today.

A Case for lex specialis for Banks

Simultaneously, there is an argument supporting the application of "lex speciallis" to banks. Variances exist in bank resolution and insolvency laws worldwide between "lex generalis" where banks are treated similarly to other corporations, and "lex specialis", which applies specific insolvency or resolution frameworks to banks.[60] The IMF/World bank report claims that the primary objective of a bank insolvency framework is (i) to safeguard the stability of the financial system (including the smooth functioning of the payment system), (ii) the protection of the depositing public and (iii) the preservation of the credit function.[61]

[58] Ben Broadbent "Central Banks and Digital Currencies" (2 March 2016), https://www.bankofengland.co.uk/-/media/boe/files/speech/2016/central-banks-and-digitalcurrencies.pdf?la=en&hash=8D9B0F2911064BD7570B10370DF521FAE174217D. Accessed 20 January 2023.

[59] Huertas "Are Banks Still Special?", 1.

[60] Lastra International Financial, 165.

[61] IMF/World Bank "An Overview of the Legal, institutional and regulatory Framework for Bank Insolvency" (17 April 2009). Christos Gortsos claims the main objectives of resolution are: (1) continuity of critical functions, (2) avoiding significant adverse effects on financial stability, (3) protecting public funds minimizing reliance on public finance, (4) protect depositors and investors covered by depositor guarantee systems, and generally avoiding bail out. "The European Banking Regulation Handbook", Volume I (Palgrave Macmillan 2023), 52. See also Martin Cihak and Erlend Nier "The Need for Special Resolution Regimes for Financial Institutions—The Case of the European Union" IMF Working Paper No. 2009/200, Available at https://www.imf.org/en/Publications/WP/Issues/2016/12/31/The-Need-for-Special-Resolution-Regimes-for-Financial-Institutions-The-Case-of-the-European-23286; See also David Muñoz "Restructuring, resolution and insolvency: shift of tasks from judicial to administrative authorities" ECB

Similarly, Gortsos claims that an "individual bank's insolvency, which may be associated, *inter alia*, with deposit behaviour, the macroeconomic conjecture, its financial structure and/or business model, can lead to the default of other banks through various contagion channels) and destabilize the banking sector with a serious negative impact on the functioning of the real economy".[62]

Bankruptcy in the banking sector differs from corporate bankruptcy primarily due to three key factors. Firstly, the value of a bank's franchise diminishes rapidly when doubts arise about its financial viability. Secondly, unlike in corporate bankruptcies where "automatic stays" may restrict creditors' rights to payment, banks must prioritize honouring deposit withdrawals and check payments, which are central to their operations. This necessity would essentially halt the bank's business activities. Thirdly, the negative externalities of a bank's failure can be substantial, especially if the bank is large or if multiple banks fail simultaneously. Additionally, it's exceedingly difficult to restructure a bank's balance sheet through traditional bankruptcy proceedings while simultaneously keeping the business operational. Overall, the costs associated with bank bankruptcy are typically higher than those of corporate bankruptcies.[63]

Furthermore, the functions of insolvency are different from resolution. While the first are "fair and predictable treatment" of creditors and "maximization of assets" in the interest of creditors, the bank resolution functions are the "safety and soundness" of the financial system and the "integrity of the payment systems".[64]

As Wojcik states corporate insolvency proceedings "are usually not speedy enough; they usually cannot ensure the continuation of the critical functions of a financial institution; they lead to the destruction of value of assets and may thus impact on the real economy. In short, their application to a credit institution will most often not sufficiently preserve financial stability".[65]

Legal Conference on "Restructuring, resolution and insolvency: shift of tasks from judicial to administrative authorities", Available at https://www.bankingsupervision.europa.eu/press/speeches/date/2017/html/ssm.sp170905.en.html.

62 Gortsos "The European Banking Regulation", 45.

63 John Armour, Dan Awrey, Paul Davies, Luca Enriques, Jeffrey Gordon, Colin Mayer, and Jennifer Payne *Principles of Financial Regulation* (Oxford 2016), 343.

64 Lastra "International Financial", 141.

65 Wojcik "Bail in in the European Union", 92.

Delimiting insolvency and illiquidity might be difficult to establish in the banking sector, especially the trigger point of the insolvency. As Lastra claims, a bank is deemed to have failed when regulatory authorities mandate the cessation of its operations and activities, but authorities often hesitate to liquidate a bank and instead opt to rehabilitate it.[66]

Besides, failure of banks is of public interest mainly because of its functions (giving credit to real economy and ensuring the payment system) which need to be carried out by competent authorities.

Liquidation is costly, mainly by dissipating the depositor's base, disrupting community-banking services and damaging confidence.[67] Occasionally, a liquidation of one bank may trigger a bank run in another one. In summary, bank insolvency procedures will "most often not sufficiently preserve financial stability".[68]

Additionally, the risk of contagion is particularly important where the size of the bank is significant: the "too big to fail problem".[69] The contagion of healthy banks by the failure of another bank will depend on the degree of interconnection between them. What the 2007–2009 crisis has demonstrated was that financial institutions were indeed connected and there were four main transmission mechanisms: (1) the inter-bank, inter-institution, inter-instrument channel, (2) payment system channel, (3) information channel, and (4) psychological channel.[70]

All these channels are exacerbated when the bank is part of an international group or conglomerate, where cross-border externalities may arise. The consequences of a large international bank failure may affect depositors, creditors, counterparties and the economy of other countries.[71]

[66] Lastra "International Financial", ibid., 141.

[67] Lastra ibid,, 167.

[68] Wojcik "Bail in in the European Union" 92.

[69] Michael Schillig "Bank Resolution Regimes in Europe-Part I: Recovery and Resolution Planning, Early Intervention, *European Business Law Review*, Vol. 24, No. 6, N/A, (2013), 755.

[70] Lastra "International Financial", 183–192.

[71] Charles Randall "The FSB's "Key Attributes": The Road to Cross-Border Resolution of Financial Institutions" Scoping Paper Prepared for the Cross-Border Resolution Symposium Bingham Centre for the Rule of Law (2012), 5.

2.3 Triple Classification

This section will analyse a tripartite classification of financial institutions according to three different drivers.

A first classification relies on the commercial activities performed by the group ("Commercial classification"). The commercial activities will vary according to jurisdiction. It is common to distinguish between:

- Banking groups,
- Mixed conglomerates,
- Financial conglomerates.

A second classification relies on the legal and operational separateness of FCs ("Structural classification") and was first developed by Herring and Santomero in 1990. They distinguish between:

- Complete Integration model or German model,
- Bank Parent, non-bank subsidiaries or British model,
- Holding Company model or US model,
- Holding Company parent, complete operational separateness.

A third classification relies on categories of systemic importance ("Regulatory classification"). A first subdivision of classification distinguishes between:

- G-SIBs,
- G-SIIs and
- NBNI G-SIFIs.

At a local level, the subdivision comprises:

- D-SIBs
- D-INBIs

As of 2023 there is no FSB framework for Domestically Important Insurers (D-SIID-SIIs), nor a framework for Domestically Non-Bank-Non-Insurance Systemically Important Financial Institutions (D-NBNI SIFIs). Also, the proposed methodologies for NBNI G-SIFIs have not been approved either.

The G-SIBs framework does not "capture the systemic impact of insurance subsidiaries of banking groups".[72] At the same time the IAIS excludes bank-owned insurance subsidiaries from the G-IIs network.[73] The result, apart from a gap in macro-prudential regulation, is the lack of clashes between G-SIBs and G-SIIs.

At national level, FSB rules were applied in different ways. After the GFC one of the major institutional reforms in the USA was the creation by the DFA of a systemic risk regulator, the FSOC. It has among others the responsibility "to identify risks to the financial stability of the United States that could arise from the material financial distress or failure, or ongoing activities, of large, interconnected bank holding companies or nonbank financial companies, or that could arise outside the financial services marketplace".[74] FSOC's main power is to designate the "SIFI label" to non-bank financial institutions and to FMU.[75]

According to the DFA there are three different "systemic importance" categories: (i) banking SIFIs: those whose assets are beyond USD 50 billion; (ii) non-banking SIFIs: those non-banking financial institutions whose material financial distress—or the nature, scope, size, scale, concentration, interconnectedness, or mix of its activities—could pose a threat to US financial stability and (iii) Financial Market Utilities.[76]

In Europe the CRD framework[77] determined another classification of systemic importance: Global systemically important institutions (G-SIIs),

[72] Basel Committee on Banking Supervision. "Consultive Document. Global Systemically Important Banks-Revised Assessment Framework" (March 2017), 5, https://www.bis.org/bcbs/publ/d402.pdf. Accessed 20 January 2023.

[73] Ibid.

[74] DFA.

[75] About FMUs see Federal Reserve (2015), https://www.federalreserve.gov/paymentsystems/designated_fmu_about.htm. Accessed 2023.

[76] DFA§ 165(a)(1) and §115; Cheryl D. Block "A Continuum Approach to Systemic Risk and Too Big to Fail", 6 Brook J. Corp Fin &Com L (2012), 289; Christina Parajon Skinner "Regulating Nonbanks: A Plan for SIFI Lite", *105 Geo. L.J.* (2017), 1379.

[77] CRD.

and other systemically important institutions (O-SIIs).[78] Member states will have to identify both kinds of institutions according to the EBA methodologies. According to the EBA Guidelines of disclosure of indicators of global importance, institutions with an overall exposure of EUR 200 billion will be subject to the disclosure requirements.[79]

At the same time, at the SSM level there is a test of significance in order to determine the scope of supervision of the European Central Bank (ECB) which is determined by: (1) size (the total value of its assets exceeds €30 billion); (2) economic importance (for the particular EU country's economy); (3) cross-border activities (total assets exceed €5 billion and the ratio of its cross-border assets/liabilities to its total assets/ liabilities is more than 20%); (4) public financial assistance (from the ESM or the EFSF). If banks fulfil at least one of these criteria, they may be referred to as "significant" and be directly supervised by the ECB.[80]

Therefore, ECB supervises significant institutions which are all "banking groups". The ECB also supervises cross-border institutions and groups, and it participates in the supplementary supervision of FCs by way of supervising the credit institutions which integrate the same and assumes the responsibilities of the coordinator referred to in FICOD.[81]

Every year the ECB reviews the list of authorized banks in order to assess its status. It may change because of normal business activity or because of mergers and/or acquisitions. For instance, if a significant bank fails to meet the significant test criteria three years in a row, it may be reclassified as "less significant".[82]

[78] Directive 2013/36/EU, article 131.

[79] EBA *Guidelines on disclosure of indicators of global systemic importance EBA/GL/ 2022/12* (2022).

[80] SSM Regulation.

[81] ECB *Guide to Banking Supervision* (2022). Lastra "International Financial", 363; Jens-Hinrich Binder "Banking Union and the Governance of Credit Institutions—A Legal Perspective" (2015) Working Paper No. 96, Leibniz Institute for Financial Research SAFE; List of supervised banks, https://www.bankingsupervision.europa.eu/ecb/pub/pdf/ssm.listofsupervisedentities202310.en.pdf?eae0f06beeb6b8c0b2a7f975a3241055. Accessed 3 November, 2023.

[82] ECB "What Makes a Bank Significant?", https://www.bankingsupervision.europa.eu/banking/list/criteria/html/index.en.html. Last modified 1 June 2023.

Commercial Classification

The first classification comprises banking groups, FCs and mixed conglomerates.

What Is a Banking Group?

In modern economy banks tend to expand into different countries and into different activities. In order to accomplish the internationalization process, banks organize themselves in groups of companies.[83]

The general definition of "group of companies" applies generally to banking groups or financial groups.[84] The essential difference between the group of companies in general and the definition of "banking group" and "financial group" arises from the special activities banks and financial institutions provide.

Groups of companies are valid ways of organizing a business. They are generally recognized in company law as useful.[85] At the same time, different companies that form the group maintain their corporate personality and "lifting the veil" are exceptional.[86] As Easterbrook and Fischel famously stated, "'piercing' seems to happen freakishly. Like lightning, it is rare, severe, and unprincipled".[87]

A group of companies encompasses some general problems which are solved in various ways. In the first place, intra-group transactions are subject to restrictions due to the prevention of conflict of interest. In the second place, there might be some type of protection for individual company of the groups' interest, minority investors' interest, and creditors of the different companies' interest.[88] In the third place, there are techniques to avoid the parent undertaking from taking advantage of its

[83] According to the Oxford Dictionary a group is "A Commercial Organization Consisting of Several Companies Under Common Ownership", https://en.oxforddictionaries.com/definition/group. Accessed 20 January 2023.

[84] Eddy Wymeersch "Financial Institutions as Members of Company Groups in the Law of the European Union" (European Business Organization Law Review 2001), 2.

[85] Ibid.

[86] Eva Hupkes "Form Follows Function—A New Architecture for Regulating and Resolving Global Financial Institutions", *European Business Organization Law Review* (2009), 372–377.

[87] Frank H. Easterbrook and Daniel. R. Fischel "Limited Liability and the Corporation", *The University of Chicago Law Review* (1985), 89.

[88] See Wymeersch "Financial Institutions", 3.

"dominant influence" over the subsidiary or branch ("private benefits"). These private benefits might be: transfer pricing agreements, provision of non-market price services, and appropriation of corporate opportunities,[89] among others.[90] In the fourth place, company law generally deals with directors' fiduciary duties, which are owed to the company involved and not to the group as a whole.[91]

As Lastra, Ayadi, Olivares-Caminal and Russo contend "the very definition of banking group is contentious".[92] One of the reasons for this is the lack of harmonization and regulatory convergence in the international arena. In the EU there is a reference to "banking groups" in the recital 48 of Directive No. 36 of 2013: "In the case of groups with diversified activities where parent undertakings control at least one subsidiary, the competent authorities should be able to assess the financial situation of each credit institution or investment firm in such a group. The competent authorities should at least have the means of obtaining from all undertakings within a group the information necessary for the performance of their function".[93] A group according to this concept would integrate parent undertakings, and subsidiaries (and branches), which apply diversified activities.

In the UK, The Banking Act 2009 (Banking group Companies) Order 2014 defines a "banking group of companies". As the explanatory note states: "A banking group company may be a parent or subsidiary undertaking of the bank or another company in the same group. There are excluded from the meaning of "banking group company"—a mixed

[89] Marcelo Sheppard Gelsi "Desvío De Oportunidades De Negocios De La Sociedad Anónima: Un supuesto de responsabilidad de los directores", *Revista de Derecho, Universidad de Montevideo* (2007), 105–119.

[90] See Wymeersch "Financial Institutions", 3.

[91] See Hupkes "Form Follows Function", 372–377, and Eddy Wymerersch, "Financial Institutions as Members of Company Groups in the Law of the European Union", *European Business Organization Law Review* (2001), 81–99.

[92] Rosa Lastra, Rym Ayadi, Rodrigo Olivares-Caminal, Costanza Russo "The Different and Operational Structures of Banking Groups in the Euro Area, and Their Impact on Banks 'Resolvability'" (European Parliament 2016), 5–21. Binder states referring to the EU "there is no such thing as a European group law for the financial industry in a technical sense either." Jens-Hinrich Binder "Financial Services Groups under EU Law" in G. Okutan Nilsson *Comparative Corporate Group Law. Conference in Honour of Prof. Dr. Unal Tekinalp's 80th Birthday* (Twelve Plates Publishing 2018).

[93] Directive No. 36 of 2013.

activity holding company where the bank is a subsidiary of an intermediate financial holding company; a subsidiary of such a mixed activity holding company, other than a parent or subsidiary of the bank, if it is neither a financial institution nor a subsidiary of a financial institution; and a covered bond vehicle or securitization company which is not an investment firm or a financial institution…".[94] The definition of the Banking Act 2009 includes, then, the complete "family tree" of the bank.[95]

The German Supervision of FCs Act refers to a group as different companies which include a parent, its subsidiaries and the entities in which the parent or a subsidiary holds an investment; or at least two companies connected in such a way that (1) they are under common control on the basis of a statutory provision or a contract or (2) the majority of their administrative, management or supervisory bodies are made up of the same persons who hold office during the financial year, if they have or should have consolidated accounts (horizontal group of companies).[96]

One of the consequences of the existence of banking groups in general is consolidated supervision. In the EU, the Banking Directive[97] requires consolidated supervision to every credit institution holding a credit institution or financial institution as subsidiary or hold a participation is such institution. Additionally, it requires consolidated supervision if a credit institution has a parent financial holding company. The Capital Adequacy Directive required consolidated supervision to groups including investment firms, which mirrors the EU Banking Directive.[98]

As Gruson affirms, consolidated supervision is not required for credit institutions and investment firms, which are subsidiaries of companies that

[94] The Banking Act 2009 (Banking group Companies) Order 2014.

[95] Anthony Pavlovich "Banking Group Companies: Which Entities Are Caught by the Special Resolution Regime?", *Journal of International Banking & Financial Law* (2015), 97. See also Código de Comercio (Spain), https://www.boe.es/eli/es/rd/1885/08/22/(1)/con. Accessed 14 July 2023.

[96] FC Supervision Act—FKAG, Available at http://www.gesetze-im-internet.de/fkag/__2.html. Last modified 20 January 2023. See also Code monétaire et financier, partie législative https://www.legifrance.gouv.fr/codes/texte_lc/LEGITEXT000006072026/. Accessed 20 January 2023. In Mercosur, the four founding members, Brazil, Argentina, Uruguay and Paraguay, have included some types of banking group regulations in their internal law.

[97] Banking Directive.

[98] Michael Gruson "Supervision of Financial Conglomerates in the European Union" in *Current Developments in Monetary and Financial Law, Vol. 4*, (IMF, 2008), 1–35.

are not credit institutions, investment firms or financial holding companies. Practically, consolidated supervision deals with consolidated financial situation in areas such as consolidated calculation of own funds, solvency ratio, adequacy of own funds to cover market risks, control of large exposures and restrictions on investments in the non-bank sector.[99]

In the US the DFA leave the Federal Reserve System as the unified consolidated regulator, covering holding companies owning insured depositories as well as holding companies that are considered potentially systemic.[100]

Financial groups are groups of companies which engage in financial activities. Wymeersch defines financial groups—before the FICOD—"as groups in which one or more components, legally independent companies, engage in offering financial services to the public, acting as a bank, a broker, an insurance company, an investment adviser or in any other capacity, offering their services to individuals, professional investment managers or other business firms".[101]

This definition of a financial group, which was adopted before the rise of the FICOD in Europe in 2002, leads us to analyse in more detail the definition of the "financial conglomerate".

What Is a Financial Conglomerate?

The increasing relevance of international FCs poses a double complexity due to its cross-sectoral and cross-jurisdiction dimensions.[102] The definition of a FC varies according to the practices and legislation within different jurisdictions.[103] The cross-sectoral dimension of the FC is the key element that distinguishes the banking group from the FC.[104]

[99] Ibid.

[100] Ashok Vir Bhatia "Consolidated Regulation and Supervision in the United States" IMF Working Paper Monetary and Capital Markets Department Strategy, Policy, and Review Department (2011).

[101] Wymeersch "Financial Institutions", 1.

[102] Rosa Lastra and Rodrigo Olivares-Caminal "Cross Border Insolvency: The Case of financial conglomerates in J. Raymon Laborsse, R. Olivares-Caminal and D. Singh *Financial Crisis Management and Bank Resolution*, (Informa, 2009), 269. Daniele D'Alvia "Law and the Market: Private Actors and Self-Regulation", Towards a New Role of Public International Law' European Business Law Review (2018), 938.

[103] Ibid.

[104] Lastra, Ayadi, Olivares-Caminal, Russo "The different", 5–21.

It is fair to say the notion of a conglomerate might have been confused with the notion of "industrial conglomerate" before the term "financial conglomerate" was widely used by the financial sector. Such a misunderstanding was strengthened by the fact that one of the recognized features of the industrial conglomerate is "conglomerate diversification". This is defined as "a diversification into completely different activities with a completely different technology oriented towards markets".[105] As FCs involve sectors that might be complementary and tend to explore synergies, the term "conglomerate diversification" would not apply to FCs.[106]

The term "conglomerate" means "a thing consisting of a number of different and distinct parts or items that are grouped together" and "a large corporation formed by the merging of separate and diverse firms".[107] In the FC there is an element of differentiation on the activities performed by it, and at the same time an element of unity in the formation of a "unit".[108]

According to Walker, "the term conglomerate can be used to refer to any form of business structure that involves at least two distinct forms of industrial activity or service provision".[109]

A FC is defined by the Tripartite Group of Bank, Insurance and Securities Regulators as "any group of companies under common control or dominant influence, including any financial holding company, which conducts material financial activities in at least two of the regulated banking, securities or insurance sectors".[110] As stated by Lastra, Ayadi,

[105] Lutgart Van den Berghe *Financial Conlomerates. New Rules for New Players?* (Klewer Academic Publishers 1995), 14.

[106] Ibid.

[107] Oxford dictionaries, https://en.oxforddictionaries.com/definition/conglomerate. Accessed 20 January 2020.

[108] Arend J. Veermat "Defining Financial Conglomerates" in Van den Berghe, "Financial Conlomerates", 21.

[109] George Walker "The Law of Financial Conglomerates: The Next Generation", (1996), 30 and see generally: James Maycock, *Financial Conglomerates: The New Phenomenon* (Gower Publishing Company, 1986); Charles R. Spruill *Conglomerates and The Evolution of Capitalism*, (Southern Illinois University Press 1982); Harry Mcvea, *Financial Conglomerates and The Chinese Wall: Regulating Conflicts of Interest* (OUP 1993).

[110] Bank of Financial Settlements "The Supervision of Financial Conglomerates" (A Report by the Tripartite Group of Bank, Securities and Insurance Regulators 1995), 13.

Olivares-Caminal and Russo, "a financial conglomerate may be characterized primarily as a securities, insurance or a banking structure. The character would be determined by the sector represented at the holding company level and by the type of activity that constitutes the major business of the conglomerate".[111]

As stated above, under SSM, ECB supervises significant banking groups which are determined by size, economic importance, cross-border importance, cross-border activities and public financial assistance. In 2023 ECB supervises 111 entities, which reflects how influential the supervision of ECB is for primarily banking FCs and how the supervisor is shaping the type of banking groups the EU will have in the near future.[112]

In 2002 the EU adopted the FICOD in order to tighten supervision of this kind of groups and to ensure the strength of the financial system.[113]

According to Article 2(14) of the FICOD, a financial conglomerate "means a group or subgroup, where a regulated entity is at the head of the group or subgroup, or where at least one of the subsidiaries in that group or subgroup is a regulated entity, and which meets the following conditions:

a. Where there is a regulated entity at the head of the group or subgroup:
    i. that entity is a parent undertaking of an entity in the financial sector, an entity which holds a participation in an entity in the financial sector, or an entity linked with an entity in the financial sector by a relationship;
    ii. at least one of the entities in the group or subgroup is within the insurance sector and at least one is within the banking or investment services sector; and
    iii. the consolidated or aggregated activities of the entities in the group or subgroup within the insurance sector and of the entities within the banking and investment services sector are both significant; or

[111] Lastra, Ayadi, Olivares-Caminal and Russo, "The Different", 7.

[112] ECB "List of Supervised entities", 1 January 2023, https://www.bankingsupervision.europa.eu/ecb/pub/pdf/ssm.listofsupervisedentities202302.en.pdf. Accessed 8 April 2023.

[113] FICOD.

b. where there is no regulated entity at the head of the group or subgroup:

   i. the group's or subgroup's activities occur mainly in the financial sector;
   ii. at least one of the entities in the group or subgroup is within the insurance sector and at least one is within the banking or investment services sector; and
   iii. the consolidated or aggregated activities of the entities in the group or subgroup within the insurance sector and of the entities within the banking and investment services sector are both significant."

According to the FICOD, a "group" means a set of undertakings which consists of a parent undertaking, its subsidiaries and the entities in which the parent undertaking or its subsidiaries are defined according to the Consolidated Accounts Directive.[114]

In order to be considered a FC by EU law they must: (1) contain at least one regulated entity in an EU member state; (2) comprise at least one entity in the insurance sector and at least another in banking/securities sectors; (3) include "significant" cross-sectorial activities. To assess the significant test, the banking/securities sector together must be significant, as well as the insurance sector assessed alone. The "relative criterion" assesses the relevance of the sector in the group's total assets and solvency requirements, which need to be more than 10%. The "absolute criterion" determines that when the small sector as assessed by the relative criterion has a balance sheet of more than € 6 billion, it is also categorized as significant.[115]

In the case where there is no regulated entity at the head of the groups or subgroup's activities, the FICOD established they must "occur mainly in the financial sector". For the purposes of determining whether the activities of a group mainly "occur in the financial sector", the ratio of the balance sheet total of the regulated and non-regulated financial sector

[114] FICOD article 2(12).

[115] Frank Dierick "The Supervision of Mixed Financial Services Groups in Europe", Occasional Paper Series No 20, *ECB* (2004), 11; FICOD, articles 2 and 3.

entities in the group to the balance sheet total of the group as a whole should exceed 40%.[116]

At the same time, when a conglomerate involves an industrial or commercial company and a regulated company it is known as a mixed conglomerate.[117]

Main Features of Each Financial Sector

As stated before, FCs combine two of the three sectors of the financial sector: banking, insurance and securities.

Each sector has a set of characteristics that differ from each other, comprising a different balance sheet structure, involving different risks and different supervision processes.

As specified above, banks engage in transforming short-term liabilities into long-term assets.[118] The bank-customer relationship tends to happen in a net of branches, while the main risk involved in its activity is credit and liquidity risk.[119] According to the Joint Forum,[120] "risk for banks has historically been credit risk - which can be amplified by concentration risk - on the asset side of the balance sheet. Risk arises on the liability side as well, in the form of liquidity risk posed by maturity mismatches between short-term deposits and long-term loans. Other banking risks include market risk (including volatility in the trading book), interest rate risk in the banking book, foreign exchange risk, funding risk, operational risk, country and transfer risk, legal risk, and reputation risk".[121]

Insurance companies underwrite risks for a premium, providing a safety net when adverse events arise.[122] In order to achieve their objectives, insurance companies rely on managing risks through "diversification and the law of large numbers". They can diversify policy liabilities by contracting reinsurance, and they rely on statistical calculations to

[116] FICOD article 3.1.

[117] European Commission "Towards an EU Directive on the Prudential Supervision of FCs", MARKT/3021/2000 (EC, 2000).

[118] Beck et al. "Bailing Out", 9; Padoa Scioppa, "The Transformation", 7; Lastra, "International Financial", 141.

[119] Dierick "The Supervision", 12.

[120] Joint Forum history https://www.bis.org/bcbs/jointforum.htm. Last modified 20 January 2023.

[121] Joint Forum *Core Principles: Cross-Sectorial Comparison* (2001), 9.

[122] Dierick "The Supervision", 12.

estimate liabilities.[123] The typical risks of the insurance sector are underwriting risks, meaning that the technical provisions or premiums are below the real needs of a company to comply with their contracts, and the investment risk, meaning that the investments the firm engages are insufficient to fulfil their obligations.[124] Typically insurance assets tend to be less risky, e.g. government bonds, and risk-linked bonds (catastrophe bonds) are uncommon. Therefore, insurance companies are assessed as "less fragile" than banks.[125]

The securities sector "is sensitive to macroeconomic factors in that there is typically a predictable correlation between macroeconomic indicators and market sentiment. Extreme macroeconomic conditions can lead to rapid changes in confidence, resulting in, for example, runs on assets by fund managers or rapid unwinding of futures positions with leverage on equity values".[126] The asset side of the balance sheet comprises inter alia receivables secured by securities and financial instruments, while the liabilities side includes payables to consumers. The assets and liabilities are both short term and market to market on a daily basis, "reflecting their true financial position".[127] The main risks involved in the securities sector are market and liquidity risk.[128] Generally, security firm regulators tend to ensure firms adopt correct record keeping and can easily distinguish their own assets from client assets.[129]

What Is a Mixed Conglomerate?

As stated above, a mixed conglomerate is a group of companies where at least one company engage in an activity of a commercial or industrial nature, and at least one company is a regulated financial institution.

[123] See Joint Forum "Core Principles", 10.

[124] See Dierick "The Supervision", 12.

[125] Indrek Saapar and Farouk Soussa "Financial Consolidation and Conglomeration: Implications for the Financial Safety Net" in Lisa Halme, et al. ***Financial Stability and Central Banks Selected Issues for Financial Safety Nets and Market Discipline*** (Bank of England 2000), 71–94.

[126] Joint Forum "Core Principles", 11.

[127] Saapar and Soussa "Financial Consolidation", 71–94; See generally Charles Goodhart, Philippe Hartmann, David Llewellyn, Liliana Rojas-Suarez, Steven Wesibrod *Financial Regulation: Why, How and Where Now?* (Routledge 1997).

[128] Dierick "The Supervision", 12.

[129] Ibid.

Traditionally, Anglo-Saxon countries relied on a separation between banks and commercial and industrial companies, as well as other financial companies. On the other hand, continental European, Latin American and Asian countries tended not to impose strict restrictions on non-banking corporations owing commercial or industrial companies. In recent years, Anglo-Saxon countries have converged with the other regions in accepting FCs.[130]

The links between banks and commercial and industrial companies vary according to the bank's role in the economy. Two models are identified. The first is the so-called Anglo-Saxon model or capital market system. In this model the members of the public invest in shares of companies which may be traded individually or through institutional investors via the stock exchange. Companies rely on capital markets for financing. Banks, at the same time, have a role in "arm-length financing", mergers and acquisitions, and internal corporate restructuring.[131] On the other hand, the Continental European/Latin American/Asian model ("Continental model") or bank-based system comprises the following features: (1) banks generally own equity in corporations; (2) banks act as "commercial and investment bankers to their clients"; (3) bank representatives may serve as directors for their clients; (4) banks may own industrial groups; and, (5) capital markets play a "limited role in financing corporations".[132]

The two systems help to understand why traditionally the Anglo-Saxon world intended to separate commerce from banking, while the continental approach favoured it.

When the Bank of England was founded in 1694 it expressly forbade trade in merchandise.[133] The same can be said in the US. Even though the Manhattan Company—a water provider in NYC—in 1799 created the Bank of Manhattan Company as a subsidiary,[134] some years later the law forbade a commercial company from performing banking activities. In 1825 the New York Statute stated banks would "possess all incidental

[130] Schooner and Taylor "Global Bank Regulation", 112.

[131] Ibid.

[132] Ibid., 113.

[133] Bank of England Act, 1694, article XXVI, http://www.legislation.gov.uk/aep/WillandMar/5-6/20/section/XXVI. Accessed 20 January 2023.

[134] JPMorgan Chase "The History of JPMorgan Chase & Co. 200 Years of Leadership in Banking", https://www.calameo.com/read/000046992b7e1be4117b9. Accessed 20 January 2018; Schooner, "Global Bank Regulation", 114.

and necessary powers to carry on the business of banking...but the said company shall have and possess no other powers whatsoever...".[135]

On the other hand, the European Continental model relied on banks to finance industry undertakings. For instance, a Deutsche Bank statute reads "the object of the company is to transact banking business of all kinds, in particular to promote and facilitate trade relations between Germany, other European countries and overseas markets". But soon it became the financier of industrial groups in Germany.[136] Sraffa understood in 1921 that bank financing of the industry was indispensable due to the shortage of capital in Italy, the unwillingness of households to invest their savings in the industry and the "timidity and ignorance" of capitalists in the country.[137] In Japan the *Keiretsu* model always includes a bank. The "*keiretsu*" is a group of industries "with one- and two-way agreements to favor each other in business deals and share in shouldering temporary burdens that would otherwise cause instability for the group... Like all *keiretsu*, there is a bank as a member, although it has less pull in a vertical orientation".[138]

Although traditionally the separation between commerce and banking existed in the Anglo-Saxon model, today both England and the US allow mixed conglomerates to operate, converging into the Continental approach. Legislation, as Effros points out, has been a driver for the

[135] William C. Bryant *The Legislative History of Banking in the State of New York, During the Period of Fifty Years, from A.D. 1791 to A.D. 1841* (1855) 19; See Schooner, "Global Bank Regulation", 114.

[136] Deutsche Bank "Deutsche Bank History Chronicle—From 1870 Until Today", https://www.db.com/files/documents/Deutsche-Bank-History--Chronicle-from-1870-until-today.pdf. Accessed 20 January 2023.

[137] Piero Sraffa "The Bank Crisis in Italy", *Economical Journal* (1922), 194.

[138] "Matt Jancer "How Eight Conglomerates Dominate Japanese Industry", Smithonian.com, 7 September 2016, https://www.smithsonianmag.com/innovation/how-eight-conglomerates-dominate-japanese-industry-180960356/ Accessed 20 January 2023; Jean McGuire and Sandra Dow "Japanese keiretsu: Past, Present, Future", *Asia Pac J Manag* (2009), 333–351; Lance Eliot Brouthers, Yan Gao and Stuart Napshin "Keiretsu Centrality—Profits and Profit Stability: A Power Dependence Perspective", *Journal of Business Research* (2014), 2603–2610; Rungrudee Suetorsak "Keiretsu and Risk: An Examination of the Risk Exposure of Keiretsu Banks in Japan", *J Econ Finan*, Vol. 31 (2007), 268; Jongmoo Jay Choi, Takato Hiraki and James A. Landi "The Value of Multinationality and Business Group for Japanese Firms", *Journal of Corporate Finance* (2014), 88–110.

historical (relative) further development of capital markets in the US and Japan as opposed to Germany.[139]

One key aspect to understand the relevance of banking in the economy is to compare banking assets with the Gross domestic product (GDP) of different countries. The results reflect Europe, Asia and Brazil rely on banking much more than the US.[140]

A question that has been raised is whether banks should be allowed to perform commercial activities. While the debate was first centred on whether the same bank would be permitted to perform commercial activities, the rational for forbidding mixed activity remains valid for mixed conglomerates.

According to Effros the rationale behind forbidding banks performing commercial activities is threefold. In the first place, allowing the banks to compete with their consumers would imply that their decision-making regarding loans to their competitors would be impartial. Secondly, as credit is a limited resource, if allocated in an impartial manner, society would pay "an economic penalty" for the "less than optimal allocation" of such credit. Thirdly, the safety and soundness of the bank might be endangered since bank officers might not have the experience to run a commercial activity. At the same time, customers of the bank would trust the investments of the bank are safe and not of a risky nature, as might be the case in the commercial business.[141]

Sraffa has explained banks with strong links with industrial or commercial companies might engage in long-term loans, increasing the maturity transformation risk. The main reason for this is banks would "immobilize" a large amount of funds where the short-term debts would still be there to be triggered at any moment.[142]

[139] Effros "Central Bank", 8. Also see generally Rafael La Porta, Florencio Lopez-De-Silanes, Andrei Shleifer and Robert W. Vishny "Legal Determinants of External Finance, *The Journal of Finance* (1997), 1131–1150.

[140] For EU data see EU Report on Financial Data, https://www.ecb.europa.eu/pub/pdf/other/reportonfinancialstructures201610.en.pdf; For US see https://fred.stlouisfed.org/series/TLAACBW027SBOG. Accessed 20 January 2023.

[141] Effros "Central Bank", 5.

[142] Sraffa "The Bank Crisis", 194.

Another problem is "insider lending" or lending in preferential terms to the commercially or industrially favoured company.[143] This has in turn two main concerns. Firstly, the lack of adequate assessment of lending risk, since the parent company may impose undue pressure on the board of the linked company, and secondly, the portfolio may be "insufficiently diversified".[144] Another perverse consequence of the ownership link between banks and commercial companies is the so-called tunnelling effect, by way of which majority shareholders appropriate assets of their own bank through fake lending, loan guarantees and other illegal methods.[145]

Even though there are several arguments to disfavour the engagement of banks in commercial and industrial activities, the scholarly "consensus"[146] in forbidding this type of activity in the 1980s and 1990s in the US has now changed direction, and mixed conglomerates may be found both in the UK and the US, as well as in the EU, Latin America and Asia.[147]

Structural Classification Organizational Structures of FCs

Herring and Santomero were the first to incorporate the distinction of legal and operational separateness and to draw a classification of FCs. For them, legal separateness implies "different products provided by separate corporate entities, each of which has its own management structure, set

[143] Gustavo A. Del Angel "The nexus between business groups and banks: Mexico, 1932–1982" *Business History* (2016), 122; Rafael La Porta, Florencio López-de-Silanes and Guillermo Zamarripa "Related Lending" *The Quarterly Journal of Economics*, (2003), 231–268; Noel Maurer and Stephen Haber "Related Lending and Economic Performance" *The Journal of Economic History* (2007), 551–581; Luc Laeven "Insider Lending and Bank Ownership: The Case of Russia" *Journal of Comparative Economics* (2001), 207–229; Robert Cull, Stephen Haber and Masami Imai "Related lending and banking development", *Journal of International Business Studies*, (2011), 406–426.

[144] Schooner "Global bank regulation", 121.

[145] Simon Johnson, Rafael La Porta, Florencio Lopez-de-Silanes and Andrei Shleifer "Tunneling", *The American Economic Review*, (2000), 22–27; Kee-Hong Bae, Jun-Koo Kang and Jin-Mo Kim "Tunneling or Value Added? Evidence from Mergers by Korean Business Groups", *The Journal of Finance* (2002), 2695; Yuan George Shan "Can Internal Governance Mechanisms Prevent Asset Appropriation? Examination of Type I Tunneling in China", *Corporate Governance: An International Review* (2013), 225–241.

[146] Effros "Central Bank", 4.

[147] This book will not assess the Commercial classification per se since it is merely descriptive, contrary to the structural and Regulatory classifications.

of accounts, board of directors, and capital. Its shareholders are legally protected from disastrous outcomes in the separate corporate entity by limited liability". On the other hand, operational separateness implies "self-imposed restrictions" or Chinese Walls that prevent the "integrated production" of different products within the group.[148] The building of firewalls within the group may prevent intra-group credit and information sharing and may also impose different distribution channels for some of the products of the conglomerate.[149]

Herring and Santomero classified FCs in four different models: 1) the "complete integration" model or German model; 2) the "bank parent, non-bank subsidiaries" or British model; 3) the "holding company parent, all activities as subsidiaries" model or US model, and 4) holding company parent, complete operational separateness model or complete operational separateness model.[150]

Complete Integration or German Model

The Complete Integration or German model comprises a single corporate entity which may provide several financial activities such as insurance,

[148] Richard J. Herring and Anthony M. Santomero "The Corporate Structure of Financial Conglomerates", *Journal of Financial Services Research* (1990), 223–224.

[149] Ibid., 223.

[150] Ibid., 223–228. The following scholars also refer to the same or similar classification as used by Herring and Santomero: Kazuhiko Koguchi and Giancarlo Forestieri, *Financial Conglomerates* (Organization for Economic Co-operation and Development 1993); Anthony Saunders and Ingo Walter Universal *Banking in the United States. What Could We Gain? What Could We Lose?*" (OUP 1994); João Santos "Commercial Banks in the Securities Business: A Review", *Journal of Financial Services Research* (1998); Lutgart Berghe and Kurt Verweire *Creating the Future with All Finance and Financial Conglomeartes* (Klewer Academics Publishers 1998); Bernard Shull and Lawrence J. White "The Right Corporate Structure for Expanded Bank Activities", *Banking L.J.* (1998), 446; Saapar and Soussa "Financial Consolidation"; Harold Skipper "Financial Services Integration Worldwide: Promises And Pitfalls" in *Insurance Regulation, Liberalisation and Financial Convergence* (OECD 2001); Howell E. Jackson and C. Half "Background Paper on Evolving Tends in the Supervision of Financial Conglomerates", *Harvard Law School* (2002); Rudi Vander Vennet "Cost Efficiency of Financial Conglomerates and Universal Banks in Europe" *Journal of Money, Credit and Banking* (2002); Dierick "The Supervision"; Douglas Arner *Financial Stability, Economic Growth, and the Role of Law* (Cambridge University Press 2009); Lastra and Olivares Caminal "Cross Border Insolvency"; Valentina Peleckiene, Kestutis Peleckies, Gitana Dudzeviciute "New Challenges of Supervising Financial Conglomerates" *Intellectual Economics* (2011).

banking and securities.[151] The Complete Integration model allows the conglomerate to engage in such activities even without firewalls or Chinese walls to separate distinct functions within it.[152] Therefore, the German model may involve no legal or functional separateness. Some scholars prefer to use the term "universal bank" to define such model.[153]

The main advantage of the German model is the maximization of synergies between different activities producing a "mix of outputs" at a lower cost.[154]

On the other hand, the German model may have the potential of maximizing anticompetitive behavior,[155] conflict of interests[156] and "disruptive shocks".[157]

Centralizing all three financial activities in one single corporate entity would give more chances for management to restrict, prevent or distort competition in all three markets.

Conflict of interest "exists whenever one is serving two or more interests and can put one person in a better position at the expense of another".[158] When the same institution is serving more groups of customers the potential for conflict of interest increases.

The consequences of the collapse of a German model FC would be wider in scope since the disruption of its functions would encompass a wider scope of activities.

At the same time the FC may expand the safety net and "implicit subsidies" to non-banking activities. This would violate the policy behind these

[151] Lastra and Olivares Caminal "Cross Border Insolvency", 271.

[152] Herring and Santomero "The Corporate", 481.

[153] Santos "Commercial Banks", 46; Shull and White, "The Right Corporate Structure", 467; Arner, "Financial Stability", 278.

[154] Herring and Santomero "The Corporate", 481; Shull and White "The Right Corporate Structure", 470.

[155] Herring and Santomero "The Corporate", 482; Peleckiene, Peleckies, and Dudzeviciute, "New Challenges", 300.

[156] Santos "Commercial Banks", 47. Herring and Santomero "The Corporate", 482.

[157] Herring and Santomero, "The Corporate", 482.

[158] Franklin. R. Edwards "Banks and Securities Activities: Legal and Economic Perspectives on the Glass-Steagall Act" in Lawrence. G. Goldbergand and Lawrence. J. White *The Deregulation of Banking and Securities Activities*, (Lexington, MA, Lexington Books 1979), 273–294.

regulations which protects banking activity due to its specialty.[159] Also, the risks associated with non-banking activities might endanger the safety and soundness of the bank, triggering the insolvency or resolution of the entity.[160] Finally, the German model would be more difficult to regulate than other models where each function is performed by a different institution[161] and would imply an expansion of regulation to other non-banking activities,[162] which would be "costly and imprecise".[163]

In fact, contrary to traditional wisdom in Germany the most common model comprises a Banking/securities company, with an insurance subsidiary.[164] Some scholars distinguish between complete integration and "partial integration" in order to include this kind of arrangement. By partial integration these scholars mean the existence of at least two activities provided by the same legal entity.[165] In Germany this process has been left to the "dwarfing" of securities' activities which were absorbed by the banks. The result is that independent securities firms are lacking in Germany and the security business is subsumed under banking.

Bank Parent, Non-bank Subsidiaries or British Model

The second model includes a banking parent company and non-banking subsidiaries that may provide insurance and securities activities, among others. According to Herring and Santomero, this model may be referred to as the British model.[166]

[159] Shull and White "The Right Corporate Structure", 471; Herring and Santomero, "The Corporate", 482.

[160] Shull and White "The Right Corporate Structure", 470.

[161] Herring and Santomero "The Corporate", 482.

[162] Shull and White "The Right Corporate Structure", 470.

[163] Herring and Santomero "The Corporate", 482; Verweire and Van den Berghe, "Creating the Future",62.

[164] Act on the Supervision of Insurance Undertakings Section 15(1); https://www.bafin.de/SharedDocs/Downloads/EN/Aufsichtsrecht/dl_vag_en_va.html?nn=8356586. Accessed 20 January 2023; Directive 92/49/EEC, Article 8 1 b; Vander Vennet "Cost Efficiency", 260; Ingo Walter " Universal Banking: A Shareholder Value Perspective" *European Management Journal* (1996), 345; Institute of International Bankers "Global Survey 2014", https://cdn.ymaws.com/sites/iib.site-ym.com/resource/resmgr/Docs/2014GlobalSurvey.pdf. Accessed 20 January 2023.

[165] Walter "Universal Banking: A Shareholder", 345; Skipper "Financial Services Integration", 5.

[166] Herring and Santomero "The Corporate", 225.

One advantage of the British model is that it might allow a functional regulation of banking activity which would reduce the costs of supervision. Secondly, legal separateness would protect the banking parent from potential bad business of its subsidiaries.[167] Thirdly, as the subsidiary is "trapped" below the parent, its income will "naturally flow up" to the bank in times of necessity.[168]

The first disadvantage would be that even though legal separateness may isolate the parent from its subsidiaries' losses, parent solvency might be seriously affected by the failure of a subsidiary. This may be the case in at least four scenarios: (1) the creditors of the failed subsidiary obtain to "pierce the corporate veil" and seize the parent assets; (2) the bank suffers reputational damage and loses clients; (3) the parent makes "sizable loans" to the subsidiary; and, (4) the parent tries to avoid the subsidiary's failure by relocating assets into it.[169] This might trigger the need to bail out the subsidiary in order to prevent further damage.[170]

Secondly, the confidence of the market in that the parent company will provide liquidity assistance to its subsidiary in times of trouble strengthens the subsidiaries' creditworthiness. However, while this could reduce funding costs of the FC, it may cause competition distortion and difficult regulation and supervision.[171]

Thirdly, separating activities through an independent subsidiary would prevent a full maximization of the synergies and diversification advantages of the German model.[172]

Fourth, legal separateness would also demand capitalizing the subsidiary, which increases the costs of the group functioning. At the same time, it might create "agency problems" since there would be various management bodies involved.[173]

Fifth, creditors of the parent company would be able to seize all the assets of the company, which will include bank assets as well as securities

[167] Ibid.

[168] Shull and White "The Right Corporate Structure", 475.

[169] Ibid., 471.

[170] Herring and Santomero "The Corporate", 226.

[171] Ibid.

[172] Jackson and Half "Background Paper", 6; Dierick "The Supervision", 18; Koguchi and Forestieri, "Financial Conglomerates", 25.

[173] Dierick "The Supervision", 18.

unit capital (which is an asset of the bank), theoretically increasing the chance of recovering their investment. This would not be automatically the case if the lines of business were legally separated. From the group perspective, this would be a disadvantage of the British organizational form.[174]

Holding Company Model: The US Model

In the Holding Company model, since 1956, independent banking and non-banking activities are functionally and legally separated under a holding company "umbrella" at the top of the structure, which is the owner of the banking, securities and insurance companies.[175]

Usually, the holding company would perform common group functions such as risk management, capital raising and allocation, auditing and information technology.[176]

The Holding Company model would theoretically have the "least likelihood" of internal contagion because of functional and legal separateness.[177]

Herring and Santomero argue the advantages of the legal separateness of the Holding Company model are: (1) limited liability allows the FC to limit the losses of a particular subsidiary or line of business; (2) independent subsidiaries can be funded more cheaply if the market believes the parent will aid the subsidiary in times of distress; (3) in cases of Mergers and Acquisitions, maintaining the existing corporate structures may allow the taking advantage of "reputational capital" of the existing company; (4) maintaining separate corporations may facilitate managerial control and balancing compensation packages to meet different lines of business that may differ considerably; and, (5) clients might be more comfortable in a separate entity if they feel they are protected from conflicts of interest that may arise if activities are provided by the same entity.[178]

174 Santos "Commercial Banks", 48.

175 Saapar and Soussa "Financial Consolidation", 83; Herring and Santomero, "The Corporate", 227.

176 Dierick "The Supervision", 18.

177 Saapar and Soussa "Financial Consolidation", 83.

178 Herring and Santomero "The Corporate", 231.

An additional advantage of the separate line of business approach (banking, securities, insurance) is that it prevents culture clashes. Managerial business styles may be different in each financial sector.[179]

Also, legal separateness in the holding model may limit the safety net implicit coverage easier than in an integrated or German model, aligning the regulatory purpose (i.e. lender of last resort) with the actual banking activities.[180]

However, as stated above, the first advantage is weakened by the fact that the market does not perceive the subsidiary to be different from the group as a whole.[181] Walter Wriston, former chairman of Citicorp, stated some decades ago: "it is inconceivable that any major bank would walk away from any subsidiary of its holding company. If your name is on the door, all your capital funds are going to be behind in the real world. Lawyers can say they have separation, but the market place is persuasive, and it would not see it that way". Former FRB Chairman Paul Volcker stated "the practical realities of the market place and the internal dynamics of a business organization under central direction drive bank holding companies to act…as one business entity, with the component parts drawing on each other for marketing and financial strength. Certainly, the market conceives of a bank holding company and its components in that way. And if market participants tend to consider the bank holding company as an integrated entity, problems in one part of the system will inevitably be transmitted to other parts".[182] Also, some regulatory measures like consolidated financial reporting may strengthen the market perception that the group acts as an entity and therefore would aid subsidiaries in need.[183]

Finally, legal separateness may involve "costs of its own". Firstly, the FC must capitalize the different subsidiaries. Secondly, it limits its capacity to fully achieve the scope of economies. Thirdly, similar to the British

[179] Koguchi and Forestieri "Financial Conglomerates", 25.

[180] Santos "Commercial Banks", 48.

[181] Ibid., 47.

[182] Arthur Wilmarth "Controlling Systemic Risk in an Era of Financial Consolidation", *Current Developments in Monetary and Financial Law*, Vol. 3 (IMF 2005), 603.

[183] Santos "Commercial Banks", 47–48.

model, legal and functional separateness determines possible agency problems since the FC needs to create different managing teams. It may also stimulate conflicts of interest between the different subsidiaries.[184]

Holding Company Parent, Complete Operational Separateness
Herring and Santomero complete their classification with this fourth model, where there is a complete operational and legal separateness. In this model, there is a complete loss of economies of scope to producers and clients and operating synergies. The only remaining advantage would be the diversification of income to the holding company. As Herring and Santomero conclude, this model is not common in the financial industry.[185]

Assessment of the Structural Classification
The main attraction of the structural classification is its focus on legal separateness and operational separateness. The structural classification may help the regulator to understand the different implications of risk assessment, taxation and resolution. It relies on objective and palpable data, which makes it easy to understand and to study.

After the GFC, the structural classification has gained a new relevance, since the resolution strategies for G-SIFIs would be defined among the corporate structures of the financial group. According to the FSB, "The Key Attributes require the development of a resolution strategy for G-SIFIs that establishes an approach for resolving the failing firm in a way that protects its critical functions, government funds and systemic stability, and achieves other relevant resolution objectives. The resolution strategy is a key component of the overall resolution plan required under the Key Attributes".[186] The two resolution strategies are the Single Point of Entry Resolution (SPOE) and the Multiple Point of Entry Resolution (MPOE), respectively, in which resolution powers are applied to the top of a group by a single national resolution authority, and "in which resolution tools are applied to different parts of the group by two or more

[184] Ibid.

[185] Herring and Santomero "The Corporate", 487.

[186] FSB *Recovery and Resolution Planning for Systemically Important Financial Institutions: Guidance on Developing Effective Resolution Strategies* (FSB 2013), 5.

resolution authorities acting in a coordinated way".[187] In 1990, when Herring and Santomero instituted the structural classification the new resolution strategies were far from existing. Nevertheless, it now proves its resilience in a way its authors would not have expected.

Van den Berghe has pointed out Herring and Santomero's classification has certain drawbacks. Firstly, he states the classification is "rather theoretical" and less "practical" for business managers. Secondly, he states the "German model doesn't exist" in practice, since "the production of insurance by banks and of banking services by insurers is generally prohibited in all countries". Thirdly, the author contends there are other forms of conglomerates which are based on weaker links such as joint ventures or marketing agreements that are not included in the classification. Fourth, Herring and Santomero focus strongly on FCs where "banks are dominant", whereas there are many FCs where insurance is dominant. Fifth, Van den Berghe argues the main concern of Herring and Santomero is legal separateness (even though they mention operational separateness) and therefore "the single use of legal distinction may be misleading and may be based on false hypothesis".[188]

The first argument is weak since the value of a classification should not be based on its practical relevance to managers of FCs, but on how they may help to understand its object and the consequences legislators and regulators can draw from it.

The second issue is true in Europe and may be solved by including a subdivision of the Complete Integration or German model by comprising a Partial Integration model which contains the actual structure of European FCs, where insurance is structured as a separate subsidiary.

The third topic is related to what the literature calls "horizontal groups". While horizontal groups exist and are regulated at the European level, the importance of such groups tends to be less significant than the other classifications. The Herring and Santomero Classification might be enlarged by adding a fifth category which would include "horizontal groups". In this sense, in 1993 Koguchi and Forestieri proposed a classification based on Herring and Santomero's model but added "joint venture" and "sales agreement" as supplementary categories of FCs.[189]

[187] Ibid.

[188] Verweire and Van den Berghe "Creating the Future", 63.

[189] Koguchi, and Forestieri "Financial Conglomerates", 25.

The fourth qualification remains true. While Herring and Santomero's classification underlines the bank as the epicentre of the FC, it is true there are FCs that are insurance-centred. This book, as stated in the Introduction chapter, will focus on the importance of bank FCs, given the specialty of banks and the challenges they pose to the whole economy.

The fifth point raised by Van der Berghe is also relevant. While operational separateness is present in Herring and Santomero's classification, legal separateness is central to their work. That said, the classification remains relevant as structured by the authors. Stating that "single use" of the classification may be based on "false hypothesis"[190] tends towards exaggeration. The classification always relies on an angle of the concept. FCs are enormous creatures and one classification would not encompass all of its expressions.

Finally, even when a FC chooses to structure itself in certain ways, there are forces in place far beyond its control. For instance, certain legal doctrines, such as the doctrine of the "source of strength" in the US, might change the way in which the group business strategies work. While in theory, the US model would help the holding company to "abandon" the subsidiary at any time, the source of strength doctrine would imply the need for the group to aid them in cases of distress.

Regulatory Classification

After the GFC, regulatory bodies designed new regulations to prevent systemic risk and enhance macro-prudential regulation. Until the GFC the issue of the size of banks and the implicit guarantees provided by governments were comprised in the Too Big to save doctrine. The GFC forced new regulations that ended up with new categories of financial institutions.

The rational being financial regulation differs from general company law, in that the former seeks the preservation of financial stability and not primarily the protection of creditors and shareholders, although they regulate similar problems.[191]

The FSB has emerged with a new system of unilateral "designation" of certain groups of companies as "globally systemically important". The

[190] Verweire and Van den Berghe "Creating the Future", 63.

[191] Binder "Financial Services Groups", 113.

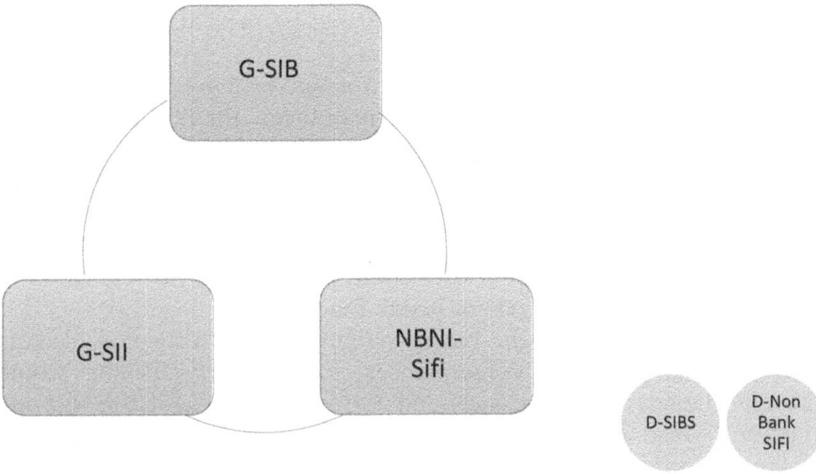

Fig. 2.1 Regulatory classification

new system has two pillars: (1) a unilateral designation system; and (2) the application of certain policies to those designated entities in order to tackle its systemic implications. The unilateral designation system is labelled as a "binary rule". A binary rule acts as an on–off switch (it applies or not), and so there is no graduation as in the continuous rule.[192]

Regulators such as Federal Reserve Board Daniel Tarullo affirm the "ideal approach would be a continuous function" and "systemic importance is not a binary determination but one of degree. A related point is that it is generally better to avoid cliff effects, whereby significant regulatory consequences ensue based on relatively modest differences among firms".[193] The DFA when addressing systemic importance includes two binary rules: (1) Bank Holding Company (BHC) with 50 billion or more in assets will be subject to enhanced supervision and early remediation;

[192] Block "A Continuum Approach", 325; Skinner "Regulating Nonbanks", 1379.

[193] Daniel Tarullo "Regulating Systemically Important Financial Firms" (Speech 3 June 2011), https://www.federalreserve.gov/newsevents/speech/tarullo20110603a.htm. Accessed 14 March 2023.

and, (2) non-banking institutions designated by the FSOC as SIFIs will also be subject to the same consequences.[194]

In the US the "cliff effect" of the automatic banking SIFI labelling is that banks now have an incentive to remain below the 50 billion thresholds in order to avoid enhanced supervision. This is particularly important in the US, since non-banking SIFI institutions will be subject to Federal Reserve supervision instead of the Securities and Exchange Commission (SEC) (i.e. investment banks and broker-dealers) or instead of state regulation (i.e. insurance companies) or limited or directly no regulation in some cases like asset managers of hedge funds.[195]

As Skinner points out, the binary system in the US for non-banking SIFIs has the following consequences. Firstly, SIFI labelling would endanger the relationship between industry actors and regulators through litigation, which may impede optimal supervision.[196] Secondly, financial institutions may find incentives to restructure in order to avoid labelling,[197] changing business strategies with potential repercussions for consumers. Thirdly, there is a risk of politicizing regulators' decisions, where those institutions designated as SIFIs would object to the designated "room for manouvre" of regulators. Likewise, as FSB also designates SIFIs, there might be a perceived risk that FSOC would coordinate their agenda with an entity that has a political nature too, since FSB's actions are designed by prerogatives of the G-20.[198]

[194] Block "A Continuum Approach", 325, See also James B. Thomson "On Systemically Important Institutions and Progressive Systemic Mitigation" *DePaul Business and Commercial Law Journal* (2009), 136.

[195] Block ibid., 325. For a summary of the roles of regulatory entities see US Department of the Treasury, *Blueprint for a Modernized Financial Regulatory Structure* (UST 2008), 3172.

[196] MetLife sued FSOC in 2015, see *MetLife, Inc. v Fin. Stability Oversight Council, 177 F. Supp 3d 219 (D.D.C 2016) (No. 15-0045).*

[197] GE restructured in order to avoid the SIFI label. In 2015 it announced selling most of GE Capital Assets, see GE "GE To Create Simpler, More Valuable Industrial Company by Selling Most Ge Capital Assets; Potential To Return More Than $90 Billion To Investors Through 2018 In Dividends, Buyback & Synchrony Exchange", https://www.ge.com/news/press-releases/ge-create-simpler-more-valuable-industrial-company-selling-most-ge-capital-assets. Accessed 14 March 2023.

[198] Skinner "Regulating Nonbanks", 1379.

The application of new policies to the designated financial institutions would trigger the possibility of bank-like prudential regulation, capital requirements, enhanced supervision and resolvability requirements.[199]

The new labels for systemically important institutions according to FSB are: G-SIBs, G-SIIs, NBNI G-SIFIs, and D-SIBs. Maybe in the future regulators would develop new titles such as D-SIIs and Non-Bank Non-Insurance Domestically-SIFI (NBNI D-SIFI) in order to complete the whole dimension of alternatives. However, at the EU and US levels, there are systems in place to address domestic systemically important non-bank financial institutions.[200]

The new designation system is a result of the evolution of the "Too big to fail" doctrine and the impact of the GFC which has focused regulatory action on addressing systemic risk and macro-prudential regulation.

While in the US non-banking institutions may be labelled as SIFIs and supervised by the Federal Reserve System, in the EU, only banks and banking groups may be labelled as SIFIs and supervised by the ECB.

The US, through DFA, developed a test of significance which assesses a "threat of financial stability to the US" by analysing material financial distress, the nature, scope, size, scale, concentration, interconnectedness or mix of activities. The lens is posed on financial stability. On the other side of the Atlantic Ocean, the EU developed a test of significance (SSM Regulation) for credit institutions only, which assesses (i) the total value of their assets; (ii) the importance for the economy of the country in which they are located or the EU as a whole; the scale of their cross-border activities; whether they have requested or received public financial assistance from the ESM or EFSF. Although both parties seconded FSB proposals, the lack of harmonization in the international arena of two major players may prove problematic when a crisis arises in the future (Fig. 2.1).

SIFIs

In April 2009 the G-20 Leaders required the FSB, IMF and BIS to develop a guide for national authorities to assess the systemic importance of financial institutions, markets and instruments. The main reason for

[199] FSB "2017 List of Global Systemically Important Banks (G-SIBs)", http://www.fsb.org/wp-content/uploads/P211117-1.pdf. Accessed 20 January 2023; Skinner "Regulating Nonbanks", 1382.

[200] Dodd Frank Act, and CRD V.

this request was a response to an "unprecedented reach of the financial crisis that began in August 2007 and the growing awareness that the macroprudential orientation of financial stability policy would need to be strengthened".[201]

The key criteria for identifying the systemic importance of financial institutions identified by the FSB, IMF and BIS in the 2009 G-20 leader's report are: size, substitutability and interconnectedness. As stated in the report, "for institutions, the size of exposures, volumes of transactions or assets managed are indicative of the extent to which clients and counterparties could be disrupted. Clusters of institutions can be individually small but collectively significant because they fall into distress at the same time. Some institutions, for example those providing key services such as clearing and settlement, lack immediate substitutes for this role. Interconnectedness captures situations when distress in one institution raises the likelihood of distress in others".[202]

In 2010 the FSB issued the Report 'Reducing the moral hazard posed by systemically important financial institutions. FSB Recommendations and Time Lines', where it refers to SIFIs as those financial institutions "whose disorderly failure, because of their size, complexity and systemic interconnectedness, would cause significant disruption to the wider financial system and economic activity".[203]

As Lastra states the "definition of a SIFI is dynamic: what is systemic today is not necessarily what will be systemic in the future".[204] The key criteria for identifying a SIFI have been widened by the inclusion of other criteria like scope, nature, concentration and provision of mix of activities that could pose a threat to financial stability.

This is the case in the US. The FSOC, which is in charge of determining if the SIFI in the US is subject to Federal Reserve supervision, "may determine that a nonbank financial company will be supervised by

[201] FSB, IMF, BIS "Report to G-20 Finance Ministers and Governors Guidance to Assess the Systemic Importance of Financial Institutions, Markets and Instruments: Initial Considerations" (2009), http://www.fsb.org/wp-content/uploads/r_091107c.pdf?page_moved=1. Accessed 20 January 2023.

[202] Ibid., 2.

[203] FSB "Reducing the Moral Hazard Posed by Systemically Important Financial Institutions. FSB Recommendations and Time Lines" (2010), http://www.fsb.org/wp-content/uploads/r_101111a.pdf?page_moved=1. Accessed 20 January 2023.

[204] Lastra "International Financial", 194.

the Board of Governors and be subject to prudential standards if the Council determines that (1) material financial distress at the nonbank financial company could pose a threat to the financial stability of the United States…or (2) the nature, scope, size, scale, concentration, interconnectedness, or mix of the activities of the nonbank financial company, could pose a threat to the financial stability of the United States".[205]

In 2011 the BIS added two different categories of systemic importance for the assessment of global systemic banks: cross-jurisdictional activity and complexity.[206]

As stated above, policy-makers have focused on the enhancement of regulation and supervision of SIFIs to tackle moral hazard arising from these kinds of institutions that are regarded as too big, or "too complex" or "too interconnected to fail".[207] After the GFC the international regulatory bodies started looking for a methodology to assess the systemic importance of banking institutions, insurance institutions and other non-banking, non-insurance financial institutions. This is how the notions of G-SIBs, G-SIIs and NBNI G-SIFIs—which assess finance companies, security firms and investment funds—were born.[208]

What Is a G-SIB?

In November 2011 the Basel Committee published a framework for G-SIBS. The Basel Committee has issued a number of reforms in order to enhance the safety and soundness of banks. One of the main reforms focused on capital requirements. The Basel Committee stated the capital adequacy measures applied to international banks may have a special

[205] FSOC "Authority to Require Supervision and Regulation of Certain Nonbank Financial Companies," [2011] Second Notice of Proposed Rulemaking and Proposed Interpretive Guidance, Federal Register, ps. 64264-83, available at https://www.federalregister.gov/documents/2011/10/18/2011-26783/authority-to-require-supervision-and-regulation-of-certain-nonbank-financial-companies#p-265. Accessed 20 January 2023.

[206] BCBS Consultative Document "Global Systemically Important Banks: Assessment Methodology and the Additional Loss Absorbency Requirement" (2011), Available at https://www.bis.org/publ/bcbs201.pdf. Accessed 20 January 2023.

[207] Daniel Gros "Too Interconnected to Fail = Too Big to Fail: What Is in a Leverage Ratio?" in *Vox.org* (January 2010), http://voxeu.org/article/too-interconnected-fail-too-big-fail. Accessed 20 January 2023. Andreas Jobst "Systemic Risk in the Insurance Sector. A Review of Current Assessment Approaches, *The Geneva Papers on Risk and Insurance*, (2014), 440.

[208] Ibid.

impact on G-SIBs since they are active in trading and capital markets—which are more affected by the "enhanced risk coverage of the capital framework". Nevertheless, capital adequacy measures might not be sufficient to cover the "negative externalities posed by G-SIBs". Therefore, the Basel Committee emphasizes the need for additional measures.[209] G-SIBS are designated by the FSB or the national authority.

FSB has designated G-SIBs for the years 2022–2023 (see Table 2.1). The main characteristic of G-SIBs is that they are subject to three main policies: (1) resilience and buffer facilitating results; (2) resolvability requirements; and, (3) higher supervisory expectations.[210]

One of the main proposals of the framework was the classification of G-SIBs into different categories of "systemic importance" based on the score produced by the "indicator-based measurement approach". The indicator-based system approach classifies five categories of systemic importance: (1) size; (2) cross-jurisdictional activity; (3) interconnectedness; (4) substitutability; and (5) complexity.

Each of them has a weight of 20%. G-SIBs will be allocated to several "buckets" according to their scoring, which will be subject to different levels of additional loss absorbency requirements (1–3.5%).[211]

The second relevant set of policies for G-SIBs is special resolvability requirements. FSB determines the requisite of "group-wide resolution planning and regular resolvability assessments". The resolvability of each G-SIB is examined according to the FSB Resolvability Assessment Process (RAP) by Crisis Management Groups.[212]

The FSB framework developed two different resolution strategies; (1) SPOE; and (2) MPOE.

SPOE is the resolution strategy where the resolution authorities apply the resolution tools at the top holding or parent company by only

[209] Basel Committee on Banking Supervision (BCBS) "Global systemically important banks: updated assessment methodology and the higher loss absorbency requirement" (2013), https://www.bis.org/publ/bcbs255.pdf. Accessed 20 January 2023.

[210] FSB "FSB publishes 2021 G-SIB list", https://www.fsb.org/wp-content/uploads/P211122.pdf. Accessed 9 April 2023; FSB, "Evaluation of the Effects of Too-Big-To-Fail Reforms Final Report" (2021), https://www.fsb.org/wp-content/uploads/P010421-1.pdf. Accessed 9 April 2023.

[211] See BCBS "Global Systemically Important Banks".

[212] FSB "2020 Resolution Report "Be Prepared" (2020), https://www.fsb.org/wp-content/uploads/P181120.pdf. Accessed 8 April 2023.

Table 2.1 G-SIBs from 2022 to 2023

Bucket	*2023*	*2022*
5 (3.5%)	Empty	Empty
4 (2.5%)	JP Morgan Chase	JP Morgan Chase
3 (2%)	Bank of America Citigroup HSBC	Bank of America Citigroup HSBC
2 (1.5%)	Agricultural Bank of China Bank of China Barclays China Construction Bank Deutsche Bank Goldman Sachs Industrial and Commercial Bank of China Mitsubishi UFJ FG UBS	Bank of China Barclays BNP Paribas Deutsche Bank Goldman Sachs Industrial and Commercial Bank of China Mitsubishi UFJ FG
1 (1%)	Bank of Comunications (BoCom) Bank of New York Mellon Groupe BPCE Groupe Crédit Agricole ING Mizuho FG Morgan Stanley Royal Bank of Canada Santander Société Générale Standard Chartered State Street Sumitomo Mitsui FG Toronto Dominion Wells Fargo	Agricultural Bank of China Bank of New York Mellon China Construction Bank Credit Suisse Groupe BPCE Groupe Crédit Agricole ING Mizuho FG Morgan Stanley Royal Bank of Canada Santander Société Générale Standard Chartered State Street Sumitomo Mitsui FG Toronto Dominion UBS UniCredit Wells Fargo

Source Based on FSB data (FSB, https://www.fsb.org/wp-content/uploads/P211122.pdf, https://www.fsb.org/2023/11/fsb-publishes-2023-g-sib-list/. Accessed 10 December 2023)

one resolution authority (i.e. where the global consolidation supervision of the financial group). Losses are absorbed by the company at the top of the structure by bail in. If the top company has sufficient loss absorbency capacity, its subsidiaries would continue operating without being resolved.[213]

MPOE is the resolution strategy where various resolution authorities apply the resolution tools to different companies of the group where the most probable outcome would be the spin-off of the financial group. Possible outcomes would be the division of the group within national or regional boundaries, or by business lines, or both. Resolution authorities will be free to apply different resolution tools, but would need to coordinate across borders in order to prevent conflicts of interest, run of assets and contagion among the whole group.[214]

Both resolution strategies would fit different groups depending on various factors that would facilitate resolution and maintain the critical functions of the group.[215]

The third special policy applicable to G-SIBs by FSB is the necessity of higher supervisory expectations. These include "supervisory expectations for risk management functions, risk data aggregation capabilities, risk governance and internal controls".[216] The timetable for meeting these requirements was included in the updated 2013 FSB document.[217]

[213] FSB "Review of the Technical Implementation of the Total LossAbsorbing Capacity (TLAC) Standard", 2 July 2019, https://www.fsb.org/wp-content/uploads/P020719.pdf. Accessed 1 November 2023.

[214] Ibid.

[215] See Chapter 6 for the analysis of resolution strategies in different FC models.

[216] FSB "Reducing the Moral Hazard Posed by Systemically Important Financial Institutions FSB Recommendations and Time Lines" (2010), http://www.fsb.org/wp-content/uploads/r_101111a.pdf?page_moved=1. Accessed 20 January 2023.

[217] FSB "2013 update of group of global systemically important banks (G-SIBs)" (2013), http://www.fsb.org/wp-content/uploads/r_131111.pdf. Accessed 20 January 2023.

In the US, the system is hybrid. Banking companies are considered SIFIs if they have over 50 billion in assets.[218] However, for non-banking SIFIs, the FSOC is mandated to designate "nonbank financial institutions" as systemically important.[219]

What Is a G-SII?

The experience of the GFC showed the TBTF doctrine, which mainly focused on banking and size, had not contemplated all the perils other financial institutions posed to financial stability. In the insurance sector AIG was the main example of that.

In 2010 the FSB recognized insurance companies should be covered by the SIFI framework. In July 2013, the IAIS set up a methodology in order to identify "global systemically important insurers" (G-SIIs). The IAIS "has developed an assessment methodology to identify insurance-dominated FCs whose distress or disorderly failure, because of their size, complexity and interconnectedness, would cause significant disruption to the global financial system and economic activity".[220]

As stated above, in the US the FSOC designates the "non-bank systemically important institutions". In July 2013, the Council of FSOC voted to designate American International Group, Inc. and General Electric Capital Corporation. Prudential Financial, Inc. was included in 2013, and MetLife in 2014. On September 29, 2017, the FSOC rescinded the designation of American International Group, Inc.[221]

[218] Even though the DFA does not adopt the term SIFI, the Federal Reserve papers refer to these institutions as SIFIs: D.E. Nolle "US Domestic and International Financial Reform Policy: are G20 Commitments and the Dodd Frank Cat in Sync?" 2 No4 (Board of the Federal reserve Sys.; International Finance Discussion papers No. 1024 (2011); See DFA, Section 165 a). Andy Winkler "Primer: FSOC's SIFI Designation Process for Nonbank Financial Companies. (AAF, 2014), https://www.americanactionforum.org/research/primer-fsocs-sifi-designation-process-for-nonbank-financial-companies/. Accessed 7 March 2023; Skinner "Regulating Nonbanks", 1381; Arthur. E. Wilmarth Jr. "The Dodd Frank Act: A Flawed and Inadequate Response to the Too-Big-to Fail Problem", 89 *Or.L. Rev* (2011), 1009.

[219] DFA Section 124 Stat 1395 (2012).

[220] IAIS "Global Systemically Important Insurers: Initial Assessment Methodology" (July 2013), https://www.iaisweb.org/file/34257/final-initial-assessment-methodology-18-july-2013. Accessed 20 January 2023.

[221] US Department of the Treasury. "Designations", https://www.treasury.gov/initiatives/fsoc/designations/Pages/default.aspx. Accessed 20 January 2023.

In July 2013, the FSB, in consultation with IAIS and national authorities, created a list of G-SIIs (9), applying the assessment methodology developed by the IAIS[222] (Table 2.2).

G-SIIs are Globally Important Insurance Companies designated by the FSB in consultation with IAIS. FSB has identified G-SIIs from 2013 to 2016. G-SII's are subject to the following main policies: (1) higher loss absorbency (HLA); (2) enhanced group-wide supervision, and (3) group-wide recovery and resolution planning and regular resolvability assessments.[223]

The first policy which applies to G-SIIs is a higher loss absorbency rule. The IAIS has created new capital requirement framework rules for G-SIIs in order to address the need to avoid further bailouts. To do so, it has established two new capital requirement frameworks, (1) the Basic Capital Requirement (BCR) in 2014, and (2) HLA in 2015. According to the IAIS the third step would be to complete the capital requirement

Table 2.2 List of G-SIIs 2015–2016

2015	*2016*
Aegon N.V.	Aegon N.V.
Allianz Se	Allianz SE
American International Group, Inc	American International Group, Inc
Aviva Plc	Aviva plc
Axa S.A.	Axa S.A.
Metlife, Inc	MetLife, Inc
Ping An Insurance (Group) Company Of China, Ltd	Ping An Insurance (Group) Company of China, Ltd
Prudential Financial, Inc.	Prudential Financial, Inc.
Prudential Plc	Prudential plc

Source FSB data (FSB in coordination with IAIS has decided not to publish lists after 2017 G-SII list. FSB "FSB statement on identification of global systemically important insurers" (2017), http://www.fsb.org/2017/11/fsb-statement-on-identification-of-global-systemically-important-insurers/. Accessed 20 January 2023)

[222] FSB "2016 List of Global Systemically Important Insurers (G-SIIs)", http://www.fsb.org/wp-content/uploads/2016-list-of-global-systemically-important-insurers-G-SIIs.pdf. Accessed 20 January 2023.

[223] Ibid.

network with "the development of a risk-based group-wide global Insurance Capital Standard (ICS)", and to "be applied to Internationally Active Insurance Groups (IAIGs)".[224]

The second main policy applied to G-SIIs is enhanced group-wide supervision, which includes the exercise by the supervisor of "direct powers over holding companies" and to "oversee the development and implementation of a Systemic Risk Management Plan and a Liquidity Management Plan".[225]

The third main policy applicable to G-SIIs is that they will be subject to the recovery and resolution planning requirements of the FSB's Key Attributes of Effective Resolution Regimes. Those applicable to G-SIIs are: (1) the formation of a Crisis Management Group (CMG); (2) the implementation of a recovery and resolution plan (RRP), and a liquidity risk management plan; (3) being subject to the CMG for resolvability assessments, and (4) the development of cross-border cooperation agreements between relevant resolution authorities for the specific G-SII.[226]

The FSB determines a framework for resolving insurers: "A resolution strategy should make it feasible to resolve an insurer while protecting vital economic functions, without severe systemic disruption or exposing taxpayers to loss, through mechanisms that make it possible for shareholders and unsecured creditors to absorb losses. Key Attributes II-Annex 2 (Resolution of Insurers) sets out the specific objective of protecting the insurer's policyholders, beneficiaries and claimants (collectively, 'policyholders')".[227]

In 2017 and 2018 the FSB, decided not to publish a new list of G-SIIs because it relied on IAIS work to develop an activities-based approach

[224] IAIS "Basic Capital Requirements for Global Systemically Important Insurers" (2014), https://www.iaisweb.org/uploads/2022/01/IAIS_Basic_Capital_Requirements_for_G-SIIs.pdf.pdf. Accessed 20 January 2023.

[225] FSB "Global systemically important insurers (G-SIIs) and the policy measures that will apply to them", July 2013, http://www.fsb.org/wp-content/uploads/r_130718.pdf?page_moved=1. Accessed 20 January 2023.

[226] Ibid.

[227] FSB "Developing Effective Resolution Strategies and Plans for Systemically Important Insurers" (2016), http://www.fsb.org/wp-content/uploads/Final-guidance-on-insurance-resolution-strategies.pdf. Accessed 20 January 2023; FSB "II-Annex 2—Resolution of Insurers" (2011) https://www.fsb.org/wp-content/uploads/II-Annex-2-Resolution-of-Insurers.pdf. Accessed 20 January 2023.

to systemic risk. IAIS adopted the "holistic framework" in 2019, after which FSB decided to suspend G-SII identification as of the beginning of 2020.[228] In 2022 FSB in consultation with IAIS decided to discontinue the annual identification of G-SIIs. Going forward it will rely on the IAIS Holistic Framework to "inform its considerations of systemic risk in the insurance sector".[229]

What Is a NBNI G-SIFI?

After the GFC, in November 2011 the G-20 Leaders requested the FSB, in consultation with IOSCO, incorporate methodologies for systemically important non-bank non-insurer financial entities.[230]

The framework would not have been completed if other financial institutions other than banks and insurers were not covered. Major players in the financial sector such as asset managers, investment funds, market intermediaries and finance companies were not within the consideration of the FSB framework. At the local level, this is currently not the case. In the USA, for instance, the FSOC has the power to designate a broad category of "non-bank systemically important banks".[231]

[228] NAIC "Global Systemically Important Insurers (G-SIIs)" (2021), https://content.naic.org/cipr_topics/topic_global_systemically_important_insurers_G-SIIs.htm. Accessed April 4, 2023.

[229] FSB (2022) "The FSB endorses an improved framework for the assessment and mitigation of systemic risk in the insurance sector and discontinues annual identification of global systemically important insurers (G-SIIs)" https://www.fsb.org/2022/12/the-fsb-endorses-an-improved-framework-for-the-assessment-and-mitigation-of-systemic-risk-in-the-insurance-sector-and-discontinues-annual-identification-of-global-systemically-important-insurers/. Accessed 10 December 2023; FSB "Global Systemically Important Financial Institutions (G-SIFIs)" https://www.fsb.org/work-of-the-fsb/market-and-institutional-resilience/global-systemically-important-financial-institutions-g-sifis/ accessed 10 December 2023. "From 2023 onwards, the FSB will publish in its Annual Resolution Report a list of insurers that – according to member authorities' assessment and self-reporting – are subject to resolution planning and resolvability assessments consistent with the FSB Key Attributes of Effective Resolution Regimes for Financial Institutions (KAs)".

[230] FSB-IOSCO "Consultative Document (2nd) Assessment Methodologies for Identifying Non-Bank Non Insurer Global Systemically Important Financial Institutions Proposed High-Level Framework and Specific Methodologies" (2015), 4–56, http://www.fsb.org/wp-content/uploads/2nd-Con-Doc-on-NBNI-G-SIFI-methodologies.pdf. Accessed 20 January 2023.

[231] See DFA.

In January 2014 the FSB-IOSCO published a document for public consultation outlining a proposal with methodologies for identifying NBNI G-SIFIs. These included a "operational framework for identifying G-SIFIs that would apply across all NBNI financial entities, and detailed NBNI sector-specific methodologies for (1) finance companies; (2) market intermediaries (securities broker-dealers); and, (3) investment funds (including hedge funds)".[232] Most of the responses from the public were concentrated on the methodology for investment funds and its risks; risks associated with asset management entities; and leverage as a category of systemic risk in the investment fund industry.[233]

In view of these responses, the FSB-IOSCO published a second public consultation paper in March 2015 which took into account most of the comments and suggestions of the public. However, while the paper engaged in special methodologies, it did not propose designation of specific entities, as in the G-SIB and G-SII systems.[234]

In July 2015 the FSB announced it has suspended the assessment methodologies for NBNI G-SIFIs until it finishes the financial stability risks from asset management activities.[235]

In January 2017 the FSB published the "Policy Recommendations to Address Structural Vulnerabilities from Asset Management Activities", where it proposes fourteen policy recommendations to address certain asset management structural vulnerabilities such as "liquidity mismatch between fund investments and redemption terms and conditions for open-ended fund units; leverage within investment funds; operational risk and challenges at asset managers in stressed conditions; and securities lending activities of asset managers and funds".[236] The NBNI G-SIFI proposed framework would be based on the following two principles:

[232] See FSB-IOSCO "Consultative Document", 4–56.

[233] Ibid.

[234] Ibid.

[235] FSB "Next Steps on the NBNI G-SIFI Assessment Methodologies" (2015), http://www.fsb.org/2015/07/next-steps-on-the-nbni-g-sifi-assessment-methodologies/. Accessed 20 January 2023.

[236] FSB "Policy Recommendations to Address Structural Vulnerabilities from Asset Management Activities" (2017), http://www.fsb.org/wp-content/uploads/FSB-Policy-Recommendations-on-Asset-Management-Structural-Vulnerabilities.pdf. Accessed 20 January 2023.

1. The main objective is to identify NBNI financial entities whose "distress or disorderly failure, because of their size complexity and systemic interconnectedness, would cause significant disruption to the global financial system and economic activity across jurisdictions".
2. The new framework needs to be consistent with G-SIBs and G-SIIs methodologies, "i.e., an indicator-based measurement approach where multiple indicators are selected to reflect the different aspects of what generates negative externalities and makes the distress or disorderly failure of a financial entity critical for the stability of the financial system (i.e., "impact factors" such as size, interconnectedness, and complexity)".[237]

The proposed methodologies identify five impact factors: (1) size; (2) interconnectedness; (3) substitutability; (4) complexity; and (5) global activities (cross-jurisdictional activities).[238]

The document identifies five main groups of NBNI which would be subject to different methodologies, applying to them the five categories of systemic importance: (1) finance companies; (2) market intermediaries (Securities Broker-Dealers); (3) investment funds; (4) asset managers; and (5) other NBNI[239] (Fig. 2.2).

The document proposed certain limits to the amount of assets the institution shall have in order to be a NBNI G-SIFI.[240]

While the process of acquiring data is in effect, the industry has opposed the methodology. Stevens, president of the Investment Company Institute, stated in 2017 "If the FSB engages in an evidence-based analysis, we believe the FSB will conclude—at a minimum—that there is no basis for considering regulated funds and their managers for possible G-SIFI designation".[241]

237 See FSB-IOSCO "Consultative Document", 4–56.

238 Ibid.

239 Ibid.

240 Ibid.

241 Investment Company Institute "Consultative Document; Proposed Policy Recommendations to Address Structural Vulnerabilities from Asset Management Activities" (2016), https://www.fsb.org/wp-content/uploads/Investment-Company-Institute-ICI1.pdf. Accessed 9 April 2023.

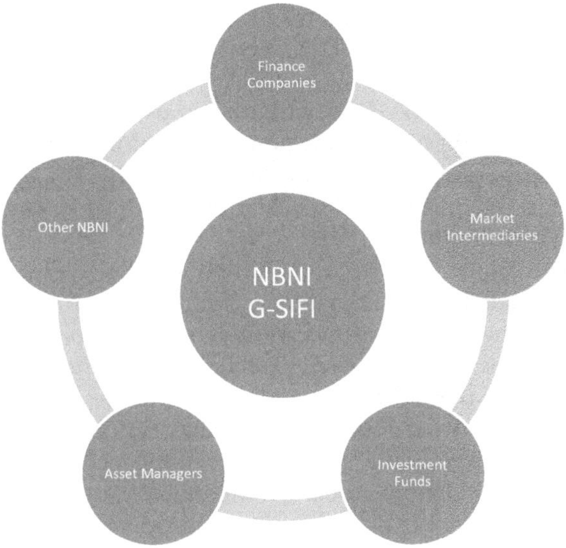

Fig. 2.2 Regulatory classification

As stated above, in the US the FSOC has the power to designate non-banking financial institutions. It has designated in the past three insurance-based groups (Prudential, AIG and MetLife) and a savings and loans-based group (General Electric Capital Corporation). So far, no asset managers, finance companies, or investment funds have been designated.

What Is a Domestically Important Financial Institution?

The regulatory classification deals with both a global and a domestic dimension. The BCBS has issued a framework for dealing with domestic systemically important banks. As of today, the BCBS has not prepared a framework for other financial institutions. However, at the level of both the EU and the US, regulations regarding domestic systemically important financial institutions are in place.

In October 2012 the BCBS issued a "Framework for dealing with domestic systemically important banks" with the aim of addressing negative externalities which apply at a domestic level. The rationale behind the new framework is that certain banks, although not significant on the global level, nevertheless have a wide impact on the local or regional financial system and economy (some of these may well have cross border externalities, though not global) if they are compared to "non-systemic institutions".[242]

The D-SIB framework deals with the impact that the "distress or failure of banks" might have on the domestic economy. Therefore, it gives the national authorities a degree of discretion in the implementation of the assessment and policy tools chosen by it, which diverges from the prescriptive G-SIB framework.[243]

The framework establishes a minimum of twelve principles which might be extended by the national authorities, or the "minimum approach".[244] The scope of application of the principles is designed to consolidate groups and subsidiaries, while the national authorities may include branches if they want to.[245,246]

The BCSB framework has been internalized in different jurisdictions. In the EU, CRD has established member states need to designate the authority which will identify global systemically important institutions (G-SIIs), on a consolidated basis and, on "an individual, sub-consolidated or consolidated basis, as applicable, other systemically important institutions (O-SIIs)".[247] O-SIIs are the equivalent of D-SIID-SIIs at the European level. National authorities may require each O-SII to maintain an "O-SII buffer" of up to "2% of the total risk exposure amount", which needs to be CET1 capital.[248] In April 2016 the EBA published the first list of O-SIIs in the EU[249] and disclosed another list in March 2017.[250] For D-SIBD-SIBs maintaining the D-SIB capital surcharge, it is very important since they are requested to meet it at any time, whereas the capital

[242] BCBS *A Framework for Dealing with Domestic Systemically Important Banks* (BIS 2012), 1.

[243] Ibid., 2.

[244] Patrick Brämer and Horst Gischer "An Assessment Methodology for Domestic Systemically Important Banks in Australia" *The Australian Economic Review* (2013), 140–59.

[245] See BCBS "A Framework" 2.

[246] Ibid., 4.

[247] See CRD V, article 131.

[248] See CRD V, article 131 (5).

[249] EBA "EBA Discloses First List of O-SIIs in the EU" (2016), https://www.eba.europa.eu/-/eba-discloses-first-list-of-o-siis-in-the--1. Accessed 9 March 2023.

[250] EBA "EBA discloses".

conservation buffer and counter-cyclical capital buffer are requested when the institution has "severe downturns".[251]

In the US, as stated above, the Dodd Frank Act—Section 165—authorizes the Board of Governors of the Federal Reserve System to impose enhanced prudential standards on bank holding companies with over $50 billion in total consolidated assets and on non-bank financial companies that the FSOC has designated for supervision by the Federal Reserve.[252] In a peculiarity of the American system, the US "considers the US G-SIBs to be those that would be designated as US D-SIBs".[253] As the BCBS emphasized, the US D-SIB framework is aligned to the Basel Committee D-SIB's principles, since it replicates the G-SIB assessment methodology. The US does not actually designate any D-SIB beyond the designated G-SIBs.[254]

Assessment of the Regulatory Classification

In order to assess the regulatory classification, it is important to bear in mind its birth is a consequence of the lack of focus in systemic risk and macro-prudential regulation before the GFC. The new focus on systemic risk and macro-prudential regulation is always a supplement to, not a substitution for micro prudential regulation.

The first question is whether the binary designation, or "shame and blame" system, is the best in order to avoid systemic risk. The literature on binary regulation and systemic risk concludes that binary regulation is flawed. The main reasons for this, as previously stated, are the increase of litigation and erosion of relations between the industry and the regulators; the increase in restructuring of labelled institutions; and the politicization of the process.[255]

The binary regulation has two different families of risks. First, there are risks derived from the lack of inclusion of true SIFIs. Under-inclusion would prevent a realistic measure of systemic risk. At the same time, a SIFI which is not regulated as such would create more systemic risk than

[251] Clieve Briault "D-SIB Designation and Capital Surcharges", KPMG (2016).

[252] See DFA.

[253] BCBS *Regulatory Consistency Assessment Programme (RCAP) Assessment of Basel III G-SIB Framework and Review of D-SIB Frameworks United States* (BIS, 2016), 16.

[254] Ibid., 5.

[255] Skinner "Regulating Nonbanks", 1381.

a labelled entity since it would not be subject to regulatory restraints. Also, these institutions would be able to take competitive advantages over-regulated SIFIs.[256] Secondly, there are risks derived from including non-systemically important institutions as SIFIs. Over-inclusion would for some commentators enhance moral hazard, since the labelling would create in the market a perception the government would bail out the institution if it were to fail, lowering borrowing costs and giving them a competitive advantage against non-designated SIFIs. Another danger of over-inclusion is the fact that regulating SIFIs with banking-like regulations would force non-bank institutions to act like banks even though their nature is different. The cost of regulation would be very dangerous for a non-systemic entity, especially with regard to capital rules.[257]

The second question is whether or not non-banking activities pose systemic risk. While there is a consensus within the literature that core insurance does not pose a systemic risk, some non-core activities—which resemble banking activities—may pose a systemic risk.

Assessing systemic risk in the asset manager industry is difficult since there are still data gaps.[258] According to Elliot there "are no true SIFIs in most of the financial sectors, including: private equity, venture capital, hedge funds, property casualty insurance, and mutual funds management, with the possible exception of money market funds".[259] On the other hand, OFR introduce some factors that need to be analysed case by case in order to assess the final degree of systemic risk of these institutions. While some commentators have disputed these factors, even Blackrock understands leverage is a better metric to screen systemic importance.[260]

[256] Douglas Elliot and Robert Litan "Identifying and Regulating Systemically Important Financial Institutions: The Risks of Under and Over Identification and Regulation" *Brookings Institutions Policy Brief* (2011), 1–20.

[257] Ibid.

[258] Office of Financial Research Report (2013), https://www.financialresearch.gov/annual-reports/files/office-of-financial-research-annual-report-2013.pdf. Accessed 23 March 2023.

[259] Douglas Elliot "Designating Systemically Important Financial Institutions: Balancing Costs and Benefits". Testimony Before the House Financial Services Subcommittee on Financial Institutions and Consumer Credit (2012), https://www.brookings.edu/wp-content/uploads/2016/06/16_sifis_elliott-1.pdf. Accessed 23 March 2023.

[260] Blackrock "Comments on the Consultative Document of Assessment Methodologies for Identifying Non-Bank, Non-Insurer Global Systemically Important Financial Institutions" (2014), 9.

The question is, then, whether banking-like regulation is appropriate to tackle systemic risk of non-banking SIFIs. This book contends regulators should avoid "tarring all birds with the same brush".[261] Because of the different natures of banking and asset management capital, leverage-based tools might not be appropriate to tackle market failures.[262] At the asset manager level, the capital requirements are not meaningful since they do not engage in proprietary trading and client assets are generally segregated, while these tools at the fund level would violate the asset manager fiduciary duty to follow client instructions.[263]

A different approach, focused on regulating similar activities along the entire industry,[264] instead of focusing on binary regulation or a "SIFI lite"[265] regulation which aligns a continuum regulation with enhanced supervision as a first step, and banking-like tools as a second step—only if necessary—would be a better approach, respecting the asset manager and core insurance nature better than "catch-all" FSB banking tools.

2.4 Summary

Table 2.3, summarizes the three different models analysed in this book in Chapters 3, 4 and 5. The purpose of this table is to provide a synopsis of these three chapters (plus additional information obtained in the annex)

[261] Andrew Haldane "The Age of Asset Management" (BIS Central Bank Speech LSE, 2014), 1–15. For an analysis if there is common ground for cross-sectoral resolution regime see Jens-Hinrich Binder "Resolution Regimes in the Financial Sector. In Need of Cross-sectoral Regulation?" in Veerle Colaert, Danny Busch, and Thomas Incalza *European Financial Regulation: Levelling the Cross-Sectoral Playing Field* (Bloomsbury, 2019).

[262] Haldane "The age", 1–15; Joshua Wan "Systemically Important Asset Managers: perspectives on Dodd-Frank's Systemic designation Mechanism" *Columbia Law Review* (2016), 804–841; Jean-Pierre Zigrand Jon Danielsson "Are Asset Managers systemically important" *Vox* (2015); PIMCO Submission to the Consultative Document (2nd), Assessment Methodologies for Identifying Non-Bank Non- Insurer Global Systemically Important Financial Institutions (2015), 1–27; Doulglas Elliot *Systemic Risk and the Asset Management Industry* (The Brookings Institution 2014), 1–16; Skinner "Regulating Nonbanks", 1381.

[263] PIMCO" Submission", 1–27.

[264] Dan Waters *Financial Stability and Regulated Funds* (ICI Global 2014); PIMCO "Submission", 1–27; Wan, "Systemically Important", 804–841.

[265] Skinner "Regulating Nonbanks", 1381.

regarding the main aspects of BBFC based on key characteristics (e.g. type of capitalism, type of BBFC, resolution corporate development, etc.).

This will inform the reading of Chapters 3, 4 and 5. Finally, it is worth stressing that this comparative analysis will be developed in Chapter six and the conclusions.

2.5 Concluding Remarks

This chapter has proposed a conceptual framework which identified the FCs by way of examining three classifications: the first one relying on the commercial activity they perform (commercial classification), the second relying on the legal separateness (structural classification) and the third relying on categories of systemic importance (regulatory classification).

Drawing on the practices of various countries this chapter has analysed the definition of a bank through the lens of these three different approaches: the list of activities approach, the formula approach, and the hybrid of intermediation approach. Following a description of the first two approaches, the book pointed out the need to allow regulators some "room for maneuver", or discretion to adapt the definition and description of bank activities to a fast-changing reality challenged by technology.

The commercial classification relies on the commercial activities performed by the group: banking groups, mixed conglomerates, and FCs.

By way of comparing the definitions of banking groups in different jurisdictions, it can be concluded banking groups are a group of banking organizations consisting of several companies under common ownership or other links. As part of a group of companies, they are subject to company law, which regulates the protection of minority shareholder's interests, as well as intra-group transactions and the avoidance of private benefits.

FCs are defined as groups of companies under common control which conduct material activities in at least two regulated banking, securities or insurance sectors. In Europe, the FICOD has established the conditions for a group of companies to be considered a FC. In order to understand the main features and risks of each sector, this book briefly examines the balance sheet structures and risks involved in the banking, insurance and securities sectors.

Table 2.3 Summary

Key features of the different BBFC models

Key features		*Germany*	*UK*	*US*	*France*
Type of capitalism		Bank-based	Hybrid	Capital market-based	Hybrid
Philosophical foundations		Saint Simon	Classic liberalism	Federalism	Originally Saint Simon, State centred system
BBFC model		German model	British model	Us model	German model-hybrid
Types of BBFC		– Commercial banks – Saving Banks cooperatives	– Banks – Credit unions – Building societies – Investment or Merchant banks	– Commercial banks – Thrifts – Credit Unions	– Banks – Cooperatives – Municipal Banks – Finance Companies – State Owned banks
Resolution	Sample entity	DB	Barclays	Citi	Credit Agricole
	Branches or subsidiaries	Both	Both	Both	Both
	Centralized or decentralized	Centralized	Centralized	Both	Centralized
	Retail or no retail	No retail	No retail	Hybrid	No retail
	Universal or Territorial approach to resolution	Universal	Universal	Universal for US BBFC and Territorial for US branches of foreign BBFC	Universal
	SPOE or MPOE	SPOE	SPOE	SPOE	SPOE

While mixed conglomerates—or groups of companies where at least one company engage in activities of a commercial or industrial nature—were historically disfavoured in the Anglo-Saxon world, today both Continental and Anglo-Saxon traditions allow certain mixed activity. This Continental/Asian/Latin American tradition of relying on banks to fund commercial activities has been a driver for the further development of capital markets in the US as opposed to continental Europe.

The structural classification incorporates the distinction of legal and operational separateness. When Herring and Santomero first proposed the classification in 1990 they would have not imagined the resilience of their work, since after the GFC the resolution strategies of G-SIFIs would be defined according to the corporate structure of the FCs. Their classification has the advantage of helping regulators to understand the implications of risk, tax and resolution. The original classification might be updated with some improvements such as the inclusion of a "partial integration" model in order to adapt it to the new structure or European FCs. Another improvement would be to include a fifth category to include horizontal groups, joint ventures and sales agreements.

The regulatory classification is a by-product of the evolution of the Too Big to Fail Doctrine. After the GFC the focus has turned to macro-prudential regulation and systemic risk. FSB has proposed a designation or binary regulation which implies the entities labelled as SIFIs will have to apply banking-like regulations. The different entities are G-SIBs, G-SIIs, NBNI G-SIFIs, D-SIBS and D-Non-Bank SIFIs. This book concludes binary regulation is flawed since its disadvantages outweigh its advantages. Litigation, politicization of the process, and forced restructuring are among the most weighted arguments. Also, the costs of "under inclusion" and "over inclusion" of an entity in the system are reasons for the regulator to adopt a more nuanced regulation, such as an activity-based regulation or "SIFI lite" regulation. These kinds of regulations would help to tackle potential systemic risk associated with those banking-like activities of non-banking groups such as money market funds, finance companies, and some non-core insurance activities.

Finally, banking-like regulations founded on capital requirements base their rationale on the nature and needs of banks. If the nature of non-bank SIFIs is different from banking, then the rationale of the regulation needs to adapt to the new recipient. If that is not the case, non-bank SIFIs will have to bear the cost of banking-like regulations without benefiting from the protection of banking regulation such as Lender of Last Resort

(LORL) and deposit insurance. Potentially, this would have non-intended consequences for competition and consumer welfare.

CHAPTER 3

German Model

3.1 Complete Integration or German Model

According to Herring and Santomero's classification, the Complete Integration or German model allows the service provider to deliver insurance, banking and securities activities in one FC.[1]

Due to historic and to some extent philosophical reasons, universal banking developed primarily in Germany and, after the Second Banking Directive and the Investment Services Directive, into the European Community at large.[2]

[1] Lastra and Olivares Caminal, "Cross Border Insolvency", 271.

[2] See Second Council Directive 89/646 of 15 December 1989 See Council Directive 93/22/EEC of 10 May 1993; Franco Fiordelisi and Ornella Ricci *Bancassurance in Europe. Past, Present and Future* (Palgrave Macmillan Studies in Banking and Financial Institutions, 2012), 7; Michael Gruson and Werner Nikowitz "The Second Banking Directive of the European Economic Community and Its Importance for Non-EEC Banks", *Fordham International Law Journal* (1988), 215; Neil. B. Murphy "European Union Financial Developments: The Single Market, the Single Currency, and Banking", *FDIC Banking Review* (2000), 4; Jennifer Manvell Jeannot "An International Perspective on Domestic Banking Reform: Could the European Union's Second Banking Directive Revolutionize the Way the United States Regulates Its Own Financial Services Industry?" *American University International Law Review* (1999), 1734; George. S. Zavvos "Banking Integration and 1992: Legal Issues and Policy Implications", *Harvard International Law Journal*, Vol. 31 (1990), 480. Vander Vennet "Cost Efficiency", 255;

M. J. Sheppard Gelsi, *Corporate Structure and Banking Resolution*, Palgrave Macmillan Studies in Banking and Financial Institutions,
https://doi.org/10.1007/978-3-031-59948-4_3

In Sect. 3.1 the chapter will examine what universal banking is, the reasons why it developed and will provide a short overview of the history of universal banking in Germany.

In Sect. 3.2 the chapter will analyse the links between banking and industry in Germany and the three pillar banking structure of the German financial system.

Definition of Universal Banking

Universal Banking is defined as a system in which a single FC or institution provides different activities such as banking, insurance and securities.[3] Universal banks differ from specialized banks—those which limit their activities to selected types of business (building societies, home loan savings banks, etc.).[4]

Universal banking can be defined as "the conduct of a range of financial services comprising deposit taking and lending, trading of financial instruments and foreign exchange (and their derivatives) underwriting of new debt and equity issues, brokerage, investment management and insurance".[5]

According to Effros, the question of the scope of permissible activities for banks may be analysed under a narrow or broad vision. The financial sector comprises three fields of activities: banking, insurance and securities. For Effros "it is not clear that insurance should necessary be outside the sphere of bank activity", while in many countries, securities business is considered to be "a normal and traditional banking activity".[6] Universal banking would be defined by the type of scope of permissible activities performed by a bank rather than by applying the "formula approach" of

Adam Dixon *The New Geography of Capitalism: Firms, Finance and Society* (Oxford Scholarship Online, 2014), 19.

[3] Diemo Dietrich, and Uwe Vollmer "Are Universal Banks Bad for Financial Stability? Germany During the World Financial Crisis", *The Quarterly Review of Economics and Finance* (2012), 123; Saunders and Walter "Universal Banking", 84; George J. Benston "Universal Banking", *Journal of Economic Perspectives* (1994), 121.

[4] Rudolf Faltermeier "The German Banking System-Types of Banks and Experience from the Crisis", *Universitätsverlag Potsdam* (2013), 15; see generally Jordi Canals *Universal Banking: International Comparison and Theoretical Perspectives* "Universal Banks versus Specialized Banks" (OUP 1997).

[5] Saunders and Walter "Universal Banking", 84; Benston "Universal Banking", 121.

[6] Effros "Central Bank", 5.

"accepting deposits and making loans". Universal banking would encompass a broad vision of the scope of permissible activities of banks, which includes commercial, insurance and securities.

Some authors define universal banking as the combination of banking and securities activities, without mentioning the insurance sector.[7] Morrison defines universal banks as "institutions that combine the lending and payment services of commercial banks with a wider range of financial services. In particular universal banks underwrite securities, and hence offer their clients firms access to a broader range of sources of funds that can specialist commercial or investment banks".[8] The focus on the banking and securities sectors (without mentioning insurance) may have an explanation in that since Directive 92/49/EEC, the Complete Integrated model has been restricted in the EU, since the insurance activities need to be developed in a separate subsidiary.[9]

In terms of the scope of permissible activities a universal bank can do, there is generally a catalogue of services offered anchored around a "core of traditional deposit-financed lending business".[10]

Steinherr, Huveneers and Vander Vennet argue the key feature of the universal bank is the repertoire of activities performed and particularly the capacity of being holders of equity shares of corporations large enough to be able to monitor them.[11]

[7] Zavvos "Banking Integration", 480. Michael Gruson and Uwe H. Schneider "The German Landesbanken", *Columbia Business Law Review* (1995), 340; Caroline Fohlin "Universal Banking Networks in Pre-war Germany: New Evidence from Company Financial Data", *Research in Economics* (1997), 203.

Jeremy Edwards and Sheilagh Ogilvie "Universal Banks and German Industrialization: A Reappraisal", *Economic History Review* (1996), 428; Daniel Verdier *Moving Money: Banking and Finance in the Industrialized World* (CUP 2003), 102.

[8] Alan Morrison "Universal Banking" in Allen N. Berger, Philip Molyneux, and John O.S. Wilson *The Oxford Handbook of Banking* (OUP 2010), 171; Gruson and Schneider "The German Landesbanken", 340.

[9] Directive 92/49/EEC, Article 8 1 b.

[10] Deutsche Bundesbank Monthly Report April 2015 "Structural Developments in the German Banking Sector" (2015), 36.

[11] Alfred Steinherr and Christian Huveneers "On the Performance of Differently Regulated Financial Institutions: Some Empirical Evidence", *Journal of Banking and Finance* (1994), 273; Vander Vennet "Cost Efficiency", 255.

The German banking system has been identified as the prototype of universal banking,[12] mainly because it was in this country that the main characteristics of the model developed over time, namely: (1) universal banking means a bank may provide all kinds of financial services to its customers; (2) universal banking means a bank is permitted to own equity interests in other commercial and industrial firms or financial firms; (3) universal banking means non-financial firms may invest in, and own, 100% of shares or control a bank if the regulator approves the transaction.[13] The key historical, philosophical and political foundations of universal banking are examined in the next section.

Historical and Philosophical Foundations of Universal Banking

The evolution of universal banking in Germany is linked to its history from 1648 to 1815. Germany had been in the middle of the battlefield in Europe during these years and suffered "spoliation and devastation" throughout as a consequence of the campaigns of Louis XIV, the Spanish War of Succession, the Seven Years' War and the war against Napoleon.[14] From 1815 to 1848 the country engaged in the rehabilitation of its economy.

According to Riesser's classic study of the *Grossbanken* (great banks), by 1845 England was engaging in a transition to becoming a great industrial country supplying more than 50% of the "world requirements". An estimation made in that year showed the ratio of capital per head in Prussia was 720 marks while the same ratio in England was 2860 marks.[15] In Prussia, in 1843, the percentage of people engaged in agriculture ranged from 60.84% to 61.34%. 23.37% of people were involved in industrial pursuits while only 0.97% of people were employed in commerce.[16]

[12] Bernard Schull "The Separation of Banking and Commerce in the United States: An Examination of Principal Issues", OCC Economics Working Paper (1999), 25.

[13] Theodore Baum and Michael Gruson "The German Banking System-System of the Future? *Brooklyn Journal of International Law* (1993), 113.

[14] Jacob Riesser *The German Great Banks and Their Concentration in Connection with the Economic Development of Germany* (National Monetary Commission 1911), 27.

[15] Ibid.

[16] Von Reden *Vergleichende Kulturstatistik* (1848), 412, cited by Riesser "The German Great Banks".

At the time, private bankers, who "were called money changers", mainly carried on with commission business and forwarding business. A good example of the dimension of the industry can be shown by the total number of employees in the state of Prussia during 1858. The total amount of employees amounted to 1774 in 602 enterprises (where 602 were overseers and the rest assistants).[17] In general, these private banks were unincorporated partnerships and operated with their own capital. At this time private banks based their business on the reliance on personal relationships and involvement with local firms. The fact they had a low capitalization and they had limited liability determined a low-risk strategy.[18] The most famous *Privatbanken* was founded by Mayer Amschel Rothschild (1744–1812).[19]

In the beginning of the 1850s the State of Prussia started a fast development of the railway system as well as the mining and machine industries. According to Riesser, the rise of the mining and smelting industries was "mainly responsible for the spread of capitalism and the development of large-scale production, as well as the gradual and radical change in the general economic conditions of the country". Following the new railway enterprises there arose a new number of joint stock companies, which included banks.[20]

The sums needed to fund the railways tended to exceed the resources of private bankers, who needed to create syndicates. As the formation of such syndicates were, practically speaking, difficult to form, the private bankers needed to seek an alternative source of funding such as large incorporated banks.[21] These banks were the *Kreditbanken* (credit banks),

[17] Werner Sombart, *Die Deutsche Volkswirtschaft,* (2d ed. 1909), 190–191 cited by Riesser "The German Great Banks".

[18] Marco Da Rin "Understanding the Development of the German Kreditbanken, 1850–1914: An Approach from Economics on Information", *Financial History Review* (1996), 32. Timothy Guinnane "Delegated Monitors, Large and Small: Germany's Banking System, 1800–1914", *Journal of Economic Literature* (2002), 96.

[19] Guinnane "Delegated Monitors", 96.

[20] Riesser "The German Great Banks", 45.

[21] Richard Tilly "German Banking, 1850–1914: Development Assistance for the Strong", *The Journal of European economic History* (1986), 119; Alfred Chandler and Takashi Hikino and *Scale and Scope: The Dynamics of Industrial Capitalism* (Harvard University Press, 2009), 415–416.

a number of which later became the *Grossbanken* that have dominated the German finance system since then.[22]

The first credit bank was formed in 1848 with the name Abraham Schaaffhausen'scher Bankverein of Cologne (A. Schaafhausen), as a result of the reorganization of the old banking of Abraham Schaaffhausen, with the purpose of financing railways in the Lower Rhine.[23] However, the model of the credit banks was the famous Societé General de Crédit Mobilier (Credit Mobilier) which opened its doors in Paris in 1852.[24] Credit Mobilier influenced the foundation of the Bank für Handel and Industrie in 1853 with headquarters in Darmstadt.[25]

Saint Simon and the Philosophical Foundations of Universal Banking

Credit Mobilier was chartered by a decree of Napoleon III on November 1852, two weeks before of the proclamation of the Second Empire. The founders of the Credit Mobilier idea were the Pereire brothers. Emile and Isaac Pereire were Portuguese Jews who settled in Bordeaux. They became active members of the Saint Simonian Brotherhood.[26]

Claude Henri de Saint Simon thought the mission of banks was strictly defined in servicing the development of industries, which was ultimately realizing the general interest.[27] He understood that the "industrial class is completely organized around the bank".[28] He thought the only way to maintain public peace was to place the industrial class in charge of managing public wealth.[29] According to Saint Simon "work is the source

[22] Chandler and Hikino "Scale and Scope", 416.

[23] Riesser "The German Great Banks", 46; Chandler and Hikino "Scale and Scope", 416.

[24] Chandler and Hikino "Scale and Scope", 416.

[25] Richard Tilly "Universal Banking in Historical Perspective", *Journal of Institutional and Theoretical Economics* (1998), 13; Hugh Neuberger and Houston H. Stokes "German Banks and German Growth 1883–1913: an Empirical View", *The Journal of Economic History* (1974), 712; Chandler and Hikino "Scale and Scope", 416; Riesser "The German Great Banks", 46.

[26] Rondo Cameron "The Credit Mobilier and the Economic Development of Europe", *The Journal of Political Economy* (1953), 465.

[27] Frank Yonnet "Claude-Henri de Saint Simon, L'Industrialisme et les banquiers", *Cahiers d' économie Politique* (2004), 154.

[28] Yonnet "Claude-Henri de Saint Simon", 155.

[29] Henri de Saint Simon *Catecismo Político de los Industriales* (Aguilar, 1960), 56.

of all virtues; the more useful jobs should be the most considered; accordingly, both divine and human morals call the industrial class to perform the first role in society".[30]

For Saint Simon banks had a hierarchical status. The role of banks was to be "general agents of the industry".[31] According to Saint Simon, the industrials (all active citizens involved in production) are hierarchized in different steps. In the lower step he positioned the entrepreneurs or workers. In the second step he located the great industrial or commercial capitalists. In the third step he placed the bankers, who are the elite leaders of the industrial class. In the final step he situated the Banque de France, which had the mission of being the unifier and centralizing force of the industrial class.[32]

Banks, in Saint Simon's opinion, underpin a social order based on confidence. For him the bank is a means by which the relationships of the "idles" and the "workers" are determined. Lending puts capital at the disposition of workers, which is distributed according to workers' capacities. Banks play a role in the ordering and vigilance of labour relations.[33]

With this in mind, the Pereire Brothers founded Credit Mobilier. The influence of the Saint Simon doctrine is palpable in Credit Mobilier bylaws. The new bank's founding documents stated "considering the important services that the establishment of a bank may favour the development of the industry…"[34] The French government welcomed the formation of Credit Mobilier, as well as the general public, since they believed the new bank would be a counterpoise to the private banks, especially the House of Rothschild.[35]

[30] Saint Simon "Catecismo", 85.

[31] Michel Ballet "Saint-Simonism and Utilitarianism: The History of a Paradox. Bentham's Defense of Usury Under Saint-Amand Bazard's Interpretation", *Working paper GATE* (2011), 13.

[32] Henri de Saint Simon *L'Industrie*, 1966, 137 cited by Yonnet "Claude-Henri de Saint Simon", 156.

[33] Sebastien Charlety *Historia del Sansimonismo* (Alianza Editorial, 1969), 47.

[34] Decret No. 7433 "Decret portant autorisation de la Societé anonyme formé a Paris sous la denomination de Societé Generale de Crédit Mobilier", *Bulletin des lois de la Republique Francaise*, 11 Dic 1852, 783.

[35] Riesser "The German Great Banks", 50.

The organization, growth and rapid decline (in 15 years) of Credit Mobilier made people in the 1910s designate the *Grossbanken* as "Credit Mobilier banks".[36] As stated above, Credit Mobilier directly participated in the formation of the Bank für Handel *und Industrie* in Darmstadt. All the other great German banks were modelled directly upon the Darmstadt bank, and therefore indirectly upon Credit Mobilier.[37]

In the first business report of the Bank für Handel und Industrie it stated "it is in no way the task of the bank to pave the way for stock-jobbing operations, and to stimulate capitalists to unproductive gambling on change. On the contrary, the bank is expected to promote sound and extensive undertakings by its own operations and by investing outsider's funds entrusted to its care. By means of its imminent position and clear insight into the whole situation of German industry it is fitted to assist to the fullest extent of its powers in directing capital and the spirit of enterprise into the channels corresponding to the requirements of the moment".[38]

The influence of Saint Simon and his disciples in the formation of Credit Mobilier, and indirectly through the formation of *Bank für Handel und Industrie* and the other great German banks can be traced to the bylaws and other corporate documents. Cameron thinks the influence was much stronger, since Credit Mobilier was a "potent force for economic development in the environment in which it existed".[39] This opinion turns the section to the analysis of the influence of universal banking in the development of Germany.

Universal Banking and Germany's Economic Development

Since Alexander Gerschenkron's seminal work *Economic Backwardness in Historical Perspective*, many economic historians have attributed universal

[36] Ibid., 51.

[37] Cameron "The Credit Mobilier", 256.

[38] Riesser "The German Great Banks", 49.

[39] Rondo Cameron "Founding the Bank of Darmstadt", *Explorations in Entrepreneurial History* (1956), 113.

banks a leading role in the development of the industry in Germany,[40] especially if compared to other jurisdictions such as the US and the UK.[41]

Gerschenkron argued Germany and many other countries in the continent had to lead with a state of "backwardness". In a country with a state of relative backwardness like Germany, where capital was scarce and disseminated, universal banks played a very important role.[42] While in England banks were obsessed with liquidity and lent on a short-term basis, firms that required capital for industrial investment had to rely on other sources of financing such as family wealth or friends, and growing firms had to rely on retained earnings. Another source of financing was the issue of equity and bonds, something that was underdeveloped in Germany.[43]

German banks were structured to build miles of railways, establish mines and build ports. The Pereire brothers' business enterprises started in France but expanded into Spain and Russia and clearly influenced the German Great Banks. According to Gerschenkron the most important effect of the Pereire brothers was in the business environment. The Pereire brothers engaged in a conflict with representatives of "old money", especially with the Rothschilds. The Pereire brothers could not form a Credit Mobilier in Austria (Credit-Anstalt) only because the Rothschilds were predisposed to create a bank like Credit Mobilier, which would invest in building railways and develop the industry in the country.

[40] Chandler and Hikino "Scale and Scope", 415; John Cable "Capital Market Information and Industrial Performace: The Role of West German Banks", *The Economic Journal*, Vol. 95 (1985), 129–130; Cameron "Founding", 113; Sandeep Baliga and Ben Polak "Banks Versus Bonds: A Simple Theory of Comparative Financial Institutions", *Cowles Foundation Discussion Paper* (1995), 1; Charles W. Calomiris "Corporate-Finance Benefits from Universal Banking: Germany and the United States 1870–1914", *NBER Working Paper* Series (1993), 1–21; Riesser "The German Great Banks", 49; Werner Sombart *Volkswirtschaft im neunzehnten Jahrhundert* (Georg Bondi, 1909) cited by Caroline Fohlin "Universal Banking in Pre-World War I Germany: Model or Myth?" *Explorations in Economic History* (1999), 307.

[41] Guinnane "Delegated Monitors", 74.

[42] Alexander Gerschenkron "Economic Backwardness in Historical Perspective" (Harvard University Press, 1962), 1–15.

[43] Guinnane "Delegated Monitors", 77; Gerschenkron "Economic Backwardness", 1–15; Riesser "The German Great Banks", 772.

This was disruptive in the sense that the "old money" was developing the industry.[44]

The German banks combined short-term financing, common in the English commercial banks, with strong links with industrial firms.[45] According to Gerschenkron, German banks had provided more help to industry than English banks because "the German Banks, and along with them the Austrian and Italian Banks, established the closest possible relations with industrial enterprises. A German Bank, as the saying went, accompanied an industrial enterprise from the cradle to the grave, from establishment to liquidation throughout all the vicissitudes of its existence."[46] Until the World War I the primary activity of German banks was the financing of the extraction of coal, steal production, electrical engineering and heavy industry in general.[47] Available data based on Bairoch's index of Industrialization shows the estimated per capita levels of industrialization[48] in the United Kingdom in 1830 ascended to 25 points against 9 in Germany (considering the United Kingdom in 1900 ascended to 100 points). In 1880 the United Kingdom moved to 87 points while Germany grew to 25 points. By 1913 the United Kingdom had 115 points while Germany moved to 87 points.[49]

Another interesting index shows the total manufacturing output of 20 leading world powers. In 1860 the UK was the leader with 45 points, while Germany was in the 11th position with 11 points. In 1913 the leading position was taken by the US with 298 points, Germany was second with 138 points, and the UK third with 127. In 1980 the US remained first with 3475 points, Russia second with 1630, Japan third with 1001 points and West Germany fourth with 590 points. The UK appeared in the 6th position with 441 points.[50]

[44] Gerschenkron "Economic Backwardness", 1–15.

[45] Ibid.

[46] Gerschenkron "Economic Backwardness", 14; Jeremy Edwards and Klaus Fischer *Banks, Finance and Investment in Germany* (CUP, 1994), 9.

[47] Ibid.

[48] For Bairoch levels of industrialization mean the volume of manufacturing output per capita. Paul Bairoch "International Industrialization Levels from 1750 to 1980", *The Journal of European Economic History* (1982), 294.

[49] Ibid.

[50] Bairoch "International Industrialization", 284.

Tilly shows between 1870 and 1913 the value of ***Kreditbanken*** assets rose from 600 million to over 17.5 billion marks, of which almost half were located in the largest Berlin banks. In 1913 the three largest incorporated companies were banks, and 17 of the largest companies were banks. According to Tilly "those figures reflect a degree of prominence which can be found in the banking institutions of no other major industrial country at the time".[51]

Both German industrialization indexes increased between 1830 and 1880. The question here is if the two indexes are related by a causal link. According to Gerschenkron there is a causal link, which characterized the German industrialization scenario in the period.

Gerschenkron's views have been labelled as the "orthodox view" by Fohlin, who argues financial institutions in Germany were not just a response to economic backwardness but a result of social, political and regulatory environments. She also argues the benefits of universal banking requires a "careful reexamination" since many of the "growth and efficiency-enhancing features" of the German financial system arose only during industrialization and many of those features were unrelated to German banks' universal structure.[52] In the same line of thinking, T. Guinnane argues Gerschenkron erred since he focused on the Great German Banks and not on the whole German financial system which comprises various types of complimentary financial institutions which had not been present in the UK or the US. He also pointed out the great universal banks were "much the product as the cause of economic growth" and the consideration of the financial system as a whole sharpens the understanding of today's financial intermediation system.[53] A similar conclusion was reached by Deeg, who affirms all types of financial institutions taken together played a major role in industrialization in Germany, something that did not happen in the UK.[54]

Tilly focused his analysis on universal banking "development assistance for the strong". He concludes the great German banks were interested in aiding large and strong businesses. Gustav Mevissen, a Rhenish

[51] Tilly "German Banking", 114.

[52] Fohlin "Universal Banking", 306.

[53] Guinnane "Delegated Monitors", 74.

[54] Richard Deeg "On the Development of Universal Banking in Germany" in Douglas J. Forsyth, and Daniel Verdier *The Origins of National Financial Systems Alexander Gerschenkron Reconsidered* (Routledge, 2002), 87.

entrepreneur and co-director of A. Schaaffhausen and Bank of Darmstadt instructed the management of the latter, stating:

> A basic principle of our bank is that it is to conduct business only with banking firms of the highest rank and with industrialists of importance, furthermore that it must in principle reject any ongoing connection which does not promise to generate a business volume of at least 50.000 Gulden per year.[55]

These instructions explain the focus of great German Banks on large-scale heavy industries in the "take off" period from 1840 to 1870.[56] In Tilly's opinion, this focus "systemically neglected an important part of their country's financial business".[57]

Neuburger and Stokes' findings suggested the credit allocation policy of the *Kreditbanken* in the take off period inhibited the German economy. They pointed out banks' biases in favour of heavy industry and "against light industry", as well as a bias in favour of export industries and national defence industry.[58] In a similar vein, Feldenkirchen states he could not dispute the "pioneering role of banks" in formation and financing firms in the heavy industry sector but "we should not overrate" the influence of banks on the "economy in general".[59]

Edwards and Ogilvie explained the available evidence does not support the argument that universal banks extensively financed German industrial joint stock companies. The fact that a large amount of non-joint stock industrial firms existed, and banks which were not *Kreditbanken* also existed, combined with the fact universal banks did not broadly support

[55] Provisional Norms for Management of the Bank and Commerce and Industry Darmstadt in Tilly "German Banking", 121.

[56] Ibid.

[57] Ibid., 150.

[58] Neuburger and Stokes "German Banks and German Growth", 729.

[59] Wilfried Feldenkirchen "Banking and Economic Growth: Banks and Industry in Germany in Robert Lee *The Nineteenth Century and Their Changing Relationship During Industrialization*" in *German Industry and German Industrialization. Essays in German Economic and Business History in the Nineteenth and Twentieth Centuries* (Routledge 1991), 121.

joint stock industrial companies, led these authors to conclude the role of universal banks had been exaggerated.[60]

Germany and the Evolution of Capital Markets

1850 marked the commencement of a "truly global securities market". Capital markets moved beyond government debt instruments and started to deal with the financing of business. By 1900 national securities markets became integrated and international as in no other stage of history.[61]

While in the UK securities as part of national assets stood at 22% during the period 1850–1900, in Germany the percentage was only 3.7%[62].

Verdier explains Anglo-Saxon countries (US and UK) in the period 1850–1913 had specialized commercial banks and large markets, while Germany had universal banking and small markets.[63] He argues the development of the securities market in Germany was affected by the action of government taxation and legislation. In 1881 a turnover tax was introduced and in 1896 prohibited buying and selling for future delivery as "being tantamount to speculation". This legislation was not revised until 1908, favouring London as a centre for trading in securities. Part of the securities business that was not channelled outside Germany was internalized between the German Grossbanken. "Such links help explain the development of integrated commercial and investment banking in Germany, as that shielded activity in securities from both taxation and external scrutiny. The combination of taxation and legislation, the direct participation of the banks in the stock exchanges, and the nationalization of the railway system impeded the development of the German securities market. Instead, German banks were forced to play a greater role in meeting the financial needs of the economy through extending long-term loans to their business customers whilst banks elsewhere were retreating from such practices because of the risks involved if depositors rushed to

[60] Edwards and Ogilvie "Banks, Finance and Investment in Germany", 444.

[61] Ranald Michie *The Global Securities Market: A History* (OUP 2006), 84.

[62] Michie "The Global Securities Market", 84; Raymond. W. Goldsmith *Comparative National Balance Sheets* (University of Chicago Press, 1985) Table 47, 134.

[63] Verdier "Moving Money: Banking and Finance", 117.

withdraw their savings during a financial crisis."[64] Fohlin, on the other hand, understands the tax effect on the increasing of universal banking and substitution of universal banking services for securities market trading "is not tremendously robust" since there is no evidence of shift of business from the market to universal banks.[65]

While a causal relation might be difficult to prove, there remain a twofold fact. First, there was a great growth of universal banking from the period 1850–1913. Second, the development of the securities market in Germany in the same period was weaker than the UK and the US.

The index of securities as part of national assets in Germany in the period 1911–1912 was 11.1%, while the UK index was 41.4% and the US was 18.5%. The period 1927–1930 shows Germany with a 4.6% index, UK with 47.4% and the US with 28%. The period 1947–1955 saw Germany decreasing to 4.4%, the UK 33.3% and the US 24.2%. Between 1970 and 1973, Germany obtained 6.7%, the UK 17.8% and the US 19.1%.[66]

However, as some authors remind us, provisions in the German Civil Code that established onerous requirements on the transferability of securities impeded the development of a deep capital market "à la americana".[67] Effros argued that Glass-Steagal Act[68] permitted this development of vibrant capital markets separate from money/banking markets.[69]

In the mid-1980s a consortium of big German banks launched the idea of the creation of a *Finanzplatz Deutschland* to encourage the increase of securities markets in Germany, and particularly the city of Frankfurt as a

64 Ibid. See also Tilly "German Banking", 125; Riesser "The German Great Banks", 772.

65 Caroline Fohlin "Regulation, Taxation and the Development of the German Universal Banking System 1884–1913", *European Review of Economic History* (2002), 252.

66 Michie "The Global Securities Market", 127.

67 In Germany, "limitations on transferability of ownership are less pronounced. However, the transfer of control is restricted by rights of workers and managers, and the power of banks." Julian Franks, Colin Mayer, Jeremy Hardie and Edmond Malinvaud "Capital Markets and Corporate Control: A Study of France, Germany and the UK", *Economic Policy* (1990), 209.

68 Act of June 16, 1933, 48 Stat. 162.

69 Effros "Central Bank", 2–10.

financial centre. This was to some extent a fruit of the internal market and the work of internalizing European directives,[70] and the realization that to compete with the UK reform was needed.[71] The government accompanied the initiative by issuing some new laws on the promotion of financial markets. Nevertheless, the role of securities markets in Germany still played a restricted role. By 2010 outstanding bonds amounted to 145 billion euros, while outstanding bank loans in 2012 stood at 1,474 billion euros. On the other hand, market capitalization in 2010 was equal to 43% of GDP (below 67% in the EU and 119% in the US). Finally, the number of citizens that held shares was 3.9 million in 2011, despite the effort of the government in developing an "equity culture".[72]

The following section analyses the benefits and costs of universal banking from the perspective of the bank and of the regulators.

Benefits and Costs of Universal Banking

The costs and benefits of universal banking may be analysed from the viewpoint of the banks and from the viewpoint of public policy.

From the perspective of the bank, the literature has examined a list of arguments in favour of universal banking: (1) universal banks enjoy advantages of economies of scale and scope; (2) universal banks benefit from being a "one-stop supplier" for various financial services; (3) the existence of alternative revenue sources and a reduction of economic risk due to diversified activities; (4) universal banking may encourage the creation of long-term relationships, easing monitoring.[73]

[70] Sigur Vitols "Changes in Germany's Bank-Based Financial System: A Varieties of Capitalism Perspective", *WZB Discussion Paper* (2004), 6; James. H. Jr. Freis "An Outsider's Look into the Regulation of Insider Trading in Germany: A Guide to Securities, Banking, and Market Reform", *Finanzplatz Deutschland, Boston College International and Comparative Law Review* (1996), 28.

[71] Freis "An Outsider's", 10.

[72] Daniel Detzer, Nina Dodig, Trevor Evans, and Eckhard Hein "The German Financial System", FESSUD (2013), 85; Deutsche Bundesbank "The Shadow Banking System: Small But Internationally Connected", *Financial Stability Review* (2012), 1.

[73] See Canals "Universal Banking", 103; Dietrich and Vollmer "Are Universal Banks", 124; Guinnane "Delegated Monitors"; Caroline Fohlin "Financial Systems and Economic Development in Historical Perspective", *Johns Hopkins University and Emory University* (2014), 6; Baum and Gruson "The German Banking System", 101–129; Alexandre Tombini "Universal Banking: The View of Brazil" *The Quarterly Review of Economics and*

From the perspective of the public policy viewpoint there are concerns about universal banking costs: (1) universal banks may increase the risk of financial instability; (2) universal banks might injure stock markets; (3) universal banks might engage in anticompetitive behaviour, concentration of power and/or monopoly practices; (4) Universal banks might lead to abuse of information or conflicts of interest. From the perspective of the bank itself, there are organizational costs of its own.

The literature on benefits and costs of universal banking can be traced back to two different moments in time: first, in the 90s with the discussion in the US of the liberalization of the Glass-Steagal Act. A second trend of literature can be found after the GFC, where the Vickers Commission and the ring-fence proposals inter alia looked at universal banking from a different perspective, watering down in part the enthusiasm for the phenomena of some scholars in the 90s. An analysis of the costs and benefits of universal banking follows.

Benefits of Universal Banking from the Perspective of the Bank

1. Economies of Scope and Scale

According to this argument, universal banking would benefit from economies of scale. Economies of scale exist if assuming a constant product mix; the bank faces "declining average costs as its size expands".[74] Universal banks would have potential for scale economies attributable to administrative overhead, agency problems and other cost factors if the bank is sufficiently big.[75] On the other hand, economies of scope exist if the total cost of offering different services in different units are bigger than offering the same services together.[76] Universal banks would bring scope economies to firms in need of funding. If the

Finance (2012), 154; Karl-Hermann Fischer, Christian Pfeil "Regulation and Competition in German Banking: An Assessment" in Jan P. Krahnen, and Reinhard H. Schmidt *The German Financial System* (OUP 2004), 291–350; Vander Vennet "Cost Efficiency", 255; Benston "Universal Banking", 121. Steinherr and Huvenners "On the Performance", 273; Calomiris "Corporate-Finance", 1–21; Hans-Jacob Krümmel "German Universal Banking Scrutinized. Some Remarks Concerning the Gessler Report", *Journal of Banking and Finance*, Vol. 4 (1980), 33–55.

[74] Vander Vennet "Cost Efficiency", 257.

[75] Walter "Universal Banking: A Shareholder", 6.

[76] Canals "Universal Banking", 104.

universal bank has a close relationship with the firm, it would be easy and cost efficient for the bank to perform due diligence for underwriting purposes. This is a case of reutilization of information. Another example of economies of scope is the use of "spillovers" of reputation acquired in one business to use in another. Additionally, a universal bank can "amortize the fixed costs" of setting up a relationship over different products among the business lines of the bank. Finally, a universal bank may find easier ways to fund itself than specialized banks, for instance by combining lending activities with fee activities such as securities business.[77]

However, empirical studies performed to examine economies of scale in universal banks are not categorical.[78] De Young explains the statistical tools to measure scale economies deliver the most accurate results for average firms. As in the banking sector, the size distribution of firms is enormous; statistical estimates of scale economies can be sensitive to the financial result of just one of the largest firms. Also, using models designed for small banks to make conclusions of large banking companies might be misleading.[79] In the same sense, the empirical evidence of economies of scope is also unclear.[80] Economies of scope are not always found immediately since the management of universal banks has become very complex.[81]

2. Benefits of One-Stop Shopping

One argument in favour of universal banks is that they can offer a wide range of financial products under the same roof. The possibility of offering

[77] Raghuram Rajan "The Entry of Commercial Banks into the Securities Business: A Selective Survey of Theories and Evidence", NYU (1995), 10; Fohlin "Universal Banking", 319.

[78] Walter "Universal Banking: A Shareholder", Exhibit 4. For a literature review on economies of scale in the US and Europe see Elena Becalli, Mario Anolli, Giuliana Borello "Are European Banks Too Big? Evidence on Economies of Scale", *LSE Research Online* (2015).

[79] Robert De Young "Scale Economies Are a Distraction" The Real Issue for Policy Is Credible Resolution of Failing Financial Firms, Not Bank Size", *Scale Economies in Banking Symposium* (2010), 15.

[80] Rajan "The Entry of Commercial Banks", 12.

[81] Canals "Universal Banking", 104.

different products would help the universal bank to offer new and diversified products that might help it to gain new customers or to retain traditional ones. An example of this was the demand of investment funds in the 90s as an alternative to deposit product, which made many banks in that decade to follow the universal banking model in order not to lose this segment of customers.[82] Another feature of the one-stop shop banking would be the need to adapt to new customer financial needs by adding new services, which in turn make universal banks expand into new business.[83] Products that at the beginning were designed for sophisticated clients may be adapted to small clients at a low marginal cost for the bank.[84]

One of the benefits of one-stop shopping is universal banking centralizes a lot of infrastructure and support functions, reducing interlinkages with different providers, and thus reducing counterparty risk, while gaining transparency.[85]

However, there is little evidence customers really want one-stop shopping. There are some individual case studies like the attempt of Sears to set up financial supermarkets that did not succeed. According to Rajan, the reason might be that unlike firms, individual investors prefer to face small transaction costs to choose the best specialist for their investment.[86] Accordingly, Canals believes when a universal bank has a firm as a customer it has "great chance of satisfying a greater number of financial needs".[87]

At the end of the day, as Canals properly notes, when an organization has the "ability to adapt", it is not so important if it is universal or specialized. What really matters is the capacity and resources to adapt to the new realities and demand for new services.[88]

[82] Canals "Universal Banking", 105.

[83] Hans E. Buschgen "The Universal Banking System in the Federal Republic of Germany", *Journal of Comparative Corporate Law and Securities Regulation* (1979), 8.

[84] Jan Schildbach "Universal Banks: Optimal for Clients and Financial Stability. Why It Would Be Wrong to Split Them Up", *Deutsche Bank Research* (2012), 6.

[85] Ibid., 14.

[86] Rajan "The Entry of Commercial Banks", 11.

[87] Canals "Universal Banking", 106.

[88] Ibid.

3. Alternative Revenue Sources and Reduction of Economic Risk due to Diversified Activities

A third argument states universal banking would benefit from alternative revenue sources from different financial activities and that economic risk is reduced due to diversified activities. Revenue synergies relate to cross-selling and cross-referencing across business divisions; for instance, a sophisticated product such as derivatives for hedging risks designed for corporate clients might be offered to small customers at no extra cost.[89]

As banks need to live with risks, universal banks seek to compensate market fluctuations by offering services that do not have "parallel profit curves". Offering lending and securities activities decreases the probability of à large "overall loss" since losses in one sector would be balanced by the other.[90] The diversification benefits may arise when episodes of disintermediation (when the public raise funds directly from the markets) happen. Universal banks would be less affected by the decline of lending business by a possible increase of their underwriting and placing business. However, as Rajan affirms, there is little evidence of these effects.[91] Additionally, having access to information of a full range of financial assets would enable universal banks to obtain an "optimal diversification" of investments that specialized firms would find harder to obtain.[92]

Drawing on historical data Benston shows bank involvement in securities activities have mitigated bank failure in the pre-Glass-Steagal Act in the US.[93] Saunders and Walter devote a whole chapter using aggregated and individual firm data to conclude

> The simulation analysis based on US data suggests that there are potential risk reduction gains from allowing banks to expand their activity set in a limited fashion – and similarly for non-bank financial firms to expand their set of activities – and that these gains increase with the number of activities undertaken. The main risk reduction gains appear to rise from banks' expanding into insurance rather than securities activities. Moreover, quite

[89] Schildbach "Universal Banks", 13.

[90] Buschgen "Universal Banking System", 5.

[91] Rajan "The entry of Commercial Banks", 15.

[92] Fohlin "Universal Banking", 319.

[93] Benston "Universal Banking", 124.

> substantial risk-reduction gains ...appear to exist at the most comprehensive level of universal banking when all five areas of financial service activity are combined.[94]

Benston concludes that theory, and evidence shows permitting banks to perform securities, insurance and other financial services would reduce rather than increase the expected risks.[95]

Conclusions on the advantages of diversification on combining activities are mixed and according to Calomiris they are ill suited to measure the diversification advantages of universal banking. The main reasons for this are that combining firms is not the same as combining balance sheets; the behaviour of firms might change as a result of combining activities.[96]

4. Long-Term Relationships

One advantage of universal banking is that it fosters long-term relationships between banks and customers. This would allow the customer to change the financing of the firm as it matures, while keeping the "optimal financial arrangements" across the "life-cycle" of the firm. The long-term relationship implies a credible implicit agreement to continue the relationship over time. Initially the bank would lend to the firm, then it would underwrite the firm issuance, and probably later it would own shares of the firm. The advantage of this relationship is that banks are encouraged to lend on favourable terms from the beginning of the relationship. Monitoring costs would be spread among long periods of time, reducing

[94] Saunders and Walter "Universal Banking", 204.

[95] Benston "Universal Banking", 126.

[96] Charles Calomiris "The Costs of Rejecting Universal Banking: American Finance in the German Mirror, 1970–1914" in Naomi R. Lamoreaux and Daniel M. G. Raff *Coordination and Information: Historical Perspectives on the Organization of Enterprise* (University of Chicago Press 1995), 271.

initial costs for the firm.[97]This specific "implicit contractual arrangement" between the bank and the firm is called "*Hausebank* financing" or "relationship lending".[98]

From the bank perspective, once it has lent to the firm, it already has valuable information that would reduce the costs of underwriting. In order to prevent the firm from changing bank in the middle of its life cycle and to avoid a time consistency problem—where the firm gains a free ride by obtaining cheap financing at the beginning of its life while changing bank when it matures and is then able to obtain financing on its own—it would be wise to allow banks to hold shares and underwrite securities in the firm as a form of compensation for the bank.[99]

Long-term relationships would promote stronger and efficient investment since in these relationships a close monitoring ingredient exists. This monitoring may be facilitated by placing bank directors on the boards of the firms. This in term would substitute collateral and allow banks to finance good projects which might have insufficient collateralized assets.[100] Also, long-term relationships may help improve corporate control, since close monitoring might detect poor managers and protect good managers. However, this would be more difficult in market-based systems where mergers and acquisitions are common and in general, old managers are changed without discernment of the quality of their work.[101]

The good reputation of the underwriter might increase the market for the firm's shares, and the access to accurate information may allow a better valuation of its shares. Relationship banking would improve the efficiency

[97] Calomiris "The Costs of Rejecting", 265; Colin Mayer "New Issues in Corporate Finance", *European Economic Review* (1988), 1167–1189; Christopher James and Peggy Wier "Borrowing Relationships, Intermediation and the Cost of Issuing Pubic Securities", *Journal of Financial Economics* (1990), 148–171; Mitchell Petersen and Raghuram Rajan "The Benefits of Lending Relationships: Evidence from Small Business Data", *Journal of Finance* (1994), 3–37; Fohlin "Universal Banking", 319.

[98] Ralf Elsas and Jan Pieter Krahnen "Is Relationship Lending Special? Evidence from Credit-File Data in Germany", *Journal of Banking and Finance* (1998), 1284; Ralf Elsas and Jan Pieter Krahnen "Universal Banks and Relationships with Firms" in Krahnen and Schmidt "The German Financial System", 227.

[99] Ibid., 268; Guinnane "Delegated Monitors", 108–109.

[100] Fohlin "Universal Banking", 319.

[101] Ibid.

of securities underwriting.[102] Through bank members on the firm's board or through the acquisition of the firm's equity by the bank, the firm would gain a seal of quality that investors would be aware of when acquiring securities of the firm's shares. Formal bank relations would give the firm more options to finance, since it would have better access to lending, securities and equity underwriting.[103]

On the other hand, three arguments are offered against the advantages of long-term relationship banking based on historical facts. First, it is affirmed only joint stock enterprises had supervisory boards (where a bank appointed its representatives to the firms). While most large industrial firms were joint stocks, these kinds of firms were a small minority of industrial capital in Germany from 1800 to 1914. A second argument states that being the bank representative on the supervisory board was a "purely formal" job; they received reports, but the position of power they actually held was not quite clear. A third argument affirms the monitoring position of the supervisory board was not different from a normal bank-customer relationship, where the bank would generally request reports, balance sheets and other information that may help it determine the risks of lending.[104]

However, this is probably one of the strongest arguments that determines which type of capitalism a country chooses: one built on short-term profits à la USA or one built on a more inclusive, long-term model that many in Germany have claimed contributed to Germany's industrialization. Populism has exposed the deficiencies of being too focused on short-term profits.[105]

Costs of Universal Banking from the Perspective of Public Policy

1. Universal Banks May Increase the Risk of Financial Instability

One common feature of universal banks is that they are on average larger than specialized banks. Since size is a category of systemic importance and

[102] John H. Boyd and Edward. C. Prescot "Financial Intermediary-Coalitions", *Journal of Economic Theory* (1986), 211–232.

[103] Fohlin "Universal Banking", 321.

[104] Guinnane "Delegated Monitors", 107–108; Edwards and Ogilvie "Banks, Finance and Investment in Germany", 441.

[105] Charles Goodhart and Rosa Lastra "Populism and Central Bank Independence", *Open Economies Review* (2018), 51.

may have implications with respect of asymmetric information and agency problems, it may also increase financial instability.[106] A first implication would be universal bank might have the problems of TBTF. If the bank served different activities under the same umbrella, it would be costly for governments to permit liquidation. Bankruptcy of universal banks would be especially costly because of their complexity and interconnecting role in the financial industry.[107] If one or several universal banks were to fail it might lead to a systemic financial crisis. A second consequence of TBTF would be the incentives for managers to take excessive risks. Regulators, recognizing this danger would tighten universal banking regulation, "hindering economic efficiency" or bailout.[108] However, this has more to do to size than to specialization or universality of banks.[109] After the GFC it is now clear that size is just one of the categories of systemic importance and the focus is more placed on the interconnectedness and contagion rather than just the size of the bank. The regulatory response of the FSB and national regulators imposed new requisites on G-SIBs in order to tackle systemic risk of these type of financial institutions.

As universal banks may manage their risks in a diversified way easily reallocating funds from a business line to another, universal banks may take on riskier assets and a more fragile capital structure. This excessive risk-taking may make the universal bank more fragile. Freixas, Loranth and Morrison argue universal banks may also abuse deposit insurance and finance their securities business with insured deposits, which may increase the risk-taking in that line of business.[110] Rajan believes this argument

[106] Benston "Universal Banking", 123; Dietrich and Vollmer, "Are Universal Banks", 124. Arthur Wilmarth in his book *Taming the Megabanks: Why We Need a New Glass-Stegal Act* (OUP, 2020), 6, indicates that universal banks "are inherently dangerous because their business model promotes dangerous boom-and-bust cyles" since they use deposits to fund risky loans, and in turn package risky loans into asset-baked securities that are sold to poorly informed investors. Muge Adalet "The Effect of Financial Structure on Crises: Universal Banking in Interwar Europe", Working Paper, No. 0910, *TÜSİAD-Koç University Economic Research Forum* (2009), 15, suggests that countries with universal banking were more likely to experience crises.

[107] Dietrich and Vollmer "Are Universal Banks", 124.

[108] Ibid.

[109] Canals "Universal Banking", 128; Schildbach "Universal Banks", 4.

[110] Xavier Freixas, Gyöngyi Lóránth, and Alan D. Morrison "Regulating Financial Conglomerates", *Journal of Financial Intermediation* (2007), 479–514; Dietrich and Vollmer "Are Universal Banks", 124.

is misplaced since the actual flow of funds between divisions of the bank can be limited by "mandating firewalls" which restrict direct transactions between sub units.[111]

Another reason why universal banks may increase instability is that diversification may ease internal bank contagion. If the securities division of the bank reports large losses, the commercial division might experience financial constraints as a consequence.[112]

In addition, a focus of instability for universal banking might be reflected by the fact that universal banks hold equity stakes in firms. This would expose banks to the firms' business fluctuations and capital market volatility.[113]

2. Universal Banks May Hurt Stock Markets

One argument against universal banking states the latter would hurt capital markets since they trade and hold equity and securities discouraging the development of active stock exchanges.[114] While there is little empirical evidence of this element, Benston believes there might be different factors that may explain why Germany has a less developed capital market system than the US. First, perceived accounting rules that may lead the German individual investor to prefer other investments; second, investors might simply have less preference to invest in the stock markets than US investors; and third, pension funds were kept within firms, without pension firm investment in stocks of other firms.[115] Additionally, as stated above, Verdier believes legislative and tax restrictions might have challenged the development of capital markets in Germany. To sum up, there is no empirical evidence allowing to establish a causal link between universal banks and the injury of capital markets. However, as showed above, the comparison of German and US securities markets display a better development of the US markets, where specialized banks were the norm.

[111] Rajan "The Entry of Commercial Banks", 14.

[112] Dietrich and Vollmer "Are Universal Banks", 124.

[113] Fohlin "Universal Banking", 321.

[114] Benston "Universal Banking", 128.

[115] Ibid.

3. Universal Banks May Engage in Anticompetitive Behaviour, Concentration of Power and/or Monopoly Practices

The anticompetitive behaviour of universal banks is one of the most important arguments in terms of costs, since "mammoth entities" are more difficult to manage, supervise, and resolve and competition in banking should provide the salutary market practice that only the best succeed.

Universal banking might induce two types of anticompetitive behaviour. First, the multiple services of universal banking may lead to financial services concentration, which, if excessive may lead to market power.[116] Additionally, the capacity of competing in various markets may induce to "limit pricing" or "predatory pricing" and stave off competition from specialized intermediaries.[117] Second, universal banks may (mis)use information to lead industry cartelization. By use of strategic information of several firms in the same sector, universal banking may enhance mergers and acquisitions or "enforce cooperation".[118]

On the first issue, as stated by Baum and Gruson, under German law these problems of limit pricing and predatory pricing are dealt by the application of competition law.[119] As of the second issue, Calomiris points out two arguments. First, he states the "development and enforcement of industrial cartels by intermediaries is not a weakness peculiar to concentrated universal banking systems", while quantitative studies were not conclusive in responding the question of whether industrial cartelization was a "historically an important function of intermediaries", and that this question remains a "murky area" in economic history. In summary, Calomiris concludes even if there is an argument in favour of cartelization, the problem would be one of all forms of "interbank coalitions" and not a specific problem of universal banking.[120] Riesser, drawing on the German experience before 1911 argues the influence of banks in

[116] Fohlin "Universal Banking", 322.

[117] Benston "Universal Banking", 131; Fohlin "Universal Banking", 322.

[118] Fohlin "Universal Banking", 322; Benston "Universal Banking", 131.

[119] Baum and Gruson "The German Banking System", 128.

[120] Calomiris "The Costs of Rejecting", 274.

enhancing industry cartels was volatile; while in some cases it was decisive, in others it was "hardly perceptible".[121]

Additionally, it is argued universal banks might dominate non-banks through capital participations in non-banking firms, exercise of proxy-voting rights in shareholder's meetings and presence in supervisory and advisory boards.[122] During the 70s in Germany two official commissions studied the involvement of universal banks with non-banks: the Monopoly Commission (1976, 1978) and the Commission on Banking Structure, or Gessler Commission (1979). The Gessler Commission lasted 4 years and included 74 large corporations and 343 banking institutions by 1975. It concluded "The universal bank's total holdings in non-banks measured by nominal values are small relative to the total equity of non-banks" except in two sectors, brewing and construction.[123] Regarding proxy rights, it stated "the inquiry into the banks' proxy rights show that the banks' influential power from voting of shares is not very great compared with non-banks on the whole".[124] Concerning the domination through supervisory boards and boards of directors, the Gessler Commission affirmed "at the end of 1974 members of bank management had supervisory board seats in about 1/3 of all German joint stock companies. In 2/3 of these companies, only one banker was represented".[125] A general conclusion of the Gessler Commission reads as follows:

> The Commission could not subscribe to the undiscriminating criticism that universal banks by holding shares in non-banks reduce, to their own benefit, the independence and the scope of the action of those companies in which participations are held. Nor did it subscribe to the opinion that banks take up shares in non-banks that are, at the same time, their borrowers with the purpose of reducing their credit risks. It follows implicitly from the Commission report that banks consider their holdings mainly as independent investments. The Commission found that

[121] Riesser "The German Great Banks", 712.

[122] Buschgen "Universal Banking System", 14.

[123] Krummel "German Universal Banking Scrutinized", 48; Benston "Universal Banking", 135.

[124] Ibid.

[125] Ibid.

abuse of influence on non-banks cannot be attributed to the banking institutions.[126]

The actual debate of liberalization versus regulation and protection under the WTO in financial services rules, which has emerged again after Brexit, offers further elements to the discussion. Some argue the rules of financial services under the WTO would not be sufficient to safeguard competition since there is a broad "prudential curve out" in place under GATS rules.[127] As the Luxembourg Court of Justice recognized in the *Züchner* case, EC competition law is applicable to the banking sector.[128] The EU has enacted State Aid rules which runs parallel to competition policy.[129]

As will be stated below, *Landesbanken* in Germany had to change their *Anstaltslast* (maintenance guarantee) and the *Gewahrtragerhaftung* (guarantee obligation) in order to comply with EU State Aid and competition rules.

To sum up, problems of enhancing anticompetitive behaviour are solved by the application of competition law in the corresponding jurisdiction. With Calomiris, it can be concluded fighting cartelization requires different legal tools than mere restricting universal banking. Baum and Gruson correctly stress the importance of competition law rather than banking law to address anticompetitive behaviour.[130]

126 Ibid.

127 Prudential Curve Out Annex 2 of the Annex to Financial Services, GATS; Eric Leroux "Trade in Financial Services Under the World Trade Organization", *Journal of World Trade* (2002), 430; Bart De Meester "The Global Financial Crisis and Government Support for Banks: What Role for the GATS?" *Journal of International Economic Law* (2010), 27–63, 60; Anne Van Aaken "Prudence or Discrimination? Emergency Measures, the Global Financial Crisis and International Economic Law", *Journal of International Economic Law* (2009), 859; Mamiko Yokoi-Arai "GATS's Prudential Carve Out in Financial Services and Its Relation with Prudential regulation", *The International and Comparative Law Quarterly* (2008), 639.

128 Case 172/80 *Züchner v Bayerishce Vereinsbank (1981) ECR 2021.*

129 Lastra "International Financial", 157.

130 Baum and Gruson "The German Banking System", 128.

4. Universal Banks May Lead to Abuse of Information and Conflicts of Interest

A fourth argument against universal banking is the possible abuse of information by them. As universal banking serves commercial and investment banking under the same umbrella it could use information gathered, for instance, in the lending business to invest or disinvest in shares of the mentioned firm. A second misuse of information by universal banks might be to deliver information to a non-bank affiliate of a competing firm that is at the same time creditor of the bank. A possible solution to mitigate this risk is the use of effective Chinese Walls. Additionally, the risks of information misuse such as civil liabilities and reputation risk might also work to dissuade the misconduct by the bank. As Baum and Gruson conclude, this risk is not only a universal bank issue, but also present in the US system.[131] An example of information abuse may be present if the insurance company obtains information of a client and at the same time releases that information to the mergers and acquisitions division that is handling an operation with a firm's competitor.[132]

Traditionally the conflict of interest referred to a financial firm "benefiting one client at the expense of another".[133] Yet the concept is much broader. As stated above, when financial institutions offer more products and the scope of customers increase, the possibilities of conflicts of interest arise.[134]

With respect to commercial banks' incursions into the securities business, conflicts of interest may arise from the advisory role of the bank

[131] Ibid., 126; Buschgen "Universal Banking System", 14.

[132] See, for instance "Willis Re (Pty) Ltd Fsp: 24845 Conflict of Interest Policy" Section 2.4. http://www.willisre.com/documents/Media_Room/Publication/Willis_Re_Conflict_of_Interest_Policy_South_Africa.pdf. Accessed 20 July 2023.

[133] See e.g. *Washington Steel v TW Corp, 602 F2d. 594 (3rd cir. 1979)* abrogated by Clark v K-Mart Corp 979 F 2d 965 (3rd cir 1992); James Fanto "'Breaking Up Is Hard to Do': Should Financial Conglomerats Be Dismanteled?" *Brooklyn Law School* (2010), 553.

[134] Santos "Commercial Banks", 35–60. See also Wilmarth "Taming the Megabanks", 6.

towards its depositors. First, the bank may be tempted to promote the securities it underwrites even though there might be better investment options in the market.[135] In other words, when the bank has the power to sell an "in-house" product it may be tempted to offer it against the best interest of the customer.[136] Second, it may also have the incentive to "stuff fiduciary accounts". When a bank is acting as underwriter and it has difficulties to place the securities, it might sell the securities to manage accounts where they have discretionary authority.[137] Third, the bank may use its influence as a lender to tie-in its securities products, for instance by threatening the client to finish the lending relationship if the investment in the securities business is not closed.[138] Fourth, banks who had lent to a firm whose bankruptcy risk has risen may induce their customers to issue bonds or equity to the public, in order to repay the loan with the proceeds of the issuance. In doing so, the bank would have transferred the debt risk to the public, while earning a fee for the underwriting.[139] At the same time, this type of conflict of interest might weaken bank monitoring, since the firm might expect to be bailed out by the universal bank instead of being liquidated.[140] Fifth, as banks have evolved from being client centred to employee and shareholder centred, information might escape from compliance and other controls and used to favour themselves. An example of this is the SEC lawsuit against Goldman Sachs for favouring itself in the "structuring and sale of synthetic collateralized debt

[135] Ibid.

[136] Walter "Universal Banking: A Shareholder", 19.

[137] Ibid. Santos "Commercial Banks", 45–60.

[138] Walter "Universal Banking: A Shareholder", 19; Santos "Commercial Banks", 45–60.

[139] Walter "Universal Banking: A Shareholder", 45–60; Canals "Universal Banking", 130; Santos "Commercial Banks" 45–60. Randall S. Kroszner and Raghuram G. Rajan "Is the Glass-Steagal Act Justified? A Study of the U.S. Experience with Universal Banking Before 1933", *The American Economic Review* (1994), 814; Gregory M. Hebb and Donald R. Fraser "Conflicts of Interest in Commercial Bank Security Underwritings: United Kingdom Evidence", *Quarterly Journal of Business and Economics* (2003), 79–95; Lars Nyberg "How Do Conflicts of Interest in Universal Banking Emerge and What Are the Arguments for a Separation of Commercial and Investment Banking?" *BIS Review* (2004), 1–4.

[140] Lili Xie "Universal Banking, Conflicts of Interest and Firm Growth", *Journal of Financial Services Research*, (2007), 178.

securities".[141] Finally, after the GFC, some authors claimed the universal banks were responsible for the creation and distribution of opaque financial innovations. Securitization has enabled universal banks to increase the volume of their lending activities, and to move loans off the balance sheet, and it has permitted banks to transfer their credit risk to investors.[142] The movement of commoditization and "opaqueness" may be a problem if the universal banks place products "beyond an appropriate customer base".[143]

A second set of conflicts of interest arises from the incursion of commercial banking into the insurance sector. A first example of conflict of interest in this area can be found in

> That many sellers of various financial services offered by banks and insurance companies have traditionally been presented as investment advisors rather than salespeople. The risk of a conflict of interest lies in the fact that their suggestions for investment have been designed more to promote the seller's or the company's interests rather than to fulfil the needs of the investor.[144]

A second possible conflict of interest may be present if the bank uses its lender influence to tie in insurance products.[145]

A third group of conflicts of interest may arise from the relation of the universal bank and the non-bank company it owns. A universal bank may give credit to a non-bank firm it owns in order to increase its share value. This would be in conflict with its depositors, it may endanger the safety and soundness of the bank and the integrity of its deposit insurance fund. Likewise, a bank may purchase the debt of a company it owns

[141] *Complaint SEC v Goldman Sachs & Co. No. 1:10 cv BSJ-MHD* (SDNY filed April 16, 2010). Fanto "Breaking Up is Hard", 553.

[142] Arthur Wilmarth "The Dark Side of Universal Banking: Financial Conglomerates and the Origins of the Subprime Financial Crisis", *Connecticut Law Review* (2009), 984–991.

[143] Fanto "Breaking Up Is Hard", 566; See also Wilmarth "Taming the Megabanks", 6.

[144] Nyberg "How Do Conflicts of Interest", 1–4.

[145] Vicente Lazen Cristián Eguiluz "Conflictos De Interés En Servicios Financieros: Taxonomía y Mecanismos De Control Regulatorio", *Superintendencia de Valores y Seguros – Chile* (2006). https://www.svs.cl/sitio/publicaciones/doc/documento_trabajo_6.pdf. Accessed 20 July 2023.

to increase its share value and may even lend funds to repay the bank loans.Other combinations might be present if the bank purchases bad assets of the non-bank company it owns to protect its reputation and "future profitability".[146]

Empirical research on conflicts of interest in Germany in the late 70s by the Gessler Commission concluded

> On the whole, consideration of potential conflicts of interest in universal banking did not lead the Commission to recommend the separation of the banking functions but rather to conclude that restraints of competition caused by such conflicts of interest are small and can be remedied or abolished by provisions within the existing system.[147]

Empirical research in the 90s conducted by Kroszner and Rajan on data before the Glass-Steagal Act in the US concludes the argument that commercial banks inducing the public to invest in low quality securities are flawed, since the performance of securities underwritten by commercial and investment banks show no evidence of such attitude. For them, the "public appears to have rationally accounted for the possibility of conflicts of interest" and this has moved banks to underwrite "high quality securities".[148] A paper by Gande, Puri and Walter in the late 90s that examined debt securities underwritten by Section 20 subsidiaries of banks holding companies compared to those underwritten by investment houses found no "evidence of conflict of interest even when an issue is used to repay bank debt".[149] In 2016, Klein, Wuebker and Zoeller studied the relationship between "IPO underpricing, secondary market IPO returns and the lead underwriters bank structure". They conclude

> While the market recognizes that conflicts of interest can arise if commercial and banking are combined in one institution, our results suggest that investors are aware of those potential problems and require – and receive – an appropriate discount. For this reason, it seems unnecessary to prohibit

[146] Bernard Shull "The Separation of Banking and Commerce in the United States: An Examination of Principal Issues", *OCC Economics Working Paper* (1999), 40.

[147] Krummel "German Universal Banking Scrutinized", 33–55.

[148] Kroszner and Rajan "Is the Glass-Steagal Act Justified", 810.

[149] Amar Gande, Manju Puri, Anthony Saunders and Ingo Walter "Bank Underwriting of Debt Securities: Modern Evidence", *The Review of Financial Studies [1997]*, 1175.

the combination of commercial banking and investment banking to protect investors.[150]

As Santos explains, the real issue regarding conflicts of interest is not its mere existence, but whether the bank has incentives and opportunities to exploit them.[151] There are different mechanisms of control of conflicts of interest: market-based, regulation based or a combination of both.[152] Market-based mechanisms rely on reputational risk, credit rating monitoring and supervision by regulatory agencies. Regulation-based mechanisms rely on the implementation of "walls" between activities, such as the Glass-Steagal Act in the US.

While empirical evidence shows conflicts of interest are somehow internalized by the public and the effects of conflicts of interest can be "abolished" by mechanisms of control, the conclusion might be the mere existence of conflicts of interest, that arise not only in universal banks, but also in specialized institutions, is not a fundamental argument to prohibit the expansion of commercial banks in other financial sectors such as securities and insurance. While market-based mechanisms might be effective in some cases, a combination of market and regulation-based control mechanisms might be a useful tool to tackle the exploitation of conflicts of interest by universal banks. That being said, it is also true the sole regulatory standard would not be capable by itself to stop dishonest behaviour.[153] A whole new ethical environment should be developed, possibly based on a virtue-based system, which by definition would take time to develop, and at the end it would rely on the human conduct of leaders and employees of the banks.[154]

Insider dealing was a normal way of doing business in Germany until the advent of the EU directives forbidding it.

[150] Peter Klein, Roberr Wuebker, and Kathrin Zoeller "Relationship Banking and Conflicts of Interest: Evidence from German Initial Public Offerings", *Journal of Corporate Finance* (2016), 220.

[151] Santos "Commercial Banks", 42.

[152] Walter "Universal Banking: A Shareholder", 19.

[153] Canals "Universal Banking", 130.

[154] Rosa Lastra and Marcelo Sheppard Gelsi "Ethical Foundations of Financial Law" in Costanza Russo, Rosa Lastra and William Blair *Research Handbook on Law and Ethics in Banking and Finance* (Elgar, 2019), 55–72.

> In Germany, no regulations regarding insider trading existed before 1970. From 1970 to 1994, only voluntary guidelines existed. In 1994, the Securities Trading Act, or *Wertpapierhandelsgesetz*, was passed, prohibiting trading on private information by corporate insiders.[155]

The whole development of securities regulation in the EU mirroring the US development (albeit a few decades later in the case of the EU) was a massive change in the way Germany had to do business. Transparency and disclosure reformed German financial markets, leaving behind decades of transparency underdevelopment.[156]

Costs from the Perspective of the Bank Itself: Organizational Costs

The German model may have organizational problems of its own. First, there may be costs of coordination of the various units of the bank. Coordination may jeopardize the necessary synergies a universal bank needs to create in order to lower the general costs or increase revenues.[157] Second, there might be a "motivation problem" between managers with the same qualifications, but working in different units of the bank, such as commercial and investment banking. As the competitive features are different, the market would differ the salary and bonus scales. However, these compensation differences within the same entity may create distrust and endanger coordination between different units.[158]

A second organizational cost is the existence of "influence costs". These are activities that are not productive "which seek to modify income distribution between different groups". In order to manage the influence costs, the universal bank needs to establish ways to distribute the costs and profits within itself, which is generally controversial among managers.[159]

[155] James H. Thompson "A Global Comparison of Insider Trading Regulations", *International Journal of Accounting and Financial Reporting* (2016) 11; see also Freis "An Outsider's Look", 302, 30.

[156] Freis "An Outsider's Look", 6.

[157] Canals "Universal Banking", 119.

[158] Ibid. Wilmarth "Taming the Megabanks", 10 suggests, based in Thomas Philippon and Ariell Reshef "Wages and Human Capital in the US Finance Industry", *Quarterly Journal of Economics* (2012), 1551–1609, there is a close connection between the rise of bonuses for insiders when universal banking was deregulated in the US, in the 1920s and 1990s and 2007.

[159] Ibid. See Herring and Santomero "The Corporate", 231.

3.2 German Banking System

In 1991 a document from the Department of Treasury described the German banking model as "arguably the most liberal in the world and is generally perceived to be the model for the future in the European Community".[160] The Bush administration was looking for a new deal for US banks, arguing the Glass-Steagall Act separation was unnecessary. The German model has changed little from that time to the present and the Treasury prophecy that Germany's model would be an example for the EU was largely fulfilled. The main features of the universal banking system comprise: (1) a broad scope of allowed activities, (2) a variety of allowed investments and a scope of allowed owners.[161]

1. Permissible Activities

As stated in Chapter 2, according to the Banking Act, section 1, credit institutions "are undertakings which conduct banking business commercially or on a scale which requires commercially organized business operations" and they may offer a variety of financial services such as (1) the acceptance of funds from others as deposits [...]; (2) the granting of money loans and acceptance credits (credit business); (3) discount business; (4) principal broking services; (5) safe custody business; [...] (8) guarantee business; (9) bill collection business; (10) underwriting business; and, (12) "acting in the capacity of a central counterpart".[162] However there are some limitations. The same Act defines Financial Services Institutions, which "are undertakings which provide financial services to others commercially or on a scale which requires commercially organized business operations, and which are not credit institutions." Financial services comprise: (1) investment broking, (1a) investment advice), (1b) operation of a multilateral trading facility, 1c) the placing of financial instruments without a firm commitment basis (placement business), (...) (2) contract broking, (3) portfolio management, (4) proprietary trading, (...), (6) crypto custody business, (...), (9) factoring, (10)

[160] US Department of the Treasury "Modernizing the Financial System. Recommendations of Safer, More Competitive Banks" (1991), 54–61.

[161] See generally Baum and Gruson "The German Banking System", 101–129.

[162] Banking Act http://www.gesetze-im-internet.de/kredwg/. Accessed 2 May 2023.

financial leasing, (11) investment management, (12) asset management, (12) limited custody business.

Both entities, credit institutions and financial services require authorization pursuant to section 32 (1) of the Banking Act. Banking supervision in Germany is shared by the Bundesbank and the Federal Financial Supervisory Authority (BaFin).

A first limitation of the universal banking model is that banks may not engage in the insurance business by issuing insurance policies.[163] Insurance Companies require a licence pursuant to the Act on the Supervision of Insurance Undertakings (*Versicherungsaufsichtsgesetz*—VAG). Section 15 (1) requires

> Beyond insurance business, the insurance undertakings are only permitted to carry on such other business as is directly related with insurance business. Such a relationship shall be deemed to exist in the case of dealings in futures, options and other financial instruments if these are to serve as hedge against price and interest rate risks in connection with existing assets or future purchases of securities or if any additional return is to be generated on existing securities, without performance of delivery obligations causing a shortfall of the restricted assets.[164]

However, banks are allowed to sell insurance issued by licensed insurance companies and are allowed to own insurance companies.[165]

A second limitation is the so-called ring-fencing of banking and certain investment activities. The "Act on Ring-Fencing and Recovery and Resolution Planning for Credit Institutions and Financial Groups" of 7 August 2013 (Bank Separation Act) includes certain prohibitions in section 3(2) of the German Banking Act as of 1 July 2015. The purpose of the Bank Separation act is to ring-fence the deposit and lending business of large institutions preventing them from engaging in risky transactions.[166] The subjects of this prohibition are "CRR [Capital Requirements Regulation]

[163] Baum and Gruson "The German Banking System", 101–129, and Michel Gruson and Ralf Reisner *Regulation of Foreign Banks, United States and International* (Second Edition, 1995), 15–19.

[164] Act on the Supervision of Insurance Undertakings (Versicherungsaufsichtsgesetz—VAG). Section 15 (1).

[165] Ibid.

[166] Section 3(2) of the German Banking Act.

credit institutions and of groups of institutions, financial holding groups, mixed financial holding groups or FCs which include a CRR credit institution" where their balance sheet positions exceed EUR 100 billion (absolute threshold) in financial assets available for trading purposes and available for sale, trading portfolio and liquidity reserves. The same applies if they "amount to at least €90 billion as at the reporting date in each of the three preceding financial years, if they exceed 20% of the total assets from the preceding financial year" (relative threshold).[167]

Section 3(3) of the German Banking Act states a group exceeding one of the thresholds specified above shall, "no later than six months after exceeding one of the thresholds, identify by means of a risk analysis which of its business activities are prohibited", and, within 12 months after exceeding one of the thresholds, "discontinue such prohibited business" or "transfer it to a financial trading institution".[168] The financial trading institution must be economically, organizationally and legally independent.[169] Finally, the engagement in prohibited activity is subject to an imprisonment or a fine.[170]

2. Permissible Investments and Owners

German banks are allowed to invest in other banks, commercial and industrial company shares and insurance companies.[171] However, anyone who wants to acquire a significant holding in a credit institution must notify BaFin and the Deutsche Bundesbank.[172] A significant holding is a qualifying holding pursuant to Article 4 (1), number 36 of CRR as last amended, which defines it as a "direct or indirect holding in an undertaking which represents 10% or more of the capital or of the voting rights or which makes it possible to exercise a significant influence over the

[167] EBA "EBA Publishes an Opinion on the Perimeter of Credit Institutions" (2014). Available at https://www.eba.europa.eu/eba-publishes-an-opinion-on-the-perimeter-of-credit-institutions. Accessed 24 August 2023.

[168] Section 3(3) of the German Banking Act.

[169] Section 25f of the German Banking Act.

[170] Section 54 (1) of the German Banking Act.

[171] Baum and Gruson "The German Banking System", 101–129; Section 2c of the Banking Act.

[172] Section 2c of the Banking Act.

management of that undertaking". In the Single Supervisory Mechanism (SSM) the European Central Bank is the one that would approve such an acquisition. Also,

> Anyone who intends to dispose of a significant holding in an institution or to reduce the amount of his/her significant holding below the thresholds of 20%, 30% or 50% of the voting rights or the capital held, or to change the holding in such a way that the institution ceases to be a controlled undertaking, shall report this in writing to BaFin and the Deutsche Bundesbank without delay.[173]

In the case of intra-group transactions with mixed-activity holding companies, a

> CRR (Capital Requirements Regulation) institution which is a subsidiary of a mixed-activity holding company is to notify BaFin and the Deutsche Bundesbank of any significant intra-group transactions with mixed-activity holding companies or other subsidiaries of such mixed-activity holding companies.[174]

There are also reporting obligations for certain credit institutions to report those "borrowers whose credit volume amounts to €1,000,000 or more (threshold for loans of €1 million or more)" to the Deutsche Bundesbank on a quarterly basis (observation period).[175] Additionally, Section 18 of the Banking Act states

> A credit institution may grant a loan amounting in the aggregate to more than €750,000 or 10% of the institution's liable capital pursuant only if it requires the borrower to disclose his or her financial situation, in particular by submitting the annual accounts. The credit institution may waive this requirement if, in the light of the collateral provided or of the co-obligors, there is evidently no reason to require such disclosure.[176]

[173] Section 2c (3) of the Banking Act.

[174] Section 13c of the Banking Act.

[175] Section 14 of the Banking Act.

[176] Section 19 include "asset items" in the concept of loans regarding Sections 13, 14 and 18 of the Banking Act.

The Three Pillar Structure

As stated above, the German banking system is universal. The "three pillar structure" of the German system is formed by: (1) Commercial banks (private banks); (2) Savings banks; (3) Cooperative banks.

Commercial banks are part of the private sector and comprise the big or major banks (*Grossbanken*), regional banks and branch offices, foreign banks and banks owned by individuals. The savings banks public sector encompasses the savings banks (*Sparkassen*), the *Landesbanken* or giro central banks (*Landesbanken-Girozentralen*) and other state-owned banks (*Landesbanken*). The savings banks and *Landesbanken* are owned by government entities such as municipalities, states or other public entities. The third pillar comprises the cooperative banks and the cooperative central banks.[177] Figure 3.1 shows the structure of the three pillar system, while Table 3.1 describes the number of financial institutions as 2022.

As an EU member state, the German banking framework is based on EU directives and regulations, primarily on CRR. The main German Banking regulation is the Banking Act (*Kreditwesengesetz*, or KWG) which comprises licensing requirements, ownership control and supervision. Other laws deal with specialized institutions such as building societies (*Bausparkassen*) and investment funds (*Kapitalverwaltungsgesselschaften*).[178]

A. The First Pillar

The financial institutions that form the first pillar are subject to private law and organized generally as limited partnerships with share capital (*Kommanditgesellschaften auf Aktien*) or joint stock corporations (*Aktiengessellschaften*). Some smaller private banks are limited partnerships or even general partnerships, which are not protected by limited liability. Since the nineteenth century, these banks have been offering

[177] Faltermeier "The German Banking System", 15; Gruson and Reisner "The German Banking System", 15–21.

[178] Hendrik Haag and Jan Letto Steffen, Hengeler Mueller "Banking Regulations in Germany: Overview" in https://uk.practicallaw.thomsonreuters.com/w-007-4084?transitionType=Default&contextData=(sc.Default)&firstPage=true&comp=pluk&bhcp=1. Accessed 7 August 2023.

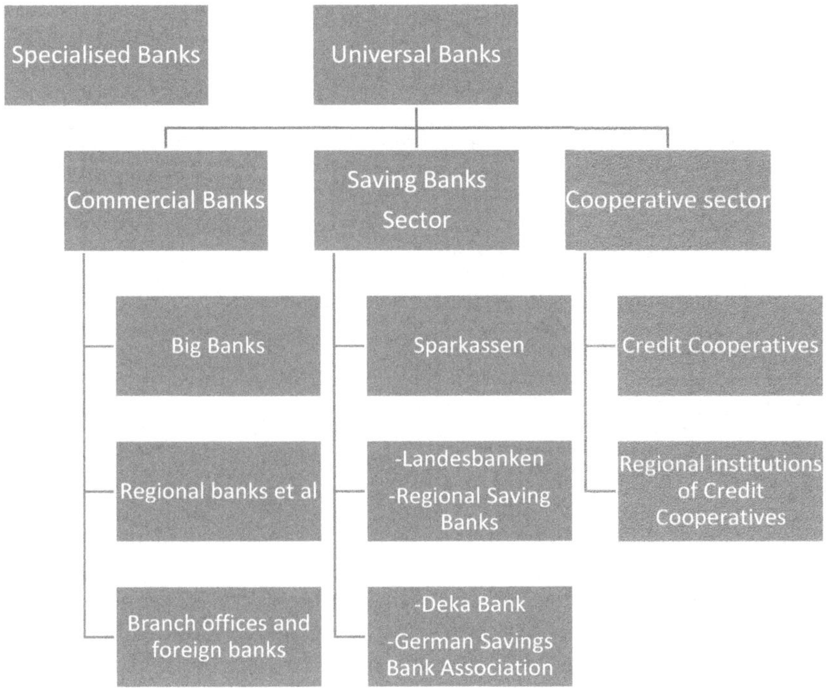

Fig. 3.1 Three pillar structure as of 2023 (Source *Bundesbank*[179])

retail, wholesale and investment banking services.[180] As licenced banks, they need to comply with the German banking regulation and banking supervision by the BaFin in cooperation with the Bundesbank.

The first group of commercial banks are the big banks. There are four *Grossbanken* in Germany: (1) Deutsche Bank Aktiengesellschaft; (2) Commerzbank Aktiengesellschaft; (3) Hypo Vereinsbank and (4) Deutsche Post (which was acquired by Deutsche Bank). In terms of assets, the four major banks account for almost 65%.[181] The big banks have

[179] Bundesbank, 2023, https://www.bundesbank.de/resource/blob/816178/1692dd2ef896b58f071cdf0525a98327/mL/bf1e00a5-data.pdf. Accessed 8 April 2023.

[180] Dietrich and Vollmer "Are Universal Banks", 127.

[181] Faltermeier "The German Banking System", 16.

Table 3.1 Number of financial institutions in Germany

Institution	*Year 2022*
Big Banks	3
Regional banks and other commercial banks	133
Branches of foreign banks	105
Landesbanken	6
Savings banks	362
Regional institutions of credit cooperatives	733
Credit cooperatives	8
Banks with special development and other central support tasks	18
Building and loan associations	18
Foreign branches	214
Foreign subsidiaries	32
Total	1632

Source *Bundesbank, 2023*[182]

traditionally acted as house banks to Germany's industrial firms, providing long-term finance, sitting on the supervisory boards, owning its shares and exercising proxy votes of other shareholders.[183] An empirical study from Elsas and Krahnen concludes that relationship lending is common "among mid-sized firms" and that it is not a "myth" but a fact, with real economic effects on the financing of corporations.[184] They also conclude that "contrary to the common presumption in the literature, evidence does not suggest that banks use proxy-voting rights as a systemic way to influence management decisions".[185] In a similar way "Studies concerned with the impact of a firm's bank dependence on performance consistently find a positive impact of direct equity holdings by banks. In contrast, proxy-voting rights and supervisory board representation by banks appear to be irrelevant for management control". The argument implies that the main advantages of house bank relationship derive from the equity holdings and not directly by proxy rights and supervisory control.[186] A

[182] Ibid.

[183] Detzer, Dodig, Evans and Herr "The German Financial System", 33; Gruson and Reisner "German Banking System", 15–19.

[184] Elsas and Krahnen "Universal Banks and Relationships with Firms", 211.

[185] Ibid.

[186] Ibid.

2018 study by the Deutsche Bundesbank affirms that after the German government abolished the capital gains tax on the divestitures of equity stakes in 2010, the German banks sold most of their equity shares in non-bank firms (75% of banks' equity was divested in the 6 years after the tax reform), but the relationship lending did not reduce as a consequence of such divestitures.[187]

However, lending by big banks to non-banks has declined from 75% of big bank assets in the 1960s to 25% in 2011. In order to turn this situation around, big banks tried to lend to small and medium size firms, but this was unsuccessful due to the strong bond between savings banks and local firms. In the interim, big banks started developing investment banking. Deutsche Bank bought the English investment bank Morgan Grenfell (1990) and in turn, Dresdner bought Kleinwort Benson (1995).[188]

The second group of commercial banks comprises smaller joint stock banks which operate on a local level. Two foreign banks are included in this group: ING and Santander Consumer Bank. Also, it comprises banks set up by industrial firms like Volkswagen Bank and Mercedes-Benz Bank.[189]

The last group comprises branches of foreign banks, which encompasses almost half of the total balance sheet assets of regional banks and almost one quarter of big bank assets.[190]

B. The Second Pillar

The second pillar comprises savings banks (or *Sparkassen*), the *Landesbanken* and DekaBank,[191] and a parallel structure of associations which comprises regional savings bank associations and the German Savings

[187] Bastian von Beschwitz and Daniel Foos "Banks' Equity Stakes and Lending: Evidence from a Tax Reform" [2018], Discussion Paper Deutsche Bundesbank No 06, 3.

[188] Detzer, Dodig, Evans and Herr "The German Financial System", 79.

[189] Ibid.; https://www.mercedes-benz-bank.de/de.html. Accessed 18 August 2018.

[190] Deutsche Bundesbank Monthly Report as of July 30, 2023, https://www.bundesbank.de/resource/blob/912862/03e9805c143c2f26b510da50b14b313c/mL/2023-07-monatsbericht-data.pdf. Accessed 18 August 2023.

[191] Detzer, Dodig, Evans and Herr "The German Financial System", 79.

Bank Association (Deutscher Sparkassen-und GiroverbandDSGV).[192] The first savings bank was founded in 1778 in Hamburg with the aim to "help the poor".[193] At the beginning the savings banks were established in towns, but later on, rural counties also founded savings banks.The aim was to give the poor the opportunity to earn interest on deposits of their savings, even though they were small. It was only in 1840 that savings banks started to provide credit to small local firms. One main feature of the savings bank from the beginning was they were not profit-motivated or shareholder-value oriented, since it was a public function of the local governments to encourage deposit taking and providing credit to "middle classes". One reason why the savings banks developed regionally was Germany did not have a central government until 1871.[194]

The legal basis of savings banks' establishment and organization are the relevant Savings Banks Act (*Sparkassengesetz*) in each state and its articles of incorporation. As credit institutions they are subject to German Banking Law (mainly the German Banking Act and Securities Trading Act).[195] As licensed banks, they are subject to bank supervision by the Federal Financial Services Authority (BaFin), in cooperation with the Bundesbank. Savings banks are generally organized as independent instrumentalities under public law, which need to fulfil a public function. However, after 1997, a few, so-called free savings banks have been formed. These are self-controlled and controlled by foundations.[196] Savings banks need to comply with the territorial principle, by which the activities and powers to create branches are restricted into an area of a county or municipality that "establishes and sponsors" the savings bank.[197]

The designation "*Sparkasse*" is protected by law. The Banking Act, section 40 states:

[192] Rym Ayadi, Emrah Arbak, Reinhard H. Schmidt, Santiago Carbó Valverde "Investigating Diversity in the Banking Sector in Europe: The Performance and Role of Savings Banks", *CEPS* (2009), 122.

[193] Guinnane "Delegated Monitors", 84.

[194] Gruson and Schneider "The German Landesbanken", 345.

[195] Peter Scherer and Sven Zeller *Banking Regulation in Germany* (German Law Publishers, 2009), 23.

[196] Ayadi et al. "Investigating Diversity", 122.

[197] Ibid.

> (1) The term "savings bank" ("Sparkasse") or a term in which the words "savings bank" appear may be used in the corporate name, as an addendum to the corporate name, to describe the business purpose or for advertising purposes only by: 1 public savings banks with authorization pursuant to section 32; 2 other undertakings which, upon this Act coming into force, were legitimately using such a term pursuant to previous provisions; 3 undertakings which are newly established by restructuring the undertakings specified in number 2 as long as they, by virtue of their articles of association or articles of incorporation, exhibit specific features (in particular, tasks geared towards public welfare and a restriction of their principal business operations to the economic area in which the undertaking is domiciled) to the same extent as before restructuring.

The wording of the disposition may be interpreted as forbidding foreign savings banks that are organized under private law, such as Spanish *cajas*, to establish themselves as *Sparkassen* in Germany. In 2006 the EC and Germany made an agreement (Agreement on Sparkasse) confirming the need to comply with European freedom of establishment (Art. 43) and free movement of capital (Art. 56). "The solution confirms the principle of neutrality of Community law as regards the decision to privatize a public enterprise (Article 295 of the Treaty). It recognizes that in the application of national law, Community law has to be respected."[198] "Such agreement was incorporated in section 41 of the Banking Act."[199]

Historically, regional regulation of savings banks tended to protect the small depositors by imposing restrictions on lending. For instance, like Bavaria in 1811, savings banks were forbidden to grant loans without real estate guarantees.[200] Nowadays, some legal acts limit the activities of its savings banks in various ways: upper limits for lending activities, limits for the acquisitions of shares and participations, restriction on risky business. The doctrine of *ultra vires* additionally restricts activities that violate the purpose of the public law institution, in that "any legal action not covered by its purpose is declared null and void".[201] While savings banks are not

[198] EC "Agreement on 'Sparkasse'", http://europa.eu/rapid/press-release_IP-06-1692_en.pdf. Accessed 15 August 2023.

[199] German Banking Act, Section 41.

[200] Guinnane "Delegated Monitors", 86.

[201] Marc Benzler "Special Institutions" in Scherer, Zeller "Banking Regulation in Germany", 26.

obliged by law to apply the regional principle, they generally observe it, by lending and operating with customers within a delimited territory.[202]

Many of the *Sparkassen* are municipal savings banks. As public law institutions *Sparkassen* have "no owner in the legal sense" but responsible institutions or "*Trager*". The *Trager* remain similar to a private owner, but present more restrictions, such as that they are not allowed to sell the bank, or that the right to take out profits is weak, since articles of association rely strongly on self-financing.[203]

The second level of savings bank sector is the regional *Landesbanken*. They are in general owned by regional associations of *Sparkassen* and the regional states. Originally the *Landesbanken* acted as bankers for the state and as central bank for the *Sparkassen* of the region.[204] Later, they added other financial activities that were difficult for local saving banks to offer due to their smaller size.[205] Nowadays, as stated above, the *Landesbanken* conduct universal banking: commercial, investment and other financial activities, as well as finance public and private projects, and "perform certain treasury functions for the states". The business of the *Landesbank* may overlap those of the *Sparkassen*. The main differences are *Sparkassen* are smaller and need to follow the territorial principle, something that is not applicable to *Landesbanken*.[206] Another feature of *Landesbanken* (together with the *Sparkassen*) was the statutory guarantee for the bank liabilities known as *Anstaltslast* (maintenance guarantee) and the *Gewahrtragerhaftung* (Guarantee obligation). *Anstaltslast* means the owners are responsible for "securing the economic basis of the institution and its function during its existence." *Gewahrtragerhaftung* means the guarantor will "meet all liabilities of the bank which cannot be satisfied from its assets". Both guarantees were not limited, and the banks did not pay any remuneration for them.[207] In the 1990s private banks challenged the system stating that it violated European competition and State Aid rules. In December 1999 the European Banking

[202] Ayadi et al. "Investigating Diversity", 119.

[203] Ibid., 119.

[204] Detzer, Dodig, Evans and Herr "The German Financial System", 79.

[205] Ayadi et al. "Investigating Diversity", 1195.

[206] Gruson and Schneider "The German Landesbanken", 353.

[207] EC Press Release "Commission Requests Germany to Bring State Guarantees for Public Banks into Line with EC Law", 8 May 2001.

Federation filed a complaint before the Directorate General of Competition of the European Commission. In May 2001, the EC proposed the German government "appropriate measures" to render the guarantee system compatible with the State Aid European rules. By letter of 11 April 2002, the German government accepted a commission's proposal, where: (1) *Gewährträgerhaftung* were abolished; (2) "*Anstaltslast*, as it exists now, shall be replaced in order to comply with the certain principles in order to comply with State Aid Rules".[208]

The third level of the savings bank sector is the DekaBank, owned by the German Bank Savings Association (DSGV) and the *Landesbanken*, and the DSGV itself. "DekaBank's roots date back to the year 1918, when Deutsche Girozentrale (DGZ) was founded. Deka as an investment company was founded in 1956; DGZ and Deka joined forces to create DekaBank in 1999." DekaBank acts as central asset manager for the savings bank sector. According to its webpage "DekaBank is the *Wertpapierhaus* of the German savings banks and, together with its subsidiaries, forms the Deka Group. With total customer assets totalling approximately €283 billion as at December 2017 and around four and a half million managed securities accounts, the Deka Group ranks among Germany's major securities service providers. It ensures access to a wide range of investment products and services for retail and institutional investors."[209] The DSGV is the "umbrella organization" of the Sparkassen-Finanzgruppe, which is a network of savings banks and "*Landesbanken*."[210]

C. Third Pillar

The third pillar comprises the largest number of institutions in the German banking system. The International Cooperative Alliance defines a cooperative bank as follows: "An autonomous association of persons united voluntarily to meet their common economic, social, and cultural

[208] EC Commission "Germany Agrees on the Implementation of the Understanding with the Commission on State Guarantees for Landesbanken and Savings Banks", https://ec.europa.eu/commission/presscorner/detail/en/IP_02_343. Accessed 13 August 2023.

[209] Deka Bank: https://www.deka.de. Accessed 15 August 2023.

[210] DSKV "Missions and Objectives", https://www.dsgv.de/en/about-us/index.html. Accessed 15 August 2023.

needs and aspirations through a jointly-owned and democratically-controlled enterprise"[211] Cooperatives are owned by their members, who receive a "profit-dependent" benefit. Their main function is to support the business of their members. As with *Landesbanken* in pillar 2, there are central institutions which provide several services to individual cooperatives.[212] Originally, cooperatives were a response to financial constraints as a result of lack of interest in other financial institutions in small craftsmen and farmers. Private bankers were focused on trade finance, commercial banks focused on manufacturers and transport, and savings banks requested collateral.[213] The cooperative societies were first founded by Frank Hermann and Friedrich Raiffeisen in 1865. The "Raiffeisen cooperatives" were a network of agricultural credit institutions that allowed their members to borrow money to pay bills before the harvest. The beginning of the cooperative business lied in the savings and short-term lending business, but it evolved into a truly universal banking system.[214] A Second type of cooperative was the "*Volksbanken*" (people's banks) that mainly functioned in cities. According to Section 39 of the Banking Act, "The term 'people's bank' ("*Volksbank*") or a term in which the words 'people's bank' appear may be newly taken up only by credit institutions operating in the legal form of a registered cooperative society and belonging to an audit association."[215] The founder of *Volksbanken* was Hermann Schulze, a former mayor of Delitzsch, Saxony.[216] The most important difference between *Volksbanken* and *Raiffeisen* cooperatives were that the former often switched to limited liability (after the 1899 Act), paid dividends, had more staff and were larger than the latter. The *Raiffeisein* cooperatives had small shares and provided long loans, which made them less

[211] ICA "Statement on the Co-operative Identity", International Cooperative Alliance website, 26 May 2007, https://www.ica.coop/en/cooperatives/cooperative-identity. Accessed 15 August 2023.

[212] Felix Hüfner "The German Banking System: Lessons from the Financial Crisis", OECD Economics Department Working Papers (2010), 92.

[213] Andreas Hackethal "German Banks and Banking Structure" in Krahnen and Schmidt, 83.

[214] Eric Owen Smith *The German Economy* (Taylor & Francis Group 2002), 330.

[215] Section 39 of the Banking Act.

[216] Rym Ayadi, David. Llewellyn, Reinhard H. Schmidt, Emrah Arbak, Willem Pieter De Groen "Investigating Diversity in the Banking Sector in Europe: Key Developments, Performance and Role of Cooperative Banks", *CEPS* (2010), 27–29.

liquid, and at the same time relied on strong enforcement mechanisms, since in rural areas members knew each other and could impose economic and extra-economic sanctions on each other.[217]

The legal form of the cooperatives in general is a "registered cooperative society" (*Eingetragene Genossenschaft*) according to the German Cooperative Act. The cooperative aim is the promotion of its members by collective business operations.[218] As licensed banks, cooperative banks need to comply with the German banking regulation and banking supervision by the BaFin in cooperation with the Bundesbank.

Several principles guide credit cooperatives' organization.[219] The "principle of self-help" means cooperatives are self-governed private organizations.[220] Members contribute their savings, which are at the same time the lending facilities for the local business. For the first 50 years of existence of cooperatives, these same members were active in monitoring borrowers, who were motivated by the fact that members were "jointly liable" for all debts of the cooperative. The principle of "identity" indicates members are their own clients. This principle was relaxed in recent years, obscuring the principle by the "so-called non-member business" which permitted cooperatives to conduct business with non-members.[221] The "democratic principle" means that, unlike corporations, cooperative members usually only have one vote, irrespective of their investment in the institution. Additionally, members cannot sell their share. The exit strategy available to members is to redeem their share at nominal value plus accumulated profits.[222] Solidarity shapes cooperatives in the sense that "by law and statute cooperative banks do not have the objective to make as large a profit as possible but rather to serve the economic interests of their members and clients".[223] From 1899 cooperatives were subject to external compulsory auditing, mainly as a request from cooperatives,

[217] Guinnane "Delegated Monitors", 90–91.

[218] Marc Benzler "Special Institutions" in Scherer and Zeller, 31.

[219] International Cooperative Alliance "Co-operative Principles". Available at https://www.ica.coop/en/whats-co-op/co-operative-identity-values-principles. Accessed 22 August 2023.

[220] Patrick Behr and Reinhard Schmidt "The German Banking System: Characteristics and Challenges", White Paper No. 32 (2015), 13.

[221] Ayadi et al. "Investigating Diversity", 15.

[222] Behr and Schmidt "The German Banking System", 13.

[223] Ayadi et al. "Investigating Diversity", 28.

which understood the need to control management in order to avoid failures and reputational risk, but at the same time preventing government interference.[224]

Many of the main characteristics of the credit cooperative today are: (i) the democratic principle, (ii) the fact members are not allowed to sell their share and (iii) the limitation of liability may weaken the incentives for a strong monitoring of management by members. From the manager's perspective, the incentives for increasing the cooperative's value are also weak, and he will not have to worry for a hostile takeover. The positive side of the system, especially the democratic principle, is that the manager may focus on helping its members, and powerful members will not be able to make managers exploit weaker members—e.g. by lowering interest rates on deposits.[225] The negative side is that managers may lack incentives to do their work.[226] The main explanations that compensate for this governance problem are twofold. First, cooperatives compete with other financial institutions; bad managers would not be able to simply underperform, since customers and staff may leave the cooperative. Second, as stated above, cooperatives are subject to a regular auditing process, which is not only an accounting procedure but a more comprehensive one, because it also audits the managerial competence. The audit process acts not only on its own behalf but on that of the institutional protection scheme, which makes the governance system even more effective.[227]

As local cooperatives had an inherent inability to diversify because of the restriction of the regional principle, they developed regional institutions that would operate with local cooperatives, accepting deposits and lending. This was the origin of central cooperatives.[228] Nowadays, local cooperative banks own the central bank, DZ BANK (Deutsche Zentral-Genossenschaftsbank—German Central Cooperative Bank). DZ Bank is a central bank, and at the same time an investment, corporate and investment bank. Additionally, the National Association of German Cooperative Banks (Bundesverband der Deutschen Volksbanken und

[224] Guinnane "Delegated Monitors", 92–93.

[225] Behr and Schmidt "The German Banking System", 13.

[226] Ayadi et al. "Investigating Diversity", 33.

[227] Behr and Schmidt "The German Banking System", 13; Ayadi et al. "Investigating Diversity", 33.

[228] Ibid.

Raiffeisenbanken—BVR) is in charge of risk monitoring and strategic coordination, and the administration of the sector's mutual protection scheme, whose goal is to protect the solvency of its member banks. Table 3.2 summerises the main features of commercial banks, saving banks and credit coorperatives in Germany.[229]

Table 3.2 Three pillar system

	Commercial banks	*Savings banks*	*Credit cooperatives*
Main German legal regulation	Banking Act	Savings Banks Act Banking Act	German Cooperative Act Banking Act
Typical legal form	Joint stock corporations Limited partnership with share capital	Independent instrumentalities under Public Law	Registered cooperative society
Ownership	Shareholders	*Trager*	Members or non-members
Territorial scope	National and/or international	*Sparkassen*: regional principle *Landesbanken*: national or international	Cooperatives: regional principle
Aim	Profit maximization	Serve public interest Profit optimization	Promotion of members Profit optimization
Exit strategy	Sale of shares	Consolidation	Redemption of shares
Way of earning profits	Dividends	Mostly self-financing	Self-financing or redemption of shares plus accumulated profits Dividends in some cases

Source Own compilation based on various authors[230]

[229] S&P Report "Cooperative Banking Sector Germany" (2022) https://www.dzbank.de/content/dam/dzbank/dokumente/de/dzbank/investor_relations/ratings/RatingsDirect_CooperativeBankingSectorGermany_51066359_Mar-25-2022.pdf. Accessed 14 August 2023. Other important cooperatives are the "Cooperative Housing Bank (Bausparkasse Schwäbisch-Hall)", one of Germany's largest building societies, and R+V-Versicherung (one of the largest insurance firms in Germany).

[230] Faltermeier "The German Banking System", 18; Benzler "Special Institutions" in Scherer and Zeller, 23–31; Ayadi et al. "Investigating Diversity", 119.

3.3 Concluding Remarks

The definition of universal banking is based on the "activities list" approach which includes commercial, insurance and securities business under the same umbrella. Universal banking is not only a way of organizing a financial group but also defines certain type of capitalism: a capitalism based on long-term relations, insider dealing and industry development. Capitalism in Germany evolved from "spoliation and devastation" due to several wars, to the rise of *Kreditbanken*, which accompanied the development of railways, mining and machine industries. Under the influence of Saint Simon, the Pereire Brothers founded Credit Mobilier, the prototype of universal banking and model of further *Grossbanken* in Germany. The main force of the newly universal banks was to favour industry development. According to several economists such as Gerschenkron, universal banks had a leading role in the development of the industry in Germany. As the saying went, the German bank accompanied the industrial firm from "cradle to the grave". This special relationship was anchored in four elements: (i) providing all kinds of financial services; (ii) owning shares in commercial and industrial firms; (iii) taking positions in supervisory bodies; (iv) controlling commercial and industrial firms via proxy rights. As it will be analysed in chapters four and five, the German model differ in many ways from the British and US Models, not only in its philosophical and historical foundations, but on the type of capitalism they founded and the organization of its banking system.

Section 3.1.5 analysed the benefits and costs of universal banking. While there are many benefits and costs, it can be concluded there is no "one fits all" type of bank for all jurisdictions alike. A universal banking system relies on long-term relationships, taking advantage of economies of scope and scale, reduction of economic risk due to diversification, and the gains of one-stop shopping. On the other hand, a natural consequence of providing all three services under one roof is the peril of creating "mammoth entities" which are difficult to manage, supervise and resolve. While universal banking is not a synonym of "systemic", the German model per se encourages the formation of entities that are bigger than their specialized counterparts. This poses additional focus on anticompetitive behaviour, abuse of information and benefiting of conflicts of interest. While banning or discouraging universal banking because of the latter may be misleading, special care needs to be taken by regulators to encourage competition and ethical behaviour.

Finally, the chapter makes a compilation of the "three pillar Structure" of the German universal banking system: (i) *Grossbanken* or big banks, (ii) savings banks and (iii) cooperative banks. Historically, the three groups have focused on serving different customers and hence underpin different business models. The big banks are organized under joint stock corporations of limited partnerships with share capital with shareholders as "owners" of the banks. Their territorial scope is national or international and their aim is profit maximization. Savings banks (the second pillar) are formed of independent instrumentalities by public law, since their responsible institutions are the *Trager*, municipalities or local governments. Their aim is to serve the public interest, while they must also look for profit optimization. They organize themselves under the regional principle (*Sparkassen*) or under a national or international scope (*Landesbanken*). Finally, cooperative banks—the third pillar—are formed under the registered cooperative society, with members or non-members as owners. Their territorial scope is regional and the principal aim is the promotion of members and profit optimization. From a systemic importance view, only one member of the first pillar falls under the G-SIB category: DB. The rest are not systemically important. From a size perspective, the regional territorial scope would segregate cooperatives and *Sparkassen* from the inclusion in the G-SIB list because they would not face cross-border issues and they would maintain a size proportional to that of the region.

Finally, the chapter makes a comparison of the three pillar Structure of the German universal banking system: the Geschäftsbanken, the [illegible] savings banks and the cooperative banks. Historically, the [illegible] three groups have focused on serving different customers and [illegible] [illegible] business models. The big banks are organized [illegible] [illegible] companies with share capital [illegible] [illegible] [illegible] [illegible] [illegible] [illegible] [illegible] Sparkassen [illegible]

CHAPTER 4

British Model

Following Herring and Santomero's classification, the British model comprises a parent-bank company with non-banking insurance and securities subsidiaries. For this reason, some authors name it the "bank-parent model".[1] However, nowadays most UK banking groups do not encompass a bank-parent company, but a holding company, which is typically a listed company holding shares of a bank. Nevertheless, many UK banking groups resemble the British model's typical structure in that the nonbanking activities depend on the bank company and not on the holding company directly, as in the case of the US. This new corporate structure may be called the British Modified model. For this reason, this chapter will analyse the UK banking system and compare the main differences with the German model. The UK also implemented a structural reform, which transformed banking groups' structure operating in the UK. Annex 1 will analyse the corporate structure of Barclays, since it is a UK G-SIB and its corporate structure resembles in part the original British model.

This chapter will examine the nature of the British banking system, a short overview of the history of banking system in the UK, and the

[1] Santos "Commercial Banks", 16.

M. J. Sheppard Gelsi, *Corporate Structure and Banking Resolution*, Palgrave Macmillan Studies in Banking and Financial Institutions, https://doi.org/10.1007/978-3-031-59948-4_4

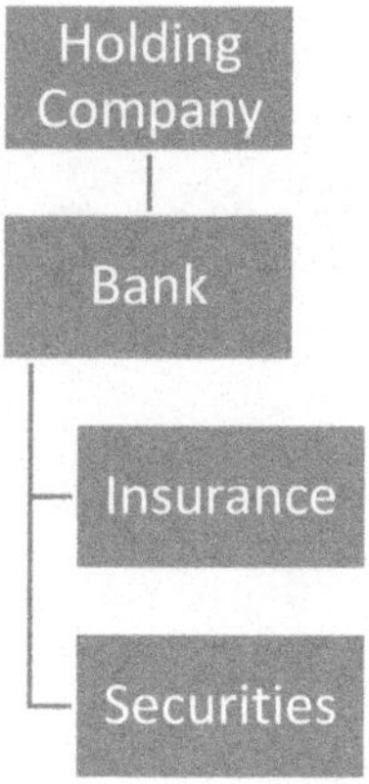

Fig. 4.1 British Modified model

alleged lack of links between banks and industry and it will survey the types of UK banking groups and structural reform (Fig. 4.1).

4.1 British Model

Historically, the British banking system (used in the broad sense to include banking—in the narrow sense as deposit taking activity—and investment banking) has been characterized by four main elements. The first is that the UK has separated the activities of the banking system into merchant banking (investment banking) and commercial banking (clearing banking). The second is that until recently, the industry was self-regulated and authorities used "moral suasion" over explicit regulation. The third is that the industry relied heavily on other sources of funding rather than using banking, like Germany does. Finally, UK banking system is shaped by the City of London. As such, it attracted foreign banks because of London's importance as a banking hub, as well as because London is the Euromarkets capital.[2]

[2] Saunders and Walter "Universal Banking", 113.

A Specialized System That Evolved into Universal Banking

The British financial system separated merchant banking, brokerage and commercial services, though not legally.[3] The British system or specialized system is often compared with the German "Universal Banking" system. Most scholars agree that the British banking system evolved from a specialized system to a universal system after a period of deregulation during the last decades of the twentieth century.[4] Offer believes that after the competition and credit control (CCC) deregulation package, a process began "that led to universal banking..."[5] Others estimate that the UE Second Banking Directive was responsible for the shift to universal banking in the UK.[6] Before this shift, the British financial system comprised a "functional specialisation" system, whereby each function was undertaken by a "different set of institutions".[7]

Although there was no regulation prohibiting banks from undertaking different finance services under the same roof, some policies helped the system to remain specialized. For instance, the Bank of England was not keen to approve certain mergers, such as the merger of the merchant bank Montagu Trust and the clearing bank Midland Bank since it feared the merged bank would be able to evade controls.[8] Also, the London Stock Exchange "restricted membership to partnerships and to those whose sole

[3] Caroline Folhlin "Banking Systems and Economic Growth: Lessons from Britain and Germany in the Pre-World War I Era", *Review, Federal Reserve Bank of Saint Louis* (1998), 39; Saunders and Walter "Universal Banking", 113; Verdier "Moving Money: Banking and Finance", 104; Geoffrey Jones *British Multinational Banking, 1830–1990* (OUP 1995), 325.

[4] Saunders and Walter "Universal Banking", 113; Charles Calomiris and Stephen Haber *Fragile by Design: The Political Origins of Banking Crisis and Scarce Credit* (Princeton University Press 2014), 147.

[5] Avner Offer "Narrow Banking, Real Estate and Financial Stability in the UK c.1870–2010" in Nicholas Dimsdale and Anthony Hotson *British Financial Crisis Since 1825* (OUP 2014), 158.

[6] Fiordelisi and Ricci "Bancassurance in Europe", 7; Gruson and Nikowitz "The Second Banking Directive", 215; Murphy "European Union Financial Developments", 4; Manvell Jeannot "An International Perspective", 1734; Zavvos "Banking Integration", 480; Vander Vennet "Cost Efficiency", 255; Dixon "The New Geography of Capitalism", 19.

[7] Offer "Narrow Banking", 158.

[8] Forrest Capie *The Bank of England: 1950s to 1979* (CUP 2010), 330.

business was the buying and selling of securities". Therefore, de facto, UK banks could not expand into the investment business.[9]

A Self-Regulated Industry

The first domestic act that regulated the conduct of banking in the UK was in 1979. Before that, the Bank of England operated through a system of moral suasion that constituted an informal supervisory body.[10] The Banking Act 1979 required that the acceptance of deposits from the public needed prior authorization by the Bank of England. This Act was a response to the First Banking Directive, which required formal authorization and supervision of the banking system.[11]

The Bank of England was founded in 1694 after the Glorious Revolution of 1689. As the government needed funds, it chartered three corporations, the Bank of England, the New India Company (1698) and the South Sea Company (1711). The chartered companies lent funds to the government, which in return received a promise of an annual payment secured by a source of revenue. The government granted a charter that gave a monopoly in certain commercial activity. As Grossman affirms, the Bank of England was born due to the government need for war funding, and not on "any desire to foster the growth of banking or to promote monetary stability".[12]

It was only in 1946 that the parliament passed the Bank of England Act, which nationalized the bank. Section 4 of this Act states, "the Bank, if they think it necessary in the public interest, may request information

[9] Ranald Michie *British Banking: Continuity and Change from 1694 to the Present* (OUP 2016), 167; Ranald Michie and Simon Mollan "British and American Banking in Historical Perspective: Beware of False Precedents", *History and Policy* (2011). www.historyandpolicy.org/policy-papers/british-and-american-banking-in-historical-perspective-beware-of-false-prec. Accessed 16 July 2023.

[10] Sue Konzelmann, Marc Fovargue-Davies and Gerhard Schnyder "The Faces of Liberal Capitalism: Anglo-Saxon Banking in Crisis?" *Cambridge Journal of Economics* (2012), 508; Charles Goodhart "The Bank of England 1970–2000" in Ranald Michie and Philip Williamson (eds) *The British Government and the City of London in the Twentieth Century* (CUP 2009), 340; Charles Proctor *The Law and Practice of International Banking* (OUP 2015), 4.

[11] Proctor "The Law and Practice", 4.

[12] Richard Grossman, *Unsettled Account: The Evolution of Banking in the Industrialised World Since 1800* (Princeton University Press 2010), 171.

from and make recommendations to bankers, and may, if so authorised by the Treasury, issue directions to any banker for the purpose of securing that effect is given to any such request or recommendation".[13] Although Section 4 gave the Bank of England such supervisory role, it generally relied "on its considerable influence in the banking sector to achieve its goals through informal discussion and persuasion".[14] According to Morton, this practice stemmed from three sources: (1) the Bank of England was the highest authority over UK money markets, hence all banks wanted to have good relations with it; (2) there were certain statutes that allowed some benefits for banks if included in certain lists. The Bank of England was the body that maintained the lists or gave input to those in charge of maintaining those lists; and, (3) the Bank of England had a moral authority as the banker and adviser of the government.[15]

Michie affirms that this self-regulated system proved to be stable: "by the late nineteenth century there was an implicit belief that the British banking system that had emerged by then was as close to perfection as it was possible to achieve...combining the virtue of stability with the ability to meet the needs of both savers and borrowers".[16] This statement was reinforced by the fact that there were no significant banking crises in the UK from 1878 to 1991.[17] Cassis suggests the last significant crisis in the UK prior to the GFC was that of Baring in 1890.[18] Grossman concurs with Cassis, stating, "The most famous English bailout of the nineteenth or twentieth century was that of Baring Brothers in 1890, although there were others. More extreme measures, in the form of a government takeover, bank moratorium, or bank holiday were never employed in England for the simple reason that such extreme measures were primarily a product of the first third of the twentieth century, and English Banking was remarkably stable during the fifty years following the

[13] Bank of England Act 1946, s 4.

[14] Guy Morton "Banking Regulation and Treatment of Foreign Banks in the United Kingdom" in M. Gruson and R. Reisner *Regulation of Foreign Banks: United States and International* (1995), 22–25.

[15] Ibid.

[16] Michie "British Banking", 16.

[17] Ibid. According to Grossman "Unsettled Account" the UK suffered banking crises in 1720 (South Sea Bubble), 1763, 1772, 1783, 1788, 1793, 1797, 1810, 1825, 1836, 1847, 1857, 1866 and 1890, before the 2007/2008 crisis, 189.

[18] Youssef Cassis *Crises and Opportunities* (OUP 2011), 4.

Baring crisis".[19] Capie also reminds us that "from 1866 onwards there were essentially a hundred years of financial stability without any financial crises".[20]

However, some authors complain about the role British banking has played on financing the long-term needs of the industry. Others understand that the British banks were London-oriented and underestimated the needs of the provinces. Further, they claim the British banks were over-conservative in their lending, which stymied economic growth.[21] Given this opinion, it is necessary to analyse the role of the British system in the development of the industry in the UK.

Banks and Industrial Finance

It is widely believed, both in economic and popular literature, that banks failed the industry in the UK. There are periods where this line of thinking arose with force: during the end of nineteenth century, before World War I, during the interwar period and after World War II.[22] Collins states,

> in Britain…it is widely accepted throughout most of the past century-and-a-half the main financial institutions- the deposit banks, the discount houses and the merchant banks-have concentrated on short-term credit provision and/or on holding their longer term assets in the form of government and public utility securities. They seem to have shied away from long-term loans and investments to domestic industry and it is this, which is said to have been in the detriment of the industry. It is in this sense that banks are alleged to 'have failed' the industry.[23]

Some commentators show that Germany outperformed the UK in this field. Clapham, Gerschenkron, Jeffreys and Kennedy believe the German

[19] Grossman "Unsettled Account", 191.

[20] Forrest Capie "British Financial Crisis in the Nineteenth and Twentieth Centuries" in Dimsdale and Hotson "British Financial Crises", 13.

[21] Michie "British Banking", 17; Michael Collins "Banks and Industrial Finance in Britain 1800–1939" (OUP 1995), 1; Herbert Somerton Foxwell "The Financing of Industry and Trade", *The Economic Journal*, Vol. 27 (1917), 505, 27; A. Gerschenkron "Economic Backwardness", 1–15.

[22] Collins "Banks and Industrial Finance in Britain", 1.

[23] Ibid., 3.

system accounted for German economic development.[24] Kennedy states, "With all their documented imperfections, by making resources available to a large group of technologically progressive industries on a scale unequalled in Britain, account for much of the difference in the economic growth performance between (Germany) and Britain in the half century after 1865".[25]

As referred to in Chapter 3, Gerschenkron showed that England was the first country to industrialize. According to him, industrialization was gradual, and the capital needs for the industry were obtained by retained earnings of agriculture, commercial and, at the end, industrial enterprises. This was not the case of continental countries with economic backwardness, where there was urgency to fund new industries and to create institutional vehicles to obtain such capital.[26] German banks were the institutional vehicles that permitted the strategic planning of industrial development. England had the appropriate banking system for the needs of the Industrial Revolution, but it did not accompany the evolution of a maturing economy.

Elbaun and Lazonick are called "institutionalists" since they allege the UK has not generated during the nineteenth-century institutions able to suit twentieth-century corporate capitalism.[27] Specifically, they suggest UK financial institutions have concentrated on short-term financing, restricting long-term finance for the industry; the City has preferred financing international trade and not domestic industry finance; and that city institutions have lobbied to use exchange rate and monetary policy to their advantage.[28]

[24] John Clapham *The Economic Development of France and Germany 1815–1914* (CUP 1936), 390; Gerschenkron "Economic Backwardness", 1–15; James Jeffreys *Trends in Business Organisations in Great Britain Since 1856, with Special Reference to the Financial Structure of Companies, the Mechanism of Investment and the Relations Between the Shareholder and the Company* (University of London 1938); William Kennedy *Industrial Structure, Capital Markets and the Origins of British Decline* (CUP 1987). 120.

[25] Kennedy "Industrial Structure", 120; Wendy Carlin and Colin Mayer "How Do Financial Systems Affect Economic Performance?" University College London and Said Business School (1999) University of Oxford, 4.

[26] Gerschenkron "Economic Backwardness", 1–15.

[27] Bernard Elbaum and William Lazonick *The Decline of the British Economy* (OUP 1986); Forrest Capie and Michael Collins *Have the Banks Failed British Industry?* (IEA 1991), 23; Collins "Banks and Industrial Finance", 8.

[28] Ibid., 10.

Others believe an explanation of the British industry decline is due to a "City-land fusion against industry". Daunton describes this historical interpretation:

> The financial sector which contributed to the reshaping of the industry in Germany and America was not involved with British industry, so that financial leverage was not available. On the contrary, the concentration of financial power in the City, and integration with the elite, produced a more coherent influence over policy than was possible for industrialists divided by sector or region; industrial problems were therefore aggravated by measures designed to benefit the City.[29]

According to them, the Industrial Revolution created two capitalisms: (1) Industrial Capitalism (economy of the provinces, "producer's England of the North, loyal to free trade and hostile to the House of Lords and "land") and (2) Commercial Capitalism (economy of the metropolis, England of the South, dominated by "ostentatious leisure" and "conspicuous waste", supporting the House of Lords and "land").[30]

Although these theoretical assumptions try to explain the reasons why the British banking system has failed the industry, it is not possible to give general explanations without understanding the historical, economic and legislative facets of the different periods during and following the Industrial Revolution. The first period runs from 1750 to 1830, the second runs from 1870 to 1914, the third is the interwar period, and the last is post World War II.

It is important to note that England's industrialization levels from 1750 to 1830, taking into account manufacturing output, were outstanding. During that period, the manufacturing output rose by a factor of seven. Taking aside the population expansion, Bairoch estimates the UK was responsible for two thirds of Europe's industrial growth of output during the period.[31] While the authors who believe banking failed industry during the Industrial Revolution do not deny this figure, they

[29] Martin Daunton *"Gentlemanly Capitalism" and British Industry 1820–1914. Past and Present* (OUP 1989), 126–127; Ewen Green "Rentiers versus Producers the Political Economy of the Bimetallic Controversy", *English Historical Review* (1998), 611; Geoffrey Inham *Capitalism Divided: The City and Industry in British Social Development* (Macmillan 1984), 9; Collins "Banks and Industrial Finance", 13.

[30] Ibid.

[31] Bairoch "International Industrialization", 294.

focus on the lack of banking lending and its probable negative impact on industrial development. During the Industrial Revolution (1760–1830) industrialists generally used their own funds—undistributed funds—and family and friends' money to fund their enterprises. "As a result, the demands on banks for long-term industrial funds were not great".[32] At that time, banks were small enterprises circumscribed to their local communities. This phenomenon is known as "country banking".[33]

Calomiris explains the laws enacted by the government in order to finance its operations "constrain the amount of credit that could be mobilised for industry".[34] First, the Bank of England was a monopoly set up to fund government spending. From 1694 to 1825 it was the "only bank in England that was able to take the form of a Joint Stock Company", while other banks could not raise capital from the public and needed to take the form of partnerships that were limited in size.[35] Second, in 1708 during the War of Spanish Succession, the English Parliament enacted a law that prohibited associations of more than six individuals from conducting banking business (issuing bank notes). Again, the act was a consequence of a Bank of England loan to the government.[36] Michie suggests this restriction on banking may have affected the development of insurance companies in the period, and that the cap "could have prevented similar companies being formed to undertake banking business".[37] Third, the Bank of England was given a

[32] Collins "Banks and Industrial Finance", 16; Gerschenkron "Economic Backwardness", 11; Calomiris and Haber "Fragile by Design", 84; Michie "British Banking", 57–58.

[33] Rondo Cameron "Banking in the Early Stages of Industrialization. A Preliminary Survey", *Scandinavian Economic History Review* (1963), 127.

[34] Calomiris and Haber "Fragile by Design", 95.

[35] Ibid.; Michie "British Banking", 51; Collins "Banks and Industrial Finance", 16.

[36] Kern Alexander "Regulating the Structure of the EU Banking Sector", *European Business Law Review* (2015) 232; Grossman "Unsettled Account", 172; Calomiris and Haber "Fragile by Design", 89; Peter Temin and Hans J. Voth *Prometheus Shackled: Goldsmith Banks and England's Financial Revolution After 1700* (OUP 2013), 181; Cameron "Banking in the Early Stages", 127; Richard Davies and Peter Richardson "Evolution of the UK Banking System", *Q4 Bank of England Quarterly Bulletin* (2010), 326; John Clapham *The Bank of England—A History, vol I 1694–1797* (CUP 1944), 79–86; Collins "Banks and Industrial Finance", 16.

[37] Michie "British Banking", 51.

monopoly over the issue of bank notes in London.[38] Additionally, the country banks were restricted from issuing small denomination notes. From 1804, they had to pay stamp duty on notes, and from 1808, they had to pay a licence fee of £30 in order to issue notes.[39]

Further, English banks were subject to usury laws,[40] which narrowed the number of clients they could obtain. If banks could not increase interest rates for new clients they did not know well, then they would limit lending.[41] As usury laws did not apply to the government, it channelled credit to itself.[42]

Another important fact was that England was in constant war with France from 1689 until 1815. War was the principal reason for the demand for new money from the government. As stated by Temin and Voth, "War increased the government's borrowing demands, crowding out private investment on a vast scale…The British 'warfare state' passed regulations that made it impossible for private finance to compete with state borrowing".[43] They conclude the increasing borrowing needs of the government reduced private lending and "industrial growth slowed markedly whenever public debt grew rapidly".[44]

During 1870–1914 there is agreement that clearing banks did not provide "long-term industrial finance in any large degree".[45] Nor did the

[38] Calomiris and Haber "Fragile by Design", 95; Grossman "Unsettled Account", 172; Temin and Voth, "Prometheus Shackled", 182.

[39] Grossman "Unsettled Account", 174. Another regulatory constraint of this period was the Bubble Act, 1720, passed as a request of the South Sea Company. The Act chartered two new companies and prohibited companies from issuing transferable shares. The Bubble Act was repealed in 1825. See Calomiris and Haber "Fragile by Design", 98.

[40] Hugh Rockoff "Prodigals and Projecture: An Economic History of Usury Laws in the United States from Colonial Times to 1900", NBER Working Paper 9742 (2003), 16; Temin and Voth "Prometheus Shackled", 73; Sybil Campbell "Usury and Annuities of the Eighteenth Century", *L. Q. Rev.*, Vol. 44 (1928), 473.

[41] Calomiris and Haber "Fragile by Design", 84; Temin and Voth "Prometheus Shackled", 73.

[42] Temin and Voth "Prometheus Shackled", 84. Contrary, Adam Smith *An Enquiry into the Nature and Causes of the Wealth of Nations* (1982 [1776]).

[43] Temin and Voth "Prometheus Shackled", 158.

[44] Ibid., 173.

[45] Collins "Banks and Industrial Finance", 28.

capital markets: "There is general agreement that the formal market institutions normally handled little of the business of the British Industry".[46] According to Bairoch's index, between 1860 and 1913 the total volume of world manufacturing output increased more than fourfold (from 226 to 933). The UK during the same period increased the absolute manufacturing output less than threefold (from 45 to 127), and hence it decreased the percentage of total manufacturing output from 19 to 13%.[47]

Have banks failed the industry, stymieing the country's industrial development during this period? According to Goodhart, in 1890 English clearing banks believed a 15% ratio of cash to deposits was recommendable.[48] This shows bankers in the period were concerned about liquidity and short-term lending. This concern was strengthened by several crises in 1847, 1857, 1866 and 1878, which made bankers become even more cautious.[49]

The period 1914–1945 witnessed three "devastating global shocks": World War I, the Great Depression and World War II. However, Britain did not suffer a "full-fledged" banking crisis.[50] At the beginning of the war, Keynes praised the British banking system: "I believe our banking system, and indeed the whole intricate organism of the city, to be one of the best and most characteristic creations of that part of the genius and virtue of our nation which has found its outlet in business".[51] This stability, nevertheless, attracted criticism from commentators that believed that the British banks reduced lending to industry.[52] In 1931, the "Macmillan Report", named after Lord Macmillan, chair of the Committee, concluded:

[46] Capie and Collins "Have the Banks Failed", 34.

[47] Bairoch "International Industrialization", 275.

[48] Charles A. E. Goodhart *The Business of Banking, 1891–1914* (Hillary House Publishers 1972), 167–191.

[49] Collins "Banks and Industrial Finance", 35.

[50] Calomiris and Haber "Fragile by Design", 135; Michie "British Banking", 125.

[51] John Maynard Keynes "The Prospectus of Money, November 1914", *Economic Journal*, Vol. 24 (1914), 633.

[52] Calomiris and Haber "Fragile by Design", 136; Haleim Park *The Conservatism of British Banks in the Interwar Period, Re-Examined* (Mineo 2012); Michie "British Banking", 125.

> Coming back now to the more general question of the relations between finance and industry, and in particular to the provision of long-dated capital, we believe that there is substance in the view that the British financial organization concentrated in the City of London might with advantage be more closely co-ordinated with British industry, particularly large-scale industry, than is now the case; and that in some respects the City is more highly organized to provide capital to foreign countries than to British industry.[53]

From this report came the term "Macmillan Gap" which referred to the lack of provision of funding to small and mid-sized enterprises and in words of Michie represented "the gulf between banking and industry in Britain".[54]

Capie and Collins show the distribution of London clearing bank assets between the wars, which confirms the "emphasis on liquidity". Cash and money at call, and on short notice, bills and "advances" were very short-term assets.[55] Investments were "holding of British Government securities", which shows how bank assets were "diverted to finance the public sector".[56]

After World War II, there was a period of "constrained banking" from 1945 to 1970. The labour government nationalized the Bank of England (1945), coalmines, civil aviation, transport, electricity generation and distribution, gas distribution and the iron and steel industry.[57] Banks were not nationalized, though. In response to the "Macmillan Gap", banks and the Bank of England formed the Industrial and Commercial Finance Corporation (ICFC). Its main aim was to provide credit to industrial and commercial business when banks or stock exchanges were not "available".[58] A World Bank dataset, which calculates private credit from deposit money banks as a percentage of GDP shows the UK was close to the worst performer in the OECD with only 19% of GDP. Germany

[53] Committee on Finance and Industry (1931) ps 161–175; Michie "British Banking", 125.

[54] Michie "British Banking", 132.

[55] Capie and Collins "Have the Banks Failed", 51.

[56] Ibid.

[57] Calomiris and Haber "Fragile by Design", 138; see also Norman Chester *The Nationalization of the British Industry 1945–51* (London: HMSO 1975).

[58] Capie and Collins "Have the Banks Failed", 66.

on the contrary was among the best performers with almost 55%.[59] During this period, the main policy to combat inflation was to constrain private credit. During the 1950s and 1960s, the Bank of England "rarely employed interest rate increases", since doing so impaired the ability to finance its expenses. The Bank of England's main instruments to control inflation were "quantity controls" over bank credits and bank "liquidity-ratio requirements".[60] In 1971, the Bolton Committee established that credit controls affected small firms and recommended the end of such policy: "Since we believe that small firms have suffered differentially from ceilings on lending, their disappearance is to be welcomed".[61] In 1971, the newly elected conservative government implemented a new regime on competition and credit control (CCC), which removed quantity constraints on bank lending and promoted interest rate targeting as the main instrument of monetary policy.[62] In the words of the governor of the Bank of England, "we have taken a major new initiative. We have put proposals to all the banks for a new approach to credit control, which...will enable us to abandon ceiling controls altogether...What we are therefore adopting is a new approach to credit control designed to permit the price mechanism to function efficiently in the allocation of credit, and to free the banks from rigidities and restraints which have for 'far too long inhibited them from efficiently fulfilling their intermediary

[59] Thorsten Beck, Asli Demirgüç-Kunt, and Ross Levine "A New Database on Financial Development and Structure", *World Bank Economic Review*, Vol. 14 (2000), 597–605; Thorsten Beck, Asli Demirgüç-Kunt and Ross Levine "Financial Institutions and Markets Across Countries and over Time: Data and Analysis", World Bank Policy Research Working Paper 4943 (2009); Martin Čihák, Asli Demirgüç-Kunt, Erik Feyen and Ross Levine "Benchmarking Financial Development Around the World", World Bank Policy Research Working Paper 6175 (2012). Financial Development and Structure Dataset (updated July 2018).

[60] Calomiris and Haber "Fragile by Design", 141; Forrest Capie *Bank of England 1950s to 1979*, Cambridge University Press; Reprint edition (2012), 271–282.

[61] John E. Bolton *Small Firms: Report of the Committee of Inquiry on Small Firms* (London Her Majesty's Stationery Office 1978), 158.

[62] Calomiris and Haber "Fragile by Design", 143–144; Capie and Collins "Have the Banks Failed", 68.

role in the financial system.'"[63] However, this new policy did not improve the Private Credit by Deposit Money Banks to GDP index.[64]

Margaret Thatcher's government imposed a shift in its main policies: it eliminated controls on deposit interest rates and foreign exchange transactions, and "permitted and encouraged the growth of universal banks".[65] After these policies were implemented, there was a rise in the Private Credit by Deposit Money Banks to GDP, which increased steadily surpassing Germany for the first time in 1988. After 2002 and until 2016, the UK leads the ranking against Germany. In 2009, the results were 99 Germany and 196 UK, while in 2016, it was 75 Germany, and 130 UK.[66]

A Banking System Shaped by the City of London

The UK banking sector is perceived as the "most successful" industry in the twenty first century. "In particular, the component of the Financial Services Sector located in the City of London was judged to be one of the most competitive in the world".[67]

According to Hutton, "In 2021, the financial services sector contributed £173.6 billion to the UK economy, 8.3% of total economic output. The sector was largest in London, where around half of the sector's output was generated".[68] Some commentators believe the City of London will continue to lead as the major European financial centre even after Brexit. "Even if the UK loses a quarter of its international financial sector as a result of Brexit, it will still be double the size of any other European business centre, according to new research which highlights the extent to which the City's dominance gives Britain a point of strength in

[63] Lucius O'Brien "Key Issues in Monetary and Credit Policy. Text of an Address by the Governor to the International Banking Conference in Munich on 28th May 1971", *Bank of England Quarterly Bulletin* (1971), 195–198.

[64] Beck, Demirgüç-Kunt and Levine "A New Database" 597–605.

[65] Calomiris and Haber "Fragile by Design", 147.

[66] Beck, Demirgüç-Kunt and Levine "A New Database", 597–605.

[67] Ranald Michie "The Emergence and Survival of a Financial Cluster in Britain" in "Learning from Some of Britain's Successful Sectors: An Historical Analysis of the Role of Government", *BIS Economics Paper, Department of Business Innovation and Skills*, Vol. 6 (2010), 87.

[68] Georgina Hutton "Financial Services: Contribution to the UK Economy", Briefing Paper, Number 6193, House of Commons Library (2022), 1–23.

negotiations over its future relationship with the EU".[69] According to the Global Financial Centres Index (GFCI 24) issued in 2023, London ranked as the second leading financial centre in the world, at just nineteen points below New York.[70]

By 1850 London was the principal financial centre in the world, as Britain was the first economy to face the Industrial Revolution and because of the stability of the country. By this time, London served the interests of the country and was not a global financial centre.[71] From 1850 to 1914, London emerged as a global financial centre. British banks not only served national interests but serviced the world economy, primarily by the use of the telegraph. Britain was by then the largest trading nation and foreign banks could use the existing network through a London-based bank.[72] After World War II New York took London's place as the most important global financial centre because it was located in the wealthiest nation, with a larger economy and most important currency.[73] During the 1950s and 1960s, London recovered and became competitive again.[74] This occurred for four reasons. First, the US imposed enforced regulations limiting interest rates on deposits (Regulation Q) and taxing interests on overseas loans (Interest Equalization Tax).[75] Second, there was an emergence and growth of the wholesale money markets, which allowed British domestic banks and merchant banks to act as principals.[76] Third, London developed the Eurocurrency market, which allowed banks

[69] Kate Allen "UK Finance Industry Dominates European Scene", *Financial Times* (London, 5 September 2018), https://www.ft.com/content/88cdec40-b03c-11e8-8d14-6f049d06439c. Accessed 21 February 2023.

[70] Z/Yen Group "The Global Financial Services Index" (Corporation of London 2023), https://www.longfinance.net/media/documents/GFCI_34_Report_2022.09.28_v1.0.pdf. Accessed February 2023.

[71] Michie "The Emergence and Survival", 91.

[72] Ibid.

[73] Ibid., 97.

[74] Mae Baker, Michale Collins "London as an International Banking Center, 1950–1980" in Youssef Cassis and Eric Bussière *London and Paris as International Financial Centres in the Twentieth Century* (OUP 2007), 247.

[75] Ibid., 251.

[76] Philip Cottrell "Established Connections and New Opportunities. London as an International Financial Centre 1914–1958" in Cassis and Bussiere "London and Paris", 175–176; Baker and Collins "London as an International Banking", 253.

to trade dollar deposits located in the city.[77] Banks did not want to trade in pounds and intended to prevent controls and interest rate caps imposed in the USA.[78] Fourth, London developed the Eurobond market. Eurobonds are bearer bonds in US dollars, issued outside the US and tax-free.[79] Cottrel explains the reasons for the rise of Eurodollar markets in London: "It offered an existing agglomeration of financial services, a reputation for stability and honesty, and freedom from tight regulation—an essential requirement, for the new markets were above all driven by the desire to escape from regulatory controls. Foreign banks were welcome to establish London branches, which did not require separate capitalization, and the Bank of England followed a flexible approach to foreign currency operations with non-residents. There were no reserve requirements or maturity constraints. There was no Glass-Steagall Act, as in the United States, to separate commercial and investment banking".[80] After the Big Bang, London has consolidated as a global financial centre. Some commentators, as stated above, believe the development of the city was to the detriment of the growth of industry.

After the GFC, the "too much finance" doctrine, which was first developed by Arcand, Berkes and Panizza in 2012, showed that the "the marginal effect of financial depth on output growth becomes negative when credit to private sector reaches 80–100%".[81] The doctrine's authors believe two possible reasons are responsible for this; first, large financial systems may lead to "large economic crashes", as predicted by Minsky; and, second the finance sector may misallocate resources from other parts of the economy, as showed by Tobin.[82] Panizza also considers

[77] David K. Sheppard *The Growth and Role of UK Financial Institutions 1880–1962* (Routledge, 2005), 12; Jones "British Multinational Banking", 320; Cottrel "Established Connections", 176; Baker and Collins "London as an International Banking Center", 249.

[78] R. Michie "The Emergence and Survival", 101.

[79] Ibid., 101; Jones "British Multinational Banking", 320.

[80] Cottrel "Established Connections", 176; see also Baker and Collins "London as an International Banking", 251.

[81] Jean-Louis Arcand, Enrico Berkes and Ugo Panizza "Too Much Finance?" IMF Working Paper WP/12/161 (2012), 6.

[82] Ibid.; Hyman P. Minsky "The Modelling of Financial Instability. An Introduction", *Hyman P. Minsky Archive*, Vol. 467 (1974), 267–272; James Tobin "On the Efficiency of the Financial System", *Lloyds Bank Review*, Vol. 153 (1984), 1–15. See also Stephen G Cecchetti and Enisse Kharroubi "Why Does Financial Sector Growth Crowd Out Real

there might be another explanations. He believes a "moral hazard fuelled bad finance", which is based in excessive housing lending and speculative risk-taking activities, may have been more important than the "good finance" as the financial sector grew. Additionally, he states there might be "political capture" by finance lobbyists who push for deregulation.[83] Sandbu, from Financial Times, on a paper on Brexit published in 2019—before the March deadline—suggests, "The rise of finance is plausibly (though partially) to blame for both small manufacturing sector and the reliance on mortgage-fuelled consumption for demand growth. There is also evidence suggesting the overgrown finance sector misallocates resources away from business investment. The tilt of the economy's centre of gravity from manufacturing to financial and professional services, moreover, has reinforced both the polarisation in the labour market and regional inequality".[84]

What is clear is the City of London has shaped the UK banking system from 1850 onwards. London's position as the leading financial centre in the world has led many academics and politicians to pose questions as to whether the City has failed industry and if too much finance has stymied economic growth. While some indicators may suggest the City may not have been active in providing long-term financing for industry in the nineteenth and most of the twentieth century, the same credit to GDP ratios show that from 1960 the UK banking system has surpassed German levels. Others focus on the long stability of the UK system during a very long period (1878–1991), something Germany lacked. Today, the City of London is the second leading financial centre in the world and has

Economic Growth?" BIS Working papers No 490 (2015); Stephen G. Cecchetti and Enisse Kharroubi, "Reassessing the Impact of Finance and Growth", BIS Working Papers No 381 (2012); Siong Hook Law, Ali M. Kutan and N.A.M. Naseem "The Role of Institutions in Finance Curse: Evidence from International Data", *Journal of Comparative Economics* (2018); Boris Cournede and Oliver Denk "Finance and Economic Growth in OECD and G20 Countries", OECD Economics Department Working Papers No. 1223 (2015). Against see William R. Cline 'Too Much Finance or Statistical Illusion?" Policy Brief PB 15-9 Peterson Institute for International Economies and William (2015). Cline "Further Statistical Debate 'Too Much Finance'", Working Paper Series WP 15-16 Peterson Institute for International Economies.

83 Ugo Panizza "Non-linearities in the Relationship Between Finance and Growth", The Graduate Institute Geneva and CEPR 9 (2017), 44–53.

84 Martin Sandbu "Brexit and the Future of UK Capitalism", *The Political Quarterly*, Vol. 2 (2019), 187–199.

proved resilient in reinventing itself and attracting foreign banks, creating vigorous money markets, taking advantage of new opportunities such as the Eurocurrency and Eurobonds markets and maintaining a pro-market financial regulation, which fostered prosperity in the City.

4.2 UK Banking System

As stated above, until 1979 the Bank of England operated an informal supervision system that relied upon moral suasion. In 1979, the parliament passed the Banking Act, which required that prior authorization was necessary to accept deposit business by the Bank of England. As stated by Lord Steyn, "Prior to the enactment of the Banking Act 1979 banking in the United Kingdom was not subject to any formalised system of regulation. Control was exercised in an informal way by the Bank of England and in an indirect manner by means of various statutory provisions which gave privileges to banks which were recognised by the Board of Trade and by the Bank".[85] The Banking Act was passed to comply with the First European Community (EC) Banking Directive.[86] In 1987 a new Banking Act was approved. It regulated who was able to carry out banking activity, but it lacked rules about the conduct of business.[87] In 1992, the UK implemented the Banking coordination (Second Council Directive) Regulations,[88] following the Second Council Directive of the coordination of laws, regulations and administrative provisions relating to the pursuit of the business of credit institutions.[89]

The most important feature of this new regulation was the "passporting" scheme, whereby an institution based on the EU should not request authorization from each country that operates through branches, it being enough to ask for authorization in the home state. During the 1980s, the UK implemented different EU directives, which internalized Basel

[85] *Three Rivers District Council v Governor and Company of The Bank of England* (2001) 2 All ER 513 (HL).

[86] 77/780/EEC, OJ L 194, 16/7/1973.

[87] Proctor "The Law and Practice", 5.

[88] See https://www.legislation.gov.uk/uksi/1992/3218/contents/made. Accessed 25 February 2019.

[89] 89/646/EEC, OJ 386 30/12/1989.

soft law into European law, and others such as the Own Funds Directive[90] and the Solvency Ratio Directive.[91] Proctor emphasizes that the early 1990s "saw a significant 'Europeanization of banking law, mainly as a harmonization measure with a view to completing the EC's single market".[92]

In 1997, the Labour government determined that central bank functions should be separated from market regulator functions, and it transferred supervisory regulation to the Financial Services Authority (FSA). In 2010, the regulatory structure was changed whereby the FSA was dismantled and transformed into two different regulators: the Prudential Regulation Authority (PRA), as a subsidiary of the Bank of England, and the Financial Conduct Authority (FCA).[93]

The European Union (Withdrawal) Act 2018 (as amended) (EUWA) entailed the modification and integration of EU and EU-related laws and regulations into the domestic legal framework of the United Kingdom. This procedure is informally referred to as "onshoring".

The next section will analyse banks and types of financial institutions that form the banking system in the UK.

Although substantive regulation under the FSMA does not explicitly distinguish between forms of banks,[94] the different credit institutions and investment banks in the UK may be classified as:

- Banks.
- Credit unions.
- Building societies.
- Investment banks or merchant banks.

[90] 89/229/EEC, OJ L 124, 5/5/1989.

[91] 89/647/EEC, OJ 386, 30/12/1989.

[92] Proctor "The Law and Practice", 6.

[93] Financial Services and Markets Act 2000ch 2, 2b.

[94] Bob Penn "Banking Regulation in the UK: Overview" (Practical Law, Thomson Reuters 2018), https://uk.practicallaw.thomsonreuters.com/w-008-0211?transitionType=Default&contextData=(sc.Default)&firstPage=true&comp=pluk&bhcp=1. Accessed 25 February 2023.

This section will examine those institutions regulated by the PRA, both credit institutions and investment firms, because of the PRA's prudential impact on the whole UK financial system.

Banks

What Is a Bank?
According to the PRA Rulebook, a bank is "means a firm with a Part 4A permission to carry on the regulated activity of accepting deposits and is a credit institution, but is not a credit union, friendly society or a building society". A "firm" means a ***PRA-authorised person*** within the meaning of section 2B (5) of the FSMA. A "PRA-authorised person" according to the FSMA means an authorized person who has permission (a) given under Part 4A, or (b) resulting from any other provision of this Act, to carry on regulated activities that consist of or include one or more PRA-regulated activities (see section 22(a)). Part 4A relates to the permission to carry on regulated activities.[95]

Section 19 imposes the general prohibition clause: "No person may carry on a regulated activity in the United Kingdom, or purport to do so, unless he is—(a) an authorised person; or (b) an exempt person. (2) The prohibition is referred to in this Act as the general prohibition". At the same time Section 22 states "an activity is a regulated activity for the purposes of this Act if it is an activity of a specified kind which is carried on by way of business and—(a) relates to an investment of a specified kind; or (b) in the case of an activity of a kind which is also specified for the purposes of this paragraph, is carried on in relation to property of any kind". FSMA refers to ***accepting deposits*** in Schedule 2, paragraph 1, without defining it. It is in the Regulated Activities Order,[96] Article 5, that "accepting deposits" is defined:

> "(1)... (a) money received by way of deposit is lent to others; or
> (b) any other activity of the person accepting the deposit is financed wholly, or to a material extent, out of the capital of or interest on money received by way of deposit.

[95] PRA Rulebook Glossary, https://www.prarulebook.co.uk/rulebook/Glossary/Rulebook/0/11-12-2023/B. Accessed 10 December 2023.

[96] The Financial Services and Markets Act 2000 (Regulated Activities) Order 2001, http://www.legislation.gov.uk/uksi/2001/544/article/5/made. Accessed 8 April 2023.

(2) In paragraph (1), "deposit" means a sum of money…
(a) under which it will be repaid, with or without interest or premium, and either on demand or at a time or in circumstances agreed by or on behalf of the person making the payment and the person receiving it; and
(b) which are not referable to the provision of property (other than currency) or services or the giving of security."

It is important to test whether the deposits are accepted by way of "business", as stated by Section 22 FSMA. In *Financial Services v Anderson* the judgement states "At its broadest it (business) may mean anything that is not done for pleasure Rolls vs. Miller (1884) L.R. 27, Ch D, 71". Without defining the term, the judgement refers to the following elements to respond to the business activity question. First, the aim was to make money. Second, the defendants took deposits over extended terms; third, the number of deposits was substantial; fourth, the amounts were large; fifth, the deposits were paid into "business bank accounts"; and sixth, the defendants described their activities as their "business".[97]

According to the PRA Rulebook, credit institution has the meaning given in point (1) of Article 4(1) of the CRR: "'Credit institution' means an undertaking the business of which is to take deposits or other repayable funds from the public and to grant credits for its own account".

Clearing Banks: The Big Four

Commentators indicate that "clearing banks", sometimes called "high street" or "retail banks", are those banks with extended networks or those participating directly in the clearing system.[98] Until 1970, the five largest UK clearing banks, known as the "big five" banks, were: (1) Barclays Bank (now part of Barclays); (2) Midland Bank (now HSBC Bank); (3) Lloyds Bank (now part of Lloyds banking group); (4) National Provincial Bank; and (5) Westminster Bank. In 1970, National Provincial and Westminster merged into NatWest, so the term "big four" was used after that.[99] By 2022, HSBC is the biggest banking group with more than $2966 billion in assets, followed by Barclays ($1513 billion), Lloyds

[97] [2010] EWHC 599 (Ch) points 51 and 52; Proctor "The Law and Practice", 10.

[98] Saunders and Walter "Universal Banking", 113; Morton "Banking Regulation", 22–27.

[99] Michie "British Banking", 78; Cottrel "Established Connections", 155.

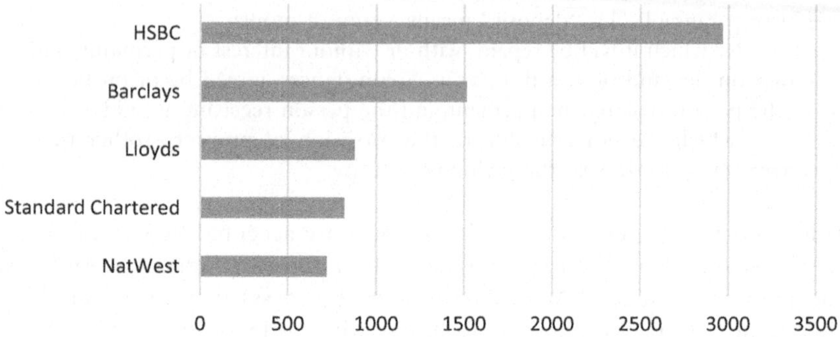

Fig. 4.2 UK Bank Assets 2022 (*Source* 2022 Annual Reports)[100]

($878 billion), Standard Chartered (820 billion) and NatWest (former RBS) ($720 billion). See Fig. 4.2.

The PRA releases lists of regulated entities every year. In 2023, they were separated as follows: (1) banks incorporated in the UK (157); (2) banks incorporated outside the UK authorized to accept deposits through a branch in the UK (123); (3) banks incorporated in the EEA entitled to accept deposits through a branch in the UK while in a Temporary Permissions regime (18); (4) building societies (42); (5) credit unions (439); (6) investment firms (8); (7) insurers (369); (8) Ring-fenced bodies (7).[101]

Foreign Banks

Historically, foreign banks have been attracted to London, as explained above. During the nineteenth century, many foreign banks started to

[100] HSBC Holdings plc's Annual Report and Accounts 2023, https://www.hsbc.com/investors/results-and-announcements/annual-report/; Barclays PLC Annual Report 2023, https://home.barclays/investor-relations/reports-and-events/annual-reports; Lloyds Banking Group Annual Report and Accounts 2023, https://www.lloydsbankinggroup.com/assets/pdfs/investors/financial-performance/lloyds-banking-group-plc/2022/full-year/2022-lbg-annual-report.pdf; Standard Chartered, https://av.sc.com/corp-en/content/docs/standard-chartered-plc-full-year-2022-report.pdf; NatWest, https://investors.natwestgroup.com/~/media/Files/R/RBS-IR-V2/results-center/17022023/nwg-annual-report-and-accounts.pdf. Accessed 8 November 2023.

[101] PRA Which Firms Does the PRA Regulate? https://www.bankofengland.co.uk/prudential-regulation/authorisations/which-firms-does-the-pra-regulate. Accessed 10 December 2023.

operate in London, such as Allied Irish (1825), Alemagne Bank Netherland (1858) and others with British connections such as the Bank of New South Wales (1853) and the Bank of New Zealand (1862). French banks arrived during the 1870s: Comptoir National d'Edspargne, Societé Générale and Crédit Lyonnais (1871). German banks arrived around the same time: Deutsche Bank (1873), Dresdner Bank (1895) and Disconto-Gellschaft (1900). By 1914, Russian, Japanese, Belgian, Chinese, Swiss and Italian banks started to operate in London too. In the 1920s, US banks arrived: Bankers Trust Company, First National City and Manufacturers Hanover Trust. During World War I, German banks abandoned London, while Italian and Japanese banks did the same during World War II. During the 1950s, foreign banks felt attracted to London again.[102] After the Second Banking Directive, passporting was granted and a new type of firm, the "EEA bank", was formed.

According to the PRA in the case of companies that serve as subsidiaries within global entities, it enforces identical regulatory standards and adheres to the same supervisory framework as it does for companies affiliated with UK-based groups. Furthermore, its supervisory approach considers the connections between the subsidiary and the broader group to which it belongs. As a branch of a foreign bank constitutes a part of a legal entity incorporated outside the UK. As it lacks its own capital or board of directors, making its operations inherently reliant on those of the overall legal entity, the PRA is receptive to hosting branches of international banks, acknowledging the efficiency advantages associated with such arrangements. Whether in the form of a branch or a subsidiary, all businesses must satisfy the same threshold conditions to receive authorization from the PRA. However, the manner in which these conditions are met will differ based on structural disparities among entities and the degree to which we may need to depend on their home state supervisor.[103]

[102] Baker and Collins "London as an International Banking", 248.

[103] PRA "The Prudential Regulation Authority's Approach to Banking Supervision" July 2023, https://www.bankofengland.co.uk/-/media/boe/files/prudential-regulation/approach/banking-approach-2023.pdf. Accessed 28 November 2023. "The Threshold Conditions are the minimum requirements that firms must meet at all times in order to be permitted to carry on the regulated activities in which they engage. They are designed to ensure that firms conduct their business in a prudent manner and are managed by persons with adequate skills, experience and propriety, which are necessary to promote

Foreign banks regulated by the PRA are those that establish a subsidiary in the UK by way of incorporation or operate in the UK via a branch. According to the PRA, a branch "means (in relation to a credit institution) a place of business which forms a legally dependent part of a credit institution and which carries out directly all or some of the transactions inherent in the business of credit institutions".[104] The definition of subsidiary is find in section 420(2) FSMA, which in turn refer to section 1162 of, and Schedule 7 to, the Companies Act 2006.

British Multinational or Overseas Banking

This panorama was not always like this. Beginning in 1830 the British banks established overseas branch networks, which focused on a "triad" consisting of Australasia, Latin America and Asia. This phenomenon was called "British multinational banking".[105] British clearers avoided international banking until the late nineteenth century and multinational banking until the twentieth. The British multinational banks of the nineteenth century did not undertake domestic business in the UK, but the London-based directors and executives took all major decisions.[106] During the 1860s, certain entrepreneurs "promoted a series of banks, including the London and River Plate Bank, the London and Brazilian Bank, the English Bank of Rio de Janeiro, and the London Bank of Mexico and South America. They established branches at the ports and in a few major inland trading centres, especially in the fast-growing River Plate region, where British mercantile interests were active in the export of wool, hides, and skins, and the import of British-manufactured textiles and other commodities....Throughout the nineteenth century and beyond, British banking activity in Latin America was confined to four countries, Argentina, Uruguay, Brazil, and Chile".[107] Many of these multinational banks consolidated, and others exist nowadays, although multinational British banking lost its prominence in the 1960s. One

safety and soundness. Threshold Conditions are crucial to the operation of our regulatory regime."

[104] PRA Rulebook Glossary: Bank, https://www.prarulebook.co.uk/rulebook/Glossary/Rulebook/0/11-12-2023/B. Accessed 28 February 2023.

[105] Jones "British Multinational Banking", 372.

[106] Ibid., 11.

[107] Ibid., 24.

example of consolidation is the acquisition by Lloyds of London and River Plate Bank in 1918. In 1923, it was merged with London and Brazilian Bank, creating the new Bank of London and South America (BOLSA) in 1923. In 1971, Lloyds merged its European and South American subsidiaries under Lloyds International Bank. On the other hand, two examples of British multinational banks that still operate are Hong Kong Bank and Standard Chartered, which survived the decline of the British Empire and two world wars. HSBC is the UK's largest bank in total assets, and Standard Charter the fifth, with £688 billion in total assets as of 2018.[108]

The second form of credit institution regulated by the PRA are the credit unions.

Credit Unions

According to the PRA Rulebook, a credit union means a credit union as defined by: (1) the Credit Unions Act 1979; or (2) the Credit Unions (Northern Ireland) Order 1985, "which is an authorised person".[109] The Credit Unions Act 1979 states: "a society may be registered under the Co-operative and Community Benefit Societies Act 2014" (the 2014 Act) as a credit union if: (i) the society has at least 21 members; (ii) it has a registered office in Great Britain; and (iii) it is regulated by the FCA.

Edmonds define credit unions as "non-profit making financial institutions based on cooperative values. A credit union is a group of people who save together and lend to each other at a favourable rate of interest. Each union is separate and autonomous although there are some national organisations which act as promoters and supply expertise, training and model rules".[110]

Credit unions are ruled by internal regulation and specific legislation. In general, trade associations prepare the internal regulation. In the UK the Irish League of Credit Unions (ILCU), the Association of British Credit Unions Limited (ABCUL), the Scottish League of Credit Unions

[108] Standard Chartered Annual Report and Account, https://www.sc.com/en/. Accessed 26 February 2018.

[109] PRA Rulebook. Glossary: Credit Union, https://www.prarulebook.co.uk/rulebook/Glossary/Rulebook/0/11-12-2023/B. Accessed 13 April 2023.

[110] Timothy Edmonds "Credit Unions" Briefing Paper Number 01034, House of Commons Library (2015) 4.

(SLCU), the Association of Independent Credit Unions (AICU) and the Ulster Federation of Credit Unions (UFCU) assist and support their members.[111]

Credit unions are "self-help cooperative financial organizations geared to attaining the economic and social goals of members and wider local communities".[112] The main characteristics of credit unions are: (1) voting is on a one-member, one-vote basis, which gives every member the same voice; (2) permitted activities are limited to membership, which is based on the common bond (e.g., belonging to a geographical place, having the same employer or following a particular occupation); (3) shareholder profit is not the principal aim of the credit union. Instead, they seek to attain the economic and social goals of their members; (4) directors are often unpaid volunteers[113]; (5) shares, other than "deferred shares", are not tradable[114]; however, members can withdraw shares[115]; (6) there are special rules for dividends: "The dividend payable on any shares of a credit union shall—(a) on its dissolution, not exceed a rate of 8 per cent per annum or such other rate as may be specified by order made by the Treasury; and (b) at any other time, not exceed that rate except to the extent that the rules of the credit union provide otherwise".[116]

According to Section 1(3) of the Credit Unions Act 1979:

> The objects of a credit union are—(a) the promotion of thrift among the members of the society by the accumulation of their savings; (b) the creation of sources of credit for the benefit of the members of the society at a fair and reasonable rate of interest; (c) the use and control of the members' savings for their mutual benefit; and (d) must be the training and

[111] Ann-Marie Ward, Donal G. McKillop "An Investigation into the Link Between UK Credit Union Characteristics, Location and Their Success", *Annals of Public and Cooperative Economics*, Vo. 76, No. 3 (2005), 463.

[112] Donal G. McKillop, Anne-M Ward & John O. S. Wilson "The Development of Credit Unions and Their Role in Tackling Financial Exclusion", *Public Money & Management*, Vol. 27, No. 1 (2010), 37–44.

[113] Ibid., 463; McKillop et al. "The Development", 37–44.

[114] Credit Unions Act 1979, s 7(2).

[115] Credit Unions Act 1979, s 7(4).

[116] Credit Unions Act 1979, s 14(4).

> education of the members in the wise use of money and in the management of their financial affairs.[117]

Credit unions require that membership “must be restricted to persons who fall within one or more common bonds appropriate to a credit union... the common bonds appropriate to a credit union are”

(a) following a particular occupation;
(b) being employed by a particular employer;
(c) residing or being employed in a particular locality;
(d) being a member of a bona fide organization or being otherwise associated with other members of the society for a purpose other than that of forming a society to be registered as a credit union;
(e) any other common bond for the time being approved by the FCA.[118]

The Legislative Reform (Industrial and Provident Societies and Credit Unions) Order 2011 broadened the common bonds in order to increase the scope of permitted activities of credit unions. It also permitted corporate members if they do not surpass 10% of total members.

According to the Bank of England, as of 2023 the total assets of all the credit unions together amount to £4678 million. The total members surpass 2 million people.[119] The next group of credit institutions are building societies.

Building Societies

According to the PRA Rulebook, a building society has the meaning given in section 119 of the Building Societies Act 1986 (BSA).[120] Section 5 of

[117] Credit Unions Act 1979 1A, https://www.legislation.gov.uk/ukpga/1979/34, Accessed 25 February 2023.

[118] Credit Unions Act 1979s 1B, amended by The Legislative Reform (Industrial and Provident Societies and Credit Unions) Order 2011, http://www.legislation.gov.uk/uksi/2011/2687/part/4/made, Accessed 25 February 2023.

[119] Bank of England Credit Union Quarterly Statistics—2023 Q3, https://www.bankofengland.co.uk/statistics/credit-union/2023/2023-q2.

[120] The Building Societies Act 1997, the Financial Services and Markets Act 2000 and the Financial Services Act 2012 have subsequently amended the 1986 Act.

this act establishes that "A society may be established under this Act if (and only if) it complies with the following requirements, namely— (a) its purpose or principal purpose is that of making loans which are secured on residential property and are funded substantially by its members; and (b) its principal office is in the United Kingdom". "Residential property" means land at least 40% of which "(a) is normally used as, or in connection with, one or more dwellings; or (b) has been, is being or is to be developed or adapted for such use".[121]

Building societies have several limitations. There are: (1) lending limits[122]; (2) funding limits[123]; and (3) restrictions to act as a market maker in securities, commodities or currencies, or to trade in commodities or currencies and enter into any transaction involving derivative investments.[124] According to Rex, "The 1997 Act gave building societies the freedom to pursue any activities set out in their memorandum, subject only to compliance with the revised principal purpose introduced by that Act, the lending and funding limits, the restrictions on powers and appropriate prudential requirements,.... In essence, it is the principal purpose, the 'nature' limits and restrictions, together with the fact that most of a building society's customers are its members, which retain a building society's fundamental character, and differentiate it from other financial institutions".[125]

Schedule 2 of the BSA states that "no person shall be a member of the society unless he is a shareholding member or a borrowing member or both. 'Borrowing member' means an individual who is indebted to the society in respect of a loan which is fully secured on land; or if the rules of the society so provide, in respect of a loan which is (within the meaning of the rules) substantially secured on land". "Shareholding member" means

[121] BSA, s 5. https://www.legislation.gov.uk/ukpga/1997/32/contents, Accessed 25 February 2023.

[122] BSA, s 6; Radha K. Shiwakoti, Abdullah Iqbal, Warwick Funnell "Organizational Form, Business Strategies and the Demise of Demutualized Building Societies in the UK", *Journal of Banking and Finance*, Vol. 94 (2018) 339: "At least 75% of building society assets must be loans fully secured on residential property and 50% of the funds must be raised from the individual members (retail depositors) of the society."

[123] BSA, s 7.

[124] BSA, s 9A (1).

[125] Simon Rex "The Building Societies Act 1986—A BSA Summary Sixth Edition", *Building Society Association* (2013), 1.

a person who holds a share in the society.[126] Schedule 2 gives the freedom to establish whether any preferential or deferred shares are to be issued and, if so, within what limits; and whose membership ceases.[127]

During the 1980s housing finance was opened, and council houses were permitted to be sold to their tenants, which extended the housing finance. Banks were permitted to engage in mortgage lending.[128] The BSA permitted mutual building societies to "demutualise" and transform into stock banks. Ten of the largest building societies abandoned the mutual form between 1989 and 2000 "transferring about 80% of the industry's assets to the banking sector".[129] Banks and building societies started competing for the same market, which drove up housing prices.[130] Households started using their properties as collateral for borrowing and "the society as a whole was becoming increasingly leveraged prior to the financial crisis".[131]

According to the Director of UK Banks and Building Societies of the Bank of England, demutualized building societies' business models proved to fail: "As I have said on other occasions, the crisis revealed deep flaws in the business model of demutualised building societies. Not one of them survives today as an independent entity".[132] Not surprisingly, it was Northern Rock, a demutualized building society that was responsible for a bank run of unprecedented dimensions in the UK in 2007.

As Lastra explains, "Northern Rock was not a victim of the subprime crisis but of its own funding structure. The credit squeeze in August 2007 following the subprime mortgage crisis in the United States, caused

[126] BSA, sch 2, s 5.

[127] BSA 1986, sch 2, s 3.

[128] Offer "Narrow Banking", n.7, 163.

[129] Shiwakoti, Iqbal and Funnell "Organizational Form", 337. These were Abbey National, Cheltenham & Gloucester, National & Provincial, Alliance & Leicester, Halifax, Woolwich, Northern Rock, Bristol & West, Birmingham & Midshires and Bradford.

[130] Offer "Narrow Banking", 167.

[131] Michie "British Banking", 223.

[132] Andrew Bailey 'Promoting a Prudent and Stable Financial System' at the Future of the Retail Banking Conference, London (Bank of England 2011), https://www.bankofengland.co.uk/-/media/boe/files/speech/2011/promoting-a-prudent-and-stable-financial-system-speech-by-andrew-bailey.pdf?la=en&hash=7C82B9E6BEC8EEA655F1AAB4629755FEABFB5B13. Accessed 28 February 2019.

serious liquidity problems in many banks that had come to rely on wholesale capital markets (markets for securitized assets) for their funding needs. Northern Rock suffered more than others because it was heavily reliant on such markets at a time when they were drying out".[133]

By 2023, building societies' total assets summed £502 billion.[134]

Investment Banks

In addition to credit institutions, the FSMA also regulates investment firms. Some major investment firms are supervised by the PRA. Under the PRA-regulated Activities Order, the PRA may designate investment firms for prudential supervision by the PRA. These are,

> [b]roadly speaking, that the person: (a) has, or has applied for, permission to deal in investments as principal; and (b) has, or would have if it were authorised, a minimum capital of €730,000, or is a broadly analogous European Economic Area (EEA) passporting firm or non-EEA firm. Under PRA Statement of policy, a person meeting the conditions in article 3(2) and (3) is referred to as an "Eligible Investment Firm". "The PRA will have regard to each of the following factors in determining whether an Eligible Investment Firm should be designated: a) whether the firm's balance sheet exceeds an average of £15 billion total gross assets over four quarters, as reported on regulatory returns; and/or b) whether the sum of the balance sheets of all Eligible Investment Firms in a group exceeds an average of £15 billion total gross assets over four quarters; and/or c) where the firm is part of a PRA group, whether the firm's revenues, balance sheet and risk-taking is significant relative to the group's revenues, balance sheet and risk-taking.[135]

[133] Rosa Lastra "Northern Rock and Banking Law Reform in the UK in F. Bruni and D.T. Llewellyn", *The Failure of Northern Rock: A Multi-dimensional Case Study* (SUERF—The European Money and Finance Forum 2009), 147.

[134] Building Societies Association: Building Society Assets, https://www.bsa.org.uk/information/consumer-factsheets/general-information/building-society-assets. Accessed 28 February 2023.

[135] PRA "Statement of Policy Designation of Investment Firms for Prudential Supervision by the Prudential Regulation Authority" March 2013 (PRA 2013), https://www.bankofengland.co.uk/-/media/boe/files/prudential-regulation/statement-of-policy/2013/designation-of-investment-firms-for-prudential-supervision-by-the-pra.pdf?la=en&hash=570F23B585B77326C308B8B45CEB157BD1ADC03D. Accessed 25 February 2023.

As of 2023, the investment firms regulated by the PRA are[136]:

- Barclays Capital Securities Limited.
- Citigroup Global Markets Limited.
- Credit Suisse Securities (Europe) Limited.
- Goldman Sachs International.
- Merrill Lynch International.
- MUFG Securities EMEA Plc.
- Morgan Stanley & Co. International Plc.
- Nomura International Plc.

According to the PRA Rulebook, an investment firm means "any person whose regular occupation or business is the provision of one or more investment services to third parties and/or the performance of one or more investment activities on a professional basis". Investment services and investment activities mean "any of the services and activities listed in Section A of Annex I to MiFID".[137] Section A, Annex I of the MiFID states, "(1) Reception and transmission of orders in relation to one or more financial instruments. (2) Execution of orders on behalf of clients. (3) Dealing on own account. (4) Portfolio management. (5) Investment advice. (6) Underwriting of financial instruments and/or placing of financial instruments on a firm commitment basis. (7) Placing of financial instruments without a firm commitment basis (8) Operation of Multilateral Trading Facilities".[138]

The origin of merchant banks was international trade. Barings (1763) started as wool merchants; Rothschilds (1808) as cotton merchants; Schroeders (1818) and Kleinworts (1855) as sugar merchants; and Morgan Grenfell (1838) as dry goods merchants. Those merchants endorsed bills of exchange of lesser-known merchants, which was known as "acceptance". Over the years, they mixed commerce and "accepting" but at the end, they concentrated on the financial activity. The name of

[136] List of Designated Firms compiled by The Bank of England January 2023, https://www.bankofengland.co.uk/-/media/boe/files/prudential-regulation/authorisations/which-firms-does-the-pra-regulate/2023/bank-of-england-designated-firms-list---january-2023.pdf. Accessed 25 October 2023.

[137] European Parliament and Council Directive on Markets in Financial Instruments (No. 2004/39/EC).

[138] Ibid., s A, Annex 1.

the institution varied over time: they were called "merchants", "merchant bankers", "accepting houses", "issuing houses", "industrial bankers" and "investment bankers". Nowadays, the most common terms are merchant banks and investment banks.[139]

While trade finance was also developed by clearing banks, it gave merchant banks the opportunity to use their experience in placing securities: investment management, underwriting, mergers and acquisitions services, financial advisory, trading of securities and bullion and personal banking.[140] In terms of a business model, Michie explains investment banks use the "Originate and Distribute model", meaning they issued stocks and bonds "on behalf of borrowers and then sold to investors. In the interval between the issue and sale of these securities, investment banks could use the stocks and bonds they held as collateral for short-term loans from retail banks, and so meet the immediate need of borrowers. Once the securities had been sold the funds borrowed from the banks could be repaid".[141]

Following the Big Bang in 1986, two of the protagonists of the financial sector in the nineteenth and twentieth centuries disappeared: multinational banking and merchant banking. Two multinational or overseas banks survive. One of them, HSBC, is the leading bank in the UK. The merchant banks "were to be taken over, one after the other, during the closing of the twentieth century, though by American and European banks rather than British".[142] One reason for this might have been the removal of exchange controls, since UK investors trusted foreign brokerage firms.[143] According to Roberts, 77 of the 225 stock firms were bought: 16 by UK merchant banks, 27 by UK clearing banks, 14 by US banks and 20 by foreign banks.[144] After the GFC, Barclays took the opportunity to buy the investment banking business of Lehman

[139] Richard Roberts "What's in a Name? Merchants, Merchant Bankers, Accepting Houses, Issuing Houses, Industrial Bankers and Investment Bankers", *Business History*, Vol. 35, No. 3 (1993), 22.

[140] Saunders and Walter "Universal Banking", 115.

[141] Michie "British Banking", 216.

[142] Cassis "Crises and Opportunities", 116.

[143] Richard Roberts "London as an International Financial Centre, 1980–2000: Global Powerhouse or Wimbledon EC2?" in Cassis and Bussiere "London and Paris", 302.

[144] Ibid.

Brothers,[145] and now it is the only British investment firm regulated by the PRA.

After the GFC the focus was centred again on the risks of providing retail and non-retail banking under the same roof. The next section will examine the structural reform in the UK.

Ring-Fencing

In response to the GFC, several developed economies adopted structural reform measures. The main feature of the three structural reform incentives, the "Volcker Rule" in the US, the Vickers Commission in the UK, and the Liikanen Report in the European Commission, was a mandatory separation of "commercial banking and certain securities market activities".[146] According to Gambacorta there was a reassessment of the costs and benefits of universal banking's involvement in proprietary trading and other securities market activities. "Many large universal banks shifted too many resources to trading books, supported by cheap funding. The complexity of many banks weakened market discipline, while their interconnectedness increased systemic risk, contributing to contagion within across firms".[147] Binder defines ring-fencing as "[a] generic concept that involves the segregation of assets, liabilities and or/business activities from

[145] Michie "British Banking", 216; Ben White and Eric Dash "Barclays Reaches $1.75 Billion Deal for a Lehman Unit", *New York Times* (New York, 17 September 2008), https://www.nytimes.com/2008/09/18/business/worldbusiness/18barclays.html. Accessed 28 February 2023; Helen Avery "The Numbers That Prove Lehman Was Deal of the Century for Barclays", *EuroMoney* (18 September 2013), https://www.euromoney.com/article/b12kjsf0lgb850/the-numbers-that-prove-lehman-was-deal-of-the-century-for-barclays?copyrightInfo=true. Accessed 28 February 2023.

[146] Leonardo Gambacorta and Adrian van Rixtel "Structural Bank Regulation Initiatives: Approaches and Implications", BIS (2013), 7–30; European Commission *Proposal for the Regulation of the European Parliament and the Council on Structural Measures Improving the Resilience of EU Credit Institutions* (2014) (Liikanen Report); FSOC, *Study and Recommendations on Prohibitions on Proprietary Trading and Certain Relationships with Hedge Funds and Private Equity Funds* (2011) (Volcker Rule). Available at https://www.federalreserve.gov/supervisionreg/volcker-rule.htm#:~:text=The%20Volcker%20rule%20generally%20prohibits,funds%20or%20private%20equity%20funds. Accessed 6 March 2023; Independent Commission on Banking, *Final Report Recommendations* (2011), https://webarchive.nationalarchives.gov.uk/ukgwa/20120827143059/; http://bankingcommission.independent.gov.uk/. Accessed 6 March 2023.

[147] Gambacorta and Van Rixtel "Structural Bank Regulation", 7–30.

specific risks with a view to protecting markets and counterparties either directly or indirectly”.[148]

The ring-fencing regulations in the UK mandate that banks holding over 25 billion in retail deposits must segregate their retail and investment operations by the start of 2019. Essentially, these banks are obligated to establish a distinct legal entity known as the ring-fenced bank (RFB).[149] The ring-fence approach in the UK is centred on a list of activities called “core activities”. Only ring-fenced banks will be able to achieve core activities. The Vickers Report is achieved by section 4 of the Financial Services (Banking Reform) Act 2013, which inserts a new Part 9B to the FSMA. “Core activities” include (i) the regulated activity of accepting deposits (whether carried out in the UK or elsewhere) and (ii) other activities designated by the Treasury when “an interruption of the provision of services provided in the UK...could adversely affect the stability of the UK financial system or of a significant part of that system, and (b) that the continuity of the provision of those services can more effectively be protected by treating the activity as a core activity”.[150] The Financial Services and Markets Act 2000 (Ring-fenced Bodies and Core Activities) Order 2014 (2014 Order), states that the following institutions are exempted from the definition of

> “ring-fenced body provisions of the FSMA:
>
> - insurance companies
> - societies registered under s. 1 of the Cooperative and Community Benefit Societies Act 2014 (which include credit unions and industrial and provident societies)
> - Northern Ireland credit unions
> - Northern Ireland industrial and provident societies
> - banks which hold less than £25 billion core deposits
> - bodies which would only have become ring-fenced bodies as a result of action being taken under the Banking Act 2009 to stabilise a bank

[148] Jens-Hinrich Binder “Ring-Fencing: An Integrated Approach with Many Unknowns”, *European Business Organization Law Review* (2015), 115.

[149] Marco Bardoscia and Raymond Ka-Kay Pang “Ring-Fencing in Financial Networks”, Bank of England (2023), https://www.bankofengland.co.uk/-/media/boe/files/working-paper/2023/ring-fencing-in-financial-networks.pdf. Accessed 1 December 2023.

[150] FSMA, s 142 B.

in financial difficulty where not more than four years has passed since the date of that action".[151]

Article 2 of the 2014 Order establishes if a deposit is not a core deposit, then the activity of accepting it is not a "core activity". A deposit is a core deposit "if it is held in an EEA account unless one or more of account holders is a relevant financial institution; a qualifying organisation; a member of a qualifying group, or an eligible individual". A qualifying organization is one the has a turnover of not less than £6.5 million; its balance sheet total is not less than £3.26 million; and it employs not less than 50 people. An eligible individual is the one that held "not less than £250,000 in assets" in a period of one year.[152,153]

After defining core activities and core services, the FSMA lists the excluded activities, which are prohibited activities for ring-fenced bodies.[154]

Goodhart believes the UK ring-fence solution is less than optimal since "[r]ing-fencing UK banks into two, or three, parts will add to transactional and operational costs for both banks and their larger clients. The ring-fenced UK retail banks will concentrate even more on financing UK property and became even more subject to the vagaries of the UK property cycle. The investment bank, i.e., the non-ring-fenced part, will face more expensive and difficult funding conditions. The idea that retail banks must be saved from liquidation, but investment banks can and should be left to fail, is dubious. A better approach would have been to require banks to hold much more equity, and to intervene earlier to stop their downward spiral, rather than to impose such a separation".[155] Binder suggests that irrespective of legal barriers the reputational risk will still be in place if similar brands and logos and marketing channels remain after modifying the banking group's structure.[156]

[151] The Financial Services and Markets Act 2000 (Ring-Fenced Bodies and Core Activities) Order 2014.

[152] The Financial Services and Markets Act 2000 (Excluded Activities and Prohibitions) Order 2014, s 2.

[153] Ibid. Core activities are listed in FSMA s 142 C.

[154] FSMA, s 142 D; Proctor "The Law and Practice", 17.

[155] Charles Goodhart "The Vickers Report: An Assessment", *Law and Financial Markets Review* (2012), 32.

[156] Binder "Ring-Fencing", 108.

The ring-fencing regime took effect on January 1, 2019. All banks falling under the scope of ring-fencing successfully carried out the required implementation activities. An amount totalling £1.2 trillion in core deposits was placed within ring-fenced banks. To align their business structures with the stipulations of structural reform, banking groups subject to these regulations underwent significant restructuring programmes from 2017 to 2018.[157]

The UK banking system is in continuous evolution.[158] While it first evolved as a specialized banking system, after the deregulation period of Margaret Thatcher and the Big Bang the system turned into a universal banking system. After the GFC, universal banks were found in part responsible for the increase of risks and interconnection, and now as Sir Vickers affirms, "(ring-fence) would end universal banking".[159] While this is part true, ring-fencing in the UK will not mandate a complete separation,[160] and permits banking groups to maintain the different activities under the same banking group and name.

4.3 Concluding Remarks

This chapter has addressed the British model banking groups. The original British model comprises a bank-parent company, which owns insurance and securities subsidiaries. Today, most British banking groups

[157] Bank of England "Ring-fencing" https://www.bankofengland.co.uk/prudential-regulation/key-initiatives/ring-fencing#:~:text=As%20part%20of%20its%20response,structural%20reform%20or%20ring%2Dfencing. Accessed 1 December 2023.

[158] The Ring fencing and proprietary Trading Independent Report concludes that the following are the package of its recommendations:

- "Keeps the core deposit threshold at £25 billion;
- Removes banks from the regime that undertake minimal excluded activities;
- Enables RFBs to undertake a small amount of excluded activities;
- Enables the authorities to remove banks from the regime that are deemed resolvable;
- Enables RFBs to provide smaller RFIs with banking services;
- Enables RFBs to provide customers outside of the EEA with banking services; and
- Makes some technical changes to improve the operation of the regime." https://rfpt.independent-review.uk/uploads/CCS0821108226-006_RFPT_Web%20Accessible.pdf. Accessed 1 December 2023.

[159] Independent Commission on Banking, Interim Report, April 2010.

[160] Goodhart "The Vickers Report", 36.

comprise a holding company at the apex of the group. Therefore, the corporate group that is composed of a holding company, which holds a Bank, which in turn owns the securities and insurance subsidiaries, may be labelled as the British Modified model.

Section 4.1 analysed the distinctive characters of the British banking system.

1. Unlike the German system, the UK system has historically been characterized by the separation of investment and retail banking. The deregulation movement that some locate in the CCC and others on the EU Second Banking Directive led the UK banking system to universal banking. After the GFC, structural reform separated retail banking from investment banking, again. This time the change was regulatory.
2. The UK banking system has relied heavily on self-regulation, a unique characteristic that is absent in the German and US models. It was only in 1979 that the Bank of England had to authorize the acceptance of deposits from the public. This self-regulated system proved to be very stable since there was a long period of more than 100 years without a significant banking crisis (1878–1991).
3. The relationship between bankers and industrialists has proven to be problematic in the different stages of history in the UK. There is acceptance that the UK banking approach was indeed different from the German system. While UK bankers provided short-term credit to the industry, their German counterparts provided long-term finance, owned the companies and were part of the boards of directors of such companies. Gerschenkron believes the main issue was that the UK faced the Industrial Revolution first, which could not accompany the evolution of a maturing economy. Germany and other backward economies had to face the Industrial Revolution via new vehicles, the *Grossbanks*. Others believe the UK institutions are to blame for the lack of long-term financing and others explain the "industry decline" due to a coalition of the City and the land against the industry. While there was no formal regulation until 1979, the Bank of England had a monopoly to fund the government and to take the form of a joint stock company, which was to the detriment of the other banking institutions. Usury laws also restrict the number of customers banks could get and increased collateral lending. Facts indicate from 1860 to 1913 the

UK manufacturing output decreased from 19 to 13% of the total manufacturing output. Additionally, there is evidence that banks before World War I were concerned with liquidity and short-term lending, and that UK foreign investment was huge. The sum of these factors might have stymied industry development in the UK. Things changed after the Big Bang. In 1988, the UK surpassed Germany for the first time in the Private Credit by Deposit Money Banks to GDP, and after 2002 Germany could not lead again against the UK. As it is analysed in Chapter 5, the UK system resembles in some way the US System in that banks did not provide sufficient financing to the industry as in Germany.

4. The UK banking system is shaped by the City, something the German model lacked. London is the second ranked financial centre in the world, below New York. Data suggest the City of London will continue to be the major financial centre in Europe after Brexit. The history of the City of London showed how London championed the financial world, first by being the imperial city. After World War II, when New York emerged as the major financial centre because it was located in the major economy and had the major currency, London demonstrated it had resilience in that it developed both the Eurocurrency market and the Eurobond Market to compete again. Some posed questions as to whether the City has failed industry in the UK, or even if the City has failed the British economy as a whole. After 2012 the "too much finance" doctrine has emerged to question if concentration of one industry may have unintended consequences such as inducing large crises and misallocating resources from other parts of the economy. Brexit has raised these questions again.

Section 4.2 makes a compilation of the UK banking system in its broad sense, including both credit institutions and investment banks. The UK banking system is comprised by: (1) banks, (2) credit unions, (3) building societies and (4) investment banks. This section defines a bank and analyses the "big four", "multinational" or "overseas" banking and foreign banks. Credit unions are non-profit financial institutions based on cooperative values. All credit unions together comprise total assets of £3.3 billion. Building societies are financial institutions with the principal purpose of making loans, which are secured on residential property and are funded by its members. During the 1980s housing finance was opened and banks were permitted to engage in mortgage lending, while at the same time building societies were permitted to demutualize. Northern Rock was one of them. These instructions were said to have deep flaws in in building societies' business models. Investment banks or merchant banks are the last category. Historically, merchant banks had a specialized banking business, which derived from international trade. Some major investment firms are regulated by the PRA. Only Barclays stands as a British PRA-regulated investment firm. Similar to Germany, the UK system includes commercial banks and institutions with a primary aim that differ from profit maximizations: Credit unions (UK) and Saving Banks and Cooperatives (Germany).

Section 4.3 examines the structural reform in the UK, which tried to break universal banking. While the aim was to separate retail banking from investment banking, the result of the ring-fencing regulation permits, under certain limits, the holding of both retail and investment banking companies under the same holding company, and under the same banking name. What the ring-fencing provisions in the UK prohibited is a German model banking group, since retail and investment banking cannot be provided under the same roof. The ring-fence provisions are centred on a list of core activities and core services that are permitted only to the ring-fenced entity.

CHAPTER 5

US Model

5.1 The US Model

Unlike the German banking system, that has always been essentially universal, the features of the US banking system have evolved over the last two centuries leading to a complex dual system (federal–state) in which banking has co-existed with capital markets and insurance businesses, and the legal form has changed often in response to crises. When Herring and Santomero classified FCs according to their legal and operational separateness, they correctly identified the US model as a holding model. From the 1950s, the US Congress introduced the holding banking system, and this structural legal form still prevails in most of the US BBFCs. The US financial system permitted universal banking from its inception as an independent nation in 1776 until the GSA in 1933. The GSA separated commercial banking from investment banking. This lasted until the deregulation period in the 1990s when Congress permitted banking groups to perform the three types of financial activities (banking, securities and insurance) under the same group, de facto permitting FCs to operate in the US market again, as in the pre-GSA period. In 1999, the Financial Services Modernization Act, also known as the Gramm-Leach-Bliley Act (GLBA), repealed provisions of the GSA that had prevented banks, securities firms and insurance companies from entering each other's markets.

M. J. Sheppard Gelsi, *Corporate Structure and Banking Resolution*, Palgrave Macmillan Studies in Banking and Financial Institutions,
https://doi.org/10.1007/978-3-031-59948-4_5

Historical and Philosophical Foundations of the US Banking System

The US banking system was shaped by its federal system and has evolved into different phases throughout history. Following the British experience, the first phase was the adoption of the charter banking system (1780–1837), which gave Congress or state legislatures the power to authorize and define permitted activities, capital and other requisites, and the period it would operate in certain territory. A second phase was the "free banking" period (1837–1865), where banks were free to engage in banking activities as long as they collaterized note issuance. A third phase comprised the "National Banking System" (1865–1913). Unlike the free banking system, where no national charters were permitted, the new system allowed banks to choose between a national and a state charter. The last phase comprises the period starting in 1913 up to the present.

After the creation of the Federal Reserve System in 1913 and its consecutive "foundings" in the words of Conti-Brown,[1] the system changed in that: (i) the new central bank was a public entity; (ii) it was given authority over the nation's payment system; and (iii) it was designed as a decentralized bank in order to prevent power concentration, and it was designed as independent from political power.[2] The Roosevelt administration responded to the Great Depression with the "New Deal Legislation". The Banking Act of June 16, 1933 (GSA) established the Federal Deposit Insurance Corporation (FDIC) to insure all accounts

[1] Peter Conti-Brown, *The Power and Independence of the Federal Reserve* (Princeton University Press 2016), 16–39. According to Conti-Brown, the Federal Reserve System had three "foundings", one in 1913 by the Federal Reserve Act of 1913, a second founding by the Banking Act of 1935 and a third founding by the Fed-Treasury Accord of 1951.

[2] Federal Reserve Bank of Minneapolis, "A History of Central Banking in the United States". https://www.minneapolisfed.org/about/more-about-the-fed/history-of-the-fed/history-of-central-banking. Accessed 5 June 2023; See generally: Rosa Lastra, *Central Banking And Banking Regulation* (Financial Markets Group of the London School of Economics and Political Science 1996); Charles Goodhart, *The Evolution of Central Banks* (MIT Press 1988); Arthur Burns, "The Independence of the Federal Reserve System" Challenge(1976); Peter Conti-Brown, "The Institution of Federal Reserve Independence", *Yale Journal on Regulation*, Vol. 32, No. 2 (2015); Ed Balls, James Howat, and Anna Stansbury, "Central Bank Independence Revisited: After the Financial Crisis, What Should a model Central Bank Look Like?" M-RCBG Associate Working Paper Series, No. 67 (2016), Mossavar-Rahmani Center for Business & Government of Harvard University; Michael Barr, Howell Jackson, and Margareth Tahyar, *Financial Regulation: Law and Policy* (Foundation Press 2018).

for depositary institutions and separated investment banking from insurance and commercial banking. Finally, the GSA prohibited the payment of interest on demand deposits.[3] In the securities front, new federal securities regulations imposed improved transparency requirements.[4]

In 1956, the US Congress passed the BHCA which introduced the "Bank Holding Company" structure.[5] At that time there were only 47 BHCs registered with 7.6% of the country's bank deposits. Fifty years later, almost 6,320 BHCs were registered, holding 94% of all bank assets.[6] The bank holding model was developed by most US BBFCs and has defined, in the words of Herring and Santomero and many others, the US model.

From April 1951 until 1965, economic growth and stable inflation was the norm in the US. After 1965, it started a period called "the great inflation", which characterized the US economy until 1982.[7] In the following years, the US banking sector was subject to interest rate controls, and later removal, and the advent of the Eurodollar market. The Eurodollar market consisted of deposits and loans issued outside of the US denominated in US dollars. They were attractive to US investors since they were outside the scope of interest rate ceilings and reserve requirements.[8]

The most important banking bills of this period were: (i) the Financial Institutions Supervisory Act of 1966[9] that expanded enforcement powers of federal banking agencies against unsafe and unsound banking practices and allowed them to remove directors who breach fiduciary duties[10]; (ii)

[3] Pub. L. No. 73–66, 48 Stat. 162.

[4] William Lovett and Michael Mallow *Banking and Financial Institutions Law in a Nutshell* (West Academic Publishing, 8th edn 2014), 16–17; Elisabeth Keller, "Introductory Comment: A Historical Introduction to the Securities Act of 1933 and the Securities Exchange Act of 1934", Ohio State Law Journal, Vol. 49 (1988), 329–352; Louis Lowenstein, "Financial Transparency and Corporate Governance: You Manage What You Measure", *Columbia Law Review*, Vol. 1335 (1996); US Securities and Exchange Commission. https://www.sec.gov/Article/whatwedo.html. Accessed 6 August 2023.

[5] Bank Holding Company Act of 1956 (12 USC § 1841, et seq).

[6] Lovett and Mallow "Banking and Financial Institutions Law", 221.

[7] Federal Reserve History https://www.federalreservehistory.org/essays/great_inflation?WT.si_n=Search&WT.si_x=3. Accessed 2 November 2023.

[8] Grossman "Unsettled Account", 264.

[9] Financial Institutions Supervisory Act of 1966 (P.L. 89–695, 80 STAT. 1028).

[10] Federal Deposit Insurance Corporation. https://www.fdic.gov/regulations/laws/important/. Accessed 2 December 2023.

the International Banking Act of 1978[11]; (iii) the Financial Institutions Regulatory and Interest Rate Control Act of 1978[12] which created the Federal Financial Institutions Examination Council that imposed limits and reporting requirements for insiders; (iv) the Depository Institutions Deregulation and Monetary Control Act of 1980,[13] which created "NOW Accounts" and "began the phase-out of interest rate ceilings on deposits",[14] while establishing the Depository Institutions Deregulation Committee; (v) the Garn-St Germain Depository Institutions Act of 1982, which strengthened the FDIC in order to help troubled banks and thrifts via the Net Worth Certificate (NWC) programme that provided funds to banks that suffered from interest rate shocks[15]; and (vi) the Competitive Equality Banking Act of 1987 (CEBA).[16]

In 1989, Congress passed the Financial Institutions Reform, Recovery and Enforcement Act,[17] also known as FIRREA. FIRREA was a response to the savings and loan crisis, which involved the failure in 1981–1983 of more than 100 savings and loan associations (S&L).[18] FIRREA tried to restore confidence in the S&L. It eliminated the Federal Savings & Loan Insurance Corporation (FSLIC), while the FDIC started insuring deposits of thrift institutions.[19]

[11] International Banking Act of 1978 (P.L. 95–369, 92 STAT. 607).

[12] Financial Institutions Regulatory and Interest Rate Control Act of 1978 (P.L. 95–630, 92 STAT. 3641).

[13] Depository Institutions Deregulation and Monetary Control Act of 1980 (P.L. 96–221, 94 STAT. 132).

[14] FDIC. https://www.fdic.gov/regulations/laws/important/. Accessed 2 November 2023.

[15] Garn-St Germain Depository Institutions Act of 1982 (P.L. 97–320, 96 STAT. 1469).

[16] Competitive Equality Banking Act of 1987 (P.L. 100–86, 101 STAT. 552). See s 5.1.6.2.

[17] P.L. 101–73, 103 STAT. 183.

[18] National Commission on Financial Institution Reform, Recovery and Enforcement, *Origins and Causes of the S&L Debacle a Blueprint for Reform* (1993), 32.

[19] FDIC. https://www.fdic.gov/regulations/laws/important/. Accessed 2 November 2023.

Two years later, the Federal Deposit Insurance Corporation Improvement Act (FDICIA)[20] was passed in order to strengthen the power of the FDIC. The FDICIA's main goals were "to recapitalize the Bank Insurance Fund of the FDIC" and (2) to reform the "deposit insurance and bank regulatory system so that taxpayer losses would be minimized".[21]

The US banking system has some distinctive features. Historically the US government constrained the growth of banks and bank holding companies via branching restrictions, holding company activity restrictions and merger regulations. These restrictions reflect a strong tradition of federalism and decentralized banking as well as prevention of undue concentration of financial resources (a classic antitrust concern).[22] While universal banking may trace its philosophical foundations to Saint Simon's ideas, which were implemented by the Pereire brothers; in America, there is no such philosophical or religious body of ideas concerning banking. While not philosophical in nature, but similar in its power to move economic agents, it can be said that federalism was the nerve which moved and shaped the US banking system from its inception, and for most of its history.[23] The fear of concentration and abuse of power which is essential to federalism was always present in the idea of decentralized "unit banks" (with no branches) which were designed to serve the needs of the communities and were not managed in a centralized way.[24]

Due to deregulation and technological advances, the Riegle-Neal Interstate Banking and Branching Efficiency Act of 1994 modified the "unit bank" model. It allowed BHCs to: i) acquire banks after 1995; ii) merge banks into a single branch network with locations in different states. It also limited the restriction of interstate branching when the

[20] Federal Deposit Insurance Corporation Improvement Act of 1991 (FDICIA, Pub. L. 102–242).

[21] Frederik Mishkin "Evaluating FDICIA" Federal Reserve Bank of New York Graduate School of Business, Columbia University and National Bureau of Economic Research, (1996), 1.

[22] Lovett and Mallow "Banking and Financial Institutions Law", 8.

[23] Ibid., 8.

[24] Burton Abrams and Russell F. Settle, "Pressure-Group Influence and Institutional Change: Branch-Banking Legislation During the Great Depression" *Public Choice* (1993), 689; Deborah Morentz Markeley, "The Impact of Financial Deregulation on Rural Capital Markets in Virginia: An Analysis of Bank Decision Making" *Virginia Polytechnic Institute and State University* (1984), 165.

national deposit market share exceeded 10%.[25] In 1999, the US Congress passed the GLBA, which repealed the GSA "granting broad-based securities and insurance powers to commercial banking companies".[26] It also allowed BHCs to take the form of financial holding companies (FHC) that are permitted to engage in securities underwriting, insurance agency and merchant banking activities.[27] The GLBA authorizes national banks to underwrite and deal in municipal revenue bonds and to own or control a financial subsidiary that may perform activities that are not permitted for national banks directly.[28] These financial subsidiaries may not engage as

[25] Patrick Mulloy and Cynthia Lasker "The Riegle-Neal Interstate Banking and Branching Efficiency Act of 1994: Responding to Global Competition" *J. Legis*, Vol. 21 (1995), 255; Robert Deyoug "Banking in the United States" in Allen Berger, Philippe Molyneux and John Wilson *The Oxford Handbook of Banking* (OUP 2012), 785; Stacey Stritzel "The Riegle-Neal Interstate Banking and Branching Efficiency Act of 1994: Progress Toward a New Era in Financial Services Regulation", *Syracuse Law Review*, Vol. 46 (1995), 165. Charlotte Tart "Expansion of the Banking Industry under the Riegle-Neal Interstate Banking and Branching Efficiency Act of 1994: Is the Banking Industry Headed in the Right Direction?" *Wake Forest Law Review* (1995), 915; Grant Buerstetta "Riegle-Neal Interstate Banking and Branching Efficiency Act of 1994" *Annual Review of Banking Law* (1995), 2; Rebecca Zarutskie "Evidence on the Effects of Bank Competition on Firm Borrowing and Investment", *Journal of Financial Economics*, Vol. 81, No. 3 (2006), 503–537; Daniel Giedeman "The Riegle-Neal Act and Local Banking Market Concentration", *International Advances in Economic Research*, Vol. 10 (2004), 245, 328; Srinvas Nippania and Kenneth.W. Green Jr. "The Banking Industry after the Riegle–Neal Act: Re-Structure and Overall Performance" *The Quarterly Review of Economics and Finance* (2002), 901–909.

[26] Deyoug "Banking in the United States", 786; Richard Cebula "Bank Failures in Light of the Gramm-Leach-Bliley Act", *Atlantic Economic Journal* (2010), 455; Jeng-Yan Tsai "The Gramm-Leach-Bliley Act: Optimal Interest Margin Effects of Commercial Bank Expansion into Insurance Underwriting", *Applied Economics Letters* (2012), 1459; Jolina Cuaresma "The Gramm-Leach-Bliley Act", *Berkeley Technology Law Journal* (2002), 497; Faith Neale and Pamela Peterson "The Effect of the Gramm-Leach-Bliley Act on the Insurance Industry", *Journal of Economics and Business*, Vol. 57, No. 4 (2005), 317–338; Abdullah Al Mamun, Kabir Hassan and Son Van Lai "The Impact of the Gramm-Leach-Bliley Act on the Financial Services Industry", *Journal of Economics and Finance*, Vol. 28, No. 3 (2004), 333–347; Matthew Restreppo "The Convergence of Commercial and Investment Banking under the Gramm-Leach-Bliley Act: Revisiting Old Risks and Facing New Problems", *Law and Business Review of the Americas* (2005), 269; Bernard Shull "Banking, Commerce and Competition under the Gramm-Leach-Bliley Act", *Antitrust Bulletin* (2002), 25.

[27] GLB 103 (a), 12 USC 1843 (K) (4); Robert Effros, *Addendum to Central Banks in an Age of Standardization* (Effros 2004), 2.

[28] 12 USC § 24a.

principal in underwriting insurance, real estate development or real estate investment activities or merchant banking activities.[29]

While not a banking fraud per se, the Enron scandal led to the Sarbanes–Oxley Act of 2002.[30] It regulated public accounting firms that audit publicly traded companies.[31] Scandals and lack of regulation were breeding grounds for the GFC.

While a multitude of causes led to the GFC, Lastra and Wood have shown the build-up to the crisis was based in part in failures of regulation and supervision. "There were plenty of regulatory and supervisory failures (as well as a degree of regulatory capture or, at the very least, excessive group-think). Rules regarding capital proved inadequate; accounting rules exacerbated problems; and the absence of rules on liquidity was unfortunate. Indeed, capital and accounting regulations actually made things worse by being procyclical, with rules on risk-weighting capital combining with mark-to-market accounting to reduce requirements in good times and raise them sharply in bad".[32]

After the deregulation period, and the following GFC, the US Congress validated the Volcker Rule and prohibited proprietary trading via the Dodd Frank Act (DFA). As Lastra and Wood contend, "one of the major 'breakthroughs' in the response to the crisis is that a distinction is now made between macro-prudential supervision and microprudential supervision". Macro-prudential supervision analyses the "trends and imbalances in the financial system and the detection of systemic risks that

[29] 12 USC § 24a (2)(B).

[30] Sarbanes–Oxley Act of 2002 (P.L. 107–204).

[31] FDIC. https://www.fdic.gov/regulations/laws/important/. Accessed 2 November 2023.

[32] Rosa Lastra and Geoffrey Wood "The Crisis of 2007–09: Nature, Causes, and Reactions", *Journal of International Economic Law*, Vol. 13, No. 3 (2010), 531–550. See also See generally James Crotty, "Structural Causes of the Global Financial Crisis: A Critical Assessment of the "New Financial Architecture"' *Cambridge Journal of Economics* Vol. 33 (2009), 563–580; Özgur Orhangazi "Financial Deregulation and the 2007–08 US Financial Crisis", FESSUD, Working Paper Series No 49 (2014); Saktinil Roy and David M. Kemmeb "The Run-Up to the Global Financial Crisis: A Longer Historical View of Financial Liberalization, Capital Inflows, and Asset Bubbles", *International Review of Financial Analysis* (2019); Helmut Anheier, Sonja Kauffman and Sebastian Ziaja, "Ten Years after the Global Financial and Economic Crisis" The Governance Report 2018, Hertie School of Governance (2018).

these trends may pose to financial institutions and the economy".[33] In the US, the macro-prudential policy response[34] and the last chapter of financial regulation of bank-based FCs led to the creation of the Financial Stability Oversight Council (FSOC) which has the responsibility of identifying risks to the financial stability of the US of large interconnected bank or non-bank holding companies. FSOC's main power is to designate the "SIFI label" to non-bank financial institutions and to financial market utilities (FMU). According to the DFA there are three different "systemic importance" categories: (i) banking SIFIs: those whose assets are beyond $50 billion; (ii) non-banking SIFIs: those non-banking financial institutions whose material financial distress—or the nature, scope, size, scale, concentration, interconnectedness or mix of its activities—could pose a threat to US financial stability; and (iii) FMU.[35]

The following sections will examine federalism in America, the evolution of banking and capital markets in the US, and some special features of the US banking system: (i) branching restrictions; and (ii) a BHC's permitted activities. Further sections will analyse the US banking structure.

Federalism in America

Federalism has shaped the banking system in the US from its inception. "The term 'federal' is derived from the Latin *foedus*, which, like the Hebrew term brit, means covenant. In essence, a federal arrangement is one of partnership, established and regulated by a covenant, whose internal relationships reflect the special kind of sharing that must prevail among the partners, based on a mutual recognition of the integrity of each partner and the attempt to foster a special unity among them".[36] A federal political system is one that constitutionally recognizes that political authority is divided between a central government and state governments,

[33] Ibid.

[34] Ben Bernanke "Implementing a Macroprudential Approach to Supervision and Regulation" speech at the 47th Annual Conference on Bank Structure and Competition, Chicago, Illinois, 5 May 2011.

[35] See Chapter 2, s 2.3.3.

[36] Daniel Elaza, *Exploring Federalism* (University of Alabama Press 1991), 5.

where people are subject to both governments at the same time, each government acting within its own sphere.[37]

Federalism refers to "a means of governing a polity that grants partial autonomy to geographical defined subdivisions of the polity".[38] The late Supreme Court Justice Antonin Scalia imagines federalism as a "midway between two extremes". At the one extreme, he poses autonomy, disunity and conflict between states; at the other, uniformity, inflexibility and monotony of a centralized government. "Federalism is meant to be a compromise between the two".[39]

John Jay explained in Federalist paper No. 2 that "[i]t is well worthy of consideration…, whether it would conduce more to the interest of the people of America that they should, to all general purposes, be one nation, under one federal government, or that they should divide themselves into separate confederacies, and give to the head of each the same kind of powers which they are advised to place in one national government…Providence has been pleased to give this one connected country to one united people…This country and this people seem to have been made for each other, and it appears as if it was the design of Providence, that an inheritance so proper and convenient for a band of brethren, united to each other by the strongest ties, should never be split into a number of unsocial, jealous, and alien sovereignties".[40] Jay recognized the need for a government and gave reasons why the most suitable form of government for Americans is a united nation and not a series of sovereign confederacies.

The framers of the US Constitution "invented a new type of federalism". Before the US constitution, federal governments were simple allies and people of the states were primarily loyal to the local government and

[37] George Bermann "Taking Subsidiarity Seriously: Federalism in the European Community and in the United States", *Columbia Law Review* Vol. 94, 331 (1994), 404.

[38] Malcolm Feeley and Edward Rubin, *Federalism: Political Identity and Tragic Compromise* (University of Michigan Press 2008), 12.

[39] Antonin Scalia "The Two Faces of Federalism" *Harvard Journal of Law and Public Policy*, Vol. 6 (1982), 19.

[40] John Jay, *Federalist Paper No 2* (1787). https://www.congress.gov/resources/display/content/The+Federalist+Papers#TheFederalistPapers-1. Accessed 2 October 2023.

not to the federal one. US federalism created a nation.[41] Since the US Constitution proved to be an effective form of government and helped to shape a nation, constitution makers in major new nations emulated it.[42] For Blumstein federalism has "indeed become *the* pervasive legal/political issue around the world".[43]

Alexis de Tocqueville in his *Democracy in America* described the American political system for French readers. He observed, "[i]t was impossible at the foundation of the states…to establish a central administration in America". For him, Americans were dispersed over an enormous geographical area and "separated by too many natural obstacles" and that "America is therefore pre-eminently the country of provincial and municipal government". Tocqueville believed that "[t]he English settlers in the United States early perceived that they were divided into a great number of small and distinct communities which belonged to non-common centre; and that it was needful for each of these little communities to take care of its own affairs, since there did not appear to be any central authority which was naturally bound and easily enabled to provide them". He also observed that the sovereignty of the people was an essential concept in the newly formed country. For him:

> [p]rovidence has given to every human being the degree of reason necessary to direct himself in the affairs which interest him exclusively-such is the grand maxim upon which civil and political society rests in the United States. The Father of the family applies to his children; the master to his servants; the township to its officers; the province to its townships; the State to its provinces; the Union to the States; and when extended to the nation, it becomes the sovereignty of the people.[44]

These observations help to explain how and why the Americans saw the federal system as so essential to their own interests. Americans lived

[41] William Riker "The Senate and American Federalism", *The American Political Science Association*, Vol. 49, No. 2 (1995), 452.

[42] Riker "The Senate": "About half the earth is presently ruled by federal governments-all of them reminiscent in one way or other of the Philadelphia invention", 452.

[43] James Blumstein "Federalism and Civil Rights: Complementary and Competing Paradigms" *Vanderbilt Law Review*, Vol. 47 (1994), 1251, 1252; Riker, "The Senate", 452.

[44] Alexis de Tocqueville *Democracy in America*, Vol I and II (The Floating Press 2009), 758.

in a great geographical space, with no other visible and accountable authority than the local one. They had to organize themselves maintaining sovereignty of the people, via a dual system, one that gave the people the power to maintain local authority while at the same time, one that gave them a sense of "nation" via a federal government. Federalism was necessary at the creation of the US since people's loyalty to their own state was stronger than their loyalty to the union.[45]

Scalia contends the individual possesses, in accordance with the Declaration of Independence, a "God-given freedom" which rejects the idea of governmental constraints. However, according to him, there is no particular governmental unit with a natural right to rule, since the decision of which unit has to rule is a pragmatic one, which would be determined by the "practicalities of the matter". The question of the limits of federal legislative or regulatory authority over a field that may be accomplished also by the State is one that has been subject to the "practicalities of the matter". Weschler argues the restraints of federal interventions flow from "the sheer existence of the states and (from) their political power to influence the action of the national authority".[46] He in turn borrows his argument from Madison's Federalist Paper no. 45 where he states that "each of the principal branches of the federal government will owe its existence more or less to the favour of the State governments" and the Congress "will be disinclined to invade the rights of the individual states or the prerogatives of their governments".[47]

During the first 70 years of the Constitution's existence, Article I, Section 8's enumeration of the powers of Congress remained a subject of discussion. The states ratified the Constitution on the understanding that the central government would only act on the powers enumerated in the Constitution.[48] Also, the Tenth Amendment enshrined this view: "[t]he powers not delegated to the United States by the Constitution, nor prohibited by it to the States, are reserved to the States respectively,

[45] Edward Rubin "Puppy Federalism and the Blessings of America" *The Annals of the American Academy of Political and Social Science*, Vol. 574 (2001), 37, 43.

[46] Herbert Weschler "The Political Safeguards of Federalism: The Role of the States in the Composition and Selection of the National Government", *Columbia Law Review*, Vol. 54 (1954), 543.

[47] James Madison *The Federalist No 45* (B. Wright ed, 1961), 327.

[48] Peter Zavodnyik *The Rise of Federal Colossus: The Growth of Federal Power from Lincoln to F.D.R* (Praeger Series on American Political Cultures 1st ed 2011), xiii.

or to the people". In early years, two schools of thought disputed the real meaning of the powers of Congress. Hamilton, Marshall, Clay and Webster gave them a broad reading, while Jefferson, Madison and Polk tended to protect the rights of the states, interpreting the powers in a narrow way. The latter prevailed during the antebellum period. After the civil war, however, the broad interpretation prevailed.[49]

The commerce clause ("[t]o regulate Commerce with foreign Nations, and among the several States, and with the Indian Tribes") was used as a way to expand federal power. The SCOTUS stated in 1824 that this power "is complete in itself, may be exercised to its utmost extent, and acknowledges no limitations other that are prescribed by the Constitution".[50] This broad interpretation changed during the first decades of the twentieth century when a body of doctrine forbade the federal government from regulating certain areas.[51]

The second avenue that would limit federal powers would be the Tenth Amendment. In 1976, the SCOTUS ruled in *National League of Cities v Usery* that the commerce clause authority does not extend to shift state power to structure employment relations in areas of "traditional governmental functions". The scope of this limit of federal power was confined to the concept of sovereignty itself.[52] In 1985, the SCOTUS overruled *National League* in *Garcia v San Antonio Metropolitan* since the category "traditional governmental functions" was unworkable.[53] Under *Garcia*, the US Congress has discretion to allocate responsibilities in areas of federal and state concurrent competence.[54] The SCOTUS ruling coincides with Weschler and Madison's views; since for SCOTUS the framers of the constitution chose to rely on a federal system in which restraints on federal power over the states rely on the national government itself "rather than in discrete limitations on the objects of federal authority". For the SCOTUS, procedural safeguards protect better state interests than judicial

[49] Ibid.

[50] *Gibbons v Ogden* 22 US (9 Wheat.) 1, 196 (1824).

[51] Feeley and Rubin "Federalism: Political Identity" 141; *United States v E. C. Knight, Co.*, 156 U.S. 1 (1895); *Hammer v Dagenhart*, 247 U.S. 251 (1918); *Carter v Carter Coal Co.*, 298 U.S. 238 (1936); *United States v Butler*, 297 U.S. 1 (1936).

[52] Bermann "Taking Subsidiarity Seriously", 418.

[53] 469 U.S. 528 (1985).

[54] Bermann "Taking Subsidiarity Seriously", 419.

limitations of federal power.[55] In 1992 in *New York v United States* the SCOTUS condemned "commandeering state regulatory apparatus" to spend their administrative resources to implement federal policies, based on the Tenth Amendment.[56]

While there is no clear doctrine distinguishing federal from state jurisdiction, some commentators believe the US is no longer federalist ("real federalism is gone"), since the reasons behind federalism, that is to say, a country with linguistic, religious and disunity, did not exist or are no longer present in the US.[57] This book argues that the US still maintains federalism. The dual banking system and the peculiar mix of state authority in insurance and federal in securities is a peculiarity of the US. While it is true that the US is now a united country and people are more loyal to the union than to the states, federalism is still present in the Constitution and that has not changed. As Scalia contends, federalism is somehow a "virtuous middle" between disunity and centralism. History has shown the system has auto-regulated the limits of federal and state jurisdiction and that the SCOTUS had a role to play in the interpretation of those limits.[58] The US is a country based on the practicalities of commerce and British Empiricism, following the Lockean school,[59] in which practical wisdom is enhanced. This practical wisdom has created a system, federalism, which is now followed by many countries around the

[55] 469 U.S. 528 (1985).

[56] 112 S. Ct. 2408 (1992).

[57] Rubin "Puppy Federalism", 49; Feeley and Rubin, "Federalism: Political Identity", 149.

[58] Jenna Bednar, William Eskridge Jr. and John Ferejohn, "A Political Theory of Federalism" in John Ferejohn, Jack Rakove and Jonathan Riley *Constitutions and Constitutionalism* (CUP 2001), 37.

[59] Larry Gerston *American Federalism: A Concise Introduction* (Routledge 2015), 22; Louis Hartz, *The Liberal Tradition in America* (Harvest 1991), 140: "Locke Dominates American Political Thought, As No Other Thinker Anywhere Dominates the Political Thought of a Nation"; Carl Becker, *The Declaration of Independence. A Study in the History of Political Ideas* (Harcourt, Brace and Co. 1922), 27: "So far as the Fathers were, before 1776, directly Influenced by Particular Writers, the Writers Were English, and Notably Locke"; Morton White, *The Philosophy of the American Revolution* (OUP 1978), 5; Elazar, "Exploring Federalism", 115; Charles Wiltse, *The Jeffersonian Tradition in American Democracy* (1960), 37; John Miller, *The Origins of the American Revolution* (Stanford University Press 1943), 491; Dumas Malone, *Jefferson and his Time Vol I.* (Little, Brown & Co. 1948), 175; Gilbert Chinard *Thomas Jefferson, the Apostle of Americanism* (The Floating Press 2011), 72.

world, and the US is home to one of the most important democracies in the world. This system has shaped banking in the US. An overview of the development of banking in the US will follow.

A. The Chartered Banking System (1780–1837)

The adoption of the new Constitution signed in 1787 and entering into force in 1789 restricted state power to print fiat paper money, but states did not lose the power to charter state banks that could issue paper money.[60] States chartered banks at a fast pace. By 1790 there were three state banks, by 1800 there were 28, by 1810 there were 102, by 1820 there were 327 and by 1835 there were 584.[61]

During the first half of the nineteenth century, corporate privileges were reserved for non-profit organizations that served the common good, e.g., libraries, schools and bridge companies. The second quarter of the century saw a rise in charters provided to profit organizations, which gave their promoters certain advantages, for instance broad powers and legal personality. However, bank and insurance charters-imposed restrictions such as unlimited liability to shareholders in the event of failure or fraud,[62] early banks were identified with the political party of their founders; "becoming a bank insider required open and dedicated service to the party".[63] Since the number of charters were limited, they became very profitable. Allegations of bribery and wrongdoing were common in the State of New York as early as 1804.[64]

[60] Richard Sylla "US Securities Markets and the Banking System, 1790–1840" Federal Reserve Bank of Saint Louis (1998), 85.

[61] Ibid., 86.

[62] Howard Bodenhorn "Bank Chartering and Political Corruption in Antebellum New York" in Edward Glaeser and Claudia Goldin *Corruption and Reform: Lessons from America's Economic History* (University of Chicago Press 2006), 233–234.

[63] Ibid.; John Wallis, Richard Sylla and John Legler, "The Interaction of Taxation and Regulation in Nineteenth-Century U.S. Banking" in Claudia Goldin and Gary Libecap *The Regulated Economy: A Historical Approach to Political Economy* (University of Chicago Press 2001), 135; Howard Bodenhorn, *State Banking in Early America: A New Economic History* (OUP 2002), 123.

[64] John Knox *A History of Banking in the United States* (Rhodes 1903), 397. Bodenhorn, "Bank Chartering", 233.

At a federal level, the first bank to receive a federal charter was the Bank of North America. It was the first fractional reserve commercial bank in the US and the first private central bank, modelled after the Bank of England.[65] It opened its doors in 1782. Despite its monopoly powers, the market perceived that its notes were inflated compared with specie. After one year of operation, the Bank of North America ended its role as central bank and obtained a bank charter by the state of Pennsylvania. All federal stock was placed in private hands and all federal debt had been repaid.[66]

Hamilton did not give up on his intention of creating a US central bank. In 1791, the First Bank of the United States (BUS or First BUS) was chartered following Hamilton's suggestion to financier Robert Morris in 1779.[67] Hamilton argued the formation of the BUS would contribute to the "augmentation of the active or productive capital of the country" and "thus by contributing to enlarge the mass of industrious and commercial enterprise, banks become nurseries of national wealth".[68] The BUS borrowed some features from the Bank of England, like the prohibition on the trade in goods, merchandize and land or the provision of a legal monopoly of the national charter for the lifetime of the BUS. However, unlike the Bank of England, the BUS was limited to twenty years.[69] The establishment of the BUS resulted in grave constitutional argument. Jeffersonians argued the Constitution gave the federal government no power to establish a bank, while Hamiltonians argued there were "implied powers" which allowed the Congress to charter the BUS.[70] The

65 Murray Rothbard *A History of Money and Banking in the United States. The Colonial Era to World War II* (Ludwig Von Mises Institute 2002), 61.

66 Ibid.

67 Grossman "Unsettled Account", 222.

68 Alexander Hamilton "Final Version of the Second Report on the Further Provision Necessary for Establishing Public Credit (Report on a National Bank), 13 December 1790" https://founders.archives.gov/documents/Hamilton/01-07-02-0229-0003. Accessed 1 July 2023.

69 Lovett and Malloy "Banking and Financial Institutions Law", 9; Grossman, "Unsettled Account", 224; Rothbard "A History of Money", 67; Edward Symons Jr and James White, *Banking Law: Teaching Materials* (1991), 12; James Wettereau "The Branches of the First Bank of the United States", *The Journal of Economic History, Supplement: The Tasks of Economic History*, Vol. 2 (1942), 66.

70 Rothbard "A History of Money", 69.

SCOTUS took Hamilton's views in *McCulloch v Maryland*.[71] However, the recharter bill was defeated by one vote both in the Senate and in the House of Representatives.[72]

During the War of 1812 (1812–1815) the government had difficulties raising federal loans while state banknotes were seen as unreliable by the market. As Ruthbard contends, "The nation could not continue indefinitely with the issue of fiat money in the hands of discordant sets of individual banks".[73] Because of these factors, the charter of the Second Bank of the US (Second BUS) (1816–1836) was established in 1816.[74] The Second BUS was modelled closely after the First BUS as a private corporation with one-fifth of the shares owned by the federal government. The aim of the Second BUS was to create a national currency, purchase public debt and receive deposits from the Treasury. Its notes were to be redeemable in specie and the federal government accepted them to pay taxes, de facto giving them "quasi-legal tender".[75] From its inception, the Second BUS had expansionary credit operations, which impelled an inflationary boom around the country. In 1818 the Second BUS contracted credit and purchased millions of dollars of specie from abroad, which led the US into a depression, which led to a series of defaults and liquidations.[76] In the aftermath of the crisis, William Gouge said, "the Bank was saved and the people were ruined".[77] In 1831, the Second BUS's President Nicholas Biddle requested the charter to be renewed. President Jackson vetoed the bill and the charter of the Second BUS expired in

[71] 17 U.S. (4 Wheat.) 316 (1819).

[72] Rothbard "A History of Money", 69; Franklin Allen and Douglas Gale, *Comparing Financial Systems* (MIT Press 2001), 32; Grossman "Unsettled Account", 225.

[73] Rothbard "A History of Money", 82.

[74] Lovett and Malloy "Banking and Financial Institutions Law", 9; Grossman, "Unsettled Account", 227; Symons Jr and White "Banking Law", 13; Bray Hammond, "Jackson, Biddle and the Bank of the United States", *The Journal of Economic History*, Vol. 7, No. (1) (1947), 1.

[75] Rothbard "A History of Money", 82.

[76] Ibid., 86.

[77] William Gouge *A Short Story of Paper Money and Banking in the United States, Including an Account of Provincial and Continental Paper Money* (T.W. Ustick 1833), 110.

1836.[78] The US did not have a central bank until three-quarters of a century later.

B. Free Banking Period (1837–1865)

From the beginning of the republic, banks in the US had been chartered by special acts of incorporation by state legislatures or by Congress (First and Second BUS).[79] Charters were comprehensive and included all sorts of issues such as value of the shares, dividend policies, the minimum number of directors, etc. Michigan (1837), New York (1837) and Georgia (1838) began to enact "free banking" acts where anyone interested in engaging in banking activities needed to complete a file and deposit the correct amount of government bonds within the corresponding authority, without legislature approval.[80] In essence, free banks were requested to grant a loan to the state government in exchange for the right to function.[81] The deposit of government bonds served as a security for all the circulating notes issued by the bank. If the bank failed to honour its notes, the state would sell the bonds and reimburse the note holders out of the proceeds.[82]

The reasons for the rise of free banking laws may be explained as an "understandable response" to the destruction of the Second BUS and

[78] Hammond "Jackson, Biddle and the Bank", 10; Ralph Catterall *Second Bank of the U.S.* (University of Chicago Press 1903), 239; Symons et al. "Banking Law", 13; Knox "A History of Banking", 69; Calomiris and Haber, "Fragile by Design", 169; Peter Temin "The Economic Consequences of the Bank War", *Journal of Political Economy*, Vol. 76 (1968), 258. On the demise of the Second BUS, see Grossman, "Unsettled Account", 228.

[79] Grossman "Unsettled Account", 229.

[80] Calomiris and Haber "Fragile by Design", 169; Grossman, "Unsettled Account", 229.

[81] Calomiris and Haber "Fragile by Design", 169.

[82] Hugh Rockoff "The Free Banking Era. A Re-Examination", *Journal of Money, Credit and Banking* Vol. 6, No. 2 (1974); Howard Bodenhorn "Entry, Rivalry and Free Banking in Antebellum America", *The Review of Economics and Statistics*, Vol. 72 (1990), 683; Kenneth Ng "Free Banking Laws and Barriers to Entry in Banking, 1838–1860", *The Journal of Economic History*, Vol. XL VIII, No. 4 (1988), 878; Gerald Dwyer Jr., "Wildcat Banking, Banking Panics and Free Banking in the United States", *Economic Review Federal Reserve Bank of Atlanta* (1996), 2; Bodenhorn, "Bank Chartering", 184.

the subsequent importance of state laws in regulating banks.[83] Additionally, economic interests of people living in cities without banks, and popular dislike of the granting of political privileges, elitism and corruption favoured the free banking movement.[84] Finally, "radical free- market or laissez-faire populism" and a general belief that more banking would promote economic growth were also elements that favoured free banking laws.[85] Free banking ended de facto in 1865 when the government imposed a tax on state banknotes.[86]

C. National Banking

In the US a dual banking system was established, in which state banks and national banks are chartered and supervised at different levels. Under the dual banking system, national banks are chartered and regulated under federal law and standards are supervised by a federal agency. State banks are chartered and regulated under state laws and standards, which includes supervision by a state supervisor. The dual banking system in the US was born during the Civil War period. President Abraham Lincoln's Treasury Secretary, Salmon Chase, led the effort to create the NBA of 1863, the main objective of which was to raise money for the North to defeat the South. This had to be done via the issuance of a common currency at the national level. Up to that point, state banknotes were in circulation. The 1863 Act created competition with state banks, and the legislators went a step further the next year by passing an amendment to tax the issuance of state banknotes.

During the Civil War, without the interference of eleven southern states, it was possible to enact stronger federal banking legislation.[87] In 1862, the federal government started issuing paper currency called "greenbacks" that held the status of legal tender. The NBA favoured the federal chartering of state banks with weak capitalization requirements, while limiting note issuance. State bank note issuance disappeared because

[83] Ibid., 142.

[84] Calomiris and Haber "Fragile by Design", 170.

[85] Bodenhorn "Bank Chartering", 191.

[86] Dwyer Jr "Wildcat Banking", 2; Bodenhorn "Bank Chartering", 183.

[87] Lovett and Mallow "Banking and Financial Institutions Law", 11.

of the 10% federal tax levied on them.[88] However, checkbook transactions replaced most currency transactions by 1880, which led to a revival of state banks.[89]

National banks were "national" in the sense they were chartered by the federal government. However, they could not operate via nationwide branches, de facto preserving a system of geographic monopolies since state laws regulated the branching of national banks. The NBA was "free banking" on a national scale.[90] The drafting of the NBA drew heavily on the New York Act.[91] For the first time in US history, national banks would be supervised by a newly created agency, the Comptroller of the Currency, under uniform charters and uniform rules.[92] The aim of the NBA was to develop a national currency, a market for federal bonds and the use of federal banks as federal depositories.[93]

In order to reduce *ex ante* the risk of a banking crisis, federal and state law in this period included capital requirements, double liability, deposit insurance and branching regulations.[94] Minimum capital requirements were introduced both at the federal and state levels, but the minimum amounts fell from an average of USD57,000 in 1865 in small populations to USD 28,000 in 1880, USD 18,800 to just USD 17,000 during World War I. The decline of minimum capital requirements may be explained by regulatory competition within states and a perception of an increase in safety in the banking system due to double liability, deposit insurance and branching.[95]

"Double liability" was imposed to shareholders of failed banks, which were called to pay not only the initial payment in capital but another amount equal to such amount.[96] For national banks, it was required

[88] Calomiris and Haber "Fragile by Design", 179; Grossman "Unsettled Account", 229.

[89] Lovett and Mallow "Banking and Financial Institutions Law", 11.

[90] Calomiris and Haber "Fragile by Design", 179.

[91] Symons Jr and White "Banking Law", 22.

[92] Grossman "Unsettled Account", 229.

[93] Symons Jr and White "Banking Law", 22.

[94] Grossman "Unsettled Account", 242.

[95] Ibid., 237.

[96] Charles A.E. Goodhart and Rosa Lastra "Equity Finance: Matching Liability to Power", *Journal of Financial Regulation* (2020), 3; Jonathan Macey and Geoffrey Miller

that "each shareholder shall be liable to the amount of the par value of the shares held by him, in addition to the amount invested in such shares".[97] Six states instituted triple liability, while others imposed unlimited liability.[98] Senator Sherman explained that the reasons for assuring double liability were the protection of creditors and that it "tend(s) to prevent stockholders and directors of a bank from engaging in hazardous operations".[99] By 1930 only four states allowed single liability.[100] The Great Depression hit both single and double liability states and by 1941 there were no double liability or triple regimes in the US. According to Macey and Miller, the reasons for the repeal of double liability rested on the following: (i) the bankruptcy of managing shareholders put pressure on politicians to change the regime; (ii) the 1929-1933 bank failures proved double liability did not adequately promote stability; and (iii) the implementation of federal deposit insurance made it redundant.[101] However, history has proved during the GFC that federal deposit insurance did not prevent the crisis. Double liability is a very interesting idea to make insiders responsible and to stop moral hazard. Recently, Goodhart and Lastra have proposed a two-tier liability system, where insiders would be subject to multiple liability depending on their involvement in the disposition of information. The aim of their proposal stems from the fact that it would "shift the costs of failure back towards those who have the responsibility for taking these decisions".[102]

Unfortunately, fragility and periodic panic were the norm until the reforms of the 1930s.[103] Defects in the banking system before that time become patent in the panic of 1907, which led the Congress to enact

"Double Liability of Bank Shareholders: History and Implications", *Wake Forest L. Rev.*, Vol. 27, No. 31 (1992), 37; Howard Bodenhorn "Double Liability at Early American Banks" NBER Working Paper No. 21494 (2015), 5–6; Richard Grossman "Fear and Greed: The Evolution of Double Liability in American Banking, 1865–1930", *Explorations in Economic History*, Vol. 44 (2007), 44, 61.

[97] National Banking Act of 1863, ch. 58, 12 Stat. 665.

[98] Grossman "Fear and Greed", 237.

[99] Cong. Globe, 38th Cong., 1st Sess. Part II 1069 (1864).

[100] Grossman "Fear and Greed", 238.

[101] Macey and Miller "Double Liability", 37; Grossman, "Fear and Greed", 238.

[102] Goodhart and Lastra "Equity Finance", 1.

[103] Lovett and Mallow "Banking and Financial Institutions Law", 13.

the Aldrich Vreeland Act of 1908.[104] The aim of this act was to permit "a greater flow" of national currency until there was a consensus for the creation of a central bank.[105]

D. The Federal Reserve System (1913–)

With agrarian objections, the Federal Reserve Act was passed in December 1913. The preamble of the Act stated that its aim was "[t]o provide for the establishment of Federal reserve banks to furnish an elastic currency, to afford means of rediscounting commercial paper, to establish a more effective supervision of banking in the United States and for other purposes".[106] The Federal Reserve System was conceived as the central bank of the US, which was the first central bank after the demise of the Second BUS, more than 75 years earlier.[107] As Bernanke affirms, "financial stability concerns were a major reason that Congress decided to create a central bank".[108] National banks had to be members of the Federal Reserve System, while state banks were allowed to join. By 1916, only 37 state banks joined the system.[109] The Board of Governors (the former Federal Reserve Board (FRB)), which leads and oversees the entire system, manages the Federal Reserve System.[110]

However, the system is federal in nature, since the law grants authority to twelve Federal Reserve banks and their branches, which operate in

[104] 35 Stat. 546. 60th Congress, 1st Session, ch 229.

[105] Symons Jr and White "Banking Law", 26.

[106] Federal Reserve Act: Public Law 63–43, 63d Congress, H.R. 7837: An Act to Provide for the Establishment of Federal Reserve Banks, to Furnish an Elastic Currency, to Afford Means of Rediscounting Commercial Paper, to Establish a More Effective Supervision of Banking in the United States, and for Other Purposes.

[107] Federal Reserve. https://www.federalreserveeducation.org/about-the-fed/structure-and-functions. Accessed 22 July 2023. Over the years, its role has expanded. Today it has three principal functions: monetary policy, banking supervision and financial services. Grossman, "Fear and Greed", 243.

[108] Ben Bernanke *The Federal Reserve and the Financial Crisis* (Princeton University Press 2013), 9.

[109] Symons Jr and White "Banking Law", 28.

[110] Federal Reserve "Structure and Functions"; Symons Jr and White, "Banking Law", 28.

twelve different districts around the country.[111] The federal nature of the bank resulted partly from American "wariness of concentrating too much financial authority within one institution".[112] Actual operations are engaged by the Federal Reserve banks "in concert" with member banks.[113] As Lastra explains, the Federal Reserve System itself does not have legal personality. Instead, the legal entities are the Board of Governors (which is a federal agency) and the twelve Federal Reserve banks, which are privately owned, and perform central banking activities and commercial banking activities.[114]

The Federal Reserve System was designed to be independent from political power.[115] Conti-Brown states, "Fed independence is the separation, by statute, of the central bankers (specifically the Fed chair) and the politicians (specifically the president) for purposes of maintaining low inflation".[116]

During the 1920s the US economy flourished. However, in 1929 the US and the world suffered the Great Depression. The US stock market crashed on 29 October 1929. From 1929 to 1932, stock prices fell 85%.[117] US GDP contracted by one third between 1929 and 1932. In 1931 the Creditanstalt collapsed, bringing down other banks in Europe. The depression in the US lasted until 1941.[118] According to some commentators, the Federal Reserve failed both on the monetary side and on the financial stability side.[119] On the monetary side, this occurred since

[111] Symons Jr and White "Banking Law", 28.

[112] Grossman "Unsettled Account", 243.

[113] Symons Jr and White "Banking Law", 29.

[114] Lastra "International Financial", 65.

[115] See generally Lastra "Central Banking"; Goodhart, "The Evolution of Central Banks"; Conti-Brown, "The Institution of Federal Reserve"; Balls, Howat and Stansbury "Central Bank Independence Revisited"; Barr, Jackson and Tahyar.

[116] Conti-Brown "The Institution of Federal Reserve", 2.

[117] Bernanke "The Federal Reserve", 19.

[118] Ibid.

[119] Bernanke "The Federal Reserve", 24; Ben Bernanke "On Milton Friedman's Ninetieth Birthday" Remarks by Governor Ben S. Bernanke at the Conference to Honour Milton Friedman, University of Chicago, Chicago, IL, 8 November 2002; Milton Friedman and Anna J. Schwartz, *A Monetary History of the United States, 1867–1960* (Princeton 1965), 444; Lovett and Mallow, "Banking and Financial Institutions Law",

it did not ease money because it wanted to maintain the gold standard and believed in the "liquidationist" theory, which stated that after an expansion the correct result is a period were excesses are "squeezed out".[120] On the financial stability side, this occurred because the Federal Reserve did not fully fulfil the lender of last resort responsibility, responding inadequately to bank runs.[121]

During the early years of 1933, many states declared banking holidays in order to free banks from redeeming deposits. On 4 March 1933, Franklin Delano Roosevelt (FDR) inaugurated his presidency and the following day he declared a national bank holiday.[122] Among a series of emergency actions, the most significant was the GSA.[123] Its most important provisions included: (i) the creation of the FDIC[124]; (ii) the "Glass-Steagall Wall" which separated investment banking from commercial banking[125]; (iii) the limit of interest payments on demand deposits;

15; Gary Richardson, "The Great Depression" https://www.federalreservehistory.org/essays/great_depression. Accessed 5 August 2023; Allan Meltzer, *A History of the Federal Reserve, volume 1: 1913–1951* (2003), 16; Peter Temin, "Lessons for the Present from the Great Depression", *The American Economic Review*, Vol. 66, No. 2 (1976), 40; Christina D. Romer "The Nation in Depression" *The Journal of Economic Perspectives*, Vol. 7, No. 2 (1993), 33.

120 Bernanke "The Federal Reserve", 24.

121 Friedman and Schwarz "A Monetary History", 407.

122 Grossman "Unsettled Account", 224.

123 Act of June 16, 1933, 48 Stat. 162.

124 According to Friedman and Schwartz "Monetary History" "Federal insurance of bank deposits was the most important structural change in the banking system to result from the 1933 panic…and…the structural change most conductive to monetary stability", 434.

125 The relevant Sections are 16, 20, 21 and 32. Effros "Central Bank", 2; Franklin Edwards "Banks and Securities Activities: Legal and Economic Perspectives on the Glass-Steagall Act" in Goldbergand, White, *The Deregulation of Banking and Securities Activities* (Lexington Books 1979), 273–294; Mathew Sherman "A Short History of Financial Deregulation in the United States", *Center for Economic and Policy Research* (2009), 10; Kroszner and Rajan "Is the Glass-Steagal Act Justified", 814; Benston "Universal Banking", 121; Roberta Carmel "Glass-Steagall: Some Critical Reflections" *Banking Law Journal* (1980), 631–641; Bernard Shull "The Separation of Banking and Commerce in the United States an Examination of Principal Issues" OCC Economics Working Paper (1999), 12; Bernard Shull and Lawrence White "Of Firewalls and Subsidiaries: The Right Stuff for Expanded Bank Activities" New York University Center for Law and Business Working Paper #CLB-98-017 (1998), 4.

(iv) giving the Federal Reserve credit control authority to prevent speculative excesses; and (v) creating the Federal Open Market Committee (FOMC) as the "central body that would make proactive decisions about the purchase of market securities, including government securities".[126] This also led to the publification/agencification of the Federal Reserve System.

Another important measure of FDR administration was the abandonment of the gold standard. Through the Banking Act of 1935, Congress expanded the powers of the FRB in order to better fulfil its functions as a central bank.[127] At the same time, the FDR government perceived the need to restore confidence in the capital markets, damaged by the Great Depression. During the 1920s approximately 20 million Americans "took advantage of post-war prosperity and set out to make their fortunes in the stock market".[128] Congress passed the Securities Act of 1933[129] with the aims of monitoring the securities industry by promoting stability in the markets and by protecting investors.[130] Many of the "New Deal" reforms persist as of today. They have shaped the US financial system and they have been essential in the development of the US economy.

Because of its federal nature, one special feature of the US banking system is how it regulated the branching of banks at both the state and federal levels. An overview of these restrictions follows.

Branching and Unit Banking

The US has a long history of restricting the geographic expansion of banking entities. Its rationale, as with antitrust, stems from preventing

[126] Conti-Brown "The Institution of Federal Reserve", 25.

[127] Lovett et al. "Banking and Financial Institutions Law", 8; Gary Richardson, Alejandro Komai, and Michael Gou "Banking Act of 1935" (2013) https://www.federalreservehistory.org/essays/banking_act_of_1935. Accessed 5 August 2023.

[128] Annette L. Nazareth "Speech by SEC Staff: "Come With Me to the SEC" Remarks before the Brown University Commencement Forum" https://www.sec.gov/news/speech/spch052403aln.htm#:~:text=During%20the%201920s%2C%20approximately%2020,fortunes%20in%20the%20stock%20market.&text=Banks%20also%20lost%20great%20sums,invested%20heavily%20in%20the%20markets. Accessed 27 November 2023.

[129] United States Code: Securities Act of 1933, 15 USC §§ 77a-77 mm (1934).

[130] US Securities and Exchange Commission https://www.sec.gov/about/advisory-committees. Accessed 5 November 2023.

abuse of power and undue concentration of financial resources.[131] While the First BUS and Second BUS were permitted to branch,[132] the NBA of 1864 was interpreted by the Comptroller of the Currency to prohibit branching by national banks.[133] State banks that already had branches were allowed to maintain those branches if they obtained federal charter, resulting in some national banks having branches. However, they could not open new branches. Similarly, many state-chartered banks faced comparable limitations. Many states prohibited branching of any kind; some states permitted only intra-city branches, and a few permitted state-wide branching.[134]

The consequence of these restrictions was a system composed mostly of individual unit banks.[135] "No other nation prevented its banks from branching as severely as the United States did, and by the beginning of the twentieth century, branching networks were nearly ubiquitous in every advanced nation except the United States".[136] The McFadden Act

[131] Bank centralization is "contrary to the spirit of American Independence". Speech by former Governor Stokes of New Jersey before Pennsylvania Bankers Ass'n at Atlantic City. 74 Cong. Rec. 1129, 1130, cited by Harvard Law Review Association "Branch, Chain and Group Banking", *Harvard Law Review*, Vol. 48, No. 4 (1935), 659. Maria Nieto and Larry Wall "Breaking Down Geographic Barriers on Banks: U.S. and EU Recent Experiences" Federal Reserve Bank of Atlanta (2015). https://www.frbatlanta.org/cenfis/publications/notesfromthevault/1507.aspx. Accessed 17 November 2023. See Calomiris and Haber "Fragile by Design". On the rational of antitrust, see Federal Trade Commission "Antitrust Laws" https://www.ftc.gov/tips-advice/competition-guidance/guide-antitrust-laws/antitrust-laws. Accessed 19 November 2023.

[132] Wettereau "The Branches", 66–100; Charles Calomiris and Carlos Ramirez "The Political Economy of Bank Entry Restrictions: Theory and Evidence from the U.S. in the 1920's" Working Paper, Columbia University (2004), 4.

[133] Dean Amel and Nellie Liang "The Relationship Between Entry into Banking Markets and Changes in Legal Restrictions on Entry", *Antitrust Bulletin* (1992), 633; Dorothy Riefler "Branch Banking and Chain Banking" *Editorial Research Reports*, Vol. 1 (1930), 1–4; Daniel Giedeman "Branch Banking Restrictions and Finance Constrains in Early- Twentieth-Century America", *The Journal of Economic History*, Vol. 65, No. 1 (2005), 129.

[134] Giedeman "Branch Banking", 129.

[135] Eugene White "A Reinterpretation of the Banking Crisis of 1930", *The Journal of Economic History*, Vol. 44, No. 1 (1984), 131.

[136] Giedeman "Branch Banking" 129; see also Caroline Fohlin, "Economic, Political and Legal Factors in Financial System Development: International Patterns in Historical Perspective" California Institute of Technology, Social Science Working paper 1098 (2000), 2.

of 1927 permitted national banks to establish branches only if state law allowed it. Even then, branching was limited to the city limits.[137] In 1986 the Douglas Amendment[138] provided no BHC might acquire a bank outside the state of its principal banking activities "unless that state specifically authorizes, by statute, such an acquisition".[139]

Calomiris explains an "agrarian Populist-Unit Banker coalition" existed in the US from the colonial era. British America was a society of small farmers that were armed and had the right to vote. The agrarian coalition believed in property rights and easy access to credit. They understood unit banks served local communities better than branches. Because of the federal nature of the American political and legal system and because the US Constitution did not explicitly give banking regulatory authority to the federal government, the "agrarian-unit bank" coalition could more easily win legislative fights at the state level. Until the twentieth century, they did not fight at a national level.[140] When this moment came, branching restrictions ceased with the passing of the Riegle-Nale Interstate Banking and Branching Efficiency Act of 1994, when the whole banking system changed.[141]

Benefits and Costs of Unit Banks

The costs and benefits of unit banking have been addressed in different stages of US history. Even before the NBA, Hamilton was distrustful of the idea of a national bank with branches.[142] Unit banks were not only favoured by the agrarian coalition, but, at least in one case, citizens

[137] Calomiris and Ramirez "The Political Economy of Bank Entry Restrictions", 5; For other legal restrictions see Amel and Liang, "The Relationship", 633.

[138] 12 USC § 1842(d).

[139] Carl Falsenfeld "The Bank Holding Company Act: Has It Lived Its Life" *Villanova Law Review* (1993), 121.

[140] Calomiris and Haber "Fragile by Design", 154.

[141] The Riegle-Niele Interstate Banking and Branching Efficiency Act of 1994 allowed the following: (i) well-managed and well-capitalized BHC's could acquire banks in any state after 29 September 1995; (ii) BHCs could merge banks in different states into a single branch group after 1 June 1997; (iii) until 1 June 1997, states could opt-out of branching provisions; and (iv) BHCs may not control more than 10% of the US's total deposits, among other requisites. Federal Reserve History, "Riegle-Neal Interstate Banking and Branching Efficiency Act of 1994" https://www.federalreservehistory.org/essays/riegle_neal_act_of_1994?WT.si_n=Search&WT.si_x=3. Accessed 27 September 2023.

[142] Wettereau "The Branches", 70.

voted for the maintenance of the unit bank system via referenda.[143] The next section analyses the benefits and costs of unit banks from a historical perspective.

A. Benefits of Unit Banks

1. Because of its unique structure unit banks may not be altered by the mismanagement of a branch

Hamilton explained that while the situation in the US would inspire the admission of a plurality of branches for the First BUS, "the argument against it is, that each branch must be under a distinct, though subordinate direction, to which a considerable latitude of discretion must of necessity be entrusted. And as the property of the whole institution would be liable for the engagements of each part, that and its credit be at stake, upon the prudence of the directors of every part. The mismanagement of either branch might hazard serious disorder in the whole".[144] While this argument is an essential note of branch banking, it does not prevent the cost effectiveness of branch banking. Moreover, the problem of mismanagement remains in the unit bank and affects all types of financial activity.

2. Small unit banks may have a more personal knowledge of customers which enhances monitoring and control

Sprague finds the most important advantage of small banks is the "extensive local knowledge…and very intimate acquaintance with the individual borrower". This advantage is greater in rural areas where loans are not so liquid and the personal element is crucial.[145]

[143] Eugene White "Voting for Costly Regulation: Evidence from Banking Referenda in Illinois, 1924", *Southern Economic Journal*, Vol. 51, No. 4 (1985), 1084.

[144] Mathew St. Claire Clarke and Karyn D. A. Hall *Legislative & Documentary History of the Bank of the United States, Reprints of Economic Classics* (Routledge 1996), 15.

[145] Oliver M. Sprague "Branch Banking in the United States", *The Quarterly Journal of Economics*, Vol. 17 (1903), 249.

While true in nature, the same effect of "local knowledge" may be theoretically present in branches of a non-unit bank.

3. Local ownership and control of unit banks focused more on local concerns and interests

Some authors from the 1920s and 1930s explained local customers were keener to be served by local unit banks than by branch banking because they believed unit banks would better attend local interests and concerns.[146] According to Morentz Markeley, "The local nature of the decision making process inherent in the independent banking structure puts the independent bank in a better position to identify the capital needs of the agricultural sector and to design bank policies that can best serve this local sector".[147]

While this subjective argument might have been present in the past in the rural areas of the US, theoretically local branches of a non-unit bank might serve local interests as well as unit banks.

4. Branch banking may lead to capital outflows from nonmetropolitan areas

Morentz Markely explains that since the decision-making process of branch banking is more centralized, "As a result, local capital needs could possibly be left unmet as capital is allocated within the holding company to less risky, higher return ventures in other areas of the state. These events could lead to capital outflows from nonmetropolitan areas, as a result of the decline in independent banks in rural areas".[148]

5. Unlike branch banking, unit banking tends not to be monopolistic in character

Comptroller Dawes raised objections to allowing branch banking before the House Committee of Banking and Currency in 1924. He contended

[146] Abrams and Settle "Pressure-Group", 689.

[147] Morentz Markeley "The Impact of Financial Deregulation", 165.

[148] Ibid.

that branch banking is "essentially monopolistic" since it may reduce interest rates until it becomes a monopoly and then reimburse the costs. He also alleged that in other countries branch banking led to bank concentration in a few banks.[149]

The monopoly argument against branch banking has been strong in the US, for the reasons Dawes explains. The development of antitrust law in the US has prevented the kind of predatory pricing-like measures described by Dawes. US law now prefers to trust in regulation to avoid monopolistic measures (predatory pricing among others)[150] and not in "anti-branch" policies as in the past.

6. Branch banking opposes federalism

Comptroller Dawes believed branch banking opposed federalism. "Branch banking is peculiarly inconsistent with the American idea of local self-government and Federal coordination. The banking system of the United States is closely analogous to the governmental structure. Under the Federal Reserve System local independent units are coordinated while branch banking proposes that they should be consolidated".[151]

Federalism as a political system is not denaturalized by the branch banking system since the way banks are structured is not an essential note of federalism. The US is and will continue to be a federal country no matter how its FCs are structured.

B. Costs of Unit Banks

1. Unit banks were inadequate to finance industrial firms

[149] House of Representatives 29 December 1924, Congressional Record House. https://www.govinfo.gov/content/pkg/GPO-CRECB-1925-pt1-v66/pdf/GPO-CRECB-1925-pt1-v66-19.pdf. Accessed 21 August 2023; Riefler, "Branch Banking", 1–4.

[150] Philipe E. Areeda and Herbert Hovenkamp *Antitrust Law* (2nd Ed 2002) paras 722–49; Philipe Areeda and Donald.F. Turner "Predatory Pricing and Related Practices under Section 2 of the Sherman Act" *Harv. L. Rev.* 697, Vol. 88 (1975); U.S. Dep't of Justice, Competition and Monopoly: Single-Firm Conduct under Section 2 of the Sherman Act (2008).

[151] House of Representatives "29 December 1929".

Evidence suggests "links between industrial firms and banks were much weaker in the United States than in other countries (notably, much weaker than in Germany's universal banking system). This reflected primarily the small size of incorporated banks relative to the large needs of industrial borrowers".[152] In 1914 in the US there were 26,000 banks, overall, not capable of establishing branches. In general, they were incapable of "financing, monitoring and disciplining large industrial borrowers".[153] On the other hand, this inability of unit banks to finance industrial growth induced innovative means of finance such as the development of commercial paper and investment banking syndicates.[154]

Not only were branching restrictions inadequate to finance large firms but also there is evidence that branch banking "hindered the development of large-scale American enterprises in the early twentieth century".[155] While there is evidence that banks did finance industry in early nineteenth century, their role was less important by the end of the century.[156]

[152] Charles Calomiris and Carlos Ramirez "Financing the American Corporation: The Changing Menu of Financial Relationships NBER Working Papers Series on Historical Factors in Long Run Growth 20" (1996), 144; See also Gaines Cartinhour *Branch, Group and Chain Banking* (Macmillan Company 1931), 266; Howard Preston "Branch Banking with Special Reference to California Conditions", *Journal of Political Economy*, Vol. 30, No. 4 (1922), 511.

[153] Calomiris and Ramirez "Financing the American Corporation", 144; see also Charles Calomiris "The Political Lessons of Depression-Era Banking Reform", *Oxford Overview of Economic Policy*, Vol. 26 (2010), 542; and Charles Calomiris "Corporate Finance Benefits from Universal Banking: Germany and the United States 1870–1914" NBER Working Paper No 4408 (1993), 6. See also Chandler and Hikino "Scale and Scope", 80.

[154] Calomiris and Ramirez "Financing the American Corporation", 21; Giedeman, "Branch Banking", 134; James Armour et al., *Principles of Financial Regulation* (OUP 2016), 438.

[155] Giedeman "Branch Banking", 148.

[156] Calomiris and Haber "Fragile by Design", 185. See also Richard Sylla "U.S. Securities Markets and the Banking System 1790–1840" Review, Federal Reserve of Saint Louis (1998), 83–84; Naomi Lamoreaux *Insider Lending, Banks, Personal Connections, and Economic Development in Industrial New England* (CUP 1994), 19; Franklin Allen, Forrest Capie, Caroline Fohlin, Hideaki Miyajima, Richard Sylla, Yishay Yafeh, and Geoffrey Wood "How Important Historically Were Financial Systems for Growth in the U.K., U.S., Germany, and Japan?" (October 25, 2010). Available at SSRN: https://ssrn.com/abstract=1701274, 1–55; Matthew Jaremski "National Banking's Role in US Industrialization, 1850–1900" Working Paper 18,789, National Bureau of Economic Research (2013), 18. Jaremski concludes that national banking acts were partially responsible for increasing the number of banks in the manufacturing belt, which "indirectly contributed to the nation's industrialization.".

In order to show the differences between the US and Germany in terms of how banks finance industry, it is useful to look at what Goldsmith defines as the "Financial Intermediation Ratio" (FIR), the ratio that "measures the importance of financial institutions in terms of resources within the financial superstructure".[157] The FIR for Germany rose from 20.3 in 1850 to 30.1 in 1929, while the FIR for the US rose from 12.5 to 16.4 over the same period. He also concludes that the participation of financial intermediaries in financing the main sectors of the economy in the US in the first half of the twentieth century "averages approximately 5 per cent for nonfarm households and agriculture, and between 12 and 15 per cent for unincorporated and corporate business and state and local governments".[158] Moreover, the specific link of banks financing industry was greater in Germany than in the US.[159]

Calomiris concludes, "American industrialists could not depend on a single banking relationship to guide them through their growing and changing financial needs over the years. They relied less on banks for credit, especially to finance large-scale projects…the small size of banks limited bank lending to large-scale firms".[160]

2. Unit banks imposed costs on large firms that had to rely on investment banking syndicates

Large firms had to rely on investment banking syndicates to finance their fixed capital investments because unit banks were incapable of borrowing such amounts.[161] According to SEC data on the fees paid to investment bankers in 1930s, external finance through security issuances were on average 20% of the value of the issue. Costs were "unusually high" compared to the fees applied by German universal banks.[162]

[157] Goldsmith "Comparative National", 134.

[158] Raymond W. Goldsmith, *Financial Intermediaries in the American Economy Since 1900* (Princeton University Press 1958), 181.

[159] Calomiris "The Costs of Rejecting", 283.

[160] Ibid., 288.

[161] Calomiris "The Costs of rejecting", 283; Armour et al. "Principles", 438.

[162] Charles Calomiris "Regulation, Industrial Structure and Instability in U.S. Banking" in M. Klasner and L. White *Structural Change in Banking* Business (One-Irwin 1993), 54.

3. Unit banks were more associated with bank panics than branch banking

According to some authors, branch banking reduced the incidence of panics.[163] Bordo's survey on panics from 1870 to 1933 explains, "[t]he United States experienced banking panics in a period when they were a historical curiosity in other countries".[164] Calomiris, comparing evidence from English-speaking countries showed unit banks were more prone to panics than branch banking institutions.[165] The reason behind these facts may be explained by the diversification of individual bank assets.[166] "Systems based on large, geographically diversified banks that engage in a variety of activities that have been the least susceptible to panic, have had a lower incidence of bank failure, and have suffered smaller losses when banks failed".[167] Bernanke and James also explain that countries with unit banking "suffered more severe banking panics".[168]

White tested the hypothesis that branch banking was better prepared to survive financial crises by comparing data from banking crises in Canada and the US in the 1920s and 1930s. While in the US in the 1920s there were 6,008 suspensions, in Canada, only one bank failed during that period.[169]

4. Unit banks hindered financial integration and diversification

There is a consensus among American scholars that disparities in regional rates of return in the nineteenth century were due to branching restrictions and "geographical dispersion of economic opportunities".[170] Unit

[163] Abrams et al. "Pressure-Group", 687; Mark Carlson and Kris Mitchener "Branch Banking as a Device for Discipline: Competition and Bank Survivorship during the Great Depression" NBER Working Paper Series (2007), 1.

[164] Michael Bordo "The Impact and International Transmission of Financial Crisis: Some Historical Evidence: 1870–1933" *Revista di Storia Economica*, Vol. 2 (1985), 41–78.

[165] Calomiris "Regulation, Industrial Structure", 11.

[166] Sprague "Branch Banking", 243; White "A Reinterpretation", 131.

[167] Calomiris "Regulation, Industrial Structure", 3.

[168] Ben Bernanke and Harold James "The Gold Standard, Deflation, and Financial Crisis in the Great Depression: An International Comparison" in Robert Glenn Hubbard, *Financial Markets and Financial Crisis* (Chicago University Press 1991), 54.

[169] White "A Reinterpretation", 131.

[170] Calomiris "Regulation, Industrial Structure", 28; See also Lance Davis "The Investment Market 1870–1914; The Evolution of a National Market" *Journal of Economic*

banks hindered interregional capital flows that in general help to equalize rates of return on loans.[171]

In addition, the high cost of gathering and transmitting information over long distances resulted in information asymmetries, which led banks to charge higher premiums on loans to customers located far away from the bank.[172] Unit banks were also less diversified and more exposed to "location-specific" shocks, such as agricultural price volatility.[173]

5. Unit banks were less able to provide services in thinly populated regions

Since the costs of establishing a branch office were much lower than establishing a unit bank, branches could operate in places where unit banks could not, expanding into new areas and diversifying bank portfolios.[174]

6. Unit banks were less efficient than branch banking in the use of capital and reserves

Historical evidence shows branch banking in certain states in the nineteenth century had lower ratios of reserves to assets and lower capital-to-asset ratios than unit banks.[175] Calomiris explains since branch banking

History, Vol. 26 (1965), 355–399; Richard Sylla, "Federal Policy, Banking Market Structure, and Capital Mobilization in the United States, 1863–1913", *Journal of Economic History*, Vol. 29 (1969), 657–686; Kenneth Snowden "Mortgage Rates and American Capital Market Development in the Late Nineteenth Century" *Journal of Economic History* (1987), 671–691; John Binder and David Brown, "Bank Rates of Return and Entry Restrictions, 1869–1914" Journal of Economic History (1991, 47–66.

171 Calomiris "Regulation, Industrial Structure", 28; Sprague "Branch Banking", 242.

172 Giedeman "Branch Banking, 148.

173 Calomiris "The Political Lessons of Depression-Era Banking Reform", 542; White, "A Reinterpretation", 131.

174 Calomiris "Regulation, Industrial Structure", 38.

175 Ibid., 39.

reduces banks' risks it also reduces banks' demands for reserves.[176] Additionally, branch banking "lowers both bank and customer costs" since they are able to produce services in "more optimally sized offices".[177]

7. Unit banks prevented competition among banks

Unit banks could only face competition by other unit banks, allowing the existence of less profitable banks which were less prepared for adverse times. Barriers of entry increased the costs of setting unit banks.[178] Furthermore, branching limits restricted the eligible candidates for acquiring or taking over banks to the same locality or state.[179] Moreover, Carlson and Mitchener showed unit banks that competed with branch banking before the Great Depression were better able to survive the crisis than unit banks that did not.[180]

8. Economic growth accelerated in states that allowed interstate branching

Jayaratne and Strahan from the Federal Reserve of New York showed upon empirical evidence that "economic growth accelerated following intrastate branching reform" and that there were no other "concurrent policy changes" to explain such "improvements in growth". They explain

[176] Calomiris "Regulation, Industrial Structure", 38; See also Charles Calomaris and Larry Schweikart, "Was the South Backward? North–South Differences in Antebellum Banking" Colombia University working Paper (1988). Sprague, "Branch Banking", 242–260.

[177] David Humphrey "Why do Estimates of Bank Scale Economies Differ?" Economic Review, Federal Reserve Bank of Richmond (1990), 38–50; See also Paul Calem, 'The Impact of Geographic Deregulation on Small Banks' 17 Federal Reserve Bank of Philadelphia (1994).

[178] Calomiris "Regulation, Industrial Structure", 38; Allen Berger et al. 'The Transformation of the U.S. Banking Industry: What a Long Strange Trip It's Been' Brooking Papers on Economic Activity (1995), 62.

[179] Berger et al. "The Transformation", 62.

[180] Carlson and Mitchener "Branch Banking", 1.

that the possible factors of growth improvement are due to "bank monitoring and screening improvements". The result of deregulation on this field was the improvement of the quality of lending.[181]

A Reaction to Unit Banks: Chain and Group Banking and Bank Holding Companies

Branching restrictions induced bankers to circumvent them via other instrumentalities such as group and chain banking.[182] Chain banking is a phenomenon of one individual, or one family or small group of persons, controlling stock in a number of banks.[183] Group banking, on the other hand, is defined by Wakefield,

> Group banking is the name that has come into common usage for this step in the evolution of the American banking system...Group banking is not simply chain banking under another name. Chains of banks under common ownership or common control usually of a single individual, have existed for generations...Group banking on the other hand is the association of a number of corporately independent institutions within a single holding company for mutual advantages, the group being built around one or more large banks of a territorial nature and its management resting in the hands of the banking interests of a territory served.[184]

The FRB characterized the group banking structure by the following features: i) the existence of a holding company which owns the stock of a number of banks; ii) a centralized direction of essential activities of the banks under the holding company; iii) an exchange of stock of the shareholders of the banks for the stock of the holding company; and iv) marketing of the existence of the group and the names of those belonging to it. By 1931, 97 banking groups controlled 978 banks.[185]

[181] Jith Jayaratne and Philip Strahan "The Finance-Growth Nexus: Evidence from Bank Branch Deregulation" The Quarterly Journal of Economics (1996), 667.

[182] Riefler "Branch Banking", 1–4; Federal Reserve Board, "Banking, Groups and Chains" (1930), 73; Harvard Law Review Association "Branch, Chain and Group Banking", 663; Amel and Liang "The Relationship", 634.

[183] Federal Reserve Board, "Banking, Groups and Chains" (1930), 73.

[184] United States Congress, 71st, 2nd Session, House Committee on Banking and Currency, Hearings on Branch, Chain and Group Banking, under H. Res. 141, 25 February 1930, 26; see also Federal Reserve Board, "Banking, Groups and Chains".

[185] Federal Reserve Board, "Banking, Groups and Chains", 5.

As it usually happens, it was a new corporate structure that gave rise to a new regulatory regime. It was not until 1956 that BHCs were regulated in the US. The relationship of the group structure and regulation is a typical chicken and egg situation.[186] The regulator reacts based upon what the private sector structures, and at the same time, the private sector tries to organize itself in a way that is economically fit and less bureaucratic in nature, which may in turn make the regulator react to impede such innovation if it finds it would harm industry.

The next section will analyse the evolution of capital markets in the US.

The US and the Evolution of Capital Markets. The Inability of the Unit Banking System to Finance the Industry

Unlike Germany, where universal banks were strongly involved in the evolution and the development of industry, in the US, unit banks were unable to finance large-scale industrial firms.[187] However, in part due to branching restrictions, capital markets were key to the US after the Great Depression. As noted by Gordon and Judge, "Central to the US story was a mismatch between growing enterprises and a stunted banking system. Political choices led to a banking system populated primarily by small local banks that were ill suited to provide financing in the amounts, or with the risk, needed to fund the railroads and the follow-on industrial firm expansion. The bond market stepped in, creating national and international channels for debt and then equity finance".[188] The results of these restrictions were the growth of bond markets first and the growth of equities markets second. Gordon and Judge correctly stress, "The role of the law here was largely repressive, facilitating the growth of capital markets

[186] Chales Morris *The Law of Financial Services Groups* (OUP 2019), 31.

[187] Naomi R. Lamoreaux "Banks, Kinship, and Economic Development: The New England Case", *Journal of Economic History*, Vol. 46, No. 3 (1986), 647. See also Bodenhorn "Bank Chartering"; Vincent Carosso *The Morgans: Private International Bankers, 1854–1913* (1987).

[188] Jeffrey N. Gordon and Kathryn Judge "The Origins of a Capital Market Union in the United States" Working Paper No. 584, The Center for Law and Economic Studies Columbia University School of Law (2018), 1–28.

by limiting bank capacity".[189] Here we find a convincing explanation of the secondary effects of the law. While the intention of US lawmakers was to restrict bank branches, the unwanted result was that US big firms had to rely on syndicates and other forms of finance to substitute bank loans, which in turn developed the bond market first, and the equity market second.

On the other hand, the depression era "New Deal" laws strengthened these markets via: (i) a strong disclosure regime; (ii) a strong regulator and enforcer, the SEC; (iii) the separation of commercial and investment banking (GSA); (iv) the creation of investment banks; and v) weak state intervention on the issuance of debt and equity. Other legal changes further helped the capital market development in the US, such as: (i) the Trust Indenture Act of 1939, which protected bondholders from expropriation in restructurings[190]; (ii) the 1940 Investment Company Act[191] that regulated the mutual industry fund, which permitted retail investors to invest in a share of a pool of diversified credit portfolios; and iii) the Employee Retirement Security Act of 1974[192] (ERISA) which pooled pension funds out of banks.[193]

One example of the inability of unit banks to finance large enterprises was railroad finance. Railroad finance took place at the beginning of the 1820s. Most of the finance was in bonds and almost a third was foreign investment.[194] Since railroad finance was risky, rates were high.[195] Gordon and Judge believe the first "junk bonds" were railroad bonds. Moreover, banks were unable to diversify the risk in their loan portfolios and they were subject to bank runs because there was no lender of last resort system at the time.[196] The consequence was that

[189] Gordon and Judge "The Origins of a Capital Market", 2. See also Calomiris, "The Costs of rejecting Universal Banking", 287.

[190] 15 USC §§ 77aaa–77bbbb.

[191] 15 USC §§ 80a-1–80a-64.

[192] 29 USC ch 18.

[193] Gordon and Judge "The Origins of a Capital Market", 3.

[194] Ibid., 13.

[195] Kenneth Snowden, "Historical Returns and Security Market Development, 1872–1925", *Explorations in Economic History*, Vol. 27 (1990), 381.

[196] Gordon and. Judge "The Origins of a Capital Market", 13.

investment banks arranged bond issuance from a national and international "catchment area".[197] Investment banks realized that credit markets were more profitable than equity markets, so they had incentives to develop market-based mechanisms of credit intermediation mainly in the form of underwriting.[198] The separation of investment banking from commercial banking led investment banks to develop a securities market-based alternative to bank-based finance.[199] As European finance has shown, a universal bank with strong commercial lending activity will be "reluctant to cannibalize its existing business through market-finance innovations".[200]

Indeed, securities as a proportion of national assets in both the US and Germany show how the US had a long-lasting superiority in the mentioned ratio, which explains the importance of US capital markets and the underdevelopment of the German counterpart.[201] The mismatch between firm size in the US and US bank fragmentation has contributed to the expansion of the bond market in the US in comparison to Germany. This has also shown a bigger loan market in Germany than in the US.[202] As stated above, bank fragmentation in the US-induced firms to find alternative ways of funding since unit banks were unable to fund big firms. They had to rely on bank syndicates and bond issuance to finance their business. That was not the case in Germany, where universal banks were able and eager to finance German industry.

Data from Beck et al. indicates that Private Credit by Deposit Money Banks to GDP (%) is higher in Germany than in the US. The same data shows that the stock market total value traded to GDP (%) for the US is

197 Ibid.; Allan Morrison and William Wilhelm, *Investment Banking, Institutions, Politics and the Law* (OUP 2008), 121. Morrison and Wilhem explain, "The capital required by the railroads, and later by the industrials, was largely raised through bond issues. Capital accumulation in America was insufficient to cover her industrialization, and as a result, America was a substantial importer of capital throughout the nineteenth century. American bond issues were therefore marketed in England and Continental Europe, as well as at home".

198 Armour et al. "Principles", 438; Jeffrey Gordon "The Empty Call for Benefit–Cost Analysis in Financial Regulation" *The Journal of Legal Studies*, Vol. 43, No. S2 (2014), 360.

199 Gordon and Judge "The Origins of a Capital Market", 2.

200 Armour et al. "Principles", 438.

201 Goldsmith "Comparative National", 134.

202 Gordon and Judge "The Origins of a Capital Market", 14.

almost 250 while for Germany it is only 50. These figures show how today the influence of the German financial system continues to be broadly bank-based, whereas the US continues to be a market-based system.[203]

Bank Holding Company Regulation

In part as a reaction to chain and group banking, the BHCA[204] was enacted in 1956. The US Congress endorsed the BHCA "to prevent possible abuses related to the control of commercial credit"[205] and its underlying philosophy was "that bank holding companies ought to confine their activities to management and control of banks and that such activities should be consistent with the public interest".[206] As the SCOTUS affirms, the BHCA "restrains undue concentration of commercial banking resources and abuses of commercial credit by regulating the activities of bank holding companies".[207] Another aim of the BCHA was to prevent banks from de facto interstate banking, since banks have used holding company with different incorporated state banks to circumvent the McFadden Act of 1927.[208]

The BCHA defines BCHs as those that "own or control" one or more banks. Ownership or control of 25% of the voting shares fulfils this purpose, or less, if the FRB believes there is controlling influence.[209] The FRB needs to approve: (i) the formation of a BHC; (ii) the formation of a subsidiary of a BHC a subsidiary of a BHC; (iii) a BHC's acquisition

[203] Beck et al. "A New Database".

[204] 12 USC § 1841, et seq.

[205] S. Rep. No. 1084, 91st Cong., 2d Sess. 24, reprinted in 1970 US. CODE Cong. & Ad. News 5519, 5541.

[206] S. Rep. No. 1095, 84th Cong., 1st Sess. 2, reprinted in 1956 US. CODE Cong. & Ad. News 2482, 2483.

[207] United States Supreme Court *Board of Governors, Frs v Dimension Financial* (1986) No. 84–1274.

[208] Saule Omarova and Tahyar Margareth "That which we Call a Bank: Revisiting the History of Bank Holding Company Regulation in the United States" 31 Review of Banking and Financial Law (2011), 129; Carl. A. Sax and Marcus Sloan III "The Bank Holding Company Amendments of 1970" 39 George Washington Law Review (1970), 1200–1202.

[209] 12 USC § 1841.

of more than 5% of the shares of a bank; iv) a BHC's acquisition of bank assets and (v) the merger of a BHC.[210]

A BHC is "any company which has control over any bank or over any company that is or becomes a bank holding company by virtue of this chapter".[211] This definition includes corporations, partnerships, business trusts, associations, trusts in general with certain exceptions and similar organizations.[212] BHCs are regulated by the FRB and are subject to the BHCA and to FRB Regulation Y, which implies reporting and compliance obligations as well as minimum capital requirements.[213] BHCs need to act as a source of managerial and financial strength for their subsidiary banks.[214] The source of financial strength means the ability of a company that directly or indirectly owns or controls an insured depository institution to provide financial assistance to such insured depository institution in the event of the financial distress of the insured depository institution.[215]

Because of prosperity in the 1960s and the eagerness of bank shareholders for growth and diversification, there was a surge of bank holding companies in 1967–1969, which augmented the conglomerate merger activity. Congress responded with the Bank Holding Company Amendments of 1970, which limited BHCs and their subsidiaries to activities that

[210] Lovett and Mallow "Banking and Financial Institutions Law", 221.

[211] 12 USC § 1841. 12 USC § 1841(b).

[212] 12 USC§ 1841(b) and 12 CFR§ 225.2(d).

[213] Regulation Y. Electronic Code of Federal Regulations.https://www.ecfr.gov/cgi-bin/text-idx?SID=0964d00e9d961703ad24e97c80394fe5&mc=true&node=pt12.3.225&rgn=div5. Accessed 2 April 2023.

[214] 12 U.S. Code § 1831o–1.

[215] 12 USC § 1831o-1(f); See also Christine M. Bradley and Kenneth D. Jones, "Loss Sharing Rules for Bank Holding Companies: An Assessment of the Federal Reserve's Source-of-Strength Policy and the FDIC's Cross Guarantee Authority" 17(4) Financial Markets, Institutions & Instruments (2008), 249–286; Paul Lee "The Source-Of-Strength Doctrine: Revered and Revisited—Part I" The Banking Law Journal (2012), 771; Paul Lee, "The Source-Of-Strength Doctrine: Revered and Revisited—Part II" The Banking Law Journal (2012), 867; See also Adam Ashcraft "Are Bank Holding Companies a Source of Strength to Their Banking Subsidiaries?" Journal of Money, Credit and Banking (2008); Steven Meyerowitz, "The Source-of-Strength Doctrine" The Banking Law Journal (2012); Steven Meyerowitz, "The Source-of-Strength Doctrine—Part II" The Banking Law Journal (2012).

are "incident to banking or managing or controlling banks".[216] From the 1980s, the Federal Reserve and the OCC have permitted BHCs to perform different activities such as the underwriting of commercial paper, securitization products and even some kind of insurance underwriting.

BCHA Section 4 and Regulation Y limit BHCs' scope of non-bank permissible activities. Permissible non-bank activities for BHCs include activities "closely related to banking" and other activities permitted by statute. The FRB has established a list of activities that are "closely related to banking". They include: (i) extending credit and servicing loans; (ii) activities related to extending credit; (iii) leasing personal or real property; (iv) operating non-bank depository institutions (industrial banking and savings associations); (v) trust company functions; (vi) financial and investment advisory activities; (vii) agency transactional services for customer investments (including securities brokerage); (viii) investment transactions as principal such as underwriting and dealing in government obligations and money market instruments; (ix) management consulting and counselling activities; (x) support services; xi) certain insurance agency and underwriting services (credit insurance and finance company subsidiary); (xii) community development activities; (xiii) money orders, savings bonds and traveller's checks services; and (xiv) data processing services.[217]

For many years, the FRB has excluded land development, real estate intermediation and travel agencies, among others.[218] Finally, in 1999, Congress passed the GLBA that allowed financial holding companies (FHCs) to operate in banking, insurance and securities markets.[219] Today virtually all big groups are registered as FHCs. While FHCs are regulated by the Federal Reserve System, the GLBA provides for functional regulation of an FHC's non-bank financial subsidiaries (i.e., broker-dealer

[216] Lovett and Mallow "Banking and Financial Institutions Law", 221.

[217] 12 CFR§ 225.28 (b) (1)-(14).

[218] Lovett and Mallow "Banking and Financial Institutions Law", 225.

[219] Kevin J. Stiroh and Adrienne Rumble "The Dark Side of Diversification: The Case of US Financial Holding Companies" *Journal of Banking & Finance*, Vol. 30, No. 8 (2006), 2131–2161; Frederick Furlong "The Gramm–Leach–Bliley Act and Financial Integration" FRBSF Economic Letter, (2000), 2000–2010.

subsidiaries of a FHC are primarily regulated by the SEC, and insurance subsidiaries by state insurance regulators).[220]

As stated above, the GLBA changed the landscape of the US banking industry since it removed many restrictions on the scope of permitted activities of BHCs. An FHC is a bank holding company that meets certain requirements. First, all depository institutions "controlled by the bank holding company must be and remain well capitalized" and well managed. Second, the BHC must have made an effective election to become an FHC.[221]

The main difference between the BHC and the FHC is that the latter may engage in a broader scope of permissible activities. These include all the activities that a BHC may engage in, and activities "financial in nature or incidental to such financial activity" or "complementary to a financial activity [that] does not pose a substantial risk to the safety or soundness of depository institutions or the financial system generally".[222]

The advantages of an FHC over a BHC may be summarized as following: an FHC may engage in activities that are banking or closely related to banking; financial in nature or complementary to financial activity while a BHC may not.[223]

According to statue, certain activities are regarded as "financial in nature" such as lending, acting as an agent or broker in life, health, property and casualty insurance, providing advisory services, securities underwriting or dealing, operating a travel agency or organizing a mutual fund, among others.[224]

The FRB may approve certain limited commercial activities that are complementary to financial activities only when "[t]he proposal could be expected to produce benefits to the public that outweigh possible

[220] Dafna Avraham, Patricia Selvaggi, and James Vickery "A Structural View of U.S. Bank Holding Companies" FRBNY Economic Policy Review (2012), 67.

[221] 12 CFR § 225.81.

[222] 12 U.S. Code § 1843 (k) (1) (A) (B); *Financial Holding Companies: Business Activities and Regulation ID 1–526-1845* (Practical Law, Thomson Reuters 2019). See also 12 U.S. Code § 1843 (k); Also, the FHC may engage in finders' activities (12 C.F.R. § 225.86(d) (1)).

[223] 12 US Code § 1843 (k) (1); *Finance Fundamentals: Bank Holding Company v Financial Holding Company* (Practical Law Note 7-521-7963, Thomson Reuters 2019).

[224] 12 CFR 225.86(b).

adverse effects"[225] and the proposal "does not pose a substantial risk to the safety or soundness of depository institutions or the financial system generally".[226]

One of the main activities that the GLBA permitted to an FHC is merchant banking. The merchant banking rule authorizes an FHC to "directly or indirectly and as principal or on behalf of one or more persons, to acquire or control any amount of shares, assets or ownership interests of a company or other entity that is engaged in any activity not otherwise authorized for the financial holding company under section 4 of the Bank Holding Company Act".[227] An FHC may invest directly (via portfolio company investments) or indirectly (via private equity funds). The merchant banking authority does not include investing in financial companies, since this is regulated under different sections of the BHCA.[228] When investing directly, FHCs are required to control a broker-dealer registered by the SEC, or control an insurance underwriter and a registered investment adviser.[229] However, an FHC and "any subsidiary (other than a depository institution or subsidiary of a depository institution) may acquire or control merchant banking investments".[230] Pursuant to 12 CFR § 225.170, merchant banking activity is "not permitted unless it is part of a bona fide underwriting or merchant or investment banking activity".[231]

The FHC structure is well suited for FCs because it allows engaging in all three financial activities, but may not be the best suited structure for core banking structures. Indeed, in 2017, Bank of the Ozarks, Inc (a BHC) merged into Bank of the Ozarks (a wholly owned subsidiary) because "the Company currently operates as the bank holding company of the Bank and conducts substantially all of its business through the Bank. The Company believes the reorganization will further improve the

[225] 12 CFR § 225.89 (b) (3).

[226] 12 U.S. Code § 1843 (k) (1) (A) (B); *Financial Holding Companies: Business Activities and Regulation* ID 1-526-1845 (Practical Law, Thomson Reuters, 2019).

[227] 12 CFR § 225.170.

[228] *Private Equity Investments by Banks (Merchant Banking) Other Methods of Making Private Equity Investments* ID 2-506-0525 (Practical Law, Thomson Reuters 2019).

[229] 12 USC § 1843(k); 12 CFR § 225.170 f (1); Private *Equity Investments by Banks (Merchant Banking) Other Methods of Making Private Equity Investments*, ibid.

[230] 12 CFR § 225.170 (d).

[231] Bank Holding Companies and Change in Bank Control. A Rule by the Federal Reserve System and the Treasury Department on 01/31/2001, 66 FR 8465.

combined entity's efficiency by eliminating redundant corporate infrastructure and activities as well as the associated supervision and oversight from the Federal Reserve Board ('FRB') applicable to registered bank holding companies"[232](Fig. 5.1 and 5.2).

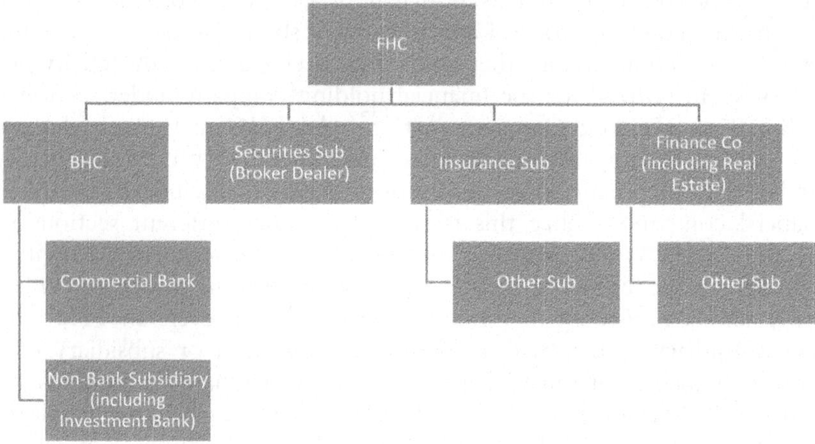

Fig. 5.1 Typical FHC structure (*Source* Federal Reserve Bank of Dallas[233])

Fig. 5.2 Typical simplified BHC structure (*Source* Federal Reserve Annual Report of Holding Companies-FR Y-6 for Merchants and Manufacturers Bank Corporation[234])

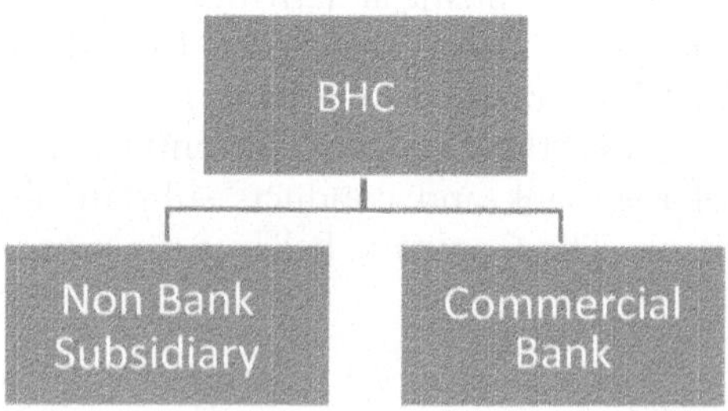

[232] SEC SCHEDULE 14A Proxy Statement Pursuant to Section 14(a) of the Securities Exchange Act of 1934, 5 May 2017.

[233] Richard W. Fisher "Ending 'Too Big to Fail': A Proposal for Reform Before It's Too Late" Federal Reserve Bank of Dallas (2013).

[234] Chicago Federal Reserve FR Y6. Merchants and Manufacturers is a typical example of a simple, one-state BHC structure.

5.2 US Banking System

Because of the federal nature of the US banking system, the banking institutions in America differ from their counterparts in Germany and most European systems. First, this is because of the dual banking system which comprises national and state banks. Second, this is because throughout US history, the GSA created de facto specialized financial institutions, with a universal banking model only arising after the GSA was eliminated in the 1990s. Third, this is because the US comprises a net of different regulators and supervisors which make the US's regulation of banking one of the most complex in the world.

This first section will analyse what a bank is. The second section will examine the structure of the US banking system.

What Is the "Business of Banking"?

In order to analyse what a bank is, this book will first examine the meaning of the phrase "business of banking". This phrase first appeared in the NYFBA, which provides: Such association shall have power to carry on the *business of banking*, discounting bills, notes and other evidences of debt, by receiving deposits, by buying and selling the gold and silver bullion, foreign coins and bills of exchange, in the manner specified in their articles of association for the purposes authorized by this act; by loaning money on real and personal security; and by exercising such incidental powers as shall be necessary to carry on such business.[235]

The NBA copies the text of the NYBA but adds the phrase "by obtaining and issuing circulating notes in accordance with the provisions of this Act".[236] This change did not alter substantially the NYFBA. The aim of the NBA was to persuade state banks to turn into national banks to create a national currency, to finance war via the placement of federal bonds and the use of national banks as depositories.[237] In 1995 the SCOTUS in *Nations Bank of North Carolina, N.A. v Variable Annuity Life Ins. Co* (VALIC) held the "'business of banking' is not limited to the enumerated powers in § 24 Seventh and that the [OCC] therefore

[235] Ch 260 § 18, 1838 N.Y Laws 245–249.

[236] Act of June 20, 1874, ch 343, §1, 18 Stat 123.

[237] Symons et al. "Banking Law", 29; Hammond "Jackson, Biddle and the Bank", 724.

has discretion to authorize activities beyond those specifically enumerated", provided that the OCC's discretion is exercised "within reasonable bounds".[238] After VALIC the OCC proposed the following test:

> "Judicial cases affirming OCC interpretations establish that an activity is within the scope of this authority [12 U.S.C. § 24(Seventh)] if the activity: (1) is functionally equivalent to or a logical outgrowth of a traditional banking activity; (2) would respond to customer needs or otherwise benefit the bank or its customers; and (3) involve risks similar to those already assumed by banks."[239]

The OCC believes, "The business of banking is an evolving concept and the permissible activities of national banks similarly evolve over time. The same holds true concerning the permissible activities of federal savings associations, subject to the applicable statutory limitations".[240] However, the SCOTUS did not address "whether the 'business of banking' includes certain essential functions, such as deposit taking, the performance of which is fundamental to the statute's purpose".[241] According to Alter, as the NBA is based on the NYFBA, it "adopted the cluster of ideas that were attached to each borrowed word in the body of learning from which it was taken".[242] Therefore, in order to examine whether there are essential functions that define the *business of banking*, the interpreter must find help in New York case law from before 1838. Several cases demonstrate how essential deposit taking was to the *business of banking*.[243] Symons concludes "the definition of the business of banking" as deposit taking, credit granting and credit exchange, though analytically

[238] *Nations Bank of North Carolina, N.A. v Variable Annuity Life Ins. Co.*, 513 U.S. 251, 258 n.2 (1995).

[239] OCC Interpretive Letter No. 684 (4 August 1995).

[240] OCC "Activities Permissible for National Banks and Federal Savings Associations, Cumulative" (2017).

[241] Daniel Alter "The 'Business of Banking'in New York—An Historical Impediment To the OCC's Proposed National 'Fintech Charter"' (2017) 36 Yale J. on Reg.: Notice & Comment. http://yalejreg.com/nc/the-business-of-banking-in-new-york-an-historical-impediment-to-the-occs-proposed-national-fintech-charter-by-daniel-s-alter/. Accessed 22 March 2023.

[242] *Sekhar v United States*, 570 U.S., 133 S. Ct. 2720, 2724 (2013).

[243] See for example *People ex rel. Attorney General v Utica Insurance Co.*, 15 Johns. 358, 390 (Sup. Ct. 1818); *People v Manhattan Co.*, 9 Wend. 351, 383 (Sup. Ct. 1832).

simple, is a key-stone in any principled elaboration of permissible banking activities".[244]

At a federal level, several cases show the centrality of deposit taking. The *McGough v Jamison* judgement stated that "[t]he very nature of the business of banking is to invite the deposits".[245] In *Commonwealth v Bilotta*, the judgement understood that "receiving deposits is…manifestly germane to and… universally associated with the business of banking".[246] The SCOTUS in *Oulton v. German Savings & Loan Society* held that "[s]trictly speaking the word bank implies a place for deposit of money, as that is the most obvious purpose of such an institution. Originally the business of banking consisted only in receiving deposits…"[247] These cases show the importance of the deposit taking function in the US, so that colloquially banks are denominated "depository institutions" whereas in the EU the common term for banks is "credit institution".[248]

As stated in Chapter One, banking business was defined by the SCOTUS in *Austen v United States Bank of New York* as a list approach.

What is a Bank?

After 1956 many statutory definitions have emerged, starting with the BHCA and ending with the Competitive Equality Banking Act of 1987 (CEBA). The evolution of the statutory definition of a bank for BHCA purposes starts with the original BHCA of 1956 and follows this path[249]: (1) the original BHCA of 1956; (2) the 1966 BHCA Amendments[250]; (3) the 1970 BHCA Amendments[251]; and (4) the CEBA of 1987.[252]

[244] Symons et al. "Banking Law", 726.

[245] *McGough v Jamison*, 107 Pa. 336, 339 (1884).

[246] *Commonwealth v Bilotta*, 61 Pa. Super. 264, 267 (1915).

[247] *Oulton v German Savings & Loan Society*, 84 U.S. 109, 118 (1872).

[248] Under US federal law, "Depository Institution" is defined under 12 USC § 1813, and "Credit Institution" is defined in point (1) of Article 4(1) of the CRR.

[249] Omarova and Tahyar "That Which We Call a Bank", 115.

[250] Act of July 1, 1966, Pub, L. No. 89–485§ 3 (c), 80 Stat. 236, 236 (1966) Codified at 12 USC § 1841 (c) 2010.

[251] BHCA Amendments of 1970, Pub. L- No 91–607, § 101 (a) 84 Stat. 1760 236 (1970).

[252] Competitive Equality Banking Act of 1987, Pub. L. No. 100–86, § 101 Stat. 552, 554 (1987).

The original BHCA defined a bank "simply on the formal charter".[253] A bank is "[a]ny national banking association or any State bank, savings bank or trust company".[254] It expressly excluded Edge Act and Agreement Corporations[255] from the definition. Initially the BHCA-regulated holding companies that hold two or more banks.[256] Congress enacted the BHCA "to prevent possible abuses related to the control of commercial credit"[257] and its underlying philosophy was "that bank holding companies ought to confine their activities to management and control of banks and that such activities should be consistent with the public interest".[258] As the SCOTUS affirms, the BHCA "restrains undue concentration of commercial banking resources and abuses of commercial credit by regulating the activities of bank holding companies".[259] Another aim of the BCHA was to prevent banks from de facto interstate banking, since banks have used the holding company with different incorporated state banks to circumvent the McFadden Act of 1927.[260]

The 1966 BHCA amendments changed the definition to include a *formula approach*. A bank "means any institution that accepts deposits that the depositor has a legal right to withdraw on demand".[261] This time the amendment excluded foreign branches and banking corporations authorized to do foreign banking business by the Federal Reserve

[253] Omarova andTahyar "That which we Call a Bank", 115–116.

[254] Bank Holding Company Act of 1956, Pub. L. No 84–511 §§ 1–12, 70 Stat 143, 135 (1956).

[255] An Edge Act and Agreement Corporation is a subsidiary of a bank or financial holding company that is authorized by the Federal Reserve to conduct foreign banking activities. (Section 25A of the Federal Reserve Act).

[256] Catherine L. McIntyre, "The Nonbank Bank Loophole to the Bank Holding Company Act of 1956–The Need for Congressional Action" 37 Alabama Law Review (1986), 713.

[257] S. Rep. No. 1084, 91st Cong., 2d Sess. 24, reprinted in 1970 US. CODE Cong. & Ad. News 5519, 5541.

[258] S. Rep. No. 1095, 84th Cong., 1st Sess. 2, reprinted in 1956 US. CODE Cong. & Ad. News 2482, 2483.

[259] United States Supreme Court, *Board of Governors, Frs v Dimension Financial* (1986) No. 84–1274.

[260] Omarova and Tahyar "That Which We Call a Bank", 129; Carl A. Sax and Marcus Sloan III "The Bank Holding Company Amendments of 1970", *George Washington Law Review*, Vol. 39 (1970), 1200–1202.

[261] S. Rep. 89–1179, 89th Cong., 2d Sess. 7 (1966).

System. The aim of the 1966 amendments was to exclude "institutions like industrial banks and nondeposit trust companies".[262] Instead of excluding explicitly industrial banks and non-deposit trust companies from the definition of a bank, the US Congress changed the entire definition to include a new test. This new test permitted certain subsidiaries to perform commercial and de facto banking activities as long as they do not accept deposits that may be withdraw on demand.

The main factor that drove the 1970 amendments was the desire to regulate the one-bank holding company, which was not included in the original BHCA.[263] The one-bank holding company combined not only a bank under the holding company but also other commercial or non-financial banks, in what was called "congenerics" or groups centred around a bank with interstate presence.[264] Edwards announced, "in 1968 a sudden- change occurred: most of our largest banks decided to form holding companies. First National City Bank of New York, Chase Manhattan, Bank of America, and six more of the twelve largest banks in the country either formed or announced plans to form one-bank holding companies".[265] Representative Patman expressed that "the entire structure of the American economy is being changed through conglomerates centered on banking institutions. This is clearly a threat to everyone-both inside and outside the financial community-and it is essential that the Congress act quickly to provide meaningful remedies".[266]

Again, the bank definition was reformulated to add a second element to the *formula approach*:

262 Ibid.

263 Paul Nadler *"The One-Bank Holding Company" Banking* (1968), 804; Franklin Edwards "The One-Bank Holding Company Conglomerate: Analysis and Evaluation" 22 Vand. L. Rev. (1969), 1275.

264 Carter H. Golembe "One-Bank Holding Companies" in Herbert Prochnow, *The One-Bank Holding Company* (1969), 66–71.

265 Edwards "The One-Bank Holding Company", 1275.

266 115 CONG. REC. 902 (daily ed. Feb. 17, 1969) cited by Edwards "The One-Bank Holding Company", 1275.

> 'Bank' means any institution organized under the laws of the United States, ... which (1) accepts deposits that the depositor has a legal right to withdraw on demand, and (2) engages in the business of making commercial loans.[267]

In practical terms, the 1970 amendments only excluded one institution, the Boston Safe Deposit and Trust Company.[268] As the formula expressed the conjunction "*and*", any subsidiary that engages in either accepting deposits with the legal right to withdraw *or* making commercial loans would not be subject to the BHCA. The consequence of this new definition was the creation of the so-called non-bank banks, which could offer banking and non-banking services, something that was prohibited for BHCs.[269]

In 1987 the Congress passed the CEBA, and this changed the bank definition for the third time. It defined a bank as an institution that:

> (i) accepts demand deposits or deposits that the depositor may withdraw by check or similar means for payment to third parties or others; and (ii) is engaged in the business of making commercial loans.

Consequently, the "non-bank banks" that were born from the 1970 BHCA amendments that were not grandfathered by them became banks.[270] As per the aforementioned bank definition, the FDIA defines insured bank as "any bank (including a foreign bank having an insured branch) the deposits of which are insured in accordance with the provisions of this Act".[271]

The list of insured banks is quite long. However, the CEBA explicitly excluded certain financial institutions from the definition of a bank; most importantly certain foreign banks, insured associations that include federal savings associations or federal saving banks, building and loan associations, trust companies, credit unions, credit card banks and industrial

[267] BHCA Amendments of 1970, Pub. L- No 91-607, § 101 (a) 84 Stat. 1760 236 (1970).

[268] Executive Session: Tuesday 13 June 1970 Hearing before the S. Comm. On Banking and Currency 91st Cong. 10 (1970).

[269] Omarova and Tahyar "That Which We Call a Bank", 142.

[270] Ibid.

[271] 12 USC. 1813(h).

banks. The main reasons for the exclusion of these financial institutions were the small size of these institutions, the fact that they were specialized in a limited range of activities and centred on consumer financial services.[272]

From a size perspective, FDIC-insured institutions in the US have been falling from 1984 from almost 18,000 to less than 6,000 in 2018. However, the total assets held by these institutions have been climbing from 337,412,063 million in 1984 to 17,943,122,396 million in 2018. According to the FDIC, the whole insured system employs more than 2 million people.[273]

A classical classification of depository institutions in the US comprises commercial banks, thrifts and credit unions.[274] Other non-bank institutions include industrial loan companies and industrial banks, credit card banks and limited purpose trust companies. A separate chapter deals with foreign banks doing business on US soil. An analysis of these institutions follows.

Commercial Banks

Using a parallel classification of the "three pillar structure" of German banks, the US banking system may be studied following a similar pattern, analysing commercial banks, followed by thrifts and credit unions.

Commercial banks may obtain a federal charter (national banks) or state (state banks). As stated above, national banks are full-service insured commercial banks chartered under the NBA. National banks are permitted to engage in general banking activities including deposit taking and lending,[275] investing in real property for their own business purposes,[276] acting as a finder,[277] personal property leasing,[278] providing

[272] Omarova and Tahyar "That Which We Call a Bank", 153.

[273] FDIC Quarterly Banking Profile. https://www.fdic.gov/bank/analytical/qbp/. Accessed 20 March 2023.

[274] Mark Labonte "Who Regulates Whom? An Overview of the U.S. Financial Regulatory Framework" (2017) Congressional Research Service; Rajesh Kumar, *Strategies of Banks and Other Financial Institutions: Theories and Cases* (Elsevier 2014), 189.

[275] 12 USC § 24 (Seventh) and 12 USC§ 371.

[276] 12 USC § 29 (First).

[277] 12 USC § 24 (Seventh).

[278] 12 USC § 24 (Seventh and Tenth).

consulting and advice,[279] corresponding banking services and payment services[280] and derivative contracts, among others.

A limitation on commercial banks activities is that national banks are subject to lending limits to one borrower. In the case of unsecured loans and extension of credit, the limit is 15% of banks' unimpaired capital and surplus. In the case of secured loans, the limit is 10%.[281] State banks are chartered by the state and are subject to the banking law of the state in which they are chartered. The scope of permissible activities is determined also by state law.

A second limitation is that "an insured State bank may not engage as principal in any type of activity that is not permissible for a national bank" under certain conditions.[282]

A third limitation is that national banks may not engage generally in underwriting and dealing in securities.[283] Regarding investments in "bank eligible securities", national banks may invest in certain government securities.[284] The amount of investments in marketable debt securities may not "exceed at any time 10 per centum of its capital stock actually paid in and unimpaired and 10 per centum of its unimpaired surplus fund".[285] However, commercial banks may engage in buying and selling securities on behalf of their customers.[286] Additionally, national banks may enter into derivative transactions as principal when the bank may "lawfully purchase and sell the underlying instrument or product for its own account as a dealer or marketmaker" or when it uses the derivative to hedge the risks arising from permissible activities, among other circumstances.[287] Moreover, the OCC affirms that banks may buy and

[279] 12 USC § 24 (Seventh).

[280] Commercial Banking (Practical Law Note 2-5070807) (Thomson Reuters 2019).

[281] 12 USC § 84.

[282] 12 USC § 1831a.

[283] 12 USC § 24 (Seventh) and 12 USC § 335.

[284] 12 USC § 24 (Seventh).

[285] According to 12 USC§ 24 (Seventh).

[286] *Securities Industry Assoc. v Comptroller of the Currency*, 577 F.Supp. 252 (D.C. Cir. 1985).

[287] *Risk Management of Financial Derivatives, Comptroller's Handbook* (OCC, 1997). https://www.occ.treas.gov/publications/publications-by-type/comptrollers-handbook/risk-mgmt-financial-derivatives/pub-ch-risk-mgmt-financial-derivatives.pdf. Accessed 3 November 2023.

"take physical possession" of certain equity securities in order to hedge "customer-driven equity derivative transactions" when certain safeguards are in place.[288]

A fourth limitation is that national banks and their subsidiaries may not "provide insurance in a State as principal except that this prohibition shall not apply to authorized products"[289] within certain exceptions.[290] They are also not allowed generally to underwrite or sell title insurance.[291] However, national banks may engage in certain insurance activities, both as agent and as principal, i.e., they act as agents and sell most kinds of insurance in populations of less than 5,000 inhabitants.

From a size perspective, the most important group of insured institutions are commercial banks. The larger commercial banks in terms of consolidated assets are JP Morgan, Bank of America, Wells Fargo, Citibank, US Bank, PNC, Capital One, Toronto-Dominion Bank (TD), Bank of New York Mellon and State Street, among others. The US has 4,687 commercial banks. One reason for the large number of commercial banks stems from the restrictions in the establishment of branches in the past, which made a unique "unit bank system", which has permitted a proliferation of many commercial banks along the US geography. The industry reacted with financial innovations such as the BHCs, which were excluded from branching restrictions. "The growth of bank holding companies has been dramatic over the past three decades. Today bank holding companies own almost all large banks, and more than 90% of all commercial bank deposits are held in banks owned by holding companies". One explanation for the fall in the number of commercial banks in the US is to be found in bank consolidation.[292] It has also been imposed

[288] *Permissible Securities Activities of Commercial Banks Under the Glass-Steagall Act (GSA) and the Gramm-Leach-Bliley Act (GLBA)* (Congressional Research Service, 2010), 12.

[289] 15 USC 6712.

[290] 15 USC 6712.

[291] 15 USC 6713 (a).

[292] Frederic Mishkin *The Economics of Money, Banking, and Financial Markets* (Pearson Education Limited 2016), 296.

by the regulatory authorities post GFC, as exemplified in the Bank of America—Merrill Lynch merger.[293]

Commercial Bank Subsidiaries
Commercial banks may form subsidiaries. US banking regulation recognizes two different types of commercial bank subsidiaries: operating subsidiaries and financial subsidiaries.

Operating subsidiaries of a national bank may conduct "activities that are permissible for a national bank to engage in directly either as part of, or incidental to, the business of banking, as determined by the OCC".[294]

An operating subsidiary of a national bank may take the legal form of a corporation, limited liability company, limited partnership or similar. It will be an operating subsidiary if: the bank has control of the management of the subsidiary; or the bank owns or control more than 50% of the voting interest, or the bank otherwise controls the operating subsidiary "and no other party controls a percentage of the voting interest of the operating subsidiary greater than the bank's interest"; and "the operating subsidiary is consolidated with the bank under generally accepted accounting principles (GAAP)".[295]

Financial subsidiaries may be subject to both national and state law. An important feature of financial subsidiaries is that they are permitted to perform certain securities and insurance activities not permitted to banks.[296] The financial subsidiary may engage only in activities that are "financial in nature" or "incidental to a financial activity" and activities that are permitted for national banks to engage in directly.[297] However, the same statute restricts the scope of permitted actives of financial subsidiaries since the following activities are forbidden: (i) "insuring, guaranteeing, or indemnifying against loss, harm, damage, illness, disability,

[293] Michael Morris and Eric Anicich "Bank of America and Merrill Lynch Merger" (2015) Columbia Business School Case Works https://www8.gsb.columbia.edu/caseworks/node/534/Bank%20of%20America%20and%20Merrill%20Lynch%20Merger. Accessed 30 November 2023.

[294] 12 CFR § 5.34.

[295] 12 CFR § 5.34 (e) (2).

[296] 12 USC § 24a (a) (2) (A) and 12 USC § 1831w; Commercial Banking (Practical Law Note 2-5070807).

[297] 12 USC 24a (a) (2)(A).

or death" and (ii) "real estate development or real estate investment activities, unless otherwise expressly authorized by law".[298]

The requirements for having a financial subsidiary are that the national bank and each depository affiliate are well capitalized and well managed and that the "the aggregate consolidated total assets of all financial subsidiaries of the national bank do not exceed the lesser of 45% of the consolidated total assets of the parent bank or USD 50,000,000,000".[299]

Financial subsidiaries may take the same legal forms as a BHC including LLCs.[300]

Thrifts

"Thrifts" or savings institutions include savings banks, savings associations (former "S&Ls") and cooperative banks.[301] Thrifts were born as state-chartered institutions with the purpose of encouraging savings and to "help persons belonging to a deserving class, whose earnings and (were) small, and with whom the slowness of accumulation discourage (d) the effort...to become...owners of homesteads".[302]

Federal regulation of thrifts was designed as a separate legal framework from commercial banking, since its aim was to encourage home ownership. The Federal Loan Act of 1932 established the Federal Home Loan Bank System (FHLBS, which was a source of liquidity for S&Ls.[303] During the Great Depression 1,700 of these institutions failed,[304] inducing a new regulatory regime under the Home Owners'

[298] 12 USC 24a (a) (2)(A) and12 CFR § 5.39(e) and (f).

[299] 12 USC § 24a.(a)(2) and 12 CFR § 5.39(g).

[300] 12 CFR § 5.39 (d)(3).

[301] Lovett and Mallow "Banking and Financial Institutions Law", 271; Ayadi et al. "Investigating diversity", 27–29; See Julie L. Williams and Scot Zesch, *Savings Institutions: Mergers, Acquisitions and Conversions* (Law Journal Press 2010).

[302] Lisa Broom and Jerry Markham, *Regulation of Bank Financial Service Activities* (4th ed, 2011), 73; Omarova et al. "That which we Call a Bank", 179.

[303] The Federal Home Loan Bank Act, Pub.L. 72–304, 47 Stat. 725; Alane Moysich, *History of the Eighties: Lessons for the Future*. Vol. 1, *An Examination of the Banking Crises of the 1980s and Early 1990s* (FDIC 1997) 170.

[304] Ibid.

Loan Act of 1933 (HOLA).[305] The HOLA empowered the FHLBB to regulate and charter S&Ls.[306] Congress specified a thrift's purpose in Section 5 "to provide for the financing of homes".[307]

As the US system is federal in nature, there are state thrifts and federal thrifts. Pursuant to the FDIA "Savings association" means "any Federal savings association; or any 'State savings association'"; "any corporation that functions as a thrift according to the OCC".[308] Federal saving associations are chartered "giving primary consideration of the best practices of thrift institutions in the United States. The lending and investment powers conferred by this section are intended to encourage such institutions to provide credit for housing safely and soundly".[309] The aim of thrifts is "the extension of credit for homes and other goods and services".[310] Federal savings associations may "raise funds through such deposit, share, or other accounts, including demand deposit accounts...and issue passbooks, certificates, or other evidence of accounts".[311]

A limitation of savings association activities is that they may not deal in lottery tickets or deal in bets.[312] Law restricts the scope of permissible activities of federal saving associations. Federal savings associations may not permit overdrafts.[313] In addition, the loan authority is restricted because some loans are limited to a certain percentage of assets, e.g., commercial loans (20%) and non-residential real property loans (400% of federal savings capital), among others.[314]

The original HOLA restricted thrifts' activities from accepting deposits: "No deposits shall be accepted and no certificates of indebtedness shall be issued except for such borrowed money as may be authorized

[305] Home Owners' Loan Act of 1933, Pub. L. No 73–43, 48 Stat. 128 (1933).

[306] Moysich "History of the Eighties", 170.

[307] HOLA Original Act, s 5.

[308] 12 USC § 1813 (b) (1).

[309] 12 USC § 1464 (a) 2.

[310] 12 USC § 1464 (a).

[311] 12 U.S. C. § 1464 (b) (1)(a)(i).

[312] 12 USC § 1463 (e) 1.

[313] 12 USC § 1464 ((b) B).

[314] 12 USC § 1464 (c) (2) (A) and (B).

by regulations of the Board".[315] It also restricted their permitted loans mainly to secured residential mortgages.[316] However, in 1980 when the US Congress passed the Depository Institutions Deregulation and Monetary Control Act, thrifts were permitted to make commercial loans, offer NOW accounts and issue credit cards.[317] In 1982, the Garn-St Germain Depository Institutions Act broadened the scope of permissible activities by permitting raising capital in the form of savings deposits, shares and other accounts.[318]

A second limitation for thrifts is that the FSA is required to be a qualified thrift lender (QTL) by HOLA.[319] The FSA must hold "qualified thrift investments (QTI) equal to at least 65 percent of the FSA's portfolio assets".[320] QTI examples are: loans to purchase, refinance, construct, improve or repair domestic residential or manufactured housing; real estate owned; home equity loans; securities backed by domestic residential or manufactured housing; and federal home loan bank stock, among others.[321]

The FSA may sell insurance through service corporations on an agency basis without geographic restriction.[322] It may also engage in securities brokerage only via a service corporation, and on agency basis.[323] A federal savings association may generally engage in transactions involving a financial derivative if it is authorized to invest in the corresponding underlying assets, and the transaction is "safe and sound".[324]

[315] HOLA Original Act, s 5 (b).

[316] HOLA Original Act, s 5 (c).

[317] Depository Institutions Deregulation and Monetary Control Act of 1980, Pub, L. 96–221§ 401–402 94 Stat. 132, 151–156 (1980); Omarova et al. "That which we Call a Bank", 180.

[318] Garn-St Germain Depository Institutions Act, Pub.L. 97–320, § 312, 96 Stat 1469 (1982) (codified as amended at 12 USC § 1464).

[319] 12 USC § 1467 a(m).

[320] OCC, "Comptroller's Handbook, Safety and Soundness" (2013).

[321] Ibid.

[322] 12 CFR § 559.4 (f) (3).

[323] 12 CFR § 545.74.

[324] 12 CFR 563.172.

The deregulation movement resulted in an S&L crisis in the 1980s.[325] During 1981–1983, 118 S&Ls failed, costing the FSLIC an "estimated $3.5 billion to resolve". Tangible net worth for the S&L industry "was virtually zero", "having fallen from 5.3 percent of assets in 1980 to only 0.5 percent of assets in 1982". One of the reasons of the S&L crisis was the "interest-rate mismatch of the institutions balance sheets".[326] The US government proved to be ill-prepared to solve the S&L crisis.[327] This was in part because there were not enough resources to close insolvent S&Ls. As thrifts were allowed to take the form of mutual saving associations or stock owned thrifts, during the 1980s thousands of mutual thrifts converted into stock owned thrifts.[328] Deregulation had unintended consequences. "The devastating consequences of adding many new institutions to the marketplace, expanding the powers of thrifts, decontrolling interest rates, and increasing deposit insurance coverage, coupled with

[325] Omarova et al. "That Which We Call a Bank", 180; FDICIA. See also generally, James Adams, *The Big Fix: Inside the S&L Scandal: How an Unholy Alliance of Politics and Money Destroyed America's Banking System* (Wiley Publishers 1990); Annual Survey Issue "Financial Institutions and Regulations, the S&L Crisis: Death and Transfiguration" (1991) 59 Fordham Law Review S1; Kathleen. Day, *S&L Hell: The People and the Politics Behind the $1 Trillion Savings and Loan Scandal* (W. W. Norton & Co. 1993); Richard De Soto and Lionelc Bascom *Bailout: The Bankrupting of America,* (Futura Press 1992); Ned Eichler, *The Thrift Debacle* (University of California Press 1989); Elisabeth Langston and Stephen Brandt, *Understanding the S&L Crisis: A Guide for Beginners and Congressmen* (Squeaky Wheel Press 1990); M. Lowy, *High Rollers: Inside the Savings and Loan Debacle* (Praeger Publishers 1991); Martin Mayer, *The Greatest-Ever Bank Robbery: The Collapse of the Savings and Loan Industry* (Charles Scribner's Sons 1990); Paul Pilzer, *Other People's Money: The Inside Story of the S&L Mess* (Simon and Schuster 1989); 'The S&L Crisis: A Chrono-Bibliography'. www.fdic.gov/resources/publications/s-and-l-crisis/index.html. Accessed 11 April 2023.

[326] FDICIA.

[327] National Commission on Financial Institution Reform, Recovery and Enforcement, "Origins and Causes", 32.

[328] Sinan Cebenoyan, Elisabeth Cooperman and Charles. A. Register "Ownership Structure, Charter Value, and Risk-Taking Behavior for Thrifts", *Financial Management*, Vol. 28, No. 1 (1999), 43–60; See generally Kenneth. A. Carow, Steven R. Cox and Diane M. Roden "The Role of Insider Influence in Mutual-to-Stock Conversions", *Journal of Money, Credit and Banking*, Vol. 39, No. 6 (2007); Fabio R. Chaddad, and Michael. L. Cook, "The Economics of Organization Structure Changes: A US Perspective on Demutualization", *Annals of Public and Cooperative Economics*, Vol. 75, No. 4 (2004); Lawrence R. Cordell, Gregor Mac Donald and Mark Wohar, "Corporate Ownership and the Thrift Crisis" *The Journal of Law & Economics*, Vol. 36, No. 2 (1993).

reducing regulatory standards and scrutiny, were not foreseen".[329] One consequence of the S&L crisis was that it induced new regulation by President George W. Bush in 1991, the FDICIA. It imposed federal banking agencies to take "prompt corrective supervisory actions" when an institution's capital declines, as well as imposed the FDIC to apply a resolution method "that minimizes the costs to taxpayers of a bank failure".[330]

Similar to commercial banks, HOLA-regulated thrift holding companies (THC). According to HOLA, "the term 'savings and loan holding company' means any company that directly or indirectly controls a savings association or that controls any other company that is a savings and loan holding company".[331] Before the GLBA, these companies could engage in "any type of activity (including insurance and manufacturing)."[332] However, the GLBA restricted the scope of their permitted activities to those activities permissible to BHCs,[333] to financial activities permitted for FHCs under certain requisites and others.[334] Nonetheless, certain grandfather unitary thrift companies may continue to engage in any activity as long as they meet certain conditions.[335]

The DFA eliminated the OTS and transferred its authority to the OCC and the Federal Reserve, and "by taking other steps effectively erase[d] regulatory differences between thrifts and banks".[336] Unitary thrift holding companies need to place all their financial activities in an "intermediate holding company" that is subject to regulation by the Federal Reserve System as an SLHC,[337] and the parent company will serve as a source of strength for the intermediate company.[338]

[329] FDICIA.

[330] Federal Deposit Insurance Corporation Improvement Act of 1991. Federal Reserve History. https://www.federalreservehistory.org/essays/fdicia. Accessed 21 January 2021.

[331] 12 USC §1467a(a)(D)(i). There are also some exceptions described under12 USC §1467a(a)(D)(ii).

[332] US Banking Law: Overview, Practical Law (2021).

[333] 12 USC §1467a(c)(2)(F)(i).

[334] 12 USC §1467a(c)(2)(H). 12 USC §1467a (c)(1)(B); 12 USC §1467a(c)(2)(F)(ii); 12 CFR § 238.53 (b) 12; 12 USC §1467a(e)(1)(A) (iii).

[335] 12 USC. § 1467a(c)(9)(C).

[336] Omarova et al. "That which we Call a Bank", 187.

[337] 12 U.S. Code § 1467b (b)(1) (A); ibid.

[338] 12 U.S. Code § 1467b (b) 3.

Also, in parallel with national banks' subsidiaries, thrifts may create their own "operative subsidiaries" and "service corporations". Operative subsidiaries may engage in the same activities as thrifts, while "service corporations" may engage in broad activities, such as business and professional services, credit-related activities, consumer services, securities activities, liquidity management and investments, among others.[339]

From a size perspective, thrifts have suffered the same trend as commercial banks. From 1990 to 2018, the number of insured savings banks has declined from 2,815 in 1990 to 691 in 2018.[340]

The third type of depositary institution in the US is the credit union.

Credit Unions

A credit union is a "non-profit financial cooperative"[341] and it has been described as a "member owned democratic institution … emphasising self-help and voluntarism".[342] Credit unions arose in the US in the first decades of the twentieth century to serve the needs of the working class.[343] The Bureau of Federal Credit Unions originally regulated credit unions in the US. In 1970, the newly created NCUA replaced the

[339] 12 CFR § 559.2, 559.3(e)(2) and 559.4.

[340] FDIC Statistics at a Glance. https://www.fdic.gov/bank/statistical/stats/. Accessed 10 April 2023.

[341] Nicholas Ryder "The Regulation of Credit Unions: A Comparative Analysis Between the USA and Great Britain" *Journal of Banking Regulation*, Vol. 6, No. 3 (2005), 261.

[342] Donal McKillop, J. Glass and Charles Ferguson "Investigating the Growth Performance of UK Credit Unions using Radial and Non-Radial Efficiency Measures" *Journal of Banking and Finance*, Vol. 26, No. 8 (2002), 1563–1591.

[343] Nicholas Ryder and Clare Chambers "The Credit Crunch-Are Credit Unions Able to Ride Out the Storm?" 11(1) Journal of Banking Regulation (2009), 76–86. US Supreme Court: "Credit unions were believed to enable the general public, which had been largely ignored by banks, to obtain credit at reasonable rates." Supreme Court, '*National Credit Union Administration, Petitioner, v First National Bank & Trust Co.*, et al.; *AT&T Family Federal Credit Union, et al., Petitioners, v First National Bank and Trust Co.*, et al., Decided 25 February 1998, Nos. 96–843, 96–847. 118 S. Ct. 927.

Bureau.[344] The NCUA is responsible for the charter and supervision of federal credit unions. It also is in charge of administering the NCUSIF.[345]

The first credit union in the US was *St.* Mary Cooperative Credit Association, in Manchester, New Hampshire, in 1909. The introducers of the credit union movement into the US were Alphonse Desjardins, Pierre Jay and Edward Filene. It was Desjardins, a Canadian journalist and politician, who organized St. Mary cooperative with the help of Jay and Filene. Jay also lobbied in Massachusetts for the instauration of a new credit union state charter. However, Filene lobbied the most and funded organizations for the promotion of credit unions throughout the country.[346]

Like credit unions in the UK, the "common bond" shapes credit unions in the US, and it is the first factor that differentiates credit unions from other depositories. The SCOTUS states:

> The common bond requirement "was seen as the cement that united credit union members in a cooperative venture, and was, therefore, thought important to credit unions' continued success." 988 F. 2d, at 1276. "Congress assumed implicitly that a common bond amongst members would ensure both that those making lending decisions would know more about applicants and that borrowers would be more reluctant to default.[347]

The requisite of the common bond helped members of the credit union to know each other and to better assess the economic prospects of the fellow members of the institution. Desjardins believed "the main security is the

[344] Ibid., 80; Public Law 91-206 (10 March 1970, 84 Stat. 49) amended sections 2, 3, and 21 of the Federal Credit Union Act. "It created the National Credit Union Administration as an independent agency and transferred all of the functions of the Bureau of Federal Credit Unions to the new Administration" (Forward).

[345] Title II of the Federal Credit Union Act, as amended.

[346] John Walter "Not your Father's Credit", *Federal Reserve Bank of Richmond Economic Quarterly*, Vol. 92, No. 4 (2006), 355–356.

[347] United States Supreme Court, *National Credit Union Administration v First National Bank & Trust Co.* (1998) No. 96-843.

fact that the association is working within a small area and that everybody knows each other".[348] Another consequence of the common bond was that it encouraged compliance. Before 1970, when federal insurance coverage was granted, if someone defaulted members of the credit union would suffer losses.[349] Additionally, a defaulting member would damage the reputation of fellow members who share a common bond. Hence, the system was designed to prevent defaults.[350]

Original Section 109 FCUA provided that federal credit union membership shall be limited "to groups having a common bond of occupation or association, or to groups within a well-defined neighbourhood, community, or rural district".[351] However, in the 1980s, many credit unions failed, and the NCUA believed one reason for this was that the common bond restricted the growth of credit unions, so they were too small to be viable.[352] In 1982, the NCUA broadened the term common bond to include "multiple occupational groups" which need only to be within a "well defined area".[353] In 1998, the SCOTUS decided that the NCUA needed to stop granting multiple-group credit union charters.[354] That same year, the US Congress passed the Credit Union Membership Access Act of 1998 where it permitted credit unions that already had multiple common bonds before February 1998 to continue operating. It also permitted additional membership groups with multiple common bonds if they do not surpass 3,000 members.[355]

[348] J. Carrol Moody and Gillbert Fite, *The Credit Union Movement: Origins and Development, 1850–1980* (Kendall/Hunt 1984), 16; Walter, "Not your Father's Credit", 357–8.

[349] Walter "Not your Father's Credit", 358.

[350] Ibid., 359.

[351] Original FCUA Section 109.

[352] Ryder and Chambers, "The Credit Crunch", 81.

[353] Interpretative Ruling and Policy Statement 82–3, 47 Red. Reg. 26,808 (22 June 1982).

[354] SCOTUS, "National Credit Union Administration".

[355] Public Law 105–219, Credit Union Membership Access Act (7 August 1998) amended sections 102a(b), 109, 202(a)(6), 202(b), 202(c), 202(h), 205(b), 206(h), 206(k), and 207(a); repealed section 116; and added new sections 107A and 216.

In 2018 the American Bankers Association (ABA) sued the NCUA[356] since, according to the ABA, the NCUA's 2016 rule "allowed community credit unions—which Congress by statute limited to serving a single 'well-defined local community, neighbourhood, or rural district'—to serve large regions encompassing multiple metropolitan areas with populations in the millions".[357] Judge Dabney Friedrich declared invalid the inclusion of "combined statistical areas" with fewer than 2.5 million people, and the definition of "rural area" to those up to 1 million people.[358]

A second factor differentiating credit unions from other depositories is the requisite of membership. Both state and federal credit unions are owners of the credit union. These might take the form of cooperatives or mutually owned institutions.[359] Contrary to commercial banks, a credit union's typical funding is via retained earnings. Credit union members, as depositors and owners, have the right to the repayment of their deposits and interests but also to access the funds that remain after the credit union is dissolved.[360]

Traditionally, credit unions have focused on "small value, nonmortgage loans to individuals and households, meaning uncollateralised loans for household expenses and the purchase of consumer durables".[361] However, within community credit unions "businesses and other legal entities within the community boundaries or rural district may also qualify for membership".[362] Likewise, credit unions that serve low-income members may accept deposits from non-members, including

[356] *American Bankers Association v National Credit Union Administration*, Civil Action No. 16–2394.

[357] ABA, "ABA Wins on Two Counts in Credit Union Field of Membership Lawsuit". https://bankingjournal.aba.com/2018/03/aba-wins-on-two-counts-in-credit-union-field-of-membership-lawsuit//. Accessed 17 April 2023.

[358] "American Bankers Association v National Credit union".

[359] According to 12 USC § 1752 (a).

[360] Walter "Not your Father's Credit", 360.

[361] Ibid., 361.

[362] 12 CFR Appendix B to part 701 Section V.

businesses.[363] From a tax perspective, credit unions are free from federal income taxes.[364]

Like banks and thrifts, credit unions are subject to lending limits. A credit union lending to only one member is limited to 10% of unimpaired capital and surplus.[365] Also, federal credit unions are subject to commercial lending limits. "The aggregate limit on a federally insured credit union's net member business loan balances is the lesser of 1.75 times the actual net worth of the credit union, or 1.75 times the minimum net worth".[366] Exceptions to this rule apply to low-income credit unions, those chartered to make business loans or those that have a history of primarily serving business loans.[367]

There are certain activities that federal credit unions are not permitted to engage in directly, but via a credit union service organization (CUSO). A CUSO is an "organization that is owned by credit unions in whole or in part that provides permitted financial services and/or operational services primarily to credit unions or members of credit unions".[368] Federal credit unions may not offer insurance or engage in securities brokerage directly, but may do so via CUSOs.[369]

From a size perspective, according to the Credit Union National Association Mutual Group, as of September 2023, there were 4740 credit

[363] 12 USC § 1757 (6).

[364] 26 USC § 501 (c) (1); John Reosti, "Do Credit Unions Still Warrant a Tax Exemption?" (2018) American Banker. https://www.americanbanker.com/news/do-credit-unions-still-warrant-a-tax-exemption; Jim Nussle, "BankThink Banker Concerns About Credit Union Mergers Are Overblown" [2019] American Banker. https://www.americanbanker.com/opinion/banker-concerns-about-credit-union-mergers-are-overblown?tag=00000157-6d0d-d460-a7f7-7f6ff5df0000. Accessed 17 November 2023; J. Walter "Not your Father's Credit", 363.

[365] 12 USC§ 1757 (5)(A) (x).

[366] 12 CFR § 723.8 (a).

[367] 12 USC § 1757a (b).

[368] Guy Messik "Credit Union Service Organizations ('CUSOs')" (*NACUSO*, 2018). https://www.nacuso.org/wp-content/uploads/2018/02/History-of-CUSOs-2-7-18.pdf. Accessed 24 April 2019; "CUSOs at a Glance" (*NCUA*, 2019). https://www.ncua.gov/files/publications/cusos-at-a-glance-2017.pdf. Accessed 24 April 2023; Andrew Downin "Ambidexterity Drives Credit Union Success, CUSOs Make it a Reality" *Credit Union Times* (12 April 2017).

[369] 12 CFR§ 712.5 (g) and 12 CFR § 712.5 (k).

unions in operation.[370] According to Wilcox and Dopico, "In 1969, when their number peaked at 23,866, credit union assets totalled $16 billion, only 3% of the assets of commercial banks and 1.6% of GDP. Since1970, there have been nearly 13,000 credit union mergers. As the number of credit unions declined, so did the number of annual mergers. Nonetheless, the annual percentage of credit unions that merged was remarkably steady, ranging from 2.5% to 3.5% in all but three years since 1984".[371]

One of the main concerns of the ABA and the banking industry is credit union concentration and expansion. In 2019 Pentagon Federal Credit Union, the third-largest credit union merged with Progressive Credit Union "that gives PenFed an open charter, allowing anyone nationwide to join".[372] Ken Clayton from the ABA stated that "[t]his merger is just the latest example of large credit unions far exceeding their original mission to serve targeted communities of modest means…This not only hurts small credit unions playing by the rules, but also taxpayers who are unknowingly subsidizing this national expansion"[373] (Table 5.1)

Other Non-bank Institutions According to the BHCA

There are certain financial institutions that are exempted from the definition of a bank according to the BHCA. They are industrial loan

370 "U.S. Credit Union Profile" (*CUNA*, 2023). https://www.cuna.org/content/dam/cuna/advocacy/cu-economics-and-data/credit-union-snapshot/National.pdf. Accessed 1 December 2023.

371 James Wilcox and Luis Dopico "Credit Union Mergers: Efficiencies and Benefits" FRBSF Economic Letter (2011).

372 Palash Ghosh and John Reosti, "PenFed Deal Feeds Bankers' Fears of Unlimited Credit Union Membership" American Banker (2019). https://www.americanbanker.com/news/penfed-deal-feeds-bankers-fears-of-unlimited-credit-union-membership?tag=00000157-6d0d-d460-a7f7-7f6ff5df0000. Accessed 17 April 2023.

373 Ibid.

Table 5.1 Comparative analysis of national banks, federal savings associations and federal credit unions

	National banks	*Federal savings associations*	*Federal credit unions*
Membership	No restrictions	No restrictions	Only serve members 12 § USC 1759
Deposit taking powers	Yes. 12 USC § 24 (seventh), 12 CFR §	Yes. 12 USC § 1464 (b), 12 CFR part 557, subpart B	May offer share certificate accounts. 12 USC § 1757 (6); 12 CFR § 701.35 (a)
Insurance	May sell liability, casualty, automobile, life, health and accident insurance on agency basis in places with less than 5,000 inhabitants. It may engage in general insurance agency functions through a financial subsidiary. 12 USC§ 92 and 24a; 12 CFR §7.1001 and 5.39	Similar to national banks but without restriction on places. Federal savings associations may sell insurance through service corporations on an agency basis without geographic restriction. 12 CFR § 559.4 (f) (3)	Federal credit unions may not offer insurance directly but may do so via a CUSO. 12 CFR§ 712.5 (g)
Securities brokerage and underwriting	National banks may engage in types of securities brokerages. 12 USC § 78c(a)(4) and (5) National banks may direct underwrite various securities. Financial subsidiaries may engage in underwriting of all types of securities. 12 USC §24 (seventh) and 24a; 12 CFR parts 1 and 12	Federal savings associations may engage in securities brokerage only via a service corporation, and on agency basis. 12 CFR § 545.74	Federal credit unions may not engage in securities brokerage directly but through a CUSO. 12 CFR § 712.5 (k)

	National banks	*Federal savings associations*	*Federal credit unions*
Derivatives	Yes. 12 USC § 24 (seventh)	Yes. 12 CFR § 563.172	Only to manage the risk of loss via long put positions on Ginnie Mae, Fannie Mae and Freddie Mac securities. 12 CFR§703.110 and 701.21 (i) (2)
Ownership	Shareholders	Shareholders or members in mutual thrifts	Members 12 USC. § 1752(1)
Aim	For profit	Depends on stock ownership or mutual thrift	Not for profit

Source US Treasury (Appendix. Comparison of Depository Institution Powers and Regulatory Requirements. https://www.treasury.gov/press-center/press.../curegapp.doc. Accessed 23 April 2023)

companies and industrial banks (ILC),[374] credit card banks[375] and limited purpose trust companies.[376]

US Regulation of International Banking

In parallel with domestic legislation, foreign banks doing business in the US are also subject to the dual regulatory regime via federal and state law. In general, foreign banks are subject to similar regulations as domestic banks.[377] The International Banking Act of 1978 (IBA) regulates non-US banks in the US and adopts the principle of "national treatment" between domestic and foreign banks.[378]

The modes of foreign bank entry into the US include: (i) US branch; (ii) agency; (iii) US bank subsidiary; (iv) representative office; (v) Edge corporation; and (vi) commercial lending company.

[374] Mindy West "The FDIC's Supervision of Industrial Loan Companies: A Historical Perspective" Supervisory Insights (2004), 5; Government Accountability Office "Industrial Loan Corporations Recent Asset Growth and Commercial Interest Highlight Differences in Regulatory Authority" (2005), 5; Keneth Spong and Eric Robbins, "Industrial Loan Companies: A Growing Industry Sparks a Public Policy Debate", *Federal Reserve of Kansas City Economic Review*, Vol. 41 (2007), 42; 12 USC §1841 (c)(2)(h)(i); James Barth and Yunfei Sun "A New Look at The Performance of Industrial Loan Corporations" Utah Center for Financial Services, The University of Utah (2018), 4. In 2017 FinTech Companies Square and SoFi applied for ILC charters, withdrawing their applications months later. Cinar Oney "Fintech Industrial Banks and Beyond: How Banking Innovations Affect the Federal Safety Net" 23 Gordham J. Corp & Fin (2018), 542; Lalita Clozel "SoFi Withdraws Bank Application in Wake of Scandal" (2017) American Banker; T. Stone, "The Past, Present and Future of the ILC Bank" (*De Banked*, 2019). https://debanked.com/2018/07/the-past-present-and-future-of-the-ilc-bank/. Accessed 24 April 2023.

[375] Omarova et al. "That which we Call a Bank", 187; *Marquette Nat'l Bank v First of Omaha Corp*, 439 US 299 (1978). See 12 USC§ 1841 (c)(2)(F).

[376] Omarova et al. "That which we Call a Bank", 173; 12 U.S. Code § 1841 2 (D); H.R. Rep. No. 261, 100th Cong., 1st Sess. 119, reprinted in 1987 U.S. Code Cong, & Admin. News 588 cited by Harvey. N. Bock "Opportunities for Nonbanking Companies to Acquire Depository Institutions in the Wake of the Competitive Equality Banking Act of 1987", *Bus. Law*, Vol. 44 (1988), 1053.

[377] US Banking Law: Overview.

[378] Pub. L. No. 95–369, 92 Stat. 607 (1978) (codified at 12 USC §§ 3101 et seq. (2010): John Carr Jr. and Thomas J. Pax, "Forms of Entry, Operation, Expansion and Supervision of Foreign Banks in the United States" in M. Gruson and R. Reisner, *Regulation of Foreign Banks. United States and International* (Michie Butterworth 1995), 1–10.

US branches—as befits the nature of a branch—are not separate legal entities in the US but the same legal foreign entity. However, in certain cases, US law treats the foreign branches differently from the whole foreign bank.[379] First, only US branches (and not the whole foreign banks) are eligible for federal deposit insurance.[380] Second, US branches are subject to BHC regulations while the foreign bank is treated as a parent, and the branch as a subsidiary.[381] Third, a foreign bank may engage in any kind of activities outside the US, even though the US branch is subject to BHC activity restrictions.[382] Fourth, state-chartered branches and federal-chartered branches are liquidated as separate legal entities under state and IBA law.[383] According to 12 USC § 3101 (b). "'Branch' means any office or any place of business of a foreign bank located in any state of the US at which deposits are received".[384] They must be approved by the Federal Reserve System.[385]

A second mode of entry is through agencies. Agencies of foreign banks may not accept deposits from US persons, but may engage in other banking activities. They may be licensed via state or federal law, and they need FRB approval.[386]

US bank subsidiaries are legal entities separate from their parent foreign bank (as all subsidiaries are). They need to charter under federal or state law. The regulation of foreign bank subsidiaries will depend on the type of banking organization the foreign subsidiary is opting for (generally national bank, BHC or FHC).[387]

A special mode of entry is the representative office. "The term 'representative office' means any office of a foreign bank which is located in any State and is not a Federal branch, Federal agency, State branch,

[379] Meeting between Federal Reserve Board Staff and Representatives of Foreign Banking Organizations 9 July 2012. https://www.federalreserve.gov/newsevents/rr-commpublic/Industry_Meeting_20120709.pdf. Accessed 9 May 2023.

[380] 12 USC§ 1815 (b).

[381] 12 USC § 1841.

[382] 12 CFR § 211.23 (f) (l).

[383] Example NY Banking Law §606 (4)(c) et seq) and 12 USC § 3102 (j) (l).

[384] 12 USC § 3101 (b).

[385] 12 USC § 3105 (d)(1).

[386] 12 USC § 3105 (d)(1).

[387] US Banking Law: Overview.

or State agency".[388] A representative office "engages solely in representational and administrative functions (such as soliciting new business or acting as liaison between the organization's head office and customers in the United States); and does not have authority to make any business decision (other than decisions relating to its premises or personnel) for the account of the organization it represents, including contracting for any deposit or deposit-like liability on behalf of the organization".[389]

Edge corporations are federally chartered entities whose business generally must be limited to international banking and financial operations. Prior approval of the Federal Reserve System must be obtained.[390] The "principal purpose of such a banking Edge Act corporation is to encourage the export of US goods and services".[391] Edge corporation subsidiaries of US banks are permitted to perform a wide range of activities abroad[392] and may also perform some activities in the US incidental to international foreign business.[393] Regulation K organizes the types of overseas investments in which BHCs, banks or Edge Corporation may engage.[394] Agreement corporations have the same functions as Edge corporations but are state chartered.[395]

Finally, a commercial lending company ("CLC") "refers to foreign banks willing to have a limited operation in NY via an 'Investment Company chartered under Article XII of the New York Banking Law". A CLC may borrow and lend money, transmit money, trade coin and bullion, among other activities.[396]

How FCs in the US Structure Themselves

Unlike the EU, where there is a directive on FCs, with clear definitions on what a FC is and how it needs to be regulated, in the US, multiple

[388] 12 U.S. Code § 3101 (15).

[389] 12 CFR § 211.2.

[390] 12 USC § 614.

[391] Carr Jr. and Pax "Forms of Entry", 1–33.

[392] 12 USC § 615.

[393] 12 CFR § 211.6.

[394] 12 CFR 211.1 to 211.605.

[395] Carr Jr. and Pax "Forms of Entry", 1–33; US Banking Law: Overview.

[396] New York Consolidated Laws, Banking Law—BNK § 508.

regulators focus on different aspects of FCs. The DFA tended to ameliorate that dispersion trying to close regulation arbitrage, putting the focus on systemic risk and establishing uniform capital adequacy standards for FCs.

Prior to the DFA the Office of Thrift Supervision (OTS) supervised THCs, which included large FCs such as AIG, Countrywide Financial, General Electric Company, General Motors Company, Merrill Lynch, Morgan Stanley and Washington Mutual.[397] Some companies that were willing to hold a depositary institution but not willing to be regulated by the Federal Reserve System via a BHC or an FHC had this option. Also, prior to the DFA, a FC could elect to be regulated by the SEC as a consolidated supervised entity (CSE) or a supervised investment bank holding company (SIBHC). According to Section 231 of the GLBA the SEC could act as a consolidated regulator of holding companies that were not regulated by bank or thrift holding companies by the Federal Reserve System or the OTS.[398] The SEC, as a reaction to the lobby of FCs that had no primary regulator implemented this regime in 2004.[399] These FCs did not want to be subject to regulation by FICOD that required competent authorities to verify whether FCs with head offices outside the EU were subject to supervision by a third-country competent authority, which was equivalent to the FICOD. The consequence of not having an equivalent regime was that those FCs would be subject to the FICOD.[400] These firms preferred the SEC regime because it offered a "preferential capital treatment".[401] Another consequence of the pre-DFA regime was that holding companies that hold industrial loan or industrial banks but do not hold a bank or a thrift or a broker-dealer were not subject to federal regulation.[402]

[397] Elisabeth Brown "The New Laws and Regulations for Financial Conglomerates: Will They Better Manage the Risks than the Previous Ones?" *American University Law Review*, Vol. 60, No. 5 (2011), 113.

[398] 15 USC § 78q(i) (2006).

[399] Ibid.

[400] FICOD, art 18.

[401] US SEC, Office of the Inspector General, Office of Audits, "SEC's Oversight of Bear Stearns and Related Entities: The Consolidated Supervised Entity Program Report" No. 446-A (25 September 2008), 4.

[402] Brown "The New Laws", 107.

After the DFA, the OTS's powers to regulate thrifts were transferred to the OCC, and the OTS's powers to regulate THCs were transferred to the Federal Reserve System. This closed the door to companies such as AIG or Merrill Lynch offering banking services via thrifts without Federal Reserve System regulation. A second consequence of the DFA was the elimination of the CSE and SIBHC regimes and the requirement for "securities holding companies" to be regulated by the Federal Reserve System.[403] Sometime before the DFA, the SEC had stopped the CSE programme due to Bear Stern financial problems.[404] In addition, the DFA enacted the "Hotel California" provision by which a FC that became a BHC or an FHC, with more than 50 billion in consolidated assets by January 2010, and received pubic aid could not avoid regulation by changing the charter of any banking subsidiary.[405] The DFA gave the Federal Reserve System the power to determine that the Board of Governors shall supervise a non-bank financial company in case it "could pose a threat to the financial stability of the United States".[406]

By doing this, the Federal Reserve System has the power to close "regulatory arbitrage" of systemic important financial institutions since from now on FCs are not able to choose regulators. For example, AIG which has chosen to be treated as a thrift would not be permitted to do that anymore according to the law.[407] Finally, the DFA adopted a provision to avoid the TBTF problem by prohibiting interstate mergers that create a depositary institution that controls more than 10% of the deposits in the US.[408]

A FC, as defined by the Tripartite group, encompasses a group of companies that engage in at least two financial activities, banking, securities and insurance.[409] FCs in the US may organize themselves via the following corporate structures:

[403] 15 USC § 78q.

[404] Brown "The New Laws", 153.

[405] 15 USC § 78q; Brown "The New Laws", 153.

[406] 12 U.S. Code § 5323.

[407] The Financial Crisis Inquiry Commission, *The Financial Crisis Inquiry Report. Final Report of the National Commission on the Causes of the Financial and Economic Crisis in the United States* (Official Government ed, 2011), 352.

[408] 12 USC § 1852.

[409] BIS "The Supervision of Financial Conglomerates", 13–65.

Via a BHC, with a broad variety of permitted banking activities, but with very limited insurance agency and underwriting activities and very limited agency transactional activities for customer investments
Via an FHC, with a broad variety of permitted insurance, securities and banking activities
Via a national bank with broad permitted bank activities, and very limited securities activities (may engage in certain types of securities brokerage and others) and insurance activities (may sell certain types of insurance in places of 5,000 inhabitants or less)
Via a national bank operative subsidiary, with broad permitted banking activities, and the power to provide title insurance as principal under certain circumstances
Via a national bank financial subsidiary, with broad permitted banking activities and certain securities (may underwrite all types of securities) and general agency insurance activities
Via a THC, with the same broad permitted activities of an FHC if they meet similar conditions as the FHC
Via a thrift, with the same permitted banking activities as national banks, with similar powers as national bank insurance activities, but without the geographic restriction of 5,000 inhabitants
Via a thrift service corporation (issuing notes, bonds, debentures, or other obligations or securities)
Via a credit union, with broad banking activity, with limited insurance and securities activities
Via a CUSO, it may broker and sell insurance and other broker securities
Via a "non-bank institutions according to BHCA" holding company, which may have banking activities via an ILC or a credit card bank, and may also include an insurance company that would be regulated by state law, and a securities firm that would generally be regulated by the SEC. In certain cases, if labelled as a SIFI, the Federal Reserve System may also regulate them
Via a non-bank financial company that has been subject to prudential supervision by the Federal Reserve System, which engages in at least two of the typical financial activities
Via a foreign bank branch, with the limitation of a BHC
Via a foreign bank subsidiary, that will have the limits of the type of charter it opts for when chartering

As stated above, most US BBFCs choose the FHC as a preferred structure since it permits engagement in banking, insurance and securities in a way that may resemble universal banks.

5.3 Concluding Remarks

1. American Federalism and a Unique "Unit Banking System"

Unlike European universal banking, which is based on an "activities list approach" that includes commercial, insurance and securities activities under the same umbrella, the evolution of BBFCs-faced different phases.

The first three phases, which comprise the charter banking system, free banking and the Federal Reserve System (until the 1930s), permitted universal banking in the US. It was only in 1933 with the GSA that traditional financial activities were separated.

While German universal banking had its philosophical foundations in Saint Simon's ideas, and the UK based its system in classic liberalism and self-regulation, federalism provides the rationale to understand the nature and evolution of the US model. Federalism shaped the banking system in the US since its inception and its regulators tended to replicate the governmental federal structure at the banking level, preventing abuse of power and undue concentration of financial resources. This is why the US banking system relied on a quite unique system of "unit banks" that were the result of heavy restrictions on branching at both the state and federal levels.

This book believes the costs of unit banks outweigh their benefits. While it is true that unit banks may have not been altered by a branch because that was not a possibility and that managers of local banks may have had better knowledge of their customers, these facts should not be enough to restrict branching altogether. Also, the fact that branch banking may lead to capital outflows from rural areas is not a defining argument if that may be compensated by other means of finance or by opening branches in those areas. The argument held by the Comptroller of the Currency in 1924 that branch banking may be monopolistic is something to take into account; nonetheless, it is not a typical note of branch banking but of big banks. The same tools that are now available to fight TBTF and trusts would apply to any institution that may present a monopolistic character. Finally, to say that branch banking opposes federalism is an outdated argument since federalism is intended, in the words of Justice Scalia, to find a midway between two extremes, disunity and uniformity. Allowing banks to freely branch among states does not undermine federalism in a way that would denaturalize its meaning. Federalism will continue to be a way of regulating the "practicalities" of US matters.

On the contrary, allowing branch banking had accelerated growth in states that permitted it, and there is evidence that unit banks were less efficient than branch banking in the use of capital and reserves. Additionally, unit banks were inadequate to finance industrial firms in the US and they hindered the development of large firms in the twentieth century. They imposed costs on large firms that had to rely on expensive investment banking syndicates. Some research believes unit banks were more associated to bank panics than branch banking. There is also evidence that unit banks hindered financial integration and diversification and they prevented competition among banks.

The unit banking system created a mismatch between big firms and unfitted small banking systems. The role of law in the US was repressive in the sense that branching restrictions stimulated the growth of capital markets. While universal banks in the German model relied on a capitalism based on long-term relations, insider dealing and industry development, in the US, a new form of capitalism emerged based primarily on capital markets. The UK has proven to rely both on capital markets and banks, while the preemince of banks is not as clear as in Germany.

2. The Chicken and the Egg Situation in American Financial Regulation

The relationship between the corporate form of BBFCs and regulation may be described as a "chicken and egg situation". Indeed, as stated above, American branching restrictions led the private sector to circumvent them via new corporate forms. The creation of chain and group banking was in part a reaction to the unit banking system. Prior to 1956, bankers started using the holding company structure as a way to have presence in different states, de facto applying interstate banking. The BHCA was partly a reaction to regulate the use of holding companies to prevent the side step of the McFadden Act. Later on, the deregulation movement built up to the GFC of 2007–2009. As a reaction to the GFC, the US legislature enacted the DFA. The DFA ended up the possibility of FCs to be regulated by the SEC. It also prevented the possibility of avoiding regulation by the Federal Bank System if a holding company holds industrial loans or industrial banks. The DFA also gave the Federal Reserve System the power to regulate non-bank financial companies in the case they could pose a threat to financial stability in the US. This way, the DFA closed regulatory arbitrage to FCs.

3. Corporate Form and American Regulators

Section 5.1.6 analyses the "business of banking" and the definition of a bank under US law as well as examining each of the traditional depository institutions in the US: (i) commercial banks; (ii) thrifts; and (iii) credit unions. One special feature of the American system is the existence of a state and federal charter of these institutions. A second feature is the existence of second level institutions, which comprise commercial bank operatives and financial subsidiaries, thrift service corporations and CUSOs. As in Germany, thrifts were born to encourage savings and help people of "deserving classes". In the US, thrifts are not independent instrumentalities of public law but private associations. Thrifts in the US may have stock ownership or mutual ownership. One special feature of thrifts in the US is that they are required to have at least 65% of their portfolio in housing-related assets. As with commercial banks, there are also THCs. Finally, credit unions are cooperatives which are governed by (i) cooperative principles of democratic vote; (ii) self-help; (iii) a common bond requirement; and (iv) mandatory membership. Similar to their European counterparts, credit unions are not for profit. Similar to the UK, the US system comprises commercial banks and credit unions. They share with Germany the existence of thrifts (saving banks) and commercial banks. Contrary to some examples in Europe, there are no globally systemically important thrifts or credit unions in the US.

Unlike the EU where there is FICOD, in the US multiple regulators focus on different aspects of FCs. The DFA focused on systemic risk and uniform capital adequacy standards. While following the deregulation period US bank-based conglomerates may choose from a variety of forms to perform banking insurance and securities, big international bank-based conglomerates have chosen primarily the FHC as their preferred structure.

4. Icarus and American Financial Regulation

In Greek mythology, Icarus is the son of Daedalus, a famous artisan who created the labyrinth on the instruction of King Minos, in order to imprison the Minotaur, a half bull-half man creature. "This labyrinth was so very intricate, that those who entered could not find their way out; and even Daedalus and his son Icarus, after many days' attempt, found they could not leave it".[410] In order to leave the labyrinth Daedalus manufactured a pair of wings for each of them made of wood, feathers and wax.

Daedalus warned Icarus not no fly too high nor too low:

> 'My Icarus!' he says; 'I warn thee fly.
> Along the middle track: nor low, nor high;
> If low, thy plumes may flag with ocean's spray;
> If high, the sun may dart his fiery ray.'[411]

Icarus flew swiftly along but forgot the warnings of his father and rose up higher and higher until he was very high, near the sun. The heat melted the wax of the feathers, and Icarus fell into the sea and drowned.

Skeel has used the image of Icarus to understand the flaws of American corporate regulation in his book *Icarus in the Boardroom: The Fundamental Flaws in Corporate America and Where They Came From.*[412] He correctly points out that American corporate regulation has consisted of federal regulatory interventions after major scandals. According to him, these scandals have two common factors: (1) Excessive risk-taking, many times influenced by competition, and (2) the manipulation of the corporate form.

A similar metaphor may be applicable to American FCs regulation. The wise warning of Daedalus is extensive to financial regulators. Do not overregulate (fly too low) because you will be limiting innovation and flexibility, and at the same time do not deregulate (fly too high) because you may endanger financial stability.

Interestingly, when considering virtues, Aristotle taught that virtue is the mean between two extremes. In one extreme, there is an excess and in the other, there is a defect. For him, "Virtue then, is a state of character concerned with choice, lying in the mean, i.e., the mean relative to us, this being determined by a rational principle, and by the principle by which the man of practical wisdom would determine it".[413] While not virtues

[410] Helene A. Guerber *Myths of Greece and Rome* (American Book Company, 1893), 254.

[411] Ibid.

[412] David Skeel *Icarus in the Boardroom: The Fundamental Flaws in Corporate America and Where They Came From* (OUP 2006), 1.

[413] Aristotle *The Nicomachean Ethics of Aristotle* (Sir D. Ross tr, OUP 1963) 1.

per se, another metaphor may be drawn here. Between overregulation and deregulation lies virtue. As with habits, which need repetition to be acquired, regulators need to repeat good practices in order to acquire the correct balance between the two extremes.

American history over the last two centuries has experienced both extremes. Branching restrictions led America to a "unit banking" system that proved to be unique. Small unit banks could not finance the needs of big industry in the US. Empirical ratios show that universal banks in Germany did provide sufficient funds and were determinant in helping the development of economic growth in that country. However, American innovation used other means for financing its industry via bank syndicates and capital markets. Branching restrictions were an indirect means of the development of capital markets in the US.

At the opposite extreme, financial deregulation may have run up the GFC. As Skeel proposed, excessive risk-taking is one typical factor of corporate scandals. The major sin of Icarus was hubris, a sober over-confidence in his capabilities that made him ignore the warnings of his father. Virtue lies in the middle, and the right balance between these two extremes is fundamental to control the potential damage of a future financial crisis. History is a good ally for regulators to find the wiser solutions, in order not to fly too low nor too high.

CHAPTER 6

Resolution of BBFCs

6.1 Resolution Planning Frameworks

In November 2011, the FSB issued the *Key Attributes of Effective Resolution Regimes for Financial Institutions (Key Attributes)* with the aim to "allow authorities to resolve financial institutions in an orderly manner without taxpayer exposure to loss from solvency support, while maintaining continuity of their vital economic functions".[1] The scope of the document is SIFIs or "systemically significant" financial institutions. As of April 2019, most FSB jurisdictions have adopted resolution planning frameworks.[2] While the Key Attributes were adopted with SIFIs in mind, different jurisdictions apply resolution planning to all banks (EU, HK) others to G-SIBs and D-SIBD-SIBs (Brazil, China, Japan, Switzerland) and others apply an "asset size threshold" that includes G-SIBs and other large financial institutions (US).[3]

[1] FSB: Key Attributes of Effective Resolution Regimes for Financial Institutions (2011), https://www.fsb.org/wp-content/uploads/r_111104cc.pdf. Accessed 4 November 2023.

[2] FSB "Thematic Review on Bank Resolution Planning. Peer Review Report", 29 April 2019.

[3] Ibid., 11.

M. J. Sheppard Gelsi, *Corporate Structure and Banking Resolution*, Palgrave Macmillan Studies in Banking and Financial Institutions, https://doi.org/10.1007/978-3-031-59948-4_6

As stated by FSB, resolution strategies and resolution tools are generally based on "type, size, complexity and significance of a bank…- Most jurisdictions report considerations related to the characteristics of the bank (i.e. structure, interconnectedness), resolution objectives and circumstances at the time of failure. In particular, consideration is given to the systemic nature of firms and factors such as bank structures, critical functions and geographical reach".[4]

There are three main resolution strategies: (i) a bail in strategy, which may be divided into SPOE and MPOE; (ii) partial transfer strategy; and (iii), a modified insolvency strategy.[5]

G-SIBs and D-SIBD-SIBs resolution strategies in general focus in maintaining the bank structure and operations intact.[6] According to the FSB 2018 *Seventh Report on the Implementation of Resolution Reforms*, 26 out of 28 G-SIBs prefer a bail in, SPOE strategy:

> In most cases a single point of entry combined with a bail-in is preferred for G-SIBs and most D-SIBs, as this enables the resolution authority to stabilise the firm and provide for continuity of its critical functions by keeping operational subsidiaries open.[7]

A second group of smaller institutions, which have less critical functions and less complex structures, may find that a transfer of assets and liabilities to a bridge bank or a third party is more appropriate for them. Also, a liquidation of the remaining of the old bank may follow.[8] Bank of England (BoE) has adopted this strategy to banks which "only critical function they supply relates to accounts relied on by customers for day-to-day payments and cash withdrawals". BoE applies this strategy to firms

[4] Ibid., 20.

[5] Morris "The Law of Financial Services Groups", 267; The Bank of England's approach to resolution October 2017, 16. For resolution tools see generally Jens-Hinrich Binder "Concepts, Requirements and Tools" in Jens-Hinrich Binder and Dalvinder Singh ***Bank Resolution: The European Regime*** (OUP 2016). Jens-Hinrich Binder "Resolution Planning and Structural Bank Reform Within the Banking Union" in Geoffrey Wood, David Mayes, and Juan Castaneda ***European Banking Union. Prospects and Challenges*** (Routledge 2015).

[6] Ibid., 20.

[7] FSB 2018 Resolution Report: "Keeping the Pressure Up". Seventh Report on the Implementation of Resolution Reforms, 15 November 2018, https://www.fsb.org/wp-content/uploads/P151118-1.pdf. Accessed 4 November 2023.

[8] FSB "Thematic Review on Bank Resolution Planning. Peer Review Report", 20.

with more than 40,000–80,000 transactional accounts if their balance sheet is less than £15 billion–£25 billion.[9]

The liquidation strategy may apply to jurisdictions that apply resolution planning to all banks, as long as it does not threat financial stability.[10] This kind of strategy count of deposit guarantee schemes, which safeguard client assets via a preferential place in credit hierarchy or via set up of trusts outside of the bank's estate.[11]

The following section will examine the bail in resolution strategy applied by BBFCs.

6.2 Resolution of a BBFCs

After the GFC, the focus of regulators has been placed on how to make FCs "safe to fail". A number of different tools have emerged in order to fulfil this objective. In 2014, the FSB announced two different "resolution strategies" based in bail in, for global systemically important banks: SPOE and MPOE strategy. The FSB allows national regulators to choose the most appropriate resolution strategy for their G-SIBs. The question here would be: What are the main elements regulators need to take into account in order to choose the most appropriate resolution strategy for their G-SIBs?

In this chapter, this book uses words like banking groups, financial institutions and banks, and FCs, whenever applicable to BBFC in order to build a workable framework.

There are certain indicators that regulators should take into account. The first indicator is how FCs/groups structure themselves, i.e. via branches, subsidiaries or a mix of both. The second indicator is the degree of centralization of global banks: centralized or decentralized type of global bank. The third indicator is the business model of the global bank; i.e. retail or wholesale banking. The fourth indicator is the territorial or unitary approach to resolution.

[9] Bank of England "The Bank of England's Approach to Resolution", 16.

[10] Ibid., 20.

[11] Morris "The Law of Financial Services Groups", 273.

First Indicator: Branches or Subsidiaries

The global bank may organize itself through branches, which are part of the same legal entity, inseparable from the parent, and therefore fully responsible for their financial obligations. Contrary to this, the subsidiary is a fully independent legal entity, which is licensed, supervised and regulated by local authorities. As such, the parent company has no legal obligation to support it in times of distress.[12]

The branch system might be more cost effective for the banking group, since there is no need for maintaining capital and liquidity buffers in each unit, which result in less need of capital and funding for the group. In addition, the global bank may mobilize funds from a healthy branch to another in times of distress, with no legal restrictions that might be present in a subsidiary model. Moreover, subsidiaries might face more costs of external funding if they borrow in their own name instead of doing so in the parent's name.[13]

On the other hand, it is recognized that in principle, the subsidiary structure may be better fitted to contain losses in the event of failure of a subsidiary.[14] In some cases, a subsidiary located in country A may continue as a going concern even if the parent or other subsidiary fails, since losses in those entities might be isolated. However, in practice, a parent might be forced to support a failing subsidiary due to reputational reasons.[15]

The subsidiary model might help to solve asymmetric information problems regarding shareholders and creditors. While shareholders might be tempted to substitute safer assets to risky assets once the lending conditions have been met, creditors might want to increase their premium or

[12] Jonathan Fiechter, İnci Ötker-Robe, Anna Ilyina, Michael Hsu, André Santos, and Jay Surti "Subsidiaries or Branches, Does One Size Fit All?", IMF Staff Discussion Note (2011), 8; Lastra, Ayadi, Olivares Caminal and Russo "The Different", 13.

[13] Fiechter et al. "Subsidiaries or Branches", 8.

[14] Jean Dermine "European Banking Integration: Don't Put the Cart Before the Horse", New York University Salomon Center, *Financial Markets, Institutions & Instruments*, Vol. 15, No. 2 (2006), 83.

[15] Eugenio Cerrutti, Giovani Dell'Ariccia, and Maria Martinez Peria "How Banks Go Abroad: Branches or Subsidiaries?", Policy Research Working Paper No. 3753 World Bank (2005), 1671; However, in some cases the cost of a bailout might be higher that the reputational risk, as shown in the cases of Nova Scotia, which did not support its argentine subsidiary Quilmes, as well as Credit Agricole with its subsidiary Banco Bisel, both in the Argentine crisis of 2002. Dermine "European Banking Integration", 83.

stop lending if they perceive these conditions will persist over time. One solution would be to create subsidiary where safe assets would be placed and therefore increase the creditors' perception that shareholders will stop risk shifting.[16]

In certain cases, where bank divisions have different compensation practices and cultures, holding separate subsidiaries might help oversight and control.[17] Another advantage of the subsidiary system is that a separate public listing of shares may make the price system more informative, since there is an increase in the number of traded securities.[18] From a group management perspective, a subsidiary model might help the managerial resistance to a merger, since it would keep in place the local structure. Also, the subsidiary model benefits from proximity. As a local entity, it might better influence the environment, i.e. by being member of the national banker's association. In terms of facilitating the merger, the subsidiary model might help to keep the business as usual after the merger, with no need to change the brand.From a tax perspective, a subsidiary model might be more flexible than a branch structure, i.e. start-up losses are more easily preserved in a subsidiary than in a branch.[19]Finally, and based on the Icelandic bank crisis, the subsidiary model would be most suitable for smaller countries with limited fiscal capacity. If a foreign branch fell into distress, the host country would have less obligations and burdens than if the failing entity were a subsidiary.[20]

From a regulatory viewpoint, home authorities are typically responsible for the supervision of foreign branches of a group, while host authorities are generally responsible for the supervision of the foreign subsidiaries.[21]

There are different reasons for why FCs/groups organize through branches or subsidiaries. According to empirical work by Cerrutti et al. on branches and subsidiaries, foreign banks tend to organize through

[16] Jacobo Carmassi and Richard J. Herring "Complexity and Systemic Risk: What's Changed Since the Crisis" in Allen Berger, Philip Molyneux, and John O. S. Wilson *The Oxford Handbook of Banking* (OUP 2015), 86.

[17] Ibid.

[18] Michele A. Habib, D. Bruce Johnsen and Narayan Y. Nail "Spinoffs and Information", *Journal of Financial Intermediation*, Vol. 6, No. 2 (1997), 153–176.

[19] Fiechter et al. "Subsidiaries or Branches", 11.

[20] Ibid., 16.

[21] IMF "Cross-Cutting Themes in Economies with Large Banking Systems" (IMF 2010), 9.

subsidiaries if the host jurisdiction limits the permitted activities and when regulation difficult the establishment of new banks. Second, banks tend to use branches in host countries with high corporate taxes, in order to maximize the shift of profits across jurisdictions. Third, there is an association between "degrees of penetration" in the host market. Subsidiaries are more common in retail business while branches are smaller and not focused on retail orientation. Finally, banking groups tend to prefer the subsidiary system when host countries present a high-risk macroeconomic environment, while the use of branches is preferred in countries that face risk of government intervention and political instability, since subsidiaries often have higher capital and reserve requirements and more local assets than branches.[22]

Although the legal definition of branch and subsidiary is in general common to all jurisdictions, from a regulatory perspective sometimes those definitions are blurred. Contrary to what happens in other jurisdictions, in the US, even though a branch is not a separate legal entity from the bank, US law treats bank branches as separate entities in various aspects. In the first place, as stated above, insolvency law treats US branches of foreign banks as separate entities.[23] Similarly, for state-chartered branches, state law has the power to liquidate the branch. For instance, State of New York law provides that the Superintendent of Financial Services has authority to seize all assets situated in NY.[24] Second, the US branch of a foreign bank is treated as a US bank under the IBA, and not the whole bank.[25] Third, the US branch of a foreign bank, and not the bank as a whole, is eligible to apply for federal deposit insurance for deposits payable at the branch.[26] Fourth, US branches of foreign banks are subject to BHCA and its limits, and the foreign company is

[22] Cerrutti et al. "How Banks Go Abroad", 11.

[23] International Banking Act of 1978, Section 4 (2) j, codified to U.S. Code § 3102. Noam Noked "Separate Entity Doctrine for U.S. Branches of Foreign Banks", Harvard Law School Forum on Corporate Governance (2012), https://corpgov.law.harvard.edu/2012/04/30/separate-entity-doctrine-for-u-s-branches-of-foreign-banks/. Accessed 17 June 2023.

[24] Meeting Between Federal Reserve Board Staff and Representatives of Foreign Banking Organizations, 9 July 2012, 1–19, https://www.federalreserve.gov/newsevents/rr-commpublic/industry_meeting_20120709.pdf. Accessed 17 November 2023; NY BANKING LAW §606 et seq.

[25] 12 USC 3102(b); "Meeting Between Federal Reserve", 1–19.

[26] 12 USC 1815(b); "Meeting Between Federal Reserve", 1–19.

treated as the holding company and the branch as its subsidiary.[27] Fifth, only US branches may apply to Federal Reserve Discount Window.[28]

Second Indicator: Centralized or Decentralized Type of Bank

Although there is no straightforward banking business model, there are two main types of global banks: centralized and decentralized. The centralized model would perform management of liquidity, capital, risk exposures, information technology and processing from the "top tier entity". Decision-making and external funding are generally positioned at the top level. Centralized banks often use branches and subsidiaries are "managed as a whole".[29] As Carmassi and Herring explain "so far regulations will permit, subsidiaries would be managed as if they were branches and lines of business will be managed to maximize the profits without regard for the legal entities in which the activities are conducted".[30] The main advantages of this type of business model are that raising funds at the top level reduces the cost of funding and provides more flexibility, and at the same time allows gains from economies of scale.[31] On the contrary, the decentralized model the top-tier entity holds various local subsidiaries under a common brand, which are usually managed by local directors, locally funded and locally incorporated.[32] Often, shares are listed in local stock exchanges.[33] The decentralized model presents various constrains on intra-group transactions.[34] The main advantage of this model is that

[27] Ibid.

[28] 12 USC 3102(b). See "Meeting Between Federal Reserve", 1–19, for further US regulation which treat the US branch of a foreign bank as separate entities for certain purposes.

[29] Dirk Schoenmaker "The Different Legal and Operational Structures of Banking Groups in the Euro Area, and the Impact on Banks' Resolvability", European Parliament (2016), 9.

[30] Jacobo Carmassi and Richard Herring "The Corporate Complexity of Global Systemically Important Banks" *Journal of Financial Services Research* (2016), 164.

[31] Schoenmaker "The Different Legal and Operational Structures", 9.

[32] Fiechter et al. "Subsidiaries or Branches", 16.

[33] Carmassi and Herring "The Corporate Complexity", 165.

[34] Fiechter et al. "Subsidiaries or Branches", 7.

cross-border exposure is limited, since subsidiaries would not normally rely on parent funding, and in times of crisis, contagion between units decreases.[35]

Third Indicator: Retail vs Non-retail Banking

BBFC may focus their business on different lines of business. One key business line is retail banking. Retail banking concentrates on the deposit taking business of households and small to medium-sized firms. The retail business will give greater importance to accessing local deposit guarantees.[36] On the contrary, where a bank focuses on other business lines such as services to large corporate clients, a branch structure would allow "cross-border inter-affiliate funding" and facilitate the provision of a broad range of activities, i.e. wholesale and investment banking. Regarding risk management, a wholesale banking may internalize the clearing and settlement of securities and cash payment obligations, reducing the total liquidity needed by the group. In contrast, a retail global bank would be more interested in managing credit risk of their retail loan books.[37]

From the public policy point of view, allowing global retail banks into a jurisdiction might imply direct competition for local retail banks, since large global retail banks may affect price and market share, while wholesaling or investment banking tend to be smaller and underdeveloped in host countries.[38]

Fourth Indicator: Territorial or Universal Approach to Resolution

There are two mainly different approaches to resolution: the universal (and also a modified universal[39]) approach, and a territorial approach. The

[35] Schoenmaker "The Different Legal and Operational", 9.

[36] Manuel Merck Martel, Adrian van Rixtel, and Emiliano González Mota "Business Models of International Banks in the Wake of the 2007–2009 Global Financial Crisis", Estabilidad Financiera Num. 22 (2012), 110; Fiechter et al. "Subsidiaries or Branches", 16.

[37] Schoenmaker "The Different Legal and Operational", 9.

[38] Cerrutti et al. "How Banks Go Abroad", 1670.

[39] The "modified universal" is a model that would give host countries the right to "bring local resolutions against local parts of a SIFI" Stijn Claessens, Richard Herring,

universal approach or principle of "unity and universality in bankruptcy", which is generally tied to the "single entity" approach[40] to resolution, implies a unique competent court in charge of the resolution or bankruptcy of the bank and a sole bankruptcy law applicable to the whole process, including the parent and branches in foreign jurisdictions.[41] In a SIFI resolution, "all creditors of the same class, wherever located, would be treated equally, pursuant to the same country rules governing the ranking of creditor classes". For universal resolution to be effective, all national resolution authorities would have to recognize the universal principle.[42]

Under the territorial approach, each unit of the SIFI would be resolved under national resolution authorities or national courts. Local bankruptcy or bank resolution laws will apply that would consider only local assets.[43] The principle of "plurality of bankruptcy", which is generally tied to the separate entity approach to liquidation, prevails. Different bankruptcy or resolution procedures would need to be initiated in each jurisdiction in which the bank holds assets or branches. Under this approach a branch of a banking group would receive a "liquidation preference" since local assets would be "segregated for the benefit of local creditors" (ring-fencing).[44] The organizational structure that best fits this approach is the subsidiary model.[45]

Dirk Schoenmaker, "A Safer World Financial System Improving the Resolution of Systemic Institutions", Geneva Reports on the World Economy 12 (2010), 88.

[40] The organizational structure that best fits universal approach would be the single entity operating via branches in different jurisdictions. Claessens, Herring, Schoenmaker, "A Safer World", 87.

[41] Rosa Lastra "Cross-Border Resolution of Banking Crisis", Paper presented at the Conference on "International Financial Instability. Cross-Border Banking and National Regulation" Sponsored by the Federal Reserve Bank of Chicago and International Association of Deposit Insurers (2006), 5; Thomas Huertas "A Resolvable Bank" in Kenneth E. Scott, Thomas H. Jackson and John Taylor *Making Failure Feasible: How Bankruptcy Reform Can End Too Big to Fail* (Hoover Institution Press 2015), 132.

[42] Claessens, Herring, Schoenmaker "A Safer World", 85.

[43] Ibid.

[44] Lastra "Cross-Border Resolution", 5.

[45] Claessens, Herring, Schoenmaker "A Safer World", 85.

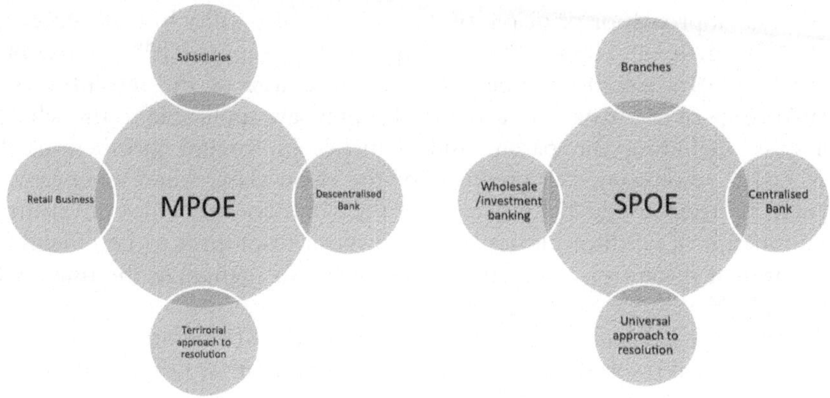

Fig. 6.1 Relationships between resolution strategies, business models, legal structural organization and approaches to resolution

Concurrence of the Four Factors

The concurrence of these four indicators allows us to make some preliminary conclusions. According to these, centralized banks tend to focus on wholesale and investment banking, while decentralized banking tends to focus on retail banking. As for the legal operational structure, centralized, wholesale and investment banking tend to rely on branches, while decentralized retail global banks tend to rely on subsidiaries. Universal approaches to resolution would best fit a SIFI organized mainly by branches, while a territorial approach would best fit the subsidiary model. While this is a general tendency, different FCs and groups organize in different ways. As stated above, there are different considerations that groups take into account such as economics, politics, tax and governance. Therefore, in practice, global FCs and or banking groups choose to branch into some jurisdictions and incorporate subsidiaries in others, which makes resolution more difficult for resolution authorities (Fig. 6.1).

The Special Case of Resolution of Insurance Companies

An additional challenge for resolution authorities would be the resolution of the insurance business of the BBFC. The outcome of resolving insurance business of a BBFC will depend on the jurisdiction involved.

At the end of 2017, the FSB conducted a survey to monitor resolvability on the insurance sector in order to evaluate the development of the *Key Attributes* and the *Developing Effective Resolution Strategies and Plans for Systemically Important Insurers*, which showed comprehensive reforms in Australia, France, Hong Kong and Singapore.[46] According to FSB, the preferred resolution strategy for many insurers is a "multiple point of entry strategy" that relies on the resolution of operative entities.[47]

In the US, the OLA permits Systemically Important insurance holding companies to be resolved under DFA. However, individual legal entity insurance company subsidiaries are resolved by the State-based resolution regime.[48] Contrary, in the EU, while there is a recovery and resolution framework in place for credit institutions and investment firms (BRRD), there is no EU legislation or resolution framework for insurers.[49] Each insurer would follow a local insolvency proceeding.[50]

6.3 Single Point of Entry and Multiple Point of Entry Strategy

As stated in the conceptual framework chapter, international regulators and soft law institutions have developed a framework of two different resolution strategies; (1) Single Point of Entry (SPOE); and (2) Multiple Point of Entry (MPOE).

The SPOE is the resolution strategy where the resolution authorities apply the resolution tools to the top holding or parent company, by

[46] FSB, www.fsb.org/2016/06/developing-effective-resolution-strategies-and-plans-for-systemically-important-insurers/. Accessed 18 June 2023; FSB "Keeping the Pressure Up".

[47] FSB "Keeping the Pressure up".

[48] IMF Country Report 18/207 "United States: 2018 Article IV Consultation – Press Release; Staff Report and Statement by the Executive Director for United States" (2018).

[49] EIOPA Opinion to Institutions of the European Union on the Harmonisation of Recovery And Resolution Frameworks for (Re)Insurers Across The Member States (July 2017), https://register.eiopa.europa.eu/Publications/Opinions/EIOPA-BoS-17-148_Opinion_on_recovery_and_resolution_for_(re)insurers.pdf. Accessed 18 June 2023.

[50] European Systemic Risk Board. Report by the ATC Expert Group on Insurance. Recovery and Resolution for the EU Insurance Sector: A Macroprudential Perspective" (August 2017), https://www.esrb.europa.eu/pub/pdf/reports/esrb.reports170817_recoveryandresolution.en.pdf. Accessed 18 June 2023. See also Andreas Dombret and Patrick Kenadjian *Resolution in Europe: The Unresolved Questions* (De Gruyter 2019).

only one resolution authority (i.e. where the global consolidation supervision of the financial group is exercised). The company at the top of the structure absorbs losses by bail-in. If the top company has sufficient loss absorbency capacity, its subsidiaries will continue operating without being resolved.[51]

The MPOE, on the contrary, is the resolution strategy where various resolution authorities apply bail-in to different companies of the group where the most probable outcome would be the spin-off of the financial group. Possible outcomes would be the division of the group within national or regional boundaries, or by business lines, or both. Resolution authorities would be free to apply different resolution tools but would need to coordinate across borders in order to prevent conflicts of interest, run of assets and contagion among the whole group.[52]

A distinctive difference between the two strategies is that under an MPOE, loss-absorbing capital is not shared across jurisdictions, and it will not need cross-jurisdictional transfers, whereas in SPOE, loss-absorbing capacity is shared and there are transfers between jurisdictions.[53]

Bolton and Oehme describe a third "hybrid" approach, whereby banking groups create intermediate national holding groups, which issue TLAC that would not be shared across the group. Therefore, there would be a shared loss-absorbing capacity, across jurisdictions, issued at the holding or parent level, and another loss-absorbing capacity issued at the "national intermediate holding" which is applied to the global parent or third-party investors.[54]

The US Federal Deposit Insurance Corporation (FDIC) approach consists of putting the holding company into receivership. The FDIC transfers holding company assets to a new bridge company. All of holding company's equity and long-term unsecured debt would be left at the

[51] FSB "Key Attributes of Effective Resolution Regimes".

[52] Ibid. See generally for EU Jean Heindrich Binder "Cross-Border Coordination of Bank Resolution in the EU: All Problems Resolved?" in Matthias Haentjens *Research Handbook on Cross-Border Bank Resolution* (Edward Elgar 2019).

[53] Patrick Bolton and Martin Oehmke "Bank Resolution and the Structure of Global Banks", Discussion paper no 778. Paul Woolley Centre Working Paper No. 59 (2018), 2.

[54] Ibid.

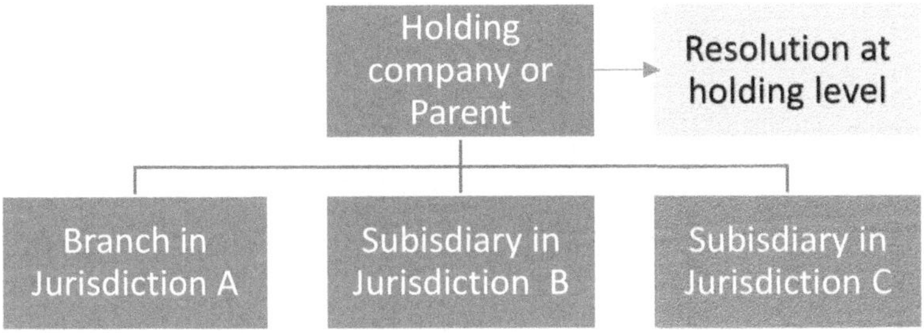

Fig. 6.2 Single Point of Entry strategy

holding company level.[55] In Europe, the BBRD admits SPOE and MPOE approaches.[56]

While at the beginning the SPOE was the preferred approach for key regulators, the TLAC regulation that proposes to "pre-position" sufficient amount of capital in each subsidiary might be a "step back" towards MPE regulation[57] (Figs. 6.2, 6.3 and 6.4).

Advantages and disadvantages of the two strategies follow.

Advantages of SPOE Strategy

1. *SPOE strategy is more efficient since it permits using lower loss-absorbing capacity*
   SPOE resolution strategy allows regulators to transfer resources between units in different jurisdictions, and therefore use a lower amount of loss-absorbing capacity.[58] A second efficiency effect would be that because of the savings anticipated by the SPOE

[55] David Skeel Jr. "Single Point of Entry and the Bankruptcy Alternative" in Martin Neil Baily and John B. Taylor *Across the Great Divide: New Perspectives on the Financial Crisis*, chapter 15 (Hoover Institution, Stanford University 2015), 312.

[56] BBRD, whereas (80) "This Directive should allow for a multiple-point-of-entry or a single-point-of-entry resolution. The MREL should reflect the resolution strategy which is appropriate to a group in accordance with the resolution plan".

[57] Ester Faia and Beatrice Weder di Mauro "Cross-Border Resolution of Global Banks", Federal Reserve Bank of Dallas Globalization and Monetary Policy Institute Working Paper No 236 (2015), 25.

[58] Ibid. Schoenmaker "The Different Legal and Operational Structures", 18; Santiago Fernandez de Liz "The Multiple-Point-of-Entry Resolution Strategy for Global Banks", BBVA Press (2015) Article, 2.

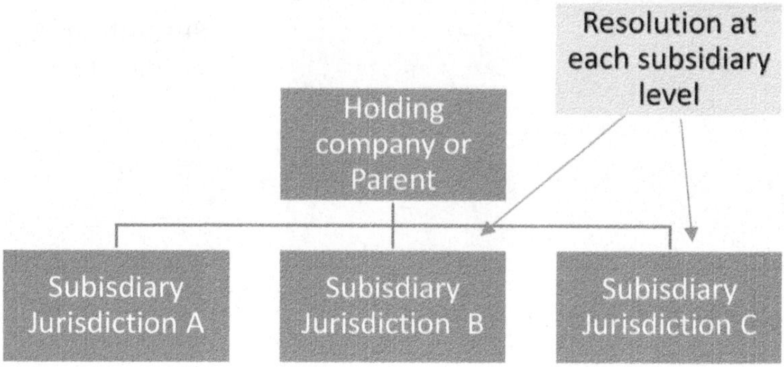

Fig. 6.3 Multiple Point of Entry resolution strategy

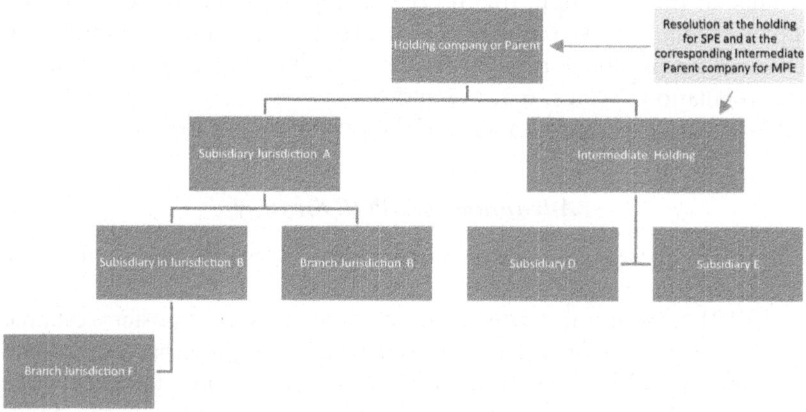

Fig. 6.4 Hybrid resolution strategy (*Source* Based on various authors[59])

[59] Bolton and Oehmke "Bank Resolution and the Structure of Global Banks", 2; Santiago Fernandez de Lis "TLAC Implementation in Retail Banks in Emerging Markets: The Multiple Point of Entry Model" European Economy, Banks, Regulation, and the Real Sector (2014), 103.

approach, the "overall losses" expected would be much less than in an uncoordinated resolution approach.[60]

2. *SPOE strategy would ensure continuity of critical functions of operating firms and of the group as a whole, and therefore reduce risks of financial stability*
As a SPOE bail-in is applied on the parent or holding level, subsidiaries will continue operating as a going concern.[61] SPOE strategy would ensure the continuity of all critical functions performed by the operating firms, thereby reducing risks of financial stability.[62] Foreign subsidiaries would be unaffected "minimizing risks of cross- border implementation",[63] thus preventing a mass termination of contracts at the subsidiary level, since the counterparties of the subsidiaries would "have little incentive" to terminate their contracts.[64] In addition, as sound subsidiaries would be open

[60] Jeoffrey Gordon and Wolf Ringe "Bank Resolution in Europe: The Unfinished Agenda of Structural Reform", ECGI Law Working Paper No 282 (2015), 11.

[61] Skeel Jr. "Single Point of Entry", 323; John Crawford "Single Point of Entry: The Promise and Limits of the Latest Cure for Bailouts", UC Hastings College of the Law Legal Studies Research Paper Series (2014), 103; Sylvester Eijffinger "Single Resolution Mechanism" in Banking Union: The Single Resolution Mechanism. Monetary Dialogue, European Parliament (2013), 56; Kwon-Yong Jin "How to Eat an Elephant: Corporate Group Structure of Systemically Important Financial Institutions, Orderly Liquidation Authority, and Single Point of Entry Resolution", *The Yale Law Journal* (2015), 1757. Howell Jackson and Stephanie Massman "The Resolution of Distressed Financial Conglomerates" *The Russell Sage Foundation Journal of the Social Sciences*, Vol. 3, No. 1 (2017), 51; FINMA "Resolution of Global Systemically Important Banks FINMA Position Paper on Resolution of G-SIBs" (2013), https://www.finma.ch/en/~/media/finma/dokumente/dokumentencenter/myfinma/finma-publikationen/diskussionspapiere/diskussionspapier-20130807-sanierung-abwicklung-global-systemrelevante-banken.pdf?la=en. Accessed 29 September 2023.

[62] FDIC-Bank of England "Resolving Globally Active, Systemically Important, Financial Institutions" [2012] A joint paper by Federal Deposit Insurance Corporation and the Bank of England, 10; Mike Konczal "Sheila Bair: Dodd-Frank Really Did End Taxpayer Bailouts" *WSJ* (New York 18 May 2013), https://www.washingtonpost.com/news/wonk/wp/2013/05/18/sheila-bair-dodd-frank-really-did-end-taxpayer-bailouts/?noredirect=on&utm_term=.b894a53ddeaf. Accessed 27 September 2023; Emilios Avgouleas and Charles Goodhart "Critical Reflections on Bank Bail-ins", *Journal of Financial Regulation* (2015), 10.

[63] Ibid., ii.

[64] Jin "How to Eat an Elephant", 1759.

and operating, contagion effects would be limited[65] and the bank would capture economies of scope and scale from shared services.[66] This would help avoiding "disruptions, destructive runs that can produce fire sale liquidations, negative asset valuation spirals and other knock-on effects".[67]

3. *SPOE strategy makes resolution transparent and credible*
SPOE strategy would be more transparent and credible than other strategies because all the bail-in-able debt is "earmarked" and "available for regulatory activation". The market would recognize the foreseeability of resolution effects and enhance transparency.[68]
4. *SPOE strategy would bundle the resolution power in one centre of control*
Unlike MPOEs, an SPOE approach would empower the home regulator avoiding multiple regulator frictions and a race for ring-fencing assets for the "protection of national creditors".[69] SPOE would avoid the need to commence different separate territorial and entity-focused resolutions, which would be "disruptive" and "difficult to coordinate".[70] This process would align incentives of resolution authorities, directors and creditors of foreign subsidiaries and branches to cooperate rather than take legal action against the bank.[71] According to Federal Reserve Governor Jerome Powell, the SPOE approach "is a classic simplifier, making theoretically possible something that seemed impossibly complex".[72]
5. *SPOE strategy would enable quick resolution*
Proponents of SPOE strategy argue it permits a fast resolution of large financial institutions. SPOE would "move very quickly from non-resolution to resolution status, while maintaining continuity of

[65] FDIC-Bank of England "Resolving Globally Active", 11.

[66] Bolton and Oehmke "Bank Resolution and the Structure of Global Banks", 14.

[67] Gordon and Ringe "Bank Resolution in Europe", 1; FDIC-Bank of England, 10.

[68] Gordon and Ringe "Bank Resolution in Europe", 9.

[69] Ibid., 11; Jackson and Massman "The Resolution of Distressed", 51.

[70] FDIC-Bank of England "Resolving Globally Active", 11.

[71] Ibid., 12.

[72] Jerome Powell "Ending Too Big to Fail", Remarks at the Institute of International Bankers Washington Conference (2013), 6.

operations".[73] SPOE resolution is supposed to be performed over the "liquidation weekend"[74] in order to apply the bail in and or other resolution tools ready for the opening of the markets the following Monday. A delay in resolution may be "catastrophic".[75]

6. *SPOE strategy is preferred by regulators in key jurisdictions*
It is important to note regulators in key jurisdictions prefer the SPOE approach. The FDIC has adopted the SPOE approach as a proposed solution to solve the TBTF problem for US G-SIBS.[76] As a way to reflect leadership, the FDIC published a joint paper in 2012 with the Bank of England describing the main features of SPOE as a viable approach for resolution of G-SIBS.[77] The UK government introduced the Financial Services (Banking Reform) in 2013, which contains the bail-in tool.[78] In Switzerland, the FINMA indicated the SPOE as a preferred strategy.[79] According to Federal Reserve Governor Gruenberg, the German BaFin also prefers SPOE strategy.[80] The Japanese Financial Services Agency has adopted SPOE for the four Japanese G-SIBS.[81] According to official information, the US, UK, Switzerland and Japan will adopt

[73] Daniel Tarullo "Toward Building a More effective Resolution Regime: Progress and Challenges" (18 October 2003), https://www.bis.org/review/r131107c.pdf, 4. Accessed 10 November 2023; Jin "How to Eat an Elephant", 1748–1786.

[74] FDIC-Bank of England "Resolving Globally Active", 4.

[75] Jin "How to Eat an Elephant", 1748–1786.

[76] FDIC "Resolution of Systemically Important Financial Institutions: The Single Point of Entry Strategy", *Federal Register*, Vol. 78, No. 243 (2013).

[77] FDIC-Bank of England "Resolving Globally Active"; "Electronic submission by The Clearing House, SIFMA, ABA,FSR, GFMA to the FDIC Re. FDIC's Notice and Request for Comments on the Resolution of Systemically Important Financial Institutions: The Single Point of Entry Strategy" (2014) (FR Docket No 2013-30057), https://www.afme.eu/globalassets/downloads/consultation-responses/joint-industry-comment-letter-on-resolution-of-systemically-important-financial-institutions-the-single-point-of-entry-strategy.pdf. Accessed 27 September 2023.

[78] Bank of England "The Bank of England's Approach to Resolution" (2017), https://www.bankofengland.co.uk/-/media/boe/files/financial-stability/resolution/boes-approach-to-resolution. Accessed 28 September 2023.

[79] FINMA" Resolution of Global Systemically Important Banks".

[80] Martin J. Gruenberg "Volcker Alliance Program", FDIC (2013), 1–7.

[81] FSA "The FSA's Approach to Introduce the TLAC Framework" (2018), https://www.fsa.go.jp/en/news/2018/20180413/01.pdf. Accessed 28 September 2023.

SPOE strategy. While BaFin did not publish an official document embracing SPOE, the only German G-SIB, Deutsche Bank, has announced in its Annual Report, stating that it prefers SPOE too. Theoretically, if key jurisdictions prefer the same approach to resolution, it would be easier for them to cooperate and coordinate a cross-border resolution of G-SIBS in these jurisdictions. In practice though, it might be more difficult because of the application of territorial approach of resolution of US branches of foreign banks in certain countries, such as the US.[82]

7. *SPOE strategy would permit the G-SIBs to organize themselves in flexible ways through branches or subsidiaries or both*
   One argument in favour of the SPOE strategy is that it respects the chosen organizational structure of the G-SIB, via branches, subsidiaries or both.[83] Instead, in an MPOE strategy the group would need to organize itself through subsidiaries. As stated above, the reasons for banking, legal and operative organization respond to different factors such as tax, economic and political environments, hence the subsidiary structure would not always be the most efficient for global banks.

Disadvantages of SPOE Strategy

1. *SPOE strategy may end up in a non-cooperative resolution and ring-fencing*
   Even though the SPOE resolution approach is theoretically more efficient than MPOE, in practice, national regulators may have incentives to ring-fence their national banking industries.[84] One of

[82] Lastra "Cross-Border Resolution", 5; Huertas "A Resolvable Bank", 139.

[83] Electronic submission by The Clearing House, SIFMA, ABA, FSR, GFMA to the FDIC, https://www.afme.eu/Portals/0/globalassets/downloads/consultation-responses/AFME-RRN-Joint-industry-comment-letter-on-Resolution-of-Systemically-Important-Financial-Institutions-The-Single-Point-of-Entry-Strategy.pdf. Accessed 28 September 2023.

[84] Bolton et al. "Bank Resolution and the Structure of Global Banks", 1–60; Skeel Jr. "Single Point of Entry" "British regulators …worry about whether US regulators will act as vigorously to recapitalize a troubled UK subsidiary as with a troubled US subsidiary", 324; Stephen Lubben and Arthur Wilmarth "Too Big and Unable to Fail", GW Law School Public Law and Legal Theory Paper No. 2016-44 (2016), 1209; Avgouleas and Goodhart "Critical Reflections on Bank Bail-ins", 21; Schoenmaker "The Different Legal

the prerequisites for a successful SPOE approach is, as the IMF contends, the need of

> [a]n effective ex ante cooperation arrangement among the authorities of relevant jurisdictions. This strategy must be underpinned by aligned incentives that create confidence their respective national interest for promoting financial stability will be protected. In the absence of such mutual trust, host authorities tend to undertake parallel resolution actions or ring-fence branches or subsidiaries in their jurisdictions, with suboptimal outcomes for all creditors of the institution/group.[85]

Avgouleas and Goodhart argue that, apart from the US-UK relationship that is based on trust, it is doubtful that "any form of non-binding bilateral arrangements, including MOUs, would hold in an event of a cross border banking crisis, involving a transfer of funds from one jurisdiction to another".[86] Even more, as argued by Bolton and Oelke, a SPOE resolution may not be followed even though it has been agreed ex ante. If the home resolution authority believes the transfer to foreign subsidiaries is too large, it may prefer to ring-fence national assets and avoid the transfer altogether. This is possibly the "biggest obstacle to a successful SPOE resolution".[87]

2. *SPOE strategy may incentive subsidiary creditors' moral hazard and may discourage market discipline*
   As the bail-in tool in a SPOE strategy is applied at the holding or top tier, shareholders and creditors of the holding company take the burden, but creditors of the subsidiaries are generally not affected by bail-in. The SPOE strategy may increase moral hazard

and Operational Structures", 10; Faia and Weder di Mauro "Cross-Border Resolution", 3; Richard Herring "The Challenge of Resolving Cross-Border Financial Institutions", *Yale Journal of Regulation*, Vol. 31 (2014), 879.

85 Giovanni Dell'Ariccia, Maria Soledad Martinez Peria, Deniz O. Igan, Elsie Addo Awadzi, Marc C. Dobler, Damiano Sandri "Trade-Offs in Bank Resolution", IMF Technical Note (2018), 31; See also Huertas "A Resolvable Bank", 132.

86 Avgouleas and Goodhart "Critical Reflections on Bank Bail-ins", 24.

87 Bolton et al. "Bank Resolution and the Structure of Global Banks", 21; Charles Randall "The FSB's Key Attributes": The Road to Cross-Border Resolution of Financial Institutions" (Discussion Draft 12.06.2012).

of subsidiaries' creditors and counterparties.[88] In this scenario, subsidiaries might obtain cheaper funding from creditors which would be willing to receive a lower yield for a perceived lower risk.[89] For the same reason, subsidiary creditor's incentives to monitor may be discouraged. A counterargument states the monitoring will shift to the creditors at the holding level, since the risk would have shifted towards them. However, it is doubtful creditors of the holding company are well positioned to monitor the whole structure effectively.[90] Additionally, as the SPOE strategy would fully commit to protect derivatives in case of resolution, derivative counterparties would also be discouraged from monitoring.[91]

3. *Regulators would not be capable of handling multiple SPOE resolutions at the same time*
According to some authors, regulators would not be able to operate "single point of entry resolutions of more than one systemically important institution at the same time".[92] Regulators would not be able to handle simultaneous SIFIs resolutions in a "resolution weekend", as the GFC has demonstrated.
4. *Loss-absorbing capacity might not be sufficient*
A challenge for a SPOE strategy is that there must be sufficient loss-absorbing capacity at the top level.[93] The key question here is if the FSB-proposed 16–20% of risk-weighted assets is sufficient or not. Crawford notes a few months before Lehman failed, it reported a 16.1% ratio of total capital-to-risk-weighted assets.[94] In a crisis scenario, insufficient loss-absorbing capacity would mean a government bailout. The result would be a failure of the system, since one

[88] Jin "How to Eat an elephant", 1765; Avgouleas and Goodhart, "Critical Reflections on Bank Bail-ins", 24. Paul Kupiec and Peter Wallison "Can the single Point of Entry Strategy Be Used to Recapitalize a Systemically Important Failing Bank?", *Journal of Financial Stability*, Vol. 20 (2015), 193; Herring "The Challenge of Resolving", 878.

[89] Stephanie Massman "The Orderly Liquidation Authority: Fanatical or Familiar? Idealistic or Unrealistic?", DASH Harvard University (2014), 39.

[90] Ibid., 40.

[91] Skeel Jr. "Single Point of Entry", 326.

[92] Skeel Jr. "Single Point of Entry", 324–326; Herring "The Challenge of Resolving", 879.

[93] Jackson and Massman "The Resolution of Distressed", 53.

[94] Crawford "Single Point of Entry", 110.

of the purposes of the SPOE strategy is avoiding taxpayer's money to resolve banking failure.

5. *SPOE strategy might encourage banking groups to issue more debt at the subsidiary level*
Since the SPOE strategy relies on the issuance of unsecured debt at the holding level, and holding creditors will request a higher yield for this debt—with a proportional increase in banking group funding costs—managers at the holding level may be encouraged to issue debt at the subsidiary level instead.[95] Even though the holding company will need to comply with the minimum total loss-absorbing capacity at the holding level, if the banks issue more debt at the subsidiary level, the minimum TLAC might not be enough in a crisis scenario, hence the possibility of a bail out might increase.
6. *Once the holding company is resolved, there might be a run by the subsidiaries' creditors*
Some authors argue the sole resolution of the holding or parent company would trigger "contagious runs" by the creditors of the subsidiaries.[96] As Avgouleas and Goodhart contend, the operating subsidiary might "suffer a flight due to reputational contagion, which triggers an irrational but quite likely panic, regardless of parent's liability to sufficiently recapitalize the operating parts of the group through conversion of bail-in-able liabilities".[97]
7. *SPOE strategy might extend support for non-core banking foreign units*
This argument is focused on the US. Before the adoption of the SPOE by the US, the "source of strength doctrine" imposed support obligations to the holding company in order to recapitalize "failing commercial banks" in trouble. In addition, a healthy bank subsidiary of the group would support the failing commercial bank via cross-guarantee provisions. The beneficiary was always

[95] Jin "How to Eat an Elephant", 1771; Joseph Sommer "Why Bail In? And How!", *Economic Policy Review* (2014), 220; Tarullo "Toward Building a More effective Resolution Regime".

[96] Lubben and Wilmarth, "Too Big and Unable to Fail", 1209; Steven Schwarcz "Beyond Bankrupcty: Resolution as a Macroprudential Regulatory Tool", *Notre Dame Law Review* (2018), 20.

[97] Avgouleas and Goodhart "Critical Reflections on Bank Bail-ins", 24.

a FDIC-insured banking subsidiary.[98] With the implementation of SPOE strategy, the scope of coverage is broader, since the support is given to any distressed affiliate, for instance insurance or securities branches or subsidiaries. This would mean any liquidity support from FDIC would indirectly support a non-insured entity. As Avgouleas and Goodhart explain, the US "would extend coverage of US deposit insurance and of the OLF to foreign depositors, probably a politically prohibitive action".[99] In the case of insurance affiliates, the support would not even go to foreign depositors but to foreign insurance policyholders or investors, which would make the US authority options much more difficult from a political perspective.

8. *Governments might face legal disputes from holding company creditors under SPOE strategy*
Given the fact that a failing subsidiary would be supported by resolving the holding company, its creditors might challenge the bail-in as an illegal appropriation. According to Kupiec and Wallison in the US,

> If the government proceeds with a SPOE liquidation to recapitalize a failing bank subsidiary, BHC creditors may have a strong legal case that their investments were illegally confiscated in the SPOE liquidation to support a failing bank subsidiary that is explicitly identified as a non-covered institution in the OLA language.[100]

Advantages of MPOE Strategy

1. *MPOE strategy enhances financial stability as proven during the financial crisis*
According to some authors, MPOE strategy has proven resilient during different financial crisis, limiting contagion. In 2001, the financial system failed in Argentina. Many banks abandoned the country and even subsidiaries of foreign banking groups were liquidated. Spanish banks stayed in the country. There was "almost no

[98] Jackson and Massman "The Resolution of Distressed", 51.

[99] Avgouleas and Goodhart "Critical Reflections on Bank Bail-ins", 25.

[100] Kupiec et al. "Can the Single Point of Entry", 189.

contagion" in the parent or other subsidiaries in the region given the limited intra-group exposure.[101] On the other hand, during the Eurozone financial crisis there was almost no contagion of Spain's liquidity problems to subsidiaries in Argentina or other Latin America's countries.[102]

2. *MPOE strategy fosters the development of local capital markets*
   MPOE strategy would foster the development of capital markets in developing countries because there would be a need of issuing capital and debt at the subsidiary level in order to fulfil the loss-absorbing capital requirements.[103]
3. *MPOE strategy would be the most efficient outcome in a non-cooperative resolution scenario*
   If, as stated above, national regulators wish to ring-fence their national banking industries, a MPOE strategy would be more efficient.[104] Subsidiaries would be capitalized, shared services such as IT would be organized on a "stand-alone" basis, all of which would help an ordered resolution of each subsidiary.[105]
4. *Under a MPOE, strategy coordination between resolution authorities is easier than in a SPOE strategy*
   While in both strategies coordination between resolution authorities is key, coordination under a MPOE strategy would not be as critical

[101] Santiago Fernandez de Lis "The Multiple-Point-of Entry Resolution Strategy for Global Banks", BBVA Press Article 25 February 2015, 1–3.

[102] Ibid.; Herman Kamil and Kulwant Rai's "The Global Credit Crunch and the Foreign Bank's Lending to Emerging Markets, Why Did Latin America Fare Better?", IMF Working paper No. 10/102 (2010), 14. Also see Robert Cull and Maria Martinez Peria "Bank Ownership and Lending Patterns During the 2008–2009 Financial Crisis", The World Bank Development Research Group Finance and Private Sector Development Team (2012), 18.

[103] Fiechter et al. "Subsidiaries or Branches", 5; Jose Pardo, Maria Mirat, Santiago Fernandez de Lis, and Victoria Santillana "Multiple Point of Entry Resolution Strategy: A Natural Approach for Decentralised Retail Banking Groups", BBVA Research (2014), 2.

[104] Bolton and Oehmke "Bank Resolution and the Structure of Global Banks", 1. Schoenmaker, "The Different Legal and Operational Structures", 12.

[105] Pardo et al. "Multiple Point of Entry Resolution Strategy", 1.

as in SPOE strategy.[106] The role of the resolution authority in the host jurisdiction would be an "executing figure" while the home jurisdiction authority would be a "coordinator figure". Cross-border cooperation agreements may be more flexible under MPOE since the resolution strategy is applied locally.[107]

5. *Decentralized business model and MPOE strategy reduces banking group complexity*

   Subsidiary model reduces "bank complexity" since accountability and transparency are enhanced. These factors lower risk perceptions in financial markets.[108] A counter-argument might exist since one of the indicators of complexity is the number of legal entities of a banking group. While it is true that more organizational complexity exists, decentralized groups generally have a simple "business complexity", which is focused on retail business. Overall, the lower interconnectedness of the subsidiary and decentralized model, and its lower business complexity would make banking groups less complex.[109]

6. *MPOE strategy enhances market monitoring and prevents moral hazard at the subsidiary level*

   One key difference between SPOE and MPOE strategies is that the bail-in is applied at different levels. In MPOE strategy bail-in would be applied at the subsidiary level, hence its creditors would have the incentive to monitor the subsidiary, with no enhancement of moral hazard.

Disadvantages of MPOE Strategy

1. *MPOE strategy is less efficient than SPOE strategy*

[106] James Chew "Multiple Point of Entry: The Forgotten Alternative", The Clearing House (2017), https://www.theclearinghouse.org/banking-perspectives/2014/2014-q1-banking-perspectives/articles/multiple-point-of-entry.

[107] Ibid.

[108] Ibid.

[109] Jacobo Carmassi and Richard Herring "The Corporate Complexity of Global Systemically Important Banks", *Journal of Financial Services Research*, Vol. 49 (2016), 175–201.

The structural design of the MPOE strategy requires more loss-absorbing capacity for the whole group.[110] The MPOE strategy has its own costs in terms of lower efficiency in capital and liquidity management.[111] Moreover, in developing economies, loss-absorbing capacity would imply higher capital requirements because subsidiaries in those countries would not be able to issue sufficient bail-in-able debt. The TLAC would need to be covered by equity, increasing the overall capital amount.[112]

2. *MPOE strategy would split the banking group*

   Normally, the result of MPOE bail-in at the subsidiary level would imply new owners at each point of entry, splitting the banking group.[113] A consequence of this splitting is the "reduction in continuation value".[114]

3. *Under MPOE strategy critical shared services should be organized independently*

   The FSB argues making a MPOE strategy effective would demand

> A degree of legal, financial and operational separation within the group, which may require changes to the way groups are structured or robust service level agreements to ensure the continuity of any critical shared services across entities subject to resolution at different points of entry.[115]

110 Bolton et al. "Bank Resolution and the Structure of Global Banks", 4.

111 Santiago Fernandez de Lis, Jose Pardo, and Victoria Santillana "Compendium on Resolution Strategies: A Multiple Point of Entry View", BBVA Regulation Outlook (2014), 4.

112 Ibid.

113 Bolton et al. above "Bank Resolution and the Structure of Global Banks", 2; Paul Tucker "Solving too Big to Fail—Where Do Things Stand on Resolution?", Speech at the Institute of International Finance October 2013; FSB "Principles on Loss-Absorbing Capacity of G-SIBS in Resolution Total Loss-Absorbing Capacity (TLAC) Term Sheet" (2015).

114 Bolton et al. "Bank Resolution and the Structure of Global Banks", 9. New bank would have a new brand if the subsidiary shared the same name as the parent company, which will entail value destruction.

115 FSB "Recovery and Resolution Planning: Making the Key Attributes Requirements Operational Consultative Document" (2012), 28.

In order to pursue this objective, banking groups with a MPOE strategy should create "separate operational subsidiaries" that would provide critical shared functions to the operating subsidiaries.[116] Under the "centralised subsidiarisation approach", a single company provides shared services, while under a "decentralised subsidiarisation approach" a separate shared services company services each subsidiary or resolution entity.[117] The first approach would need strong service agreements, which "would survive the resolution of any bank within the group and allow for that bank to leave the group if that is the consequence of its resolution".[118] The need of redundant critical shared services subsidiaries is inefficient and lacks the benefits of economies of scale.

4. *MPOE strategy restricts the organizational structure since it is designed as a subsidiary model*

   A precondition for a MPOE strategy to be effective is that the group must be structured by subsidiaries. As stated above, the subsidiary model has its advantages and disadvantages, but it is not effective for certain business models.

6.4 Which Resolution Strategy Best Fits the German Model Conglomerate?

This analysis will focus on the resolution of German model BBFC that poses systemic risk exposure to the whole system. Currently, there is only one G-SIB in Germany, which is Deutsche Bank. The main characteristics of DB are:

1. Its legal structure is complex, with parent legal entity with branches in many countries and subsidiaries in others, mainly in emerging markets.[119]

[116] Chew "Multiple Point of Entry"; Huertas "A Resolvable Bank", 164; Fernandez et al. "Compendium on Resolution Strategies", 3.

[117] Fernandez et al. "Compendium on Resolution Strategies", 5.

[118] Chew "Multiple Point of Entry".

[119] DB Annual Report 2020. Available at: https://www.db.com/ir/en/download/Annual_Report_2020.pdf. Accessed 23 April 2023.

2. Its business model is focused on wholesale banking and investment banking.[120]
3. It is a centralized type of bank.
4. Its headquarters are located in Germany, hence governed by German law, which has a universal approach to resolution.[121]

Germany is involved in the Single Resolution Mechanism (SRM), which consolidates key competences and resources at a European level for managing the failure of banks within member states participating in the banking union. The SRM operates under the SRM Regulation and the Bank Recovery and Resolution Directive (BRRD), which have been implemented in Germany through the German Recovery and Resolution Act. Additionally, the German Resolution Mechanism Act (Abwicklungsmechanismusgesetz) aligns German bank resolution laws with the SRM.[122]

Both the SRM Regulation and the German Recovery and Resolution Act mandate the development of recovery and resolution plans for banks and grant significant powers to public authorities to intervene in failing or likely to fail banks. Banks under direct supervision by the European Central Bank (ECB), such as Deutsche Bank, undergo resolvability assessments by the Single Resolution Board (SRB) which may require legal and operational adjustments to ensure their resolvability. If a bank is deemed by the ECB or the SRB to be failing or likely to fail, and certain conditions are met, the SRB is responsible for adopting a resolution scheme in

[120] Sigurt Vitols "Changes in Germany's Bank-Based Financial System: A Varieties of Capitalism Perspective", WZB Discussion Paper, No. SP II 2004-03 (2014), 5.

[121] Insolvency Statute of 5 October 1994 (Federal Law Gazette I page 2866), as last amended by Article 19 of the Act of 20 December 2011 (Federal Law Gazette I page 2854) section 335, https://www.gesetze-im-internet.de/englisch_inso/englisch_inso.html. Accessed 17 June 2023; IMF Country Report No. 16/194: Germany. Crisis Preparedness, Bank Resolution and Crisis Management Frameworks-Technical Note (2016), 27; Ian Fletcher *Cross-Border Insolvency: National and Comparative Studies: Reports* (Tubingen 1992), 107; American Bankruptcy Institute, https://www.abi.org/abi-journal/the-new-german-rules-on-international-insolvency-law. Accessed 17 June 2023.

[122] Deutsche Bank "Second Supplement Dated 23 September 2022 to the Registration Document for Secondary Issuances of Non-Equity Securities Dated 4 May 2022, As Supplemented by the First Supplement Dated 3 August 2022". See Gortsos "The Single Resolution Mechanism (SRM) and the Single Resolution Fund (SRF): Legal Aspects of the Second Main Pillar of the European Banking Union (Fifth-Extended and Fully Updated-Edition)." Available at SSRN 2668653 (2019).

accordance with the SRM Regulation. The European Commission, along with the Council of the European Union to a lesser extent, plays a role in endorsing or objecting to the proposed resolution scheme put forth by the SRB. The execution of the resolution scheme falls under the purview of the competent national resolution authorities (Bafin).[123]

Accordingly, when we refer to Germany or German authorities in the below paragraphs it should be interpreted considering the different roles taken by SRB or Bafin.

According to the four factors analysed before, a SPOE strategy would best fit the German model BBFC. However, the following preconditions need to align in order to hold an effective SPOE resolution in this particular case: (i) Germany should have effective ex ante cooperation arrangements with authorities of relevant jurisdictions (EU, UK, US, Japan). This would give them assurance that the SPOE will be respected; (ii) every country where the German SIFI has assets, branches and subsidiaries should recognize the universal approach to resolution in order to avoid ring-fencing by national regulators; (iii) German authorities need to monitor the amount of eligible liabilities to enable a sufficient bail-in. An important challenge concerns whether foreign resolution authorities would embrace the German universal resolution approach. If a foreign resolution authority would ring-fence and liquidate a SIFI German branch, it would most probably end up in the liquidation of the parent entity as well. Additionally, the US resolution proceedings—where there is a territorial approach to foreign bank distressed branches acting in the US and a universal approach to US branches acting abroad—would make the German resolution authorities' decision-making difficult. If such scenario takes place, it would have negative implications for the resolution of the remainder of the group, since all the assets of the US branches would be isolated from the SPOE resolution.

A number of conditions favour a SPOE strategy in the case of Germany. First, as stated above, the principle of universality insolvency law applies through Directive 2001/24/EC on the Reorganization and Winding-Up of credit institutions, together with the BRRD, which provides for the automatic recognition within the EU of resolution decisions adopted by other EU member states' authorities, and to a considerable degree the SRM Regulation. This favours the SPOE strategy in

[123] Ibid.

the sense that the German authority would accept the leading role of the home resolution authority. German law would apply to the whole process and German resolution authorities would be in charge as coordinator with foreign regulators and as executor of the resolution tools. German legislation requires banks "to include in financial contracts governed by third country law provisions recognizing the power to the resolution authorities to bail in debt and suspend contractual termination rights".[124] For all EU jurisdictions, BRRD guarantees that execution of bail in of the debt issued by German Banks in those jurisdictions is valid and recognized by local courts.[125] Second, DB has signed the International Swaps and Derivatives Association (ISDA) 2015 Universal protocol on Resolution Stays,[126] which address the issue of recognition of resolution action regarding temporary stays.[127] Third, as stated above, SRB prefers SPOE strategy, as detailed in their 2020 Annual Report.[128]

The SPOE strategy has plenty of advantages, as analysed above, but it also faces profound challenges for German model conglomerates and banking groups. The first and most important one is the need of ex ante agreements in order to assure the SPOE resolution will be executed as planned. Even within the most advanced and trustful regulator relationships (UK and US) there is still some doubt concerning, for example, whether the FDIC would apply the resolution tool at the holding company level to support a distressed UK subsidiary of a US G-SIB, and indirectly apply liquidity support to foreign depositors.[129]

[124] IMF "Country Report No 16/194", 9–39.

[125] Ibid., 27.

[126] DB Adherence to ISDA, November 2015, https://www.isda.org/protocol-adherence/67599/. Accessed 17 June 2023.

[127] This is particularly important in cross-border SPOE strategy where the resolution process needs international cooperation between authorities. "ISDA 2015 Universal Protocol which enables parties to amend the terms of their Protocol Covered Agreements to contractually recognize the cross-border application of special resolution regimes applicable to certain financial companies until comprehensive statutory regimes are adopted and to support the resolution of certain financial companies under the United States Bankruptcy Code", https://www.isda.org/protocol/isda-2015-universal-resolution-stay-protocol/. Accessed 22 June 2023.

[128] DB Annual Report 2020.

[129] Skeel "Single Point of Entry", 324; Avgouleas and Goodhart "Critical Reflections on Bank Bail-ins", 25.

The second challenge refers to the need to adjust the corporate structure of the German model to fully apply all the advantages of the SPOE strategy.[130] While in theory the bail-in tool may be applied to the parent company, the SPOE strategy relies heavily on a non-operative holding company, which has the advantage of not posing problems with workers, commercial creditors and other stockholders other than shareholders and bail-in-able creditors.

Two approaches might be used in order to achieve such a structure. First, by insisting in a structural change via recovery and resolution planning under BRRD, and second, via a compulsory holding company structure for all European-based SIFIs,[131] which would have a similar purpose in terms of resolution to the Intermediate Parent Undertaking in the EU.[132]

Advantages of SPOE as a preferred resolution strategy for German model conglomerates and banking groups	*Challenges of the SPOE strategy for German model conglomerates and banking groups*
Efficiency: a SPOE strategy allows cross-jurisdictional transfers and needs less loss-absorbing capacity needed as a group	Need to have ex ante agreements with other resolution authorities
Continuity as a group: critical functions assured	Doubtful that foreign jurisdictions would respect Germany's universal approach to resolution Special case of the US insolvency approaches
Flexibility: allows a flexible legal structure through branches and or subsidiaries	Need to change legal and operational structure to include a holding company on top of current parent company
Fast process: through a "liquidation weekend" Enhances transparency German Resolution authority would be in control of the process BaFin would prefer SPOE strategy Germany applies the universal approach to resolution SRB prefers SPOE as of Annual Report	

(continued)

130 Schoenmaker "The Different Legal and Operational Structures", 16. Sam Theodore and Thue Sondergaard "Total Loss-Absorption Capacity (TLAC): Does It Matter?", Scope Bank Ratings (2014), 2.

131 Gordon and Ringe "Bank Resolution in Europe", 1364–1365.

132 See Article 21b CRD V.

(continued)

Advantages of SPOE as a preferred resolution strategy for German model conglomerates and banking groups	*Challenges of the SPOE strategy for German model conglomerates and banking groups*
DB has signed the ISDA 2015 Universal protocol on Resolution Stays	

Furthermore, a possible hybrid model would be possible if Germany concludes that the branches and subsidiaries in certain jurisdictions would prefer the territorial approach. In such a disfavoured scenario, it might be possible to apply a SPOE strategy within certain jurisdictions and a MPOE with others. Since in the EU the bail-in tool is recognized and would be respected if BaFin used it in DB resolution, it would be wise to apply a SPOE strategy within these countries. If trustworthy ex ante agreements are available with the UK, Japan and the US (if certain assurances were made that SPOE strategy would be applied in both scenarios) SPOE strategy would be preferred with those countries too. On the contrary, in developing countries with a long tradition of territorial approach to resolution, such as Brazil, where branches need to have their own capital and other requisites in place as if they were subsidiaries,[133] a MPOE strategy might be possible. This hybrid model would be less efficient than the pure SPOE approach,[134] but would give assurance to BaFin that an uncoordinated "ring-fenced type" resolution would not take place (Fig. 6.5).

[133] IIF "Achieving Bank Resolution in Practice Are We Nearly There Yet?", A report of the IIF Cross-Border Resolution Working Group September (2014); 35 Cámara del Tribunal de Justicia de São Paulo, *Telenova Comunicações Ltda vs Telmex do Brasil Ltda* (6 june 2006); Jose Garcez, *Elementos Básicos de Direito Internacional Privado* (Síntese 1999), 139; Maria Noodt Taquela, "Concursos y Quiebras" in Diego P. Fernández Arroyo (Ed) *Derecho Internacional Privado de los Estados del Mercosur: Argentina, Brasil, Paraguay y Uruguay* (Zavalia 2003), 1386.

[134] Pardo et al. "Multiple Point of Entry Resolution Strategy", 13.

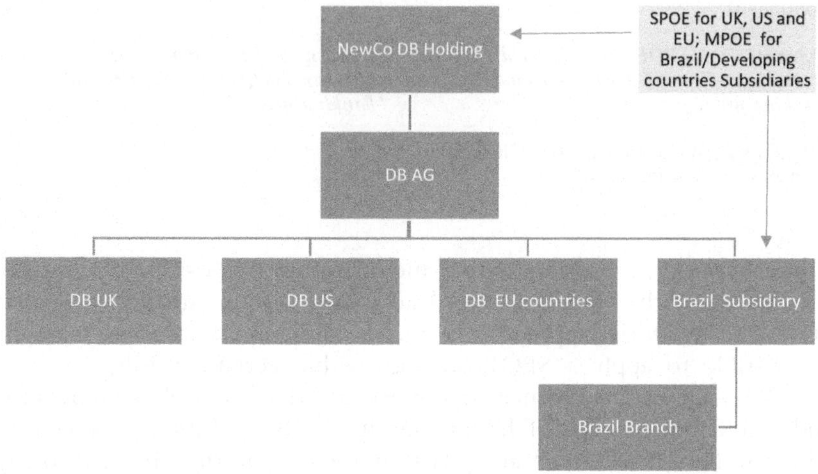

Fig. 6.5 Simplified hybrid resolution strategy for DB (*Source* Based on DB Annual report 2022)

6.5 Which Resolution Strategy Best Fits the British Model?

This section will focus on the resolution of a British model BBFC with reference to its most important institutions. In the UK, there are two G-SIBS: HSBC and Barclays. HSBC has adopted a MPOE strategy, and will be analysed along with the Santander and BBVA in Annex 1. HSBC structure is based on a holding company and different intermediate holding companies comprising each continent where they operate.[135] On the contrary, Barclay's structure remains posing the bank as holder of the insurance and securities business, even though the apex of the group is now a Holding Company. For this reason, the exam of the best strategy for the British model will focus on Barclays and not in HSBC.

Regarding the first indicator, Barclay's structure itself with both subsidiaries and branches. Units located in the following jurisdictions obtain 90% of Barclays' turnover: Canada, France, Guernsey, Hong Kong, India, Ireland, Isle of Man, Israel, Italy, Japan, Jersey, Mauritius, Monaco,

[135] HSBC Simplified group chart, https://www.hsbc.com/investors/investing-in-hsbc/group-structure. Accessed 13 March 2023.

Portugal, Singapore, Spain, United Arab Emirates, USA, UK, Luxembourg, Mexico, and Switzerland. Most of them operate through branches, with the exception of Switzerland, Mexico and Luxembourg, which operate through subsidiaries. In Hong Kong there are both branches and subsidiaries, as well as in the US.[136]

The second indicator refers to the banking business model, centralized or decentralized business model. Barclays is a centralized bank, where the investment bank model comprises 70% of risk-weighted assets. Barclays is the 7th "investment bank" in the world, and even though there are voices willing to change the model, until now the investment banking—wholesale banking prevails.[137]

The third indicator refers to retail versus no retail banking. After 2018 in the UK, Barclays is separated into Barclays UK PLC (ring fenced) bank and Barclays PLC (non-ring-fenced bank). The retail banking business of Barclays as a whole is not prevalent in the bank.

The fourth indicator deals with the universal or territorial approach to resolution. The UK embraces modified universalism, which underpins the UNCITRAL model Law on Cross-Border Insolvency, and the EC Insolvency Regulation on Insolvency Proceedings. Lord Hoffman in the UK Supreme Court *HIH Casualty & General Insurance Ltd, Re* case states

> The primary rule of private international law which seems to me applicable to this case is the principle of (modified) universalism, which has been the golden thread running through English cross-border insolvency law since the 18th century. That principle requires English courts should, so far as is consistent with justice and UK public policy, co-operate with the courts in the country of the principal liquidation to ensure that all the

[136] List of Barclays main entities (2020), https://home.barclays/content/dam/home-barclays/documents/investor-relations/reports-and-events/annual-reports/2020/Barclays-Country-Snapshot-2020-LE-Listing.pdf. Accessed 13 March 2023. See also Barclays Annual Report 2020, https://home.barclays/content/dam/home-barclays/documents/investor-relations/reports-and-events/annual-reports/2020/Barclays-PLC-Annual-Report-2020.pdf. Accessed 13 March 2021.

[137] David Crow and Stephen Morris "Investment Banking: The Battle for Barclays" *Financial Times* (London 20 January 2019).

company's assets are distributed to its creditors under a single system of distribution.[138]

In the case of *Kaupthing Bank HF*, regarding the application of EU Winding Up directive, Lord Briggs held that:

> The very essence of the universalism sought to be achieved by making the insolvency law of the home Member State applicable across the territory of all Member States depends upon that being achieved in relation to every potential home Member State in which a credit institution is regulated and has its head office regardless whether, apart from those instruments, the State's insolvency law would be anything more that domestic in its application. If that were not so, then the creation of a universally applicable law (subject to strict exceptions) for the insolvency of credit institutions, and other entities, would fall at the first hurdle, in relation to any home Member State the insolvency law which did not already have cross border effect.[139]

Theoretically, as explained by Claessens et al., the organizational structure that best fits the universal approach is the Single entity, which is "a SIFI incorporated in one jurisdiction and operating a global network composed of branch offices".[140] However, as stated above, most BBFCs structure themselves via both branches and subsidiaries.

The concurrence of the four indicators indicates SPOE would be the best solution for a "modified" British model. In the case of Barclays, it best fits because: (1) Barclays is a centralized bank; (2) which operates mainly through branches, but also via subsidiaries; (3) Its main business comprises wholesale and investment banking, with a much-reduced retail section; (4) the UK embraces universalism; (5) The apex of the banking group is a non-operative holding company.

As in the case of the German model, the following preconditions are needed for a SPOE strategy to be effective: (1) the UK should have effective ex-ante burden agreements and cooperation agreements with relevant jurisdictions (US, EU, Japan); (2) every country where Barclays holds

[138] *HIH Casualty & General Insurance Ltd, Re [2008] UKHL 21 (09 April 2008) 1 WLR 852.*

[139] *Tchenguiz &ors vs Kapthing Bank HF* [2017] *EWCA Civ 83, CA, 2017 WL 00817001.*

[140] Claessens, Herring, Schoenmaker, and Summe "A Safer World", 86.

assets need to respect the universal approach to resolution, to avoid territorial ring-fencing of assets; (3) UK authorities would need to monitor the amount of eligible liabilities to ensure bail in is applicable.

The SPOE strategy comprises certain advantages. First, the UK would lead the resolution process. Second, Barclays has adopted the ISDA 2015 Universal protocol on Resolution Stays, which address the issue of recognition of resolution action regarding temporary stays. Third, UK authorities prefer the SPOE strategy, as stated in the "US Resolution Planning 2018" document. Contrary to DB, the structure of Barclays comprises a holding company; therefore, from an organizational point of view, no structural changes are needed. In terms of efficiency, a SPOE strategy would allow regulators to transfer resources between units using a lower amount of absorbing capacity.[141] From an organizational perspective, SPOE strategy would permit the subsidiaries to continue operating as a going concern, and thus it will ensure continuity of all critical functions, reducing financial stability.[142] From a control of the resolution point of view, SPOE strategy will empower British resolution authority and avoid multiple different resolution proceedings.[143] In terms of duration, a SPOE strategy would be theoretically more expedite (it is supposed to be performed in a weekend) thus preserving stability.[144] Regulators in key jurisdictions prefer the SPOE strategy, including the US, UK, Germany, Switzerland, and Japan.[145]

As well as in the case of DB, a SPOE strategy poses challenges. First, ex ante agreements are needed in order to execute the resolution plans. There are concerns about a lack of mutual trust between home and host resolution authorities that may induce a disorderly resolution. Second, all jurisdictions in place, especially those which include foreign assets, need to

[141] Schoenmaker "The Different Legal and Operational Structures", 18; Fernandez de Liz "The Multiple-Point-of Entry", 2.

[142] Skeel Jr. "Single Point of Entry", 323; Crawford "Single Point of Entry", 103; Eijffinger "Single Resolution Mechanism", 56; Jin "How to Eat an Elephant", 1757. Jackson and Massman "The Resolution of Distressed", 51; FINMA "Resolution of Global Systemically Important Banks".

[143] FDIC-Bank of England "Resolving Globally Active", 10.

[144] Ibid., 4; Tarullo "Toward Building a More Effective Resolution Regime", 4; Jin "How to Eat an Elephant", 1764.

[145] See section "Advantages of SPOE Strategy".

respect the UK universal approach to resolution. If any jurisdiction ring-fences assets located overseas, the resolution would end up in disorder.

Advantages of SPOE as a preferred resolution strategy for the British model (Barclays)	*Challenges of the SPOE strategy for the British model (Barclays)*
Efficiency: SPOE allows cross-jurisdictional transfers and needs less loss-absorbing capacity needed as a group	Need to have ex ante agreements with other resolution authorities
Continuity as a group: critical functions assured	Doubtful that foreign jurisdictions would respect UK's universal approach to resolution
	Special case of the US insolvency approaches
Flexibility: allows a flexible legal structure through branches and or subsidiaries	Need to change legal and operational structure to include a holding company on top of current parent company
Fast process: through a "liquidation weekend"	
Enhances transparency	
UK Resolution authority would be in control of the process	
BoE and Barclays prefer the SPOE strategy	
UK applies the Universal Approach to resolution	
Barclays has signed the ISDA 2015 Universal protocol on Resolution Stays	

As with DB, a hybrid approach would be possible if the bank believes certain jurisdictions would not respect the universality principle and employ a territorial approach to resolution. In such a scenario, a SPOE strategy might be applied to certain jurisdictions (US, EU), and a MPOE to others (developing countries). This approach would be less effective due to the need to ensure shared critical functions, but would avoid an uncoordinated resolution that would be less efficient than a coordinated MPOE strategy (Fig. 6.6).

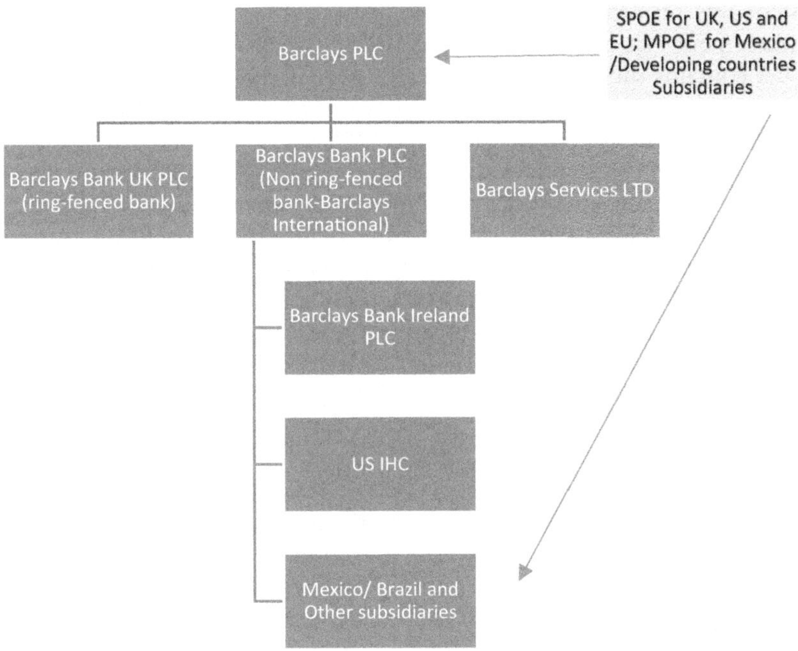

Fig. 6.6 Simplified hybrid resolution strategy for Barclays (*Source* Based on Barclays Bank UK PLC Annual Report 2022 and S&P Global Ratings, June 20, 2023)

6.6 Which Resolution Strategy Best Fits the US Model?

As Morris contents, the "true innovator" in developing a resolution regime was the US, which created the FDIC in the Great Depression and since then it has resolved thousands of banks.[146] The system evolved from simple way of returning deposits to insured depositors to a system that intended to reduce contagion, preserve public confidence in banking system and enhance financial stability.[147] The FDIC bank resolution

[146] Morris "The Law of Financial Services Groups", 254. Simon Gleeson and Randall Guynn *Bank Resolution and Crisis Management: Law and Practice* (OUP 2016), 67.

[147] Gleeson and Guynn "Bank Resolution", 67.

system was revised by the Financial Institutions Reform, Recovery and Enforcement Act of 1989 (FIRREA) during the Savings and Loan crisis. FDIA contains the US resolution statue.[148] Gleeson resumed the resolution system as "a special type of insolvency code for US insured depository institutions administered by the FDIC".[149]

As explained in Chapter 5 the US developed a unit bank system, which restricted interstate and intrastate branching. In 1956, after the enactment of the BHCA, banks moved to structure themselves via a BHC, owning a separate bank in each state. After the interstate restrictions where liberated, most of the US BBFC/banking groups maintained the US model (BHC with a non-operating company at the apex of the group). However, until the GFC the resolution system in the US only applied to insured banks.[150]

As stated above, resolution processes for US BBFCs are performed under Title I or Title II of DFA, which now includes non-insured financial institutions. Title II provides for a SPOE resolution, only if resolution under the US Bankruptcy Code is not effective.[151]

A second important change in the system was the inclusion of Section 165 of the DFA, which requires that nonbank financial companies supervised by the Federal Reserve System, and bank holding companies with assets of more than USD 50 billion to report a resolution plan. This plan must include: (i) information about how the insured company is protected from risks from other nonbank subsidiaries; (ii) descriptions of the ownership structure, balance sheet and contractual obligations, (iii) description of cross-guarantees, (iv) other information requested by the authorities.[152]

Authorities around the world have recognized the US has the means to apply successfully the SPOE resolution strategy.[153] D. Tarullo, member of the Board of Governors of the Federal Reserve System, endorsed

[148] Specially ss 11–15 of the FDIA, 12 USC ss 1821–1825.

[149] Gleeson and Guynn "Bank Resolution", 67.

[150] Gleeson and Guynn "Bank Resolution", 67.

[151] DFA Para. 203 (b)(2) and (5); ibid., 274.

[152] DFA Sec. 165, https://www.fdic.gov/regulations/reform/dfa_selections.html#1. Accessed 30 March 2023.

[153] See generally Randall D. Guynn, "Framing the TBTF Problem: The Path to a Solution" in Martin Neil Baily and John. B Taylor (Eds) *Across the Divide: New Perspectives on the Financial Crisis* (Hoover Institution 2014).

the SPOE strategy as the "best potential for the orderly resolution of a systemic financial firm under Title II".[154] J. Yellen has confirmed "right now the FDIC has the capacity and the legal authority to resolve, possibly using orderly liquidation authority, a systemically important firm that finds itself in trouble, and they have designed an architecture that I think is very promising in terms of being able to accomplish that".[155] P. Tucker has acknowledged that "in short, the US authorities have the technology – via Title II of Dodd Frank; and, just as important, most US bank and dealer groups are, through an accident of history, organized in way that lends them to top-down resolution on a group-wide basis".[156] On the academic side, a "Resolution Project" team lead by Professor T. Jackson has endorsed the SPOE strategy in his proposal to create a new Chapter 14 based on this resolution strategy.[157]

According to the FSB's "2023 list of global systemically important banks" the following G-SIBs have their headquarters and origin in the US: JP Morgan Chase, Bank of America, Citigroup, Goldman Sachs, Wells Fargo, Bank of New York Mellon, Morgan Stanley, and State Street.[158] Although JP Morgan Chase has become the largest G-SIB in the world, this book will analyse Citigroup, which appears in the second place of the FSB 2023 List. It is the third largest bank in America following JP Morgan Chase and Bank of America. The reason for this election is that Citigroup is an archetypical US model BBFC and has been the largest bank throughout its long history, until recent times, and has an impressive geographical extension (see Annex 1).

The case of Citigroup ("Citi") is illustrative of the US banking system. From its inception in 1870, it has grown to become the biggest bank in the US. However, the GFC turned the US authorities to implement one

[154] Tarullo "Toward Building a More effective Resolution Regime", 8.

[155] Janet Yellen " Hearing Before the Committee on Banking, Housing, and Urban Affairs, United States Senate, One Hundred Thirteenth Congress, First Session on Nomination of Janet L. Yellen, of California, to Be Chairman of the Board of Governors of the Federal Reserve" (2013), https://www.govinfo.gov/content/pkg/CHRG-113shrg85910/html/CHRG-113shrg85910.htm. Accessed 13 April 2023.

[156] Tucker "Solving too Big to Fail", 2.

[157] Thomas H. Jackson, "Bankruptcy Code Chapter 14: A Proposal," in Kenneth E. Scott, John B. Taylor (Eds) *Bankruptcy Not Bailout: A Special Chapter 14* (Hoover Institution Press, 2012), 14. Other members of the "Resolution Project" are A. Crockett, D. Duffie, R. Herring, W. Kroener, K. Scott (chair), G. Shultz, K. Summe, and D. Skeel.

[158] FSB 2023 list of global systemically important banks.

of the biggest bailouts in US history. Nowadays, a decade after the GFC, Citi is again in the hands of private owners and continues to be one of the most important BBFCs in the world.

The main characteristics of Citi according to the *four-factor* classification are as follows:

1. Its legal structure is complex, with parent legal entity with branches in all continents and subsidiaries all over the world.
2. Its business model is divided into *Institutional Clients Group*; *Personal Banking and Wealth Management* and *Legacy Franchises.*[159]
3. It may be characterized as a centralized BBFC since management of liquidity, capital, risk exposures and IT are processed, and decision-making is positioned at the top level.[160]
4. Citi has a hybrid business model. According to its 2022 Annual Report, Institutional Clients Group represents 54% of its total revenue, Personal *Banking and Wealth Management,* 32%, *Legacy Franchises*, 12%, and *Corporate* 2%.[161]

As of the first indicator, Citi structure includes both branches and subsidiaries. Citi's geographical expansion covers the five continents and expresses the long history of the bank. As SPOE strategy favours a flexible way of structuring the BBFCs, this would be a preferred resolution strategy if we focus on this first factor.

Contrary to Barclays, whose structure is more typical (Wholesale/Investment bank, centralized, structured mainly by branches), Citi has a hybrid approach: hybrid business model (retail/wholesale), centralized BBFC, and it operates via branches and subsidiaries with no clear pattern regarding factors 2 and 3.

The headquarters of Citibank N.A. are located in the US. From a US perspective, US applies the single entity approach to liquidation of US bank with foreign branches. As Lastra explains, the single entity approach

[159] Citi 2022 Annual Report, https://www.citigroup.com/rcs/citigpa/storage/public/citi-2022-annual-report.pdf. Accessed 19 April 2023.

[160] Ibid.

[161] Citi 2019 Annual Report, 5.

to liquidation "goes hand in hand with the principle of unity and universality of bankruptcy, which means that there is only one competent court to decide on the bankruptcy of a bank and that the bankruptcy law of the country in which the insolvency has been initiated is effective in all other countries in which the bank has assets or branches".[162] Universalism and single entity approach would facilitate the resolution of US BBFCs with branches and subsidiaries abroad, since it would favour the lead of the US resolution authority over foreign authorities.

However, the US generally applies the separate entity approach to liquidation of US branches of foreign banks.[163] Therefore, contrary to the case of Germany and Britain, the US applies a territorial bank insolvency approach for a US branch of a foreign bank, de facto permitting US authorities to ring-fence assets of such branch in the US.[164] This "ring-fence" feature of US law may prevent a SPOE resolution of a foreign bank with US branches. This is something foreign jurisdictions will have to analyse before deciding to ensure a SPOE resolution, as stated above in the case of DB and Barclays.

Under Citigroup 2023 Resolution's Plan the preferred resolution strategy is still SPOE.

> Citi's preferred Resolution strategy remains a single point of entry strategy (SPOE Strategy) under which Citigroup Inc. (Citigroup Parent) would enter bankruptcy, but Citi's material legal entities (MLEs) would continue operating for the benefit of the Citigroup Parent bankruptcy estate. Specifically, under the SPOE Strategy, Citi's Operating MLEs — which are MLEs that contain operating businesses and include Citibank, N.A. (CBNA) and certain broker dealers, among others — would be recapitalized so that they would continue operating throughout Citi's Resolution.
>
> The SPOE Strategy is designed to (i) minimize the impact of Citi's Resolution on the U.S. and global financial systems, depositors, clients, and counterparties, (ii) maintain continuity of Citi's core business lines (CBLs),

162 Lastra "International Financial", 174.

163 Lastra "International Financial", 174. After cases *Trinh v Citibank*, 850 F 2d 1164 (6th Cir 1988) and *Wells Fargo Ltd v Citibank*, 936 F 2d 723 (2d Cir 1991) New York Banking Law and Federal Reserve Act were amended to include a provision that a home office of a US bank would not have to repay a deposit held in a foreign branch in cases of government action (political risk). As Lastra stays, sometimes this is called "ring fencing" of foreign branch deposits.

164 Bolton and Oehmke "Bank Resolution and the Structure of Global Banks", 38.

> critical operations (Cos), and MLEs, and (iii) maximize the value of Citi's businesses for the benefit of the Citigroup Parent bankruptcy estate.[165]

According to the same document Citi is resolvable under the SPOE Strategy because it has: (i) a trigger framework than enables it to take actions to execute the strategy; (ii) sufficient financial resources at the appropriate Citi legal entities; (iii) the capacity for the operating MLEs to receive funds where appropriate; (iv) the capabilities to maintain the internal share services functioning; (v) "credible divestiture" options for its businesses; and (vi) a process in place, ready for resolution.[166]

Subject to the above analysis, a SPOE strategy would best fit the US model BBFCs. However, as in the case of DB and Barclays, in order to perform an effective SPOE resolution the following preconditions need to be aligned: (1) The US would have ex ante cooperation agreements in place with relevant jurisdictions; (2) jurisdictions where Citi has branches and subsidiaries would need to recognize the US universalism principles of insolvency; (3) US authorities should monitor the correct amount of eligible liabilities to assure the bail-in tool.

As in the German and British cases, a number of conditions favour a SPOE strategy in the US. First, the single entity approach to liquidation and universalism would give the US authorities the role of resolution authority. US law would apply to the whole resolution process. Additionally, Citi has signed the ISDA 2015 Universal protocol on Resolution stays, and third, Citi's preferred resolution strategy is SPOE, as stated above. Finally, and contrary to German counterpart, the corporate structure of the US model BBFCs makes a SPOE easy to apply since it relies on non-operative Holding companies at the apex of the structure.

Still, there are challenges for a SPOE strategy effective application for US model BBFCs. As in the German model and British model BBFCs, ex ante agreements are needed in order to avoid ring-fencing of assets. Another possible scenario would be that foreign authorities would not recognize American universalism since the American system recognized territorialism for US branches of foreign banks. If such reciprocity applies, a SPOE resolution would not be effective.

[165] Citigroup Inc. 2023 Resolution Plan Public Section July 1, 2023, https://www.federalreserve.gov/supervisionreg/resolution-plans/citigroup-1g-20230701.pdf. Accessed 15 November 2023.

[166] Ibid.

Advantages of the SPOE as a preferred resolution strategy for US model BBFCs	*Challenges of the SPOE strategy for US model BBFCs*
Efficiency: a SPOE strategy allows cross-jurisdictional transfers and needs less loss-absorbing capacity needed as a group	Need to have ex ante agreements with other resolution authorities
Continuity as a group: critical functions assured	Doubtful that foreign jurisdictions would respect US's universal approach to resolution
	Possible reciprocity from foreign jurisdictions since US applies territorial approach to US branches of foreign banks
Flexibility: allows a flexible legal structure through branches and or subsidiaries	Need to change legal and operational structure to include a holding company on top of current parent company
No need to change legal and operational structure to include a holding company on top of current parent company	
Fast process: through a "liquidation weekend"	
Enhances transparency	
US Resolution authority would be in control of the process	
US authorities prefer the SPOE strategy	
US applies the universal approach to resolution	
US authorities prefer the SPOE strategy as of Annual Report	
Citi has signed the ISDA 2015 Universal protocol on Resolution Stays	

Similar to the cases of DB and Barclays, Citi has physical presence in jurisdictions with territorial approach to resolution such as Brazil and others. Depending on the amount of business, turnover, and analysing the costs involved, Citi may prefer a hybrid model, applying a SPOE strategy to some jurisdictions and a MPOE strategy to others. A MPOE resolution will ensure that those jurisdictions will have its own liquidation according to local laws, assuring there is no risk of ring-fencing of assets in the mentioned jurisdictions (Fig. 6.7).

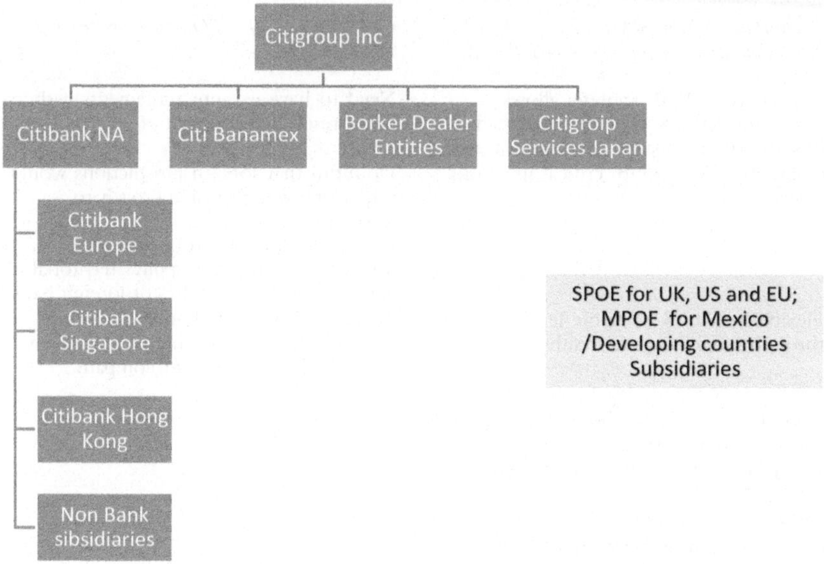

Fig. 6.7 Simplified hybrid resolution strategy for Citi (*Source* Based on 2023 Citi Resolution Plan[167])

6.7 Concluding Remarks

This book compiles a four-factor indicator which rely on: (1) how the BBFCs structure themselves (branches or subsidies); (2) on types of global banks (centralized or decentralized banks); (3) on how they develop their business (retail versus non-retail banking) and; (4) on how the jurisdictions where the head offices are incorporated apply a territorial or universal approach to resolution (territorial or universal approach to resolution). Based on these factors, the book examines the three BBFC models to find which resolution strategy best fits each one.

As of the German model BBFC (DB) there are a number of factors that favour a SPOE resolution. DB legal structure is complex comprising

[167] Citigroup Inc. 2023 Resolution Plan Public Section July 1, 2023, https://www.federalreserve.gov/supervisionreg/resolution-plans/citigroup-1g-20230701.pdf. Accessed 23 November 2023.

both subsidiaries and branches, its business model is focused on wholesale banking and investment banking, it may be defined as a centralized BBFC and as its headquarters are incorporated and situated in Germany; German law and German resolution authorities will prevail and lead the whole resolution process. The fact that DB has signed the ISDA 2015 Protocol would help "support the cross-border enforceability of resolution action",[168] that is especially important in a SPOE strategy, where cross-border cooperation is essential for effective resolution. BaFin prefers the SPOE strategy and DB argues that SPOE is the preferred resolution strategy.

However, DB faces some challenges for an effective SPOE resolution. Ex ante agreements need to be effective before a SPOE strategy is planned. While these agreements may be in place, there are no guarantees that in a "resolution weekend" jurisdictions will be cooperative and for example, apply liquidity to foreign depositors. In the same vein, there are no guarantees that foreign jurisdictions will respect the German universal approach to resolution. This is particularly important with respect to the US, which applies territorial approach to US branches of foreign banks. Finally, the SPOE strategy relies on applying bail in to a holding non-operative company at the apex of the structure. DB apex is an operative company; therefore, some kind of corporate restructuring might be necessary to achieve an effective SPOE resolution strategy. An alternative of "hybrid model" resolution might as well be established. This model would apply a SPOE with certain jurisdictions (e.g. EU, Japan) and a MPOE with jurisdictions with long tradition of territorial approach to resolution, such as Brazil.

When it comes to Barclays (British model BBFC), the four indicators show that SPOE strategy would best fit since its business model is based on wholesale, it is centralized and relies on both branches and subsidiaries. British universalism helps to ensure that British resolution authorities would lead the process. As in the case of DB, the typical preconditions of SPOE strategy need to be met in order to fulfil an effective SPOE resolution. Contrary to DB, Barclays has a non-operative company apex, which is a resolution simplifier. On the other hand, as in the case of DB, the same challenges apply to Barclays: ex ante agreements are needed, and

[168] FSB "Principles for Cross-border Effectiveness of Resolution Actions", https://www.fsb.org/wp-content/uploads/Principles-for-Cross-border-Effectiveness-of-Resolution-Actions.pdf. Accessed 22 June 2023.

the peril of foreign authorities' ring-fencing assets is still present. As in the case of DB, a hybrid resolution approach would be possible in order to separate jurisdictions that apply a territorial approach to resolution. In this case, a SPOE strategy would be granted to certain jurisdictions and MPOE to others.

Similar conclusions apply to Citi or US model BBFC. In this case, a SPOE strategy typically applies. Not only because Citi structure is constructed upon the holding model, but because US authorities prefer the SPOE strategy for US G-SIBs. The main problem for an effective SPOE strategy in the US is the dichotomy of resolution approaches. While US endorses universalism for US banks with foreign branches, it applies a territorial approach to US branches of foreign banks. This double system might jeopardize cross-border cooperation since for instance a German BBFC with US branches would not be able to fully apply a SPOE resolution for all their branches, since the US would "ring fence" and treat its US branches as local banks for resolution purposes.

While there is no "one fits all" solution for resolving G-SIBS, a careful analysis of the four indicators should be pursued by national regulators. In the first place, all G-SIBs will need to be "safe to safe" in the words of Huertas. In the second place, when the time comes to apply the resolution tools, all the preconditions of the chosen resolution strategy will have to be in place in order to maintain financial stability and to correctly balance the rights and interests of all stakeholders of the G-SIB in every jurisdiction involved.

When analysing the insurance business of the BBFC, while the FSB recognizes a preferred "multiple entry resolution", the lack of convergence of resolution of this kind of companies in different jurisdictions poses regulators with an additional problem. While in the US, significant insurance companies will be able to be resolved under DFA, in Europe there is no harmonization of recovery and resolution frameworks for insurers, which implies applying local insolvency proceedings.

CHAPTER 7

Concluding Remarks

> What's in a name? That which we call a rose By any other name would smell as sweet.
>
> *Romeo and Juliet*, William Shakespeare

7.1 The Definition of Financial Conglomerate Is Contentious

Chapter 2 of the book of Genesis tells how Adam gave names to different things

> so out of the ground the Lord God formed every animal of the field and every bird of the air, and brought them to the man to see what he would call them; and whatever the man called every living creature, that was its name. [2:20] The man gave names to all cattle, and to the birds of the air, and to every animal of the field...[1]

Human beings had not lost their capacity to give names along history. Names not only define things but also qualify them in different systems and processes.

[1] The Bible, http://www.vatican.va/archive/bible/genesis/documents/bible_genesis_en.html. Accessed 10 August 2023.

M. J. Sheppard Gelsi, *Corporate Structure and Banking Resolution*, Palgrave Macmillan Studies in Banking and Financial Institutions, https://doi.org/10.1007/978-3-031-59948-4_7

In the financial regulation sphere, modern "Adams" give names to new phenomena and are constantly trying to solve problems derived from a field that is underpinned by fast technological innovations. The term FC is one these phenomena. This book reaffirms the FC definition is contentious because of its cross-sectoral and cross-border dimensions. From a cross-sectoral perspective, the FC deals with different risks along lines of financial business that make it difficult to supervise and regulate. From a cross-border dimension, FCs are difficult to regulate since there is a lack of harmonization and regulatory convergence in the international arena.

The same concept may have different meanings analysed through different lenses. A first lens is the geographical lens. This book has examined the Commercial classification of financial institutions, which comprises banking groups, mixed conglomerates and FCs. When the geographical lens is applied to the definition of a bank, the same institution is defined in the EU and the US by pointing out one of its cores, albeit different i.e. functions as "depository institutions" (taking deposits-US), and credit institutions (granting credit-EU). Drawing on practices of different countries, this book has analysed the definition of banks through different approaches, the list of activity approach, the formula approach and the hybrid approach, and this book insists on the need of maintaining "room for manoeuvre" or discretion to adapt the definition of bank to fast-changing reality constantly challenged by technology. Although we live in times of quantitative easing and there is a potential of the creation of central bank digital currencies, this book understands that as long as critical functions of banks persist as of today, banks will continue to be special and will continue to benefit from a special status in the financial arena.

When dealing with "banking groups", there is also a broad understanding that consolidated supervision is a natural consequence of such a form of legal organization. However, when analysing how those banking groups are structured, even the meaning of "subsidiary" in the US has a different approach contrary to the conventional meaning in the rest of the western world. The definitions did not change but the law gives different effects to bank subsidiaries in the US assimilating them to branches which blurred the vision and challenge international cooperation in cross-border insolvency. Contrary, in the EU, the definition of subsidiary is critical, since the "passporting" system where banking groups are allowed to operate in the single market as far as it is authorized by one-member country only applies to branches and not to subsidiaries.

When analysing the FC, whereas there is an international doctrinal definition (Joint Forum),[2] the consequences of dealing with it will be different in the UE where supplementary supervision will apply due to the FICOD, and in the US where FC has no legal or regulatory consequence per se.

Contrary to the words that Shakespeare puts in Juliet's mouth, in financial regulation, and in law in general, names do matter, since the consequences of being a solo bank, a banking group, a FC or a SIFI will have diverse consequences.

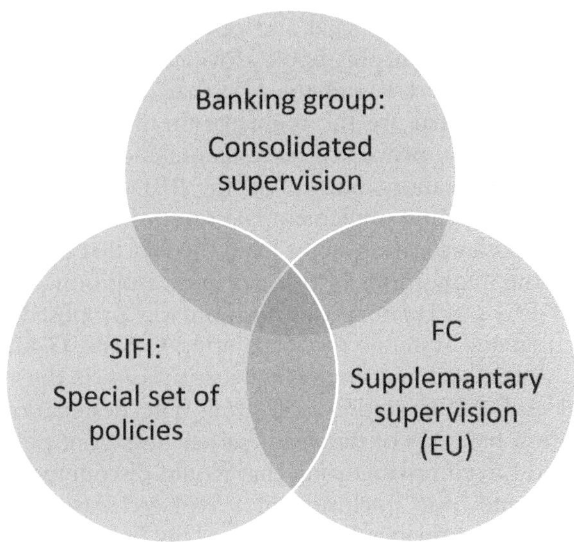

After the GFC, an additional lens was incorporated. The "systemic risk lens" was introduced to add a new perspective to old concepts. The FC and banking group definitions did lack this new perspective that added new categories such as SIFIs and G-SIIs, which complemented these definitions with new content. While in the US the SIFI labelling system under

[2] Bank of Financial Settlements "The Supervision of Financial Conglomerates", A Report by the Tripartite Group of Bank, Securities and Insurance Regulators (1995), 13.

DFA may include non-banking institutions, in the EU the system (SSM) only includes banking systemic institutions and not others (e.g. insurance companies, hedge funds) like in the US.

This book affirms the important role of soft law in integrating and providing a common language that protects international relations. Soft law and the institutions that developed those soft laws have done a lot in coordinating the effects of definitions in International Financial law. However, a lot may be done to continue the efforts of international harmonization especially between the main actors, e.g. the US, the EU and the UK.

After examining the Commercial classification, this book draws on the structural classification, first adopted by Herring and Santomero in the 1990s, that relies on the legal and operational separateness of FCs. Following this classification, this book provides a comparative analysis of BBFCs in Germany, the UK and the US, that draws some light on the concept of FCs and what are the regulatory frameworks that applies to them. This classification proved to be resilient, since after the GFC regulators took the structural organization of the BBFCs and banking groups into account to design and implement the resolution strategies for SIFIs. The beauty of this classification stems from the fact that it helps regulators to understand the implications of risk, tax and resolution.

After the GFC, a regulatory classification was proposed focusing on macro-prudential and systemic risk, separating G-SIBs, G-SIIs and Non-Bank, Non-Insurers systemic important institutions at the international level, as well as D-SIFIs at the local level. The designation system or binary regulation has a set of disadvantages as litigation, politicization of the process, and forced restructuring that would discourage it. Additional costs of "under and over" inclusion of a SIFI are reasons for the regulator to adopt a more nuanced regulation. This book believes that since there is evidence that the risks of the different lines of finance differ, the banking like regulations applied to all SIFIs need to adapt to each recipient in order not to apply the "burden" of the SIFI labelling while not "benefiting" from the protection of banking regulation such as LOLR and deposit insurance.

Along Chapter 3 (German model), Chapter 4 (British model) and Chapter 5 (US model) this book analysed different research questions. First it scrutinized the philosophical foundations of each model and if and how the banking system influenced the industry in each jurisdiction and its impact on types of capitalism. Second, it examined the way BFCCs are legally organized in each jurisdiction. Third, it answered what resolution strategy best fitted each model considering a selected BBFC-G-SIBs which represented the model in each jurisdiction.

The research has identified three different models and found that the corporate structure of BBFCs in two of them, i.e. the German and the US models, have specially influenced the type of capitalism involved in Germany and the US. The pre-eminence of German banks, which were and are generally universal, shaped the financial needs of industrial enterprises in Germany and has proven to be the preferred financial institution in Germany, even after the Government tried to develop the *Finanzplatz Deutschland* in the 1980s. In addition, it can be argued that unit banking in the US helped the development of capital markets, (which is multicausal), since big enterprises needed to find alternative sources of funding because there was a mismatch between big firms and small banks. While in the UK banks were not important in the development of the industry, the capital market is not as developed as in the US and the bank system is not as preeminent as in Germany.

As this book affirms below, it has also analysed the different philosophical and historical foundations of the different models. While Germany may root the beginnings of universal banking in Saint Simon ideas, the UK relied in self-regulation and classical liberalism, and the US in federalism.

Based on Herring and Santomero's classical structural classification, this book identified the Integrated Model or German Model and analysed how BBFCs structure themselves in that prototypical jurisdiction. While there is only one G-SIB in Germany, i.e. DB, which is universal, the other three pillar entities (saving banks and cooperatives) were key in the development and in shaping Germany as it is known today. The second model, the British model, was modified because of the influence of European law, and this book has changed the original name for Modified British model, since in general, at the apex of British BBFCs there is a holding company. The British model has also been shaped by ring-fencing regulations, which separates the core activities from other divisions of the group. British banks are classified in banks, credit unions, building societies and merchant banks. British banking developed a multinational or overseas banking which had great influence in Asia and Latin America, and which subsist in entities like HSBC. Finally, the US or holding model, the last identified model according to Herring and Santomero's classification, has developed in the US after 1956, and its features have proven to be resilient since the SPOE resolution strategy heavily relies on this structure to function well. The US classifies its financial BBFCs in banks, thrifts and credit unions, and as stated above is the only of the selected jurisdictions that has the power to label both banks and non-bank SIFIs as such.

Finally, Sect. 7.3 below summarizes the findings of the analysis of which resolution strategy best fits in each jurisdiction. In Annex 1, this book analyses the case of Credit Agricole and Santander. In the latter case, the results differ from the other cases, in that for this book the most appropriate resolution strategy for Santander is MPOE. In the other cases (i.e. DB, Barclays and Citi), the SPOE resolution strategy would best fit in each of the selected jurisdictions involved. Although there are certain preconditions that need to be in place, a SPOE resolution or a hybrid resolution, meaning a SPOE resolution for certain jurisdictions (such as the EU) and a MPOE resolution for others (i.e. Brazil) is preferred.

7.2 What Are the Philosophical Foundations of Each Model? Did the Banking Systems Finance the Industry? What Type of Capitalism Did They Represent?

Keynes famously stated

> [t]he ideas of economists and political philosophers, both when they are right and when they are wrong, are more powerful than is commonly understood. Indeed, the world is ruled by little else. Practical men, who believe themselves to be quite exempt from any intellectual influences, are usually the slaves of some defunct economist. Madmen in authority, who hear voices in the air are distilling their frenzy from some academic scribbler of a few years back.[3]

While a priori conventional wisdom would not say a banking system would be slave of a "defunct economist" but of a set of technical regulations, history shows intellectual influences are always present and are determinant to understand the present.

[3] John M. Keynes *The General Theory of Employment, Interest and Money* (London: Macmillan, 1936), 383.

The philosophical foundations of universal banking in Germany are rooted in the work and deeds of Saint Simon and his disciples, the Pereire Brothers. There are several well-documented links between the work of Saint Simon, the foundation of the Credit Mobiliere and the Grossbanken in Germany, which were built upon the same pillars of the French bank. Credit Mobilier bylaws' expressly affirm "the important services that the establishment of bank may favour the development of the industry".[4] Saint Simon thought the role of banks was to be "general agents of the industry" and that the industrial class was called to be in charge of "public wealth". By 1910 Grossbanken in Germany were called "Credit Mobilier Banks". This link between Saint Simon ideas and the creation of the first Grossbanken generated a particular type of bank, the universal bank. Universal banks in Germany (as well as in Austria and Italy) established very close relations with the industry, in the words of Gerschenkron, a German Bank "accompanied an industrial enterprise from the cradle to the grave, from establishment to liquidation throughout all the vicissitudes of its existence".[5] This special relationship in Germany, contrary to BBFCs in the US and the UK, was anchored in four elements: (i) providing all kinds of financial services (banking, securities, insurance); (ii) owning shares in commercial and industrial firms; (iii) taking positions in supervisory bodies; and (iv) controlling commercial and industrial firms via proxy rights.

Available data of Bairoch's index of industrialization show Germany grew in a faster pace than the UK, even though the UK was the leading industrial power since the Industrial Revolution. Also, from 1870 to 1913 the Grossbanken in Germany were the three most important firms in Germany. There is evidence that German banks did finance heavy industry and the *housebank* long-term relationships were key to German economy. There is also evidence that while in the period 1850–1913, the US, UK had specialized commercial banks, and large markets, Germany had universal banks and small markets. While it is difficult to prove causality, it can be said that Germany was shaped by Grossbanks—helping the industry—and a sub developed capital markets, due in part by the application of incorrect incentives (taxes and share transfer restrictions,

[4] Decret No. 7433 "Decret portant autorisation".

[5] Gerschenkron "Economic Backwardness", 1–15.

nationalization of railways) and by direct participation of banks in stock markets.

On the other hand, banking system in the UK was organized under four pillars, a specialized system that historically separated merchant banking, brokerage and commercial services, a self-regulated industry where moral suasion was used by banking authorities, the reliance of other sources of funding to finance the industry, and the prominence of the City of London.

Contrary to Germany, where universal banking had a clear philosophical foundation on Saint Simon ideas, in the UK the intellectual nerve that moved the banking system may be found in classical liberalism[6] and the primacy of private initiative and self-regulation. Lord Leslie O'Brien, Governor of the Bank of England, stated in 1973 "[t]he supremacy of London as an international banking centre is founded on a freedom from vexatious banking legislation equalled in few countries in the world".[7] It was only after the Banking Act of 1979 that the UK has a domestic formal banking regulation. Before that, the Bank of England used moral suasion to control credit institutions. Self-regulation in the UK proved to be stable from 1878 to 1991 where there was no major financial crisis in the UK. As Lord O'Brien states, another pillar of the UK banking system is the prevalence of the City of London. While not an intellectual nerve by itself, as may be the Saint Simon ideas in Germany, a differential motor of the UK banking system is the City of London. London is now the second ranked financial centre in the world second after New York. Data suggest London will be the major financial centre in Europe after Brexit. History tells how London championed the financial world, first because it was the capital of the Empire, then because it was located in a major economy and had a strong currency, and afterwards because it reinvented itself with the Eurobond market. Some posed questions on whether the

[6] Suzanne Konzelmann, Marc Fovargue-Davies, and Gerhard Schnyder "Varieties of Liberalism: Anglo-Saxon Capitalism in Crisis?", Centre for Business Research, University of Cambridge, Working Paper No. 403 (2010), 11; Peter A. Hall and David Soskice *Varieties of Capitalism: The Institutional Foundations of Comparative Advantage* (Oxford Scholarship Online 2003), 337.

[7] Leslie O'Brien "Speech by the Governor of the Bank of England", Given at the biennial dinner of the Institute of Bankers in Scotland on 22nd January 1973, https://www.bankofengland.co.uk/-/media/boe/files/quarterly-bulletin/1973/speech-by-governor-given-at-the-biennial-dinner-of-the-institute-of-bankers-scotland-22-jan-1973.pdf. Accessed 19 April 2023.

city has failed the industry in the UK, or the economy as a whole, and Brexit has posed these questions again. Opportunities for further research are now opened.

Unlike Germany, and like the US, in the UK there is a consensus that "banks failed the industry" and that financial institutions concentrated on short-term lending and/or holding their long-term assets in government and public utility securities. Also, the City has preferred financing international trade to financing local industry. During the Industrial Revolution (1760–1830), industrialists used own funds to finance their enterprises, since country banks were small and circumscribed to their constituencies. The Bank of England was the only approved Joint Stock Company until 1825, restricting other banks to raise capital from the public. In 1708, Parliament limited associations of more than six people to conduct the business of banking, aggravating the problem. Usury laws also restrict the number of customers banks could get and increased collateral lending. Data from 1860 to 1913 the UK show the manufacturing output decreased from 19 to 13% of the total manufacturing output. Before World War I there was evidence that banks were concerned with liquidity and short-term lending, and that the UK foreign investment was immense. The sum of these factors might have stymied the industry development in the UK. Things changed after the Big Bang. In 1988, the UK surpassed Germany for the first time in the Private Credit by Deposit Money Banks to GDP Index, and after 2002 Germany could not lead again against the UK.

On the other side of the Atlantic, different intellectual references other than Saint Simon's ideas were determinant to shape the banking system in the US. Federalism designed the US banking system from its inception. Its regulators tended to replicate the federal government structure at the banking level, preserving abuse of power and undue concentration of financial resources. Federalism refers to a means of governing the polity that grants partial autonomy to geographical defined subdivisions of such polity. Late Supreme Court Justice Antonin Scalia resumed federalism as a midway between two extremes, autonomy on the one side and division on the other. The US relied on a unique "unit bank" system, which was the result of heavy restrictions on branching at state and federal levels.

This book believes that restrictions on branching and the unit bank system had different outcomes when analysed from different perspectives. From a business bank perspective, the costs of unit banks outweigh its benefits. There is evidence that allowing branch banking accelerated growth in states that permitted it, and that unit banks were less efficient in the use of capital and reserves. Unit banks were more associated with bank panics than branch banking in certain regions, and there is evidence that unit banks hindered financial integration and diversification. However, from a national interest perspective, unit banks created a mismatch between big firms and unfitted small banking system that led those firms to find other sources of finance. US firms had to rely in syndicates and other forms of finance to substitute bank loans, which stimulated the bond market first, and equities market second. Anglo-Saxon capitalism or market-based capitalism in the US may trace part of its success in an unwanted effect of heavy restrictions on bank branching.

7.3 How BBFCs Are Legally Organized in Each Jurisdiction?

The second research question focuses on the legal organization of BBFCs on three selected jurisdictions, which are tied to each of the structural classification's model: Germany (German model), UK (British Modified model) and the US (Holding Company model).

In Germany the "three pillar Structure" of universal banking is represented by (i) *Grossbanken* or big banks, (ii) savings banks, and (iii) cooperative banks. Historically, each pillar served different customers, which underpinned different business models. *Grossbanken* are joint stock corporations with national or international scope and their aim is profit maximization. Savings banks are independent instrumentalities organized by public law, with municipalities of local governments as responsible institutions. Contrary to *Grossbanken*, their aim is to serve the public interest, while they must also look for profit optimization. They organize themselves under the regional principle (*Sparkassen*) or under a national or international scope (*Landesbanken*). Cooperative banks are registered cooperative societies, with members or non-members as owners, with regional scope. Their principal aim is the promotion of members and profit optimization.

From a systemic importance perspective, only DB is a member of the first pillar and falls under the G-SIB category. The rest are not systemically important. From a size perspective, the regional territorial scope would segregate cooperatives and *Sparkassen* from the inclusion in the G-SIB list because they would not face cross-border issues and they would maintain a size proportional to that of the region.

This book believes that there are several benefits and costs of universal banking. Theoretically, a universal banking system relies on long-term relationships, taking advantage of economies of scope and scale, diversification and the gains of one-stop shopping. On the other hand, the peril of creating "mammoth entities" which are difficult to manage, supervise and resolve is present in this kind of structure. While universal banking is not a synonym of "systemic", the universal banking encourages the formation of entities that are bigger than their specialized institutions. This poses additional focus on anticompetitive behaviour, abuse of information and benefiting of conflicts of interest.[8] This book sets out to show that discouraging universal banking because of the latter may not be sufficient, but special care needs to be taken by regulators to encourage competition and ethical behaviour.

On the other hand, Chapter 4 examined the British model, or what this book calls British Modified model. This new classification adapts the original classification to a more complete one that best reflects the structure of British BBFCs, including the bank company/insurance and securities subsidiaries plus a holding company at the apex of the corporate structure. The UK system comprises: (1) banks, (2) credit unions, (3) building societies and (4) investment Banks. The first group includes the "big four" clearing banks, overseas banks and foreign banks. Credit unions, as *Sparkassen* in Germany, are non-profit institutions based on cooperative values. Contrary, building societies are specialized institutions with the aim of making loans, which are secured on residential property and are funded by its members. Building societies were permitted to demutualized, being Northern Rock a renowned example. Investment banks or merchant banks had a historical origin in international trade (Barings: wool; Rothschilds, cotton; Schroeders and Kelinworts: sugar) with the aim of dealing in investments as principal or investment activities on a professional basis. After the Big Bang in the UK merchant banks were taken over by other continental and US counterparts. Nowadays, the only British Investment Bank regulated by the PRA is Barclays, after buying the investment banking division of Lehman Brothers in 2008.

From a systemic importance perspective, Barclays and HSBC are the two British-based SIFIs. The rest are not systemically important. From a size perspective, the specialized scope would segregate Building societies

[8] Ioannis Kokkoris and Rodrigo Olivares-Caminal *Antitrust Law Amidst Financial Crisis* (CUP 2010), 5.

from that list. The same applies to Credit Unions because they would not face cross-border issues and they would maintain a size proportional to that of geographical place where the common bond rules.

Chapter 5 analysed the corporate legal form of US BBFC. The US has since 1956 a Bank Holding Companies Regulation in order to enhance the control of BHCs and being consistent with the public interest. It was not until 1999 with GLBA that allowed FHC to operate in banking, insurance and securities market. Today almost all big BBFCs are registered as FHC.

The traditional classification of depository institutions in the US comprises: (1) commercial banks, (2) thrifts and (3) credit unions. One special feature of the American system is the existence of a dual banking system comprising a federal and state level. A second feature is the presence of second level institutions, which are commercial bank operative and financial subsidiaries, thrift service corporations and CUSOs. As in Germany, thrifts were intended to encourage savings and help the working class. Contrary to Germany, thrifts are not independent instrumentalities of public law, but private associations, which may take the form of stock ownership or mutual ownership. Thrifts in the US need to have at least 65% of their portfolio in Housing related assets. As in the case of commercial banks, there are also thrift holding companies. Finally, as credit unions in the UK, they are cooperatives governed by cooperative rules and non-profit aims. Contrary to, for example Credit Agricole in France, there are no globally systemically important credit unions or thrifts in the US. While after the deregulation period, US BBFCs may choose from a variety of forms to perform the three finance functions, international BBFCs have chosen the FHC as a preferred structure.

This book concludes that the dilemma in the genesis or emergence of BBFCs (the "chicken and egg situation") may describe the relationship between corporate form of BBFCs and regulation. Chain and group banking were created in order to prevent branching restrictions in the US. At the same time, the use of the holding company structure before 1956 was used to operate in different states, applying de facto interstate banking. BHCA was partly a reaction to stop the use of holding companies as a way to circumvent the Mc Fadden Act.

Half a century later, the deregulation movement somehow build up to the GFC of 2007–2009. The US legislator enacted DFA as a reaction to the GFC. The DFA ended up the possibility of FCs to be regulated by the SEC. It also prevented financial institutions that owned industrial banks from avoiding regulation by the Federal Banking System. The Federal Reserve System received the power to determine to regulate non-bank financial companies in the case they could pose a threat to financial stability in the US. In this way DFA close regulatory arbitrage to FCs. This proves banking regulation and corporate innovation feed each other and there is space to conclude the interaction in the US went on both sides.

7.4 Which Resolution Strategy Best Fits Each Model?

Chapter 6 compiles a four-factor indicator underpinned on (1) how the BBFCs structure themselves, (via branches or subsidiaries); (2) on types of global banks, (centralized or decentralized); (3) on how they develop their business, (retail versus non-retail); and (4) on the jurisdictions approach to resolution, (territorial or universal). Based on these factors, this book examines the three BBFC models to find which resolution strategy best fits each one.

The concurrence of the four factors indicates that pure models of BBFCs that rely on branches, are centralized, have a wholesale and investment banking business model and operate in jurisdictions where universal approach of resolution applies, would best fit a SPOE resolution strategy. On the other hand, BBFCs that are organized through subsidiaries are decentralized, rely on retail business and operate in jurisdictions where territorial approach to resolution applies, would best fit a MPOE resolution strategy. While this might work on pure models, BBFCs are complex structures and an in-depth analysis of each BBFC is necessary to assess the most effective resolution strategy.

As a general conclusion, the SPOE strategy prevails or best fits the three selected models. Contrary to the Santander case, studied in Annex 1, the SPOE strategy proved to be more resilient in the three chosen SIFIs: DB, Barclays and Citi.

This book insists that the SPOE strategy has weighted advantages. From a business perspective, the SPOE strategy is more efficient since it permits using lower loss-absorbing capacity and will ensure the continuity of critical functions of operating firms and of the group as a whole. It also permits the BBFC to organize itself through both branches and subsidiaries. From a market perspective, the SPOE strategy makes resolutions transparent because bail-in-able debt is earmarked and available for regulatory activation. From a resolution authority perspective, the SPOE strategy gives authorities a centre of control that avoids multiple territorial resolutions, and it would enable a quick resolution in a "liquidation weekend", which make it a preferred resolution strategy for authorities in the selected jurisdictions.

As of the first case, the German model BBFC (DB) meets elements that favour a SPOE strategy. DB's legal structure is complex and it comprises both subsidiaries and branches. As of the second indicator, DB is categorized as a global centralized bank. As for the third indicator, DB's business model is focused on wholesale banking and investment banking. As for the fourth indicator, Germany adopted the universal approach to resolution. As DB has its headquarters and it is incorporated in Germany, German law and German resolution authorities will be in charge of a resolution process. The fact that DB is a signatory of the ISDA 2015 Protocol helps to support the cross-border enforceability of the whole process. Finally, Bafin prefers the SPOE strategy, and DB authorities have stated they too prefer a SPOE strategy. Because all of this, the SPOE strategy would best fit the resolution strategy of DB.

However, this book shows DB faces certain challenges for effective resolution. First, ex-ante burden agreements need to be effective before a SPOE strategy is planned. Second, there are no guarantees that in the short window of time or "resolution weekend" jurisdictions will cooperate and apply liquidity to foreign depositors. Third, there is no guarantee that foreign jurisdictions will respect German universal approach to resolution and be tempted to ring-fence local assets. This is particularly true with the US that applies a territorial approach to resolution to US branches of foreign banks. Finally, the SPOE strategy relies on applying the bail in tool to the apex, which is in general a holding company with no operative functions. As DB apex is an operative company, some kind of restructuring might be necessary in order to achieve an effective SPOE resolution. This book states that DB might as well establish a hybrid resolution strategy, where it might apply a SPOE resolution strategy in the EU and a MPOE resolution strategy in places where the territorial approach to resolution has a long tradition, such as Brazil, where DB has a subsidiary.

The concurrence of the four indicators shows that SPOE would best fit the British Modified model BBFCs (Barclays). British universalism helps to ensure UK authorities would lead the whole resolution process. As in the case of DB, preconditions of SPOE would need to be in place to assure a swift resolution. Barclays has also signed the ISDA 2015 Universal protocol that would help the enforceability of the process. Contrary to DB, Barclays has no operative apex, which is a resolution simplifier, since no restructuring would be needed. As in the case of DB, there are still challenges: ex-ante burden agreements will need to be in place, and the peril of foreign jurisdictions ring-fencing assets may be present. As in the case of DB a hybrid solution may be possible, granting a SPOE strategy to the EU and MPOE to jurisdictions that would most probably apply territorial approach to resolution and avoid cooperation.

Similar conclusions apply to Citi or the US model BBFCs. In this case, the SPOE strategy applies not only because Citi is an archetypical example to a Holding model structure, but also because US authorities prefer the SPOE strategy for US G-SIBs. As the US applies the single entity approach to liquidation and universalism, it would give the US authorities a leading role in the resolution of a BBFCs with branches and subsidiaries operating abroad. Citi has signed the ISDA 2015 Universal protocol, which would help the enforceability of the process. The same challenges apply to Citi, with the additional issue of the US double approach to resolution. The US endorses a single entity or universalism for US banks with foreign branches, but it applies the territorial approach to foreign banks with US branches. This may jeopardize cross-border cooperation.

When it comes to international cooperation, trust relations are key in order to fulfil an effective relation. That said, when there is lack of convergence in key regulations such as universal or territorial approaches to resolution, there will always be risks since no matter how deep trust might be if the law command to ring-fence assets, no political partnership would suffice to stop an uncooperative resolution. Convergence in the EU would recommend a SPOE strategy for this territory since in many aspects the EU conducts itself as a single jurisdiction. In order to avoid uncooperative resolution processes, a hybrid resolution would be recommended, since it would not endanger financial stability and would offer tranquillity to the markets. Additional problems are added when it comes to the resolution of the insurance business of BBFCs. While in the US significant insurance companies are resolved under DFA, in the EU there is lack of harmonization of recovery and resolution frameworks, which implies different local resolutions in each member state.

The regulation of FCs is complex due to cross-sectoral and cross-border dimensions. In Chapter 5, this book formulated a metaphor based on the myth of Icarus and Daedalus. Icarus sin consisted in disobeying his father's advice not to fly too high nor too low. Flying too high can be assimilated to overregulation and flying too low to overregulation. This book argues that regulators need to fly in the middle, to respect flexibility and innovation and at the same time safeguarding financial stability and the soundness of the economy.

ANNEX 1: Case Studies: Deutsche Bank, Credit Agricole, Barclays, Citi and Santander

Case Study: Deutsche Bank

Deutsche Bank History

Deutsche Bank (DB) is the most important bank in Germany and it is viewed as a leading financial institution in Europe. DB was founded in 1870 under the leadership of Adelbert Delbrück. According to its statue "The object of the company is to transact banking business of all kinds, in particular to promote and facilitate trade relations between Germany, other European countries and overseas markets". The first two decades the DB contributed to the development of German electrical, iron and steel industries, as well as other overseas projects such as the Baghdad Railway. DB was the first bank in Germany that relied in retail deposits to finance banking, which was an important innovation at the time.[1] DB rapidly expanded into Asia and in 1914 the "Frankfurter Zeitung" announced that DB was "the biggest bank in the world".[2] From 1914 to 1932 Germany was ruled by the Weimar Republic, which

[1] Guinnane "Delegated Monitors", 102.

[2] Deutsche Bank History "Chronicle 1870 Until Today", available at https://www.db.com/company/en/media/Deutsche-Bank-History--Chronicle-from-1870-until-today.pdf. Accessed 27 August 2023.

M. J. Sheppard Gelsi, *Corporate Structure and Banking Resolution*, Palgrave Macmillan Studies in Banking and Financial Institutions,
https://doi.org/10.1007/978-3-031-59948-4

turned Germany into an inflationary process. DB merged with Disconto-Gesellschaf, its most important rival in 1929, increasing German bank concentration. From 1933 to 1945 DB had to live with the Nazi regime. As the DB official History Chronicle state, "Hitler's seizure of power in 1933 marked the beginning of the darkest chapter in the history of Deutsche Bank. By 1945, after twelve years of National-Socialist rule and six years of war, not only was the bank itself on the brink of the abyss; it had also allowed itself to become a tool of the Nazi state".[3]

After the war over, DB was divided into ten banks[4] and the name "Deutsche Bank" was forbidden. In 1952 the 10 banks were regrouped in three: Rheinisch-Westfälische (Düsseldorf), Süddeutsche Bank (Frankfurt and Munich) and Norddeutsche Bank (Hamburg). In 1957 they merged in DB again. From 1958 to 1988 a stage of internationalization begun for the bank. In the national front, the bank focused on retail banking, while on the international side, it expanded owing banks in Italy, Spain, the UK and the US.[5] In 1989, DB acquired the British merchant bank Morgan Grenfell and the New York investment bank Bankers Trust, which opened the American market for DB. DB is today a leading institution in Germany and Europe. However, in 2018 the Fed announced the DB US subsidiary failed the Fed stress test: "Concerns include material weaknesses in the firm's data capabilities and controls supporting its capital planning process, as well as weaknesses in its approaches and assumptions used to forecast revenues and losses under stress".[6] After the announcement, Standard and Poor's downgraded the bank's Credit Rating (Long-Term) to BBB-.[7]

[3] Ibid.

[4] Owen Smith "The German Economy", 324.

[5] Deutsche Bank History "Chronicle 1870 Until Today".

[6] Michelle Price, David Henry "Deutsche Bank Fails Fed Stress Test While Three U.S. Lenders Stumble" (Reuters, June 28, 2018), https://www.reuters.com/article/us-usa-fed-stresstests/deutsche-bank-fails-fed-stress-test-while-three-u-s-lenders-stumble-idUSKBN1JO33U. Accessed 27 August 2023.

[7] Deutsch Bank Ratings, Available at https://www.db.com/ir/en/current-ratings.htm. Accessed 27 August 2023. For 2021 ratings see https://www.db.com/ir/en/current-ratings.htm.

Additionally, DB is the only German G-SIB according to FSB G-SIB List, classified in Bucket 3 with Bank of America, Citigroup and HSBC.[8] In 2016, the IMF announced that DB "Deutsche Bank is also a major source of systemic risk in the global financial system. The net contribution to global systemic risk is captured by the difference between the outward spillover to the system from the bank and the inward spillover to the bank from the system based on forecast error variance decomposition. Deutsche Bank appears to the most important net contributor to systemic risks in the global banking system, followed by HSBC and Credit Suisse".[9]

In March 2017, DB announced a restructuring plan in order to take

> a decisive step forward to become stronger and grow again. Decisions agreed by the Management Board and Supervisory Board on Sunday aim to reinforce the bank's roots in its home market of Germany and its position as a leading European bank with global reach. The bank plans to combine Postbank and Deutsche Bank's Private & Commercial client's business, float a minority stake of Deutsche Asset Management and create an integrated corporate and investment bank.[10]

Three years later, in the 2020 Annual Report DB declared

> In July 2019, we announced a strategic transformation of Deutsche Bank, designed to significantly improve sustainable returns to shareholders. This strategy is underpinned by four specific objectives. First, to refocus Deutsche Bank around four core businesses, focusing on key areas of strength and on more predictable revenue sources while exiting business areas unlikely to produce adequate returns. Second, to reduce our adjusted costs and improve the efficiency and effectiveness of our infrastructure. Third, to reinvigorate the leadership and spirit of the bank by enabling faster decision-making, increasing discipline in execution and unleashing

[8] FSB 2017 list of global systemically important banks (G-SIBs), http://www.fsb.org/wp-content/uploads/P211117-1.pdf, FSB 2018 list https://www.fsb.org/wp-content/uploads/P161118-1.pdf, FSB 2019 list https://www.fsb.org/wp-content/uploads/P221119-1.pdf and FSB 2020 List, https://www.fsb.org/wp-content/uploads/P111120.pdf. Accessed 24 April 2023.

[9] IMF "Country Report No. 16/191".

[10] DB Media Release (March 5, 2017), Available at https://www.db.com/newsroom_news/2017/medien/deutsche-bank-refines-strategy-and-announces-capital-increase-en-11483.htm. Accessed 27 August 2018.

> Deutsche Bank's entrepreneurial culture. Finally, we established the Capital Release Unit to liberate capital consumed by low return assets and businesses that earn insufficient returns or that are no longer core to our strategy, by winding those down in an economically rational manner.[11]

Deutsche Bank Group

DB has its Headquarters in Frankfurt am Main, Germany, and it is the largest bank in Germany and one of the largest financial institutions in Europe, with total assets of € 1,475 billion as of 2018. DB employs 97,535 people, operates in 60 countries out of 2,425 branches. DB "provide(s) services in commercial and investment banking and retail banking as well as wealth and asset management products to corporations, governments, institutional investors, small and medium-sized businesses, and private individuals".[12] DB comprises three corporate divisions, which are supported by infrastructure functions: Corporate & Investment Bank (CIB); Private & Commercial Bank (PCB); and, Deutsche Asset Management (Deutsche AM).[13] DB operates with customers in most countries in the world, through: (1) subsidiaries and branches; (2) representative offices and or representatives assigned to serve customers.

As of 2023 "The Group consists of 521 (2021: 563) consolidated entities, thereof 200 (2021: 225) consolidated structured entities. 362 (2021: 376) of the entities controlled by the Group are directly or indirectly held by the Group at 100% of the ownership interests (share of capital). Third parties also hold ownership interests in 159 (2021: 187) of the consolidated entities (noncontrolling interests). As of December 31, 2022, and 2021, one subsidiary has material noncontrolling interests. Noncontrolling interests for all other subsidiaries are neither individually nor cumulatively material to the Group"[14] (Figs. A.1 and A.2).

According to 2020 Annual Report

> Our strategic transformation is designed to refocus our Core Bank around market leading businesses, which operate in growing markets with attractive return potential. Our Core Bank comprises our four core operating divisions, namely the Corporate Bank, the Investment Bank, the Private

[11] DB 2020 Annual Report, https://www.db.com/ir/en/download/Annual_Report_2020.pdf. Accessed 29 April 2021.

[12] DB Annual Report 2017, https://annualreport.deutschebank.com/2017/ar/servicepages/downloads/files/dbfy2017_entire.pdf. Accessed 20 April 2019.

[13] Ibid.

[14] DB 2023 Annual Report.

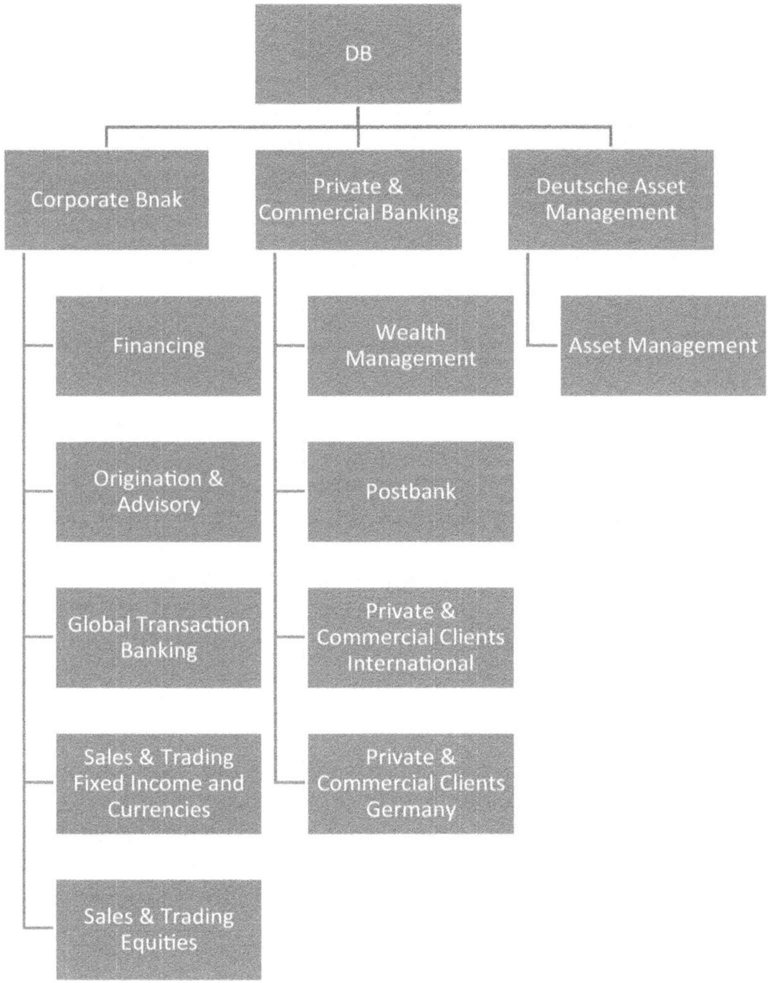

Fig. A.1 DB internal divisions 2017 (*Source* DB[15])

[15] DB Annual Report 2017, Available at https://annualreport.deutschebank.com/2017/ar/servicepages/downloads/files/dbfy2017_entire.pdf. Accessed 27 August 2023.

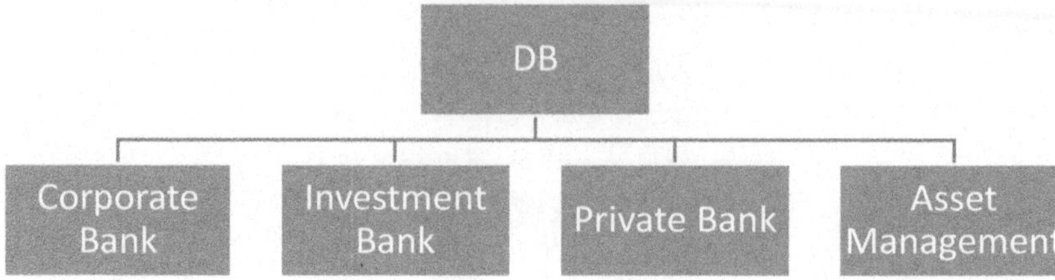

Fig. A.2 DB internal divisions 2023 (*Source* DB[16])

Bank, and Asset Management, together with the segment Corporate & Other.[17]

DB as "House Bank"

DB acted as House Bank of many companies for many years. The house bank would not only own shares of the company, it would take up of Director positions in supervisory boards and rely on "relationship lending". A "classic example" of a house bank relationship is that of DB and Daimler Benz. DB has guided the mergers of Mercedes Benz along time. Until 1994, Daimler Benz president was a senior DB official. Other example was the house bank relationship between DB and Volkswagen.[18]

Deutsche Bank and Insurance

In 1989 the DB formed the Lebensversicherungs-AG der Deutschen Bank, an insurance company: "Since September 1989 we have been offering life insurance in the Group through a newly-established company, Lebensversicherungs-AG der Deutschen Bank, Wiesbaden. Marketing is carried out mainly via our branches".[19] In 1992 DB "acquired a majority

[16] DB Annual Report 2023.

[17] Ibid.

[18] Jordi Canals *Universal Banking: International Comparisons and Theoretical Perspectives* (1997), 169; Automotive News "German Cross-Shareholding System Unwinds as Deutsche Bank Exits", http://www.autonews.com/article/20091101/ANE02/311019997/german-cross-shareholding-system-unwinds-as-deutsche-bank-exits. Accessed 12 October 2018.

[19] DB Annual Report 1989, Available at http://www.bankgeschichte.de/en/docs/1989.pdf. Accessed 27 August 2023.

interest in Deutscher Herold AG, Bonn. Deutscher Herold is an insurance group with a long tradition and a good market positioning. Its activities are centred on life insurance business with private individuals and commercial clients. It also offers a wide range of composite insurance products. In addition, we took a 30% stake in GerlingKonzern Versicherungs-Beteiligungs-AG, Cologne".[20]

As of 1995 the DB owed Deutscher Herold Allgemeine VersicherungsAG der Deutschen Bank, Deutscher Herold Lebensversicherungs-AG der Deutschen Bank, Deutscher Herold Rechtsschutzversicherungs-AG der Deutschen Bank, Globale Krankenversicherungs-AG (Germany), DB Vida – Companhia de Seguros de Vida, S.A. (Portugal) DB Vida Compañía de Seguros y Reaseguros, S.A, and DB Vita Compagnia di Assicurazioni e Riassicurazioni sulla Vita S.p.A. (Italy).[21] In 1996 the insurance companies were regrouped under the Retail and Private Client Division.[22]

In May 2014, DB "completed the sale of a 20.2% stake in Deutsche Herold AG to Zürich Beteiligungs AG, a subsidiary of Zurich Insurance Group AG. We acquired the 20.2% stake from a third party immediately ahead of selling it to Zurich".[23] In December 2016 DB completed the sale of 100% of the shares of Abbey Life Assurance Company to Phoenix Group Ltd. As a consequence of this sale all of the Group's insurance contracts business and the majority of the investment contract business were disposed of leaving only € 592 million in a remaining program".[24]

In 2018 DB and the digital insurance broker Friendsurance announced a partnership in order for DB to offer insurance products through the

[20] DB Annual Report 1992, http://www.bankgeschichte.de/en/docs/1992.pdf. Accessed 27 August 2018.

[21] DB Annual Report 1995, Available at http://www.bankgeschichte.de/en/docs/Annual_Report_1995_(Group).pdf. Accessed 27 August 2018.

[22] DB Annual Report 1996, Available at http://www.bankgeschichte.de/en/docs/Annual_Report_1996_(Group).pdf. Accessed 27 August 2018.

[23] DB Annual Report 2016, Available at https://www.db.com/ir/en/download/Deutsche_Bank_Annual_Report_2016.pdf accessed 27 August 2018.

[24] Ibid. Therefore, DB improved the Bank's CET1 ratio by approximately 10 basis points.

broker. In order "to drive this Deutsche Bank will integrate Friendsurance's digital products into its online banking portal".[25] By doing this, DB is "resurrecting" the concept of Allfinanz or bacassurance" by way of selling insurance products. While the 2016 strategy was to sell its equity in Abbey Life Insurance, the new strategy is to use its digital bank platform to offer insurance to its customers.[26]

Investment Banking Business Model

The business model for DS has changed from mainly commercial banking to investment banking from the 1980s and 1990s. "The larger for-profit banks, particularly the Deutsche Bank and Dresdner Bank. Throughout the postwar period, these banks had made most of their profits from the interest rate spread...and the interest they received on loans (most of these were made to the company sector). As has been well documented the slowing of economic growth in the 1980s and 1990s (and thus slowing demand for bank loans from companies) and increased competition among banks led to a narrowing of this interest rate spread. The main alternative to interest-based income for banks is fee-based income, such as investment banking and asset management. These activities are, however, primarily market based, and thus require growing financial markets to increase income. These banks thus became the main supporters of strengthening markets within the German financial system".[27]

Historically, DB has been able to raise money at a rate similar to that of the sovereign since it was seen as "an extension of the German state". However, after the GFC even senior bondholders may be "bailined" if a bank fails, making funding costs increase. "Paying more than big rivals such as France's BNP Paribas and JPMorgan Chase in the US leaves Deutsche's investment bank vulnerable to being priced out of business for its most important institutional clients, which would exacerbate market share declines in key trading and lending businesses, analysts say".[28]

[25] DB Media Release "Deutsche Bank Strengthens Its Insurance Business" (January 16, 2018), Available at https://www.db.com/newsroom_news/2017/deutsche-bank-strengthens-its-insurance-business-en-11763.htm. Accessed 27 August 2018.

[26] Darrel Delamaide, Yasmin. Osman, Christian Schnell "Deutsche Bank Partners with Tech Firm to Offer Online Insurance Product" Handelsblatt Global, 16 January 2018.

[27] Vitols "Changes in Germany's Bank-Based Financial System", 5.

[28] Stephen Morris, Robert Smith and Olaf Storbeck "Deutsche Bank Struggles with Rising Funding Costs" *Financial Times* (London 10 September 2018).

While some think, creating a "National Champion" via a merger with Commerzbank[29] would be a possible solution for DB, in 2019 that chance did not materialize.[30]

Recovery and Resolution Planning
According to DB 2023 Annual Report "Deutsche Bank works closely with the Single Resolution Board and the Bundesanstalt für Finanzdienstleistungsaufsicht (BaFin) who establish the Group resolution plan for Deutsche Bank, which is currently based on a single point of entry bail-in as the preferred resolution strategy. Under the single point of entry bail-in strategy, the parent entity Deutsche Bank AG would be recapitalized through a write-down and/or conversion to equity of capital instruments (Common Equity Tier 1, Additional Tier 1, Tier 2) and other eligible liabilities in order to stabilize the Group. Within one month after the application of the bail-in tool to recapitalize an institution, the BRRD (as implemented in the SAG) requires such institution to prepare a business reorganization plan, addressing the causes of failure and aiming to restore the institution's long-term viability.[31]

Case Study: Crédit Agricole

Universal Banking in France
"Saint Simonian banks" played an important role in the development of the Universal banking model during the Second Empire period due to the persistence and leadership of the Pereire brothers and *Crédit Mobilier*. Contrary to what happened in Germany, in France from 1880 to 1914 "universal banks gave up their universal bank- pattern to be turned into deposit banks (designed to serve exclusively as a source of short-term capital)".[32] Universal banks faced "massive withdrawals" at the time of

[29] Lex "Commerzbank: Waiting for Deutsche Bank" *Financial Times* (London, August 7, 2018).

[30] "Germany's Deutsche Bank and Commerzbank End Merger Talks" *DW* (Berlin, 15 April 2019) https://www.dw.com/en/germanys-deutsche-bank-and-commerzbank-end-merger-talks/a-48474225. Accessed August 15 2020.

[31] DB Annual Report 2023.

[32] M. Levy- Leboyer and M. Lescure "France" in Richard Sylla and Gianni Toniollo *Patterns of European Industrialization*, Chapter 8 (Routledge, Chapman, and Hall 1991), 164.

war in 1870 and following crisis from 1873 to 1896. In order to prevent further loses, some banks such as *Crédit Lyonais*, *Crédit Industriel et Commercial*, and *Societé Générale* limited the business to short-term loans. "The deposit banks thereby came to specialize in discounting operations as well as advances on securities and loans on securities on the stock carried over"[33] Small and mid-size manufactory firms tended not to use these joint stock banks. Levy-Leboyer and Lescare state that universal banks did not develop in France because: (i) Long-term investment come from firms themselves or family and friends; (ii) the stock market provided new financing opportunities for large firms; and (iii) local banks played an important role.[34] When universal banks were permitted to capture individual's deposits, they left the business "of investment banking to institutions especially created for that purpose, trustee banks, investment banks, and the stock market... The outcome was specialised banking".[35] The principal investment banks in the nineteenth century were *Banque de Paris et des Pays-Bas* (1872), the *Banque de l' Indochine* (1875) and the *Banque de l' Union Parisienne.*[36]

In 1945 De Gaulle nationalized *Banque de France* and the four most important banks, *Crédit Lyonnais, Société Générale*, *Comptoir National d'Escompte de Paris* and *Banque National pour le Commerce et l'Industrie.* Under Chirac government, major banks were privatized including *Société Générale*, *Crédit Commercial de France*, *Paribas* and *Suez. Crédit Lyonnais* was privatized in 1999.[37] *Caisse National de Crédit Agricole* was transformed into a stock company in 1988, which gave it independence from the State, and it was listed in 2001.[38]

Verdier explains that universal banking is commonly believed to exist before 1913 in Belgium, Germany, Austria, Italy, whereas specialized

[33] Alain Plessis "The History of Banks in France" (Elgar, 2003), 166.

[34] Idid, 166.

[35] Daniel Verdier "Explaining Cross-national Variations in Universal Banking in Nineteenth-Century Europe, North America and Australasia" in Douglas Forsyth and Daniel Verdier *The Origins of National Financial Systems: Alexander Gerschenkron Reconsidered* (Routledge, 2002), 29.

[36] Plessis "The History of Banks in France", 5.

[37] Idid, 6.

[38] Histoire Du Groupe Crédit Agricole (Crédit Agricole, 2018), https://www.Crédit-agricole.com/le-groupe/histoire-du-groupe-Crédit-agricole. Accessed 22 November 2023.

banking "was mostly encountered in France and the Anglo-Saxon countries".[39] While the development of the universal banking model in Germany and France in the nineteenth and almost all of the twentieth century was different, after 1984, French Banking Act "defined the concept of universal banking". As the *Federation Bancaire Française* affirm "French groups were subsequently able to expand to all business in the banking industry: namely, retail banking as well as corporate and investment banking".[40]

Scholars argue that France shifted from a government-based financial system to a market-based one. The change involved patterns of ownership and financing. State ownership was transferred to "cross-shareholding networks in newly privatised firms" at a first stage, and after de late 90's, to foreign shareholders.[41] O'Sullivan explains this change as follows. First, there was a contraction of the role of the state in the allocation of funds. Second, the role of financial markets in funding firms "experienced a market expansion"—from 27% of GDP in 1975 to 186% by 2001–. Third, the relevance of the banking sector decayed in comparison to other sources of funding. French deregulation started in 1984. Some believe this movement was a reaction to the "growing integration of financial markets" on the one side, and the pressure for the move to a single currency and the integration of the monetary policy in Europe, on the other.[42]

French deregulation, among other drivers, led to a new phenomenon in the financial industry called "Bancassurance".

Bancassurance

Bancassurance phenomenon first appeared in France in 1980.[43] There is not a single definition of "bancassurance" since it depends on the strategy adopted by financial institutions. Bancassurance "in its simplest form is the

[39] Vedier "Explaining Cross-National", 23.

[40] Federation Bancaire Francaise "The French Banking System" (2008), 1.

[41] Mary O´Sullivan "Acting Out Institutional Change: Understanding the Recent Transformation of the French Financial System" *Socio-Economic Review* (2017), 396.

[42] O´Sullivan, "Acting out Institutional Change", 400; Michael Loriaux France *After Hegemony: International Change and Financial Reform* (Cornell university Press 1991).

[43] Panayiotis G. Artikis, Stanley Mutenga, and Sotiris K. Staikouras "A Practical Approach to Blend Insurance in the Banking Network" *The Journal of Risk Insurance*, Vol. 9 No. 2 (2008), 107; Fiordelisi and Ricci "Bancassurance in Europe", 1.

distribution of insurance products through a bank's established distribution channels. The result is a banking corporation that can offer banking, insurance, lending and investment products to its customers".[44] In general terms, it "refers primarily to banks entering the insurance sector by offering insurance products to their retail customers".[45] According to the Cambridge Dictionary, Bancassurance is "a business activity in which banks sell services and products usually sold by insurance companies" or "the combination of banking and insurance services that is offered by many banks".[46] Oxford Dictionary defines Bancassurance as "[t]he selling of life assurance and other insurance products and services by banking institutions".[47] The Financial Times Lexicon define the term as "The combining of banking and insurance activities in one organization".[48] While originally the term was adopted to define a distribution phenomenon, today it is used to define "all kinds of relationships between banking and insurance industries".[49] The "assurfinance" phenomenon refers to insurance companies selling financial products.[50]

Gonulal, Goulder and Lester explain that bancasurance is "the process of using a bank's branches, sales network, and customer relationships to develop sales or insurance products…It is not simply a sales technique. It is a development channel". Bancassurance is the "development channel" and there is no requisite for the insurance company to be wholly owned

[44] Mohamed Nurullah and Sotiris Staikouras "The Separation of Banking from Insurance: Evidence from Europe" *Multinational Finance Journal*, Vol. 12 (2008), 159; Emilia Clipici and Catalina Bolovan "Bancassurance-Main Insurance Distribution and Sale Channel in Europe", Scientific Bulletin—Economic Sciences, Vol. 11 (2012), 54.

[45] Tobias Hoschka *Bancassurance in Europe* (St. Martin's Press, 1994), 1.

[46] Cambridge Dictionary, https://dictionary.cambridge.org, Accessed 12 November 2023.

[47] Oxford Dictionary, https://en.oxforddictionaries.com/definition/bancassurance. Accessed 12 November 2023.

[48] Financial Times Lexicon, https://markets.ft.com/glossary/searchLetter.asp?letter=B. Accessed 12 November 2023. In a similar way, Elkington defines bancassurance as the provision of and selling of banking or insurance products by the same organization under the same roof. W. Elkington *Bancassurance* [1993] Chartered Building Societies Institutions Journal (1993), 2.

[49] Fiordelisi and Ricci "Bancassurance in Europe", 5–25.

[50] Lutgart Van den Berghe and Kurt Verweire "Convergence in the Financial Services Industry" *The Geneva Papers on Risk and Insurance*, Vol. 26 No. 2 (2001), 175.

by the bank. There is "nothing intrinsic" in Bancassurance that require ownership linkages between the bank and the insurance company.[51]

The French financial sector is "concentrated and connected through cross- shareholdings" between the banking and insurer's sectors. A majority of French banks hold insurance company subsidiaries.[52]

Models of Bancassurance

There are different models of bancassurance according to the degree of integration of insurance and banking.

The first mode of entry is called "multi-tie or referral" where banks distribute insurance products for a fee.[53] Its aim is to bypass the middle agent and take advantage of the bank customer database to offer products. After the introduction of the Freedom of Services Directive in Europe, insurers avoided setting up offices but use bank branches to offer their products. These products are offered via branches, internet, apps and other supports.[54] The bank may choose more than one alliance. Generally, both parties remain autonomous.[55] Figure A.3 describes the first model, in which a single bank holds four commercial agreements with four different insurers.

The second mode of entry relies on joint ventures, where both insurers and bankers put resources together and form a separate entity (Fig. A.4), which will have to "blend cultures" and share risks.[56]

The third mode of entry is through financial conglomerates.[57] This type of bancassurance model is the most integrated one, since it involves

[51] Serap O. Gonulal, Nick Goulder, and Rodney Lester "Bancassurance- A Valuable Tool for Developing Insurance in emerging Markets" Policy Research Working Paper 6196, The World Bank, (2012), 9–10.

[52] IMF "France: Financial Sector Assessment Program—Detailed Assessment of Observance of Insurance Core Principles" (2013), 14.

[53] Artikis, Mutenga and Staikouras, "A Practical Approach to Blend Insurance", 107; Mark Teunissen "Bancassurance: Tapping into the Banking Strength" The Geneva Papers 33, (2008), 409; Philippe Trainar "La Bancassurance: Generalization ou déclin du modèle? Revue déconomie financière (2008), 53.

[54] Artikis, Mutenga and Staikouras "A practical approach to blend insurance",107.

[55] Sotiris Staikouras "Business Opportunities and Market Realities in Financial Conglomerates". The Geneva Papers (2006) 31, 139.

[56] Ibid, 119; Clipici and Bolovan "Bancassurance-Main Insurance Distribution", 54; Teunissen, "Bancassurance: Tapping into the Banking Strength", 409.

[57] See Chapter 2.

Fig. A.3 Model 1. Multi-tie or Referral

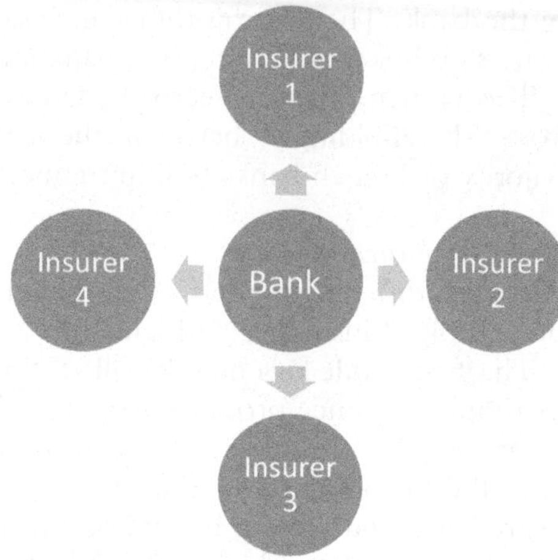

Fig. A.4 Joint venture

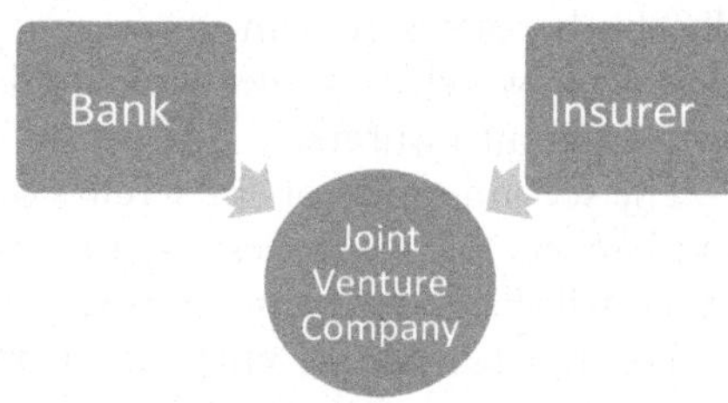

an "extended capital commitment" and "adequate pool of skilled professionals" and a strong brand. This model is the most widespread in France.[58]

Drivers of Bancassurance

Teunissen explains there are a number of drivers that underpin the development of bancassurance. In the first place, regulation permits banks to owe insurance companies and to distribute insurance products through banking networks. Second, insurers may use the bank databases as new a channel for sales, while international insurers may use local banks to enter

[58] Sotiris Staikouras "Business Opportunities and Market Realities in Financial Conglomerates, 119; Teunissen "Bancassurance: Tapping into the Banking Strength", 409.

new markets. Third, bancassurance is a new source of revenue in times of deregulation and more competition in the financial sector. Fourth, "positive fiscal" treatment of long-term saving products fosters the sale of bancassurance products. Fifth, experience shows bancassurance products are more desirable if they are simple and standardized. Sixth, the bancassurance model proved to be successful in markets where there is no strong alternative distribution channel, such as independent brokers. Seventh, the more integrated the model is, in terms of IT, product development, sales and remuneration, the more successful bancassurance would be.[59]

Particularly in France, there are certain factors that support the bancassurance model. First, the liberalization of bank's scope of actives permitted banks to expand into insurance. Second, the French tax system encourages savings, fostering the sale of certain insurance products. In the case of life insurance products, they are exempted for tax on the proceeds if they are held for a minimum period. Third, banks take advantage of the marginal cost of distributing insurance because their fixed overheads are covered by the banking activities. Fourth, banks and life insurers extend the term of their liabilities "through the creation of longer-term contracts". Fifth, Solvency I permitted a "degree of regulatory arbitrage", though it was "diluted" by the Financial Conglomerates Directive.[60]

Mutual or Cooperative Banks

The *Code Monetaire et Financier* or Money and Financial Code is the main code regulating financial institutions in France. Book V regulate Financial Service Providers. The French banking sector is composed by:

- Banks (Book V, Chapter 1),
- Mutual or Cooperative Banks (Book 5 Chapter II: *Banques Populaires, Crédit Agricole, Crédit Mutuel, Crédit Mutuel Agricole et Rural, Sociétés Cooperatives de banque, Crédit Maritime Mutuel, Caisses D'espargne* [Saving Banks]),
- Municipal Credit Banks (Book 5 Chapter IV), which "are local public lending and welfare institutions. Their role is to prevent usury

[59] Teunissen "Bancassurance: Tapping into the Banking Strength, 412–413.

[60] Gonulal, Goulder and Lester, "Bancassurance—A Valuable Tool", 9; Similar causes listed by Glenn Morgan, Andrew Sturdy, Jean Daniel and David Knights "Bancassurance in Britain and France: Innovating Strategies in the Financial Services." The Geneva Papers on Risks and Insurance (1994), 178.

through the granting of loans secured by pledge, in respect of which they have a monopoly. They may execute any transaction with the Credit institutions, accept funds from individuals and legal entities make means of payment available to them and effect related transactions".[61]

- Finance Companies (Book 5 Chapter V)
- State—owned banks:
    - *Caisse des Depôts et Consignations*, which is a "public group in the service of the country's general interest and economic development. Said group fulfils public interest duties in support of the public policies pursued by the State and the local authorities and may engage in competitive activities."[62]
    - *Trésor Public*, which is a public institution with responsibilities in collection of taxes, execution of state budget, with regulation prerogatives in banking and financial issues.[63]
    - *Banque de France,* which is the French Central Bank: "The Banque de France is the French pillar of the Eurosystem, a federal system formed by the European Central Bank and the national central banks of the euro area. Its three main missions are monetary strategy, financial stability and the provision of economic services to the community."[64]
    - Others: *La Banque Postale*, the *Institut d'emission des departaments d'autre –mer* and *Bpifrance* are also public institutions that perform banking activities.

A second category consists of the Mutual or Cooperative Banks. Contrary to Germany, where Saving Banks and Cooperatives are two different categories, in France, the Monetary and Financial Code regulate both institutions under the same chapter. The first saving banks were founded in Paris in 1818 as a private initiative; while in the nineteenth century, they were recognized as institutions of public utility. From 1950, several laws permitted saving banks to widen their scope of permitted

[61] Monetary and Financial Code, Art. 514-1.

[62] Monetary and Financial Code, Art 518-2.

[63] Olivier Hubert and Arnaud Pince, D, Banking Regulation in France: Overview (Practical Law).

[64] Banque de France https://www.banque-france.fr/en/banque-de-france/about-banque-de-france/missions, Accessed 20 November 2023.

activities, which were restricted to collect savings until then. From 1999, saving banks were induced to use the legal form of cooperative banks. As of today, saving banks exist under the *Banque Populaire Caisse d'Espargne* (BPCE), but are not organized as publicly owned banks anymore.[65]

The first cooperative bank in France was *Banque Poulaire* in the 1870s. Two rural Credit cooperatives were founded in the following years, *Crédit Mutuel* in the Alsace-Lorraine region, and *Crédit Agricole*, founded in 1890s. The cooperative banks multiplied and grew until after the Second World War, where the banking sector was nationalized. In the 80s, 90s and 2000s the law changed permitting the privatization of major French banking institutions. *Crédit Agricole* has transformed into one of the largest financial institutions in France and internationally.[66]

French banking cooperatives also commit to cooperative principles, similar to German banking cooperatives. French cooperatives have set up networks comprised by different levels of entities, conforming an "inverted pyramid structure". Local cooperatives are independent entities owned by members. These local cooperatives own regional cooperative banks, that in turn own federal or national body cooperatives (Fig. A.5).

The French cooperatives have evolved into complex structures, where the simple inverted pyramid is no longer the standard. Now, a central institution generally holds interests in different "conventional subsidiaries" turning the cooperative network into hybrid banking groups.[67] For *Crédit Agricole, Caisse d'Espargne* and *Banque Populaire*, the central institution has become a joint stock company, where regional/ local banks have remained cooperatives.[68] A second change in cooperative structures was the introduction of two innovative cooperative instruments called Associate Cooperative Certificates (CCA) and Investment Cooperative Certificate (CCI), which mix cooperative principles with capitalist ones. For instance, CCI are subscribed freely, they grant no voting rights,

[65] Dilek Bülbül, Reinhard H. Schmidt, Ulrich Schüwer "Saving Banks and Cooperative Banks in Europe" White Paper Series No. 5 Center of Excellenece Sustainable Architecture for Finance in Europe (2013), 11–12.

[66] Ayadi, Llewellyn, Schmidt, Arbak, Pieter De Groen "Investigating Diversity", 66–67.

[67] Jean-Noël Ory, Emmanuelle Gurtner, and Mireille Jaeger "The Challenges of Recent Changes in French Cooperative Banking Groups", RECMA Revue Internationale de L'Economie Sociale", No. 301 (2006) 44.

[68] Jean-Noël Ory and Yasmina Lemezeri "The French Co-operative Banking Group Model: Too Good to be True? XIXème Conférence de l'AIMS, (2010), 10.

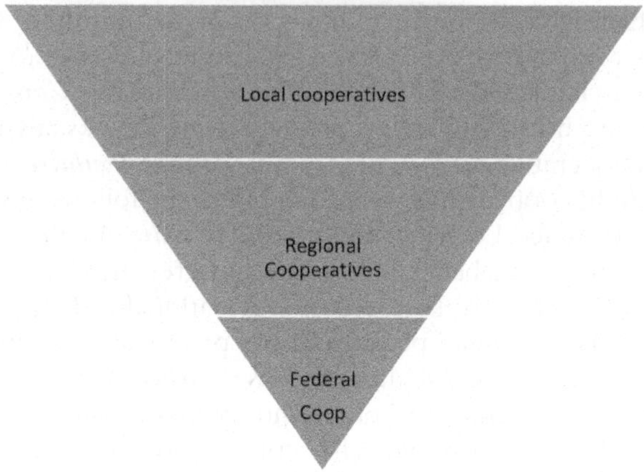

Fig. A.5 Inverted pyramid french cooperative structure

they may be sold in the market, they allow free interest withdrawals, and they act as stocks in liquidation. CCA give subscription rights to associates only, they do not grant voting rights, they grant free dividends, but in order to sell them an "order book" is required. As with CCI, CCA act as stock in liquidation.[69]

Figure A.6 describes the 2023 *Crédit Agricole* structure, which includes a listed central body, and relationships via CCA and CCI instruments.

The role of the Central bodies is regulated by Article 511-31 para 2: "They are responsible for ensuring the cohesiveness of their network and the correct functioning of the institutions affiliated with them. To this end, they shall take all necessary measures to ensure the liquidity and solvency of each said institution and of the entire network. They may also decide to prohibit or limit the distribution of dividends to the shareholders or the remuneration of the shares of the Credit institutions or investment firms affiliated with them".[70]

In general, local cooperatives have delegated functions such as treasury, risk management, mutual support, investment activities, debt issuance

[69] Spphie Nivoix "Specificities of the French Cooperative Banking Groups Facing the 2007–2012 Crisis", *China-USA Business Review*, Vol 15, (2016), 381.

[70] Monetary and Financial Code Art. 511-31.

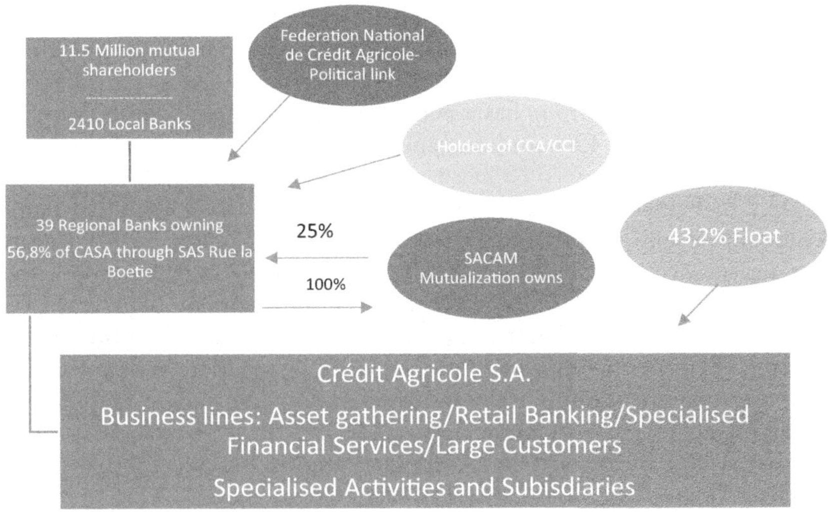

Fig. A.6 Crédit Agricole (*Source* Crédit Agricole 2022–2023 Integrated Report)[71]

and back-office IT services to central institutions.[72] Regarding mutual support, *Crédit Agricole* has a "legally binding cross-guarantee system" that enables the use of the group resources to serve the debt of regional cooperatives.[73]

The Case of Crédit Agricole

Crédit Agricole is an interesting case because it is one of French SIFIs, it is a Cooperative network, and one of the most successful cases of cross-border BBFC.

[71] Credit Agricole 2022–2023 Integrated Report, https://rapport-integre.credit-agricole.com/en/credit_agricole_group_and_its_model/the-origins-of-the-group-and-its-cooperative-foundation/. Accessed 23 November 2023.

[72] Ayadi et al. "Investigating Diversity", 66.

[73] Ayadi et al. "Investigating Diversity", 67; David Blanche "The Regulation of French Financial Co-operatives: From Local Co-operatives to Global Banking Groups Subject to the post-Crisis Regime for Banking Resolution", 11th Strasbourg European Meeting—European Parliament (2016).

Crédit Agricole S.A, (CASA) headquartered in Montrouge, is the central body of the "Crédit Agricole Network", which includes 2410 local banks, 39 regional banks, and all the CASA business lines and subsidiaries. The *Crédit Agricole Group* has a net income group share (NIGS) of €5.5 billion, presence in 42 countries, and it is the number 1 bancassurer in Europe.[74]

Only in France, the retail bank division comprises 39 Regional Banks (co-operative entities providing a comprehensive range of financial products and services), LCL, a subsidiary of Credit Agricole S.A which is one of the biggest banks in France; BforBank, CASA's online bank and LCL Private Banking, plus Credit Agricole Private Banking. The insurance & Banking division encompasses Amundi, CPR Asset Management, Credit Agricole Assurances and Credit Agricole Inmobilier, Square Habitat and Credit Agricole Titres. The specialized services division includes Leasing and Factoring, Eurofactor and Unifergie, among others. The Corporate and Investment banking division embraces Credit Agricole Corporate and Investment Bank, Caceis and CA Indosuez. Other brands include CA Grands Crus, Mozaic, Uni-editions and Pleinchamp, among others.[75]

Resolution of Crédit Agricole

Directive 2019/879 of 20 May 2019 ("BRRD2") was transposed into French law and is applicable since 28 December 2020. The law provides requisites for French cooperative banking groups. According to CA "The resolution authorities will treat the Central Body and its affiliated entities ("Network") as a whole when assessing the conditions to enter in resolution... In case of a bail-in, write-down or conversion measures will apply simultaneously to all entities within the Network".[76]

Analysing the four indicators detailed in Chapter 6, it can be concluded that:

[74] Credit Agricole 2022–2023 Integrated Report; Credit Agricole "Key Figures on Our Strategic Positioning", https://www.credit-agricole.com/en/group/group-project-and-ambitions-2022/our-strategic-positioning. Accessed 1 December 2023.

[75] Credit Agricole All Brands, https://www.credit-agricole.com/en/business-lines-and-brands/all-brands. Accessed 1 December 2023.

[76] Credit Agricole Credit Update, Available at https://www.credit-agricole.com/pdfPreview/186516.

1. *Crédit Agricole* Group is a highly complex group, which comprises not only CASA and its subsidiaries and branches, but also local and regional cooperatives.
2. CASA perform many functions delegated by local and regional cooperatives, such as management liquidity, risk management, IT services, etc. Therefore, *Crédit Agricole* may be included in the "centralised business model" category, even though as a central body it is located at the bottom of the inverted pyramid structure.
3. *Crédit Agricole* retail business amounts to 17% of its NIGS, while Large Customers and Asset gathering amounts to 68% of its NIGS. Therefore, it may be labelled as a "no retail business model" although historically it was based on retail banking, aligned with the cooperative solidarity movement.
4. France has a universal approach to resolution: "The French court tends to consider an insolvency estate as a whole (*universalité de patrimoine*). This means that the court that has jurisdiction to open insolvency proceedings also has jurisdiction over all the company's assets, whether located in France or abroad. There are some exceptions to this for assets located in EU member states, which apply when secondary proceedings are opened with respect to a company's branch(es) operating in another EU member state."[77]

While theoretically the four indicators discussed above show the SPOE strategy would be the most appropriate for *Crédit Agricole Group*, its corporate structure presents some challenges. As its structure remains a hybrid-inverted pyramid, a pure SPOE strategy would not be achievable without changing the group's nature. Applying SPOE at the central body would mean a split of the group, which would present similar effects as a MPOE.

If a pure SPOE strategy bail in tool would be applied primary to ordinary shares (most of them in hands of the regional banks) and then to holders of bail-in able debt (generally issued by the central body), so the regional banks would lose their shares in the central body.[78] The result

[77] Paul Talbourdet and Joanna Gumpelson "Restructuring and Insolvency in France: Overview", Practical Law Country Q&A 1-501-6905, Thomson Reuters, 2021.

[78] Blanche "The Regulation of French Financial Co-operatives", 73.

would be splitting the cooperative group via a de facto "demutualization"[79] of part of the group. CASA would have new shareholders, while local and regional cooperatives will continue to exist as cooperatives.

Second, *Crédit Agricole* as a consolidated group has mutual guarantee schemes in place, which ensure the transfer of funds and liquidity within the group at any moment.[80] According to the FSB, "The existence of intra-group transactions and exposures, including the use of intra-group guarantees (IGGs) ...increases interconnectedness and may impede separability of firms' transactions and legal entities. The existence of IGGs makes it challenging for a firm to transfer positions or portfolios from guaranteed entities to third parties as client consent would be required to not only transfer the trade but also to release the firm from the guarantee. Obtaining the release from the guarantee can add time and cost, e.g. price concessions or alternative Credit support. The use of IGGs also increases the likelihood that financially sound entities are caused to fail due to contagion. The insolvency of a guarantor, especially a parent, may hasten the insolvency of any guaranteed subsidiaries, thereby increasing the potential disruption to financial stability".[81] The existence of IGGs in French cooperative networks is part of its nature, so the resolution of cooperative networks would be more challenging than other banking groups with no IGGs in place.

Is it possible to apply the bail in tool to the regional or local banks? While theoretically possible since the bail in tool is legally applicable to

[79] Murray Fulton and Jean Girard "Co-operatives and Mutual Canada, Demutualization of Co-operatives and Mutuals" (COOP 2015). Demutualization according to Fulton and Girard is "Demutualisation is the conversion of a cooperative", Crédit union or mutual into an alternative organisational form (usually one owned by investors). Demutualisation can occur through the conversion of equity into investment shares, or it can occur via a merger, takeover or buyout involving companies that are not cooperatives or mutuals. Regardless of the form it takes, demutualisation involves the transfer to private investors of the capital that has been built up in the cooperative over the years".

[80] European Association of Co-operative Banks "Consultative Document "Effective Resolution of Systemically Important Financial Institutions. Recommendations and Timelines" (2011).

[81] FSB "Consultative Document Effective Resolution of Systemically Important Financial Institutions Recommendations and Timelines" (2011).

cooperative banks in France, bail-inable debt is not issued at the local or regional levels.[82]

Considering the above-mentioned elements, a pure SPOE resolution strategy applied to the current structure, would imply the split of the CA group due to the hybrid inverted pyramid structure. However, SPOE has certain advantages described in Table A.1.

In order to apply a proper SPOE strategy, the inverted pyramid structure would have to be turned upside down. This would mean the end of the cooperative structure, via a demutualization of the local and regional banks, and posing CASA at the top of the pyramid. In order to apply a "pure" SPOE resolution strategy a non-operative holding company would have to be created on top of CASA. While this option is non-viable from a practical point of view, there is room for applying a SPOE strategy taking

Table A.1 Advantages and challenges of SPOE for CA

Advantages of SPOE as a preferred resolution strategy CA	*Challenges of the SPOE strategy CA*
Efficiency: SPOE strategy allows cross-jurisdictional transfers and needs less loss absorbing capacity needed as a group	Need to have ex ante agreements with other resolution authorities
Critical functions assured	Doubtful that foreign jurisdictions would respect French's universal approach to resolution Special case of the US insolvency approaches
Flexibility: allows a flexible legal structure through branches and or subsidiaries	Need to change legal and operational structure to include a holding company on top of current parent company
Fast process: through a "liquidation weekend"	Split of the Cooperative Network. Demutualization of part of the Group
Enhances transparency	
French Resolution authority would be is in control of the process	
France applies the Universal Approach to resolution	

[82] In the hypothetical case that regional or local banks issue bail-inable debt, a number of challenges would be present: a) how to harmonize the "one member-one vote" principle with the conversion of debt into cooperative shares, b) how to harmonize the need of approval of new members by other members. IADI Resolution issues for Financial Cooperatives-Overview of Distinctive Features and Current resolution Tools" (2017).

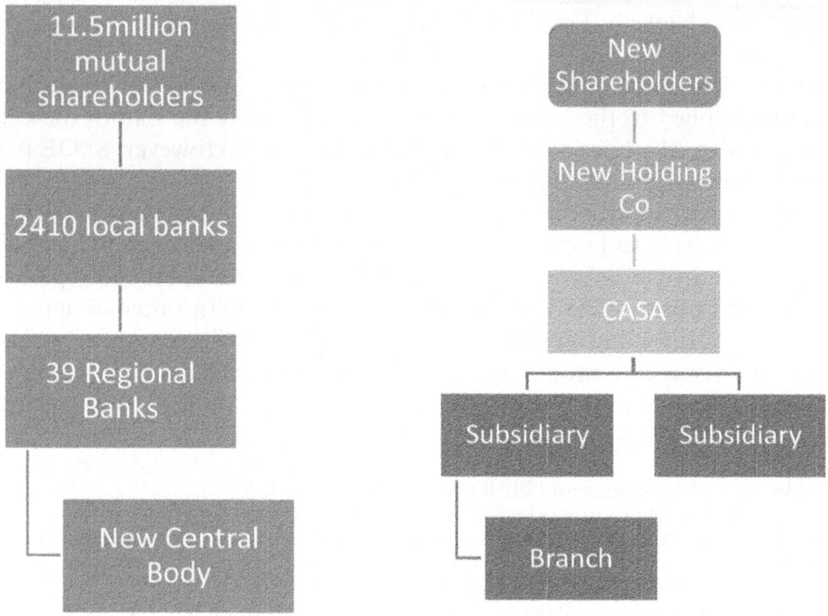

Fig. A.7 Result of applying SPOE at CASA/New Holding Co. Level

CASA as the point of entry. This option would mean at least that the local and regional banks might continue to be cooperatives (and would need to create a new central body), while the structure below CASA would split into a banking group with CASA or a holding company as the apex. Figure A.7 shows the result of applying a SPOE at CASA/New holding Co. level.

As in the case of Deutsche Bank, an alternative scenario would be to take advantage of SPOE in Europe, and to analyse a MPOE strategy for foreign subsidiaries such as Asian, African and Latin American units.

Concluding Remarks

Unlike Germany, France has not engaged in universal banking throughout its history, although the *Crédit Financier* and Saint Simon ideas were precursors of the universal banking model in Europe, and particularly in Germany. After 1980's, French financial system has changed from a governed-centred model to a market-centred one, and it has embraced universal banking model. This has underpined the insurgence of Bancassurance, a term that was first used in France, and which emerged because of deregulation and competition. Contrary to the German banking system, in France there is no "three-pillar system", since Saving banks are regulated "in tandem" with cooperative banks, and there is no clear distinction in its legal form, as in Germany. One of the most impressive developments of the French banking system is the evolution of the Cooperative banking system, which has created one of the French SIFIs, *Crédit Agricole*.

The Cooperative Network inverted pyramid structure is designed to fulfil the cooperative principles of solidarity, mutual support and democracy. While this structure has proved to assure the mentioned principles, certain challenges appear when the structure confronts a distress situation. The new resolution toolbox was designed to tackle traditional join stock banking groups. The bail in tool is planned for entities that are able to issue bail-inable debt freely and that allow the write down of shares and the conversion of debt into equity. While the traditional inverted pyramid is no longer the standard since the central body is generally a listed entity, there are still some challenges ahead. These challenges pose difficulties to maintain the cooperative network standing as a whole after the bail in is applied.

There are three theoretical options for *Crédit Agricole*. First, to change the structure, turning the inverted pyramid upside down, demutualizing both local and regional cooperatives, and changing the ownership structure to mimic a join stock universal bank as Deutsche Bank. The "pure" SPOE strategy would imply also to set up a holding company on top of CASA. This option is practically infeasible since it would denaturalize the cooperative and would be politically unattainable. A second option would be to apply the SPOE strategy at the CASA level. This option would maintain the local and regional cooperatives as such, splitting the network since the regional banks would lose their equity in CASA. The benefits of this option are that the international side of the group would remain united, and the local cooperatives would survive. The costs of this option are that unlike in a traditional SPOE strategy, the consequence will be the split of the group, which resembles the result of a MPOE strategy in this respect. A third option for *Crédit Agricole* would be a hybrid resolution strategy, whereby a SPOE resolution strategy would be applied to certain jurisdictions (e.g. the EU, USA and Japan) and a MPOE would be applicable for developing countries. This option would not be as efficient as a SPOE strategy, but would assure there is no uncoordinated "ring-fenced" type of resolution.

Case Study: Barclays

Barclays History

"Barclays traces its ancestry back to two goldsmith bankers, John Freame and Thomas Gould, who were doing business in Lombard Street, London in 1690. In 1736, Freame's son, Joseph took his brother-in-law, James Barclay on as a partner, and the name has remained a constant presence in the business ever since".[83] Foxwell states "The economist Storch said in 1815 that Great Britain was the only country in Europe in which there were any private banks. The statement requires qualification; but there is certainly no other country in which such private firms, half-bankers and half traders, can be more profitably studied, or have given rise to such remarkable developments. Nor is there any English bank better suited through all the stages of its long history than Barclays to illustrate the most characteristic features of these developments".[84]

As the Saint Simonians shaped the Credit Mobilier and the Universal banking system, Quaker religious movement shaped Barclays. "The Quakers have played a great part in English banking, nowhere more than in the Barclay group: the Huguenots may rank next; but a certain pietistic and mystical form of religious feeling seems to have characterised nearly all the original Barclay banker".[85]

In 1888 Barclay, Bevan, Tritton & Co., and Ransom, Bouverie & Co.—London agents of several country banks-united. In 1896, twenty country banks, including the Gurneys of Norwich and Backhouse of Darlington also united. In 1915, Barclays amalgamated with large centralized branch-banks of a different type.[86] In 1916, Barclays acquired the

[83] Barclays "Our history," https://home.barclays/who-we-are/our-history/. Accessed 7 March 2023.

[84] Herbert Foxwell "A History of Barclays Bank," *The Economic Journal*, Vol. 37, No. 147 (1927), 411–417.

[85] Idid; Mitchel Larson, Gerhard Schnyder, Gerarda Westerhuis and John Wilson "Strategic Responses to Global Challenges: The Case of European Banking, 1973–2000," *Business History*, Vol. 53, No. 1 (2011), 40–62.

[86] Ibid.

United Counties Bank, which "enabled Barclays to become one of the 'Big Five' clearing banks, with national coverage".[87]

In the 1920s Barclays gained control of the following banks: i) the Colonial Bank, with branches in the Caribbean and West Africa; ii) the Anglo-Egyptian Bank, with branches in Palestine, Egypt, Malta and Cyprus; and iii) the National Bank of South Africa. In 1925, these banks were merged into the newly formed "Barclays Bank (Dominion, Colonial and Overseas), "Barclays Bank DCO", and later "Barclays Bank International". In 1968, Barclays acquired Martins Bank. In 2000, Barclays acquired The Woolwich, a former building society. In 2003, it acquired Banco Zaragozano, a Spanish bank. In 2005, it acquired a majority stake in ABSA, a leading South African bank.[88] In 1986 Barclays established an investment banking operation known as Barclays Capital. Barclays Capital is now part as Barclays International. In 1995 the fund manager Wells Fargo Nikko Investment Advisers was acquired by Barclays and "was integrated with BZW Investment Management to form Barclays Global Investors". In 2008 Barclays acquired the investment banking and capital markets businesses of Lehman Brothers. In 2009, BGI was sold to BlackRock.[89]

In 2016 Barclays "announced a new strategy, designed to build on its strengths as a diversified transatlantic consumer and wholesale bank, anchored in the UK and US home markets, with global reach". In 2018, the Barclays "underwent its biggest structural changes for over 30 years, in accordance with regulatory requirements introduced by the UK government as a result of the financial crisis of 2008. The main objective was to separate or "ring-fence" the domestic retail and business bank from the international and investment bank. Barclays PLC continues as the holding company, supervising three operational subsidiaries: Barclays Bank UK PLC, comprising the UK Retail Bank, UK Barclaycard, UK Wealth and Investments and Corporate Banking for smaller UK businesses; Barclays Bank PLC comprising Corporate and Investment Banking, non-UK Barclaycard, Wealth International, the Private Bank and Overseas Services; and Barclays Services Ltd, which

[87] Barclays "Our history".

[88] Reuters: FACTBOX-What Barclays has said and done on M&A, 9 August 2007; Barclays "A Quick History", https://www.archive.barclays.com/items/show/5419. Accessed 7 March 2023.

[89] The Banker "Barclays sells BGI to BlackRock" July 6, 2009.

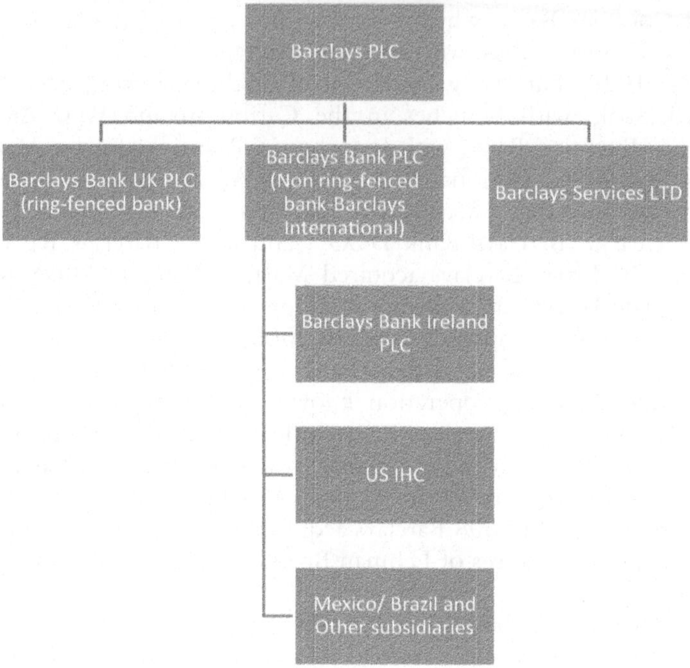

Fig. A.8 Simplified Barclays' structure (*Source* Based on Barclays Bank UK PLC Annual Report 2022 and S&P Global Ratings, June 20, 2023)

includes support services such as Group Functions, Operations and Technology"[90] (Fig. A.8).

Barclays Insurance
In the UK, Barclays Bank UK PLC arranges home insurance via Barclays Insurance Services Company Limited, a wholly owned subsidiary of Barclays Bank UK PLC. Barclays Bank UK PLC and Barclays Insurance Services Company Limited are both insurance intermediaries. Barclays Bank UK PLC is authorized by PRA and regulated by PRA and FCA.

[90] Barclays: "A Quick History" (2019).

Barclays Insurance Services Company Limited is authorized and regulated by the FCA.[91]

Barclays Investment banking

After the Big Bang, in 1985, the Bank merged its merchant bank with Zoate & Bevan and Wedd Durlacher to form BZW. A decade after, it sold its division to Credit Suisse. In 2008, Barclays purchased the US operations of Lehman Brothers under the leadership of Bob Diamond. Today, the corporate and investment banking division amounts to a 70% of total risk weighted assets of the group, while the retail bank amounts to the remaining 30%.[92] Barclays ranks on the seventh position on the world's top investment banks, being the first British bank to rank in it, before HSBC (position 9) (see Table A.2).

While some believe Barclays would be better without the investment-banking unit,[93] Barclays CEO Staley states: "I believe in universal

Table A.2 World's top investment banks

1	JPMorgan
2	Goldman Sachs
3 =	Citi
3 =	Morgan Stanley
5	Bank of America Merryll Lynch
6	Deutsch Bank
7	Barclays
8	Credit Suisse
9 =	UBS
9 =	HSBC

Source Coalition and Financial Times (Crow and Morris "Investment Banking" [20 January 2019])

[91] Barclays Important Information About Barclays Insurance Services, https://www.barclays.co.uk/content/dam/documents/premier/BAR_9914957_Cropped.pdf. Accessed 8 March 2023.

[92] Crow and Morris "Investment Banking": (20 January 2019).

[93] Ed Firth, an equity analyst at Keefe, Bruyette & Woods Inc believes: "Barclays has some truly wonderful consumer businesses, but the problem is the big investment bank. It's impossible to predict earnings in the division, which you'd accept if from time to time you made 20 to 25 percent return on equity. But we don't even have that anymore." Edward Robinson "Jes Staley Stakes Barclays's Future on Investment Banking", https://www.bloomberg.com/news/features/2018-09-26/jes-staley-stakes-barclays-s-future-on-investment-banking *Bloomberg* (New York, 26 September 2018), Accessed 11 March 2023.

banks…I believe in having a diversified portfolio of consumer and wholesale businesses. I believe you've got to have the team to execute and deliver strong returns for your shareholders. And I believe in scale. What I don't believe is this notion that only an American bank can be a bulge-bracket investment bank. That is flawed".[94]

Resolution Planning

According to the Annual Report 2022 "The BoE's preferred approach for the resolution of the Group is a bail-in strategy with a single point of entry at Barclays PLC. Under such a strategy, Barclays PLC's subsidiaries would remain operational while Barclays PLC's capital instruments and eligible liabilities would be written down or converted to equity in order to recapitalise the Group and allow for the continued provision of services and operations throughout the resolution. The order in which the bail-in tool is applied reflects the hierarchy of capital instruments under UK CRD IV and otherwise respecting the hierarchy of claims in an ordinary insolvency. Accordingly, the more subordinated the claim, the more likely losses will be suffered by owners of the claim"[95] (See Chapter 6).

Citibank Case

Historical Overview

The case of Citibank is illustrative and archetypical of the US banking system. From its inception in 1870, it has grown to become the biggest bank in the US. However, the GFC turned the US authorities to implement one of the biggest bailouts in US history. Nowadays, a decade after the GFC, Citibank is again in the hands of private owners and continues to be one of the most important banking groups in the world. As Huertas states:

> In 1870 the firm was an owner-managed entity with few employees. It operated from a single location, had a restricted customer base and a single product. Its share of the total banking industry was by any measure small. By 1920 the picture had changed dramatically. Citibank had become the

[94] Ibid.

[95] Barclays. Annual Report 2022, https://home.barclays/content/dam/home-barclays/documents/investor-relations/reports-and-events/annual-reports/2022/AR/Barclays-PLC-Annual-Report-2022.pdf, Accessed 20 November 2023.

> largest commercial bank in the country and a leading investment banking house. It had put a managerial hierarchy in place and was in the process of separating ownership from management. It was on the verge of becoming the nation's first truly modern bank.[96]

On June 16, 1812, City Bank of New York was chartered by the NY authorities with the purpose of competing with other states such as Philadelphia and Baltimore.[97] In 1865 the bank gained a national charter and changed his name to "National City Bank of New York". By then, Moses Taylor was his president, principal owner and principal customer. In 1891, Stillman was created president and changed the business model of Citibank. From being a specialized small bank, it changed the bank in terms of size and product diversification. Stillman wrote

> I firmly believe ... that the most successful banks will be the ones that can do something else than the mere receiving and loaning of money. That does not require a very high order of ability, but devising methods of serving people and [of• attracting business without resorting to unconservative or unprofitable methods, that opens limited fields for study, ability and resourcefulness and few only will be found to do it.[98]

The bank was organized through commercial, investment and trust affiliates and commenced an era of geographical expansion. In 1920, with the incorporation of Mitchel as Manager, a special compensation scheme was introduced consisting of 20% share of profits over those needed to pay dividends. This scheme separated the ownership from managerial positions and helped the expansion of the bank during that decade. In 1929 Citibank was the largest in the world.[99]

After the creation of the Federal Reserve Act in 1913, the previous perception that banks were "quasi-public entities" changes because of the creation of the central bank. The new Act permitted banks to

[96] Thomas Huertas "The Rise of the Modern Business Enterprise: The Case of Citibank" *Business and Economic History*, (1985), 146.

[97] Citibank: Timeline, https://www.citigroup.com/citi/about/timeline/. Accessed 14 May 2023.

[98] James Stillman, Letter to Frank A. Vanderlip, 12 February 1907, Vanderlip MSS, Columbia University, cited by Huertas "The Rise of the Modern Business Enterprise", 146.

[99] Huertas "The Rise of the Modern Business Enterprise", 152.

expand through international branching.[100] National City Bank took the opportunity. In terms of geographical expansion, it established offices in London, Shanghai, Manila, Yokohama and Singapore in 1902. In 1914, it opened its first South American office in Buenos Aires, followed by, Rio de Janeiro, Montevideo and Santiago de Chile. By 1917, Citibank had 35 branches and in 1998, it has expanded over 100 countries.[101]

By 1965

> Fortune magazine was describing First National City Bank as the "wave of the future" for American banking. It had surpassed its rivals in terms of local branch network; with 150 branches, it was the leading bank in the New York metropolitan area. In terms of assets, it was now America's second-largest bank after Bank of America. It was the top bank overseas, with 163 branches and affiliates in 55 countries and territories.[102]

In 1968, following McKenzie advice, Citibank took a series of measures to reorganize the business. First, a holding company "First National Citi Corporation" was created, who acquired the bank as a wholly owned subsidiary. Second, a new management structure was established, focusing on the types of customers (individuals, small and mid-sized customers, national or multinational businesses, overseas customers and high net wealthy individuals).[103]

The GFC hit Citigroup. By November 2008, Citigroup had receipt $25 billion in taxpayer-funded federal Troubled Asset Relief Program funds. On November 2018 Shares of Citigroup common stock traded below $1.00 on the New York Stock Exchange. In November 2018 Citigroup was bailout by the Treasury and the FDIC by "approximately $306 billion of loans and securities backed by residential and commercial real estate and other such assets, which will remain on Citigroup's balance sheet". Additionally, the Treasury would invest "$20 billion in Citigroup from the Troubled Asset Relief Program in exchange for preferred stock

[100] Huertas "The Rise of the Modern Business Enterprise", 149.

[101] David Baron and David Besanko "Strategy, Organization and Incentives: Global Corporate Banking at Citibank" *Journal of Industrial and Corporate Change* (2001), 12.

[102] Citibank: "Timeline".

[103] Ibid.

with an 8% dividend to the Treasury". In 2010, the Treasury sold its Citigroup shares denationalizing the bank again.[104]

According to its 2023 Annual Report,

> Citigroup is a global diversified financial service holding company whose businesses provide consumers, corporations, governments and institutions with a broad, yet focused, range of financial products and services, including consumer banking and credit, corporate and investment banking, securities brokerage, trade and securities services and wealth management. Citi has approximately 200 million customer accounts and does business in more than 160 countries and jurisdictions.[105]

Additionally, Citigroup is one of the US bank-based conglomerates included in the FSB G-SIB List (2023), classified in Bucket 3 with Bank of America, DB and HSBC[106] (Fig. A.9).

Citi has a strong presence in Latin America and the Caribbean through branches: Argentina, Bahamas, Ecuador, Salvador, Guatemala, Haiti, Jamaica, Panamá, Paraguay, Puerto Rico, República Dominicana, Uruguay, and Venezuela; and through subsidiaries in: Aruba, Barbados, Brazil, Chile, Colombia, Costa Rica, Honduras, México, Perú and Trinidad and Tobago.[107]

In Canada Citi operates through both subsidiaries and a branch.[108]

In Africa, Citi operates through branches in: Algeria, Cameroon, Democratic Republic of Congo, Egypt, Gabon, Ghana (Representative Office), Kenya, South Africa, Tanzania, Tunisia, Uganda, Zambia and subsidiaries in: Ivory Coast, Morocco, Nigeria and Senegal.[109]

[104] Tom Braithwaite and Francesco Guerrera "US Treasury Sells Remaining Citi Share" *Financial Times* (7 December 2010), https://www.ft.com/content/f8d42e04-0181-11e0-9b29-00144feab49a. Accessed 23 September 2023.

[105] Citigroup 2023 Annual Report. https://www.citigroup.com/rcs/citigpa/storage/public/citi-2022-annual-report.pdf. Accessed 23 September 2023.

[106] FSB GSIB list 2023.

[107] Citi https://www.citibank.com/. Accessed 15 April 2023.

[108] https://www.citibank.com/tts/insights/eSource_academy/docs/country_profiles/north_america/1442257821-Citi-TTS-Canada-Country-Profile-2014.pdf. Accessed 15 April 2023.

[109] Citigroup https://www.citigroup.com/citi/about/countries-and-jurisdictions/. Accessed 15 April 2023.

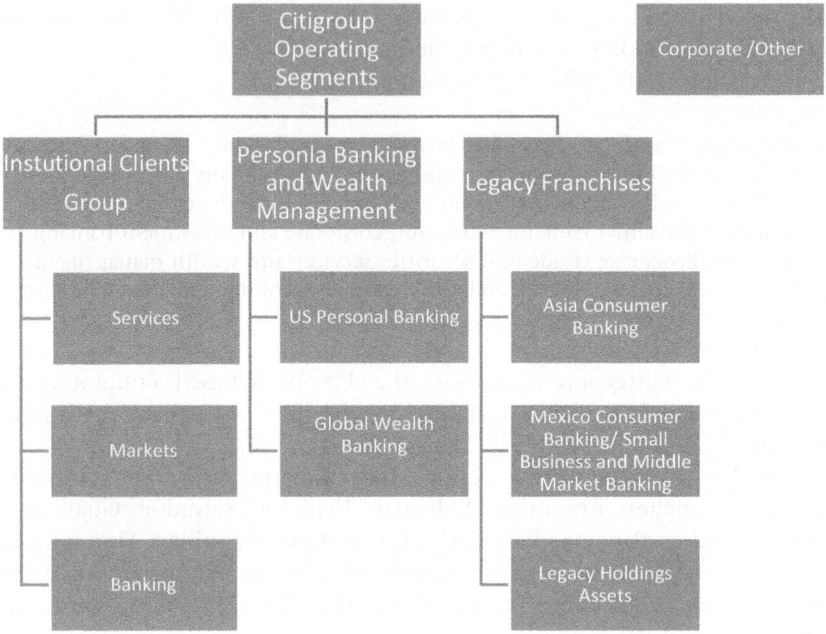

Fig. A.9 Citigroup segments (*Source* 2023 Citigroup Annual Report)

In Europe, Citi chose to operate mainly through subsidiaries. The only country where Citi functions through a branch is Italy. It acts through subsidiaries in: Austria, Belgium, Bulgaria, Czech Republic, Denmark, Finland, France Germany, Greece, Hungary, Ireland, Luxembourg, Monaco, Netherlands, Norway, Poland, Portugal, Romania, Russia, Slovakia, Spain, Sweden, Switzerland, Turkey, Ukraine and the United Kingdom.[110]

In the Middle East Region, Citi acts through branches and subsidiaries. In Bahrein, Citi operates via a branch, and has erected a subsidiary called Citi Islamic Investment Bank E.C. In Iraq it operates through a branch, as

[110] Citigroup https://www.citigroup.com/citi/about/countries-and-jurisdictions/. Accessed 15 April 2023.

well as in Israel, Jordan, Kuwait, Lebanon, Pakistan, Qatar, United Arab Emirates, and through subsidiaries in: Kazakhstan and Saudi Arabia.[111]

In the Asia Pacific region, Citi operates through branches in: Australia, Bangladesh, Hong Kong, India, Indonesia, Macau, Mauritius, New Zealand, Sri Lanka and Vietnam; and through subsidiaries in China, Korea, Malaysia and Taiwan.[112]

In Japan, Philippines, Singapore and Thailand Citi operates through branches and subsidiaries.[113]

Citi Resolution Planning

As stated in 6.6, Citi's preferred resolution strategy is SPOE.

Banco Santander Case

Banco Santander is a *rara avis* in the world of G-SIBs. Not only because of its origins in a northern province of Spain, but because of its history of internationalization, focus on retail business and family leadership for more than three generations. The Botin family, despite holding less than 3% of the shares of the bank has led the bank with intermittences since 1907, when Emilio Botin López was appointed president of the bank. Emilio Botin III who took office as president of the bank in 1986 made Banco Santander rise from the 152nd to number 10 in 2008.[114] Santander is the only Spanish G-SIB by 2023.[115]

Banco Santander was founded in 1857 in Santander, Spain. By then, Spain's economy was approximately one fourth of UK's economy and on third the size of Germany. The population of the city of Santander by 1857 was 28.907 inhabitants.[116] Competition among banks in Spain between 1874 and 1892 was intense and the main banks were Barcelona, Bilbao, Santander and Crédito Mobiliario Español. After the repatriation

[111] Ibid.

[112] Ibid.

[113] https://www.citigroup.com/citi/about/countries-and-jurisdictions/thailand.html. Accessed 25 May 2023.

[114] Adrian Tschoegl and Mauro F. Guillén *Building a Global Bank: The Transformation of Banco Santander* (Princeton University Press 2008), 2.

[115] 2023 list of G-SIBs.

[116] Tschoegl and Guillen "Building a Global Bank", 2.

of capital due to the colonial crisis of 1898 when Spain lost Cuba, the Philippines and Puerto Rico, three banks were formed: Banco Guipuozcoano, Banco Hispano-Americano, Banco de Vizcaya and Banco Español de Crédito (Banesto).[117] Banco Santander grew during the 1940s because of acquisition of Spanish banks. In 1946, Santander acquired Banco Mercantil and a year later, it opened representative offices in Cuba, Argentina, Mexico and Venezuela and a London office.[118]

During the 1960s, Emilio Botin II opened new branches taking advantage of the banking deregulation in Spain. In 1965, Santander bought *Banco del Hogar Argentino*, the first wholly owned Latin American subsidiary, and in the same year it founded Banco Intercontinental Español (Bankinter).[119] From 1977 to 1982 Santander launched subsidiaries in different Latin American locations: Santo Domingo, Costa Rica, El Salvador (1978), Nassau, Sao Paulo, Uruguay and Chile (1982).[120]

In 1976, Santander bought First National Bank of Puerto Rico, and in 1982, Banco Español-Chile. At the end of the 1980s, Santander acquired German CC-Bank. In 1988, Santander acquired shares of Banco de Comércio e Indústria (Portugal) and it started a partnership with The Royal Bank of Scotland. [121] In 1987, Metropolitan Life and Santander constitute a company, Santander-Met S.A, to operate in the insurance business.[122]

In 1989, Santander launched the "supercuenta" a high-interest check account, (11% on balances of USD 4000 or more, when the average was 6.8%) which started the so called "Guerra del pasivo" or deposits war. By 1992, it started the "Guerra del activo" or loans war with the launch of a "superhipoteca", a mortgage loan of 12% (2% less than its competitors did).

[117] Tschoegl and Guillen "Building a Global Bank", 2.

[118] Santander: Our History https://www.santander.com/en/about-us/our-history#1856-1950. Accessed 2 March 2023.

[119] Santander: "Our History".

[120] Archivo Histórico Santander, https://www.archivohistoricosantander.es/. Accessed 2 March 2023.

[121] Santander: "Our History".

[122] Archivo Histórico Santander; Jesus Cacho "Metropolitan Life y Banco de Santander crean una compañía de seguros con un capital inicial de 5.000 millones de pesetas" *El Pais* (Madrid, 7 July 1987).

An important milestone in Santander History was the acquisition of Banesto in 1994, which made Santander the biggest bank group in Spain.[123] Another big milestone took place in 1999 when Santander merge with Banco Hispanoamericano in a USD 11.35 billion deal.[124] The new bank became the 8th largest Eurozone bank.[125] The same year Santander bought Totta e Açores financial group and Crédito Predial Português.[126]

Santander Group continued with its acquisition strategy in Latin-America. It acquired Banespa in Brazil,[127] Serfín in Mexico[128] and Banco Santiago in Chile, which strengthened its position in the subcontinent.[129]

A third important milestone in Santander history was the acquisition of Abbey, the UK's sixth-largest bank.[130] It was then Europe's biggest cross

[123] Santander "Our History"; "El Santander adquiere Banesto por 313.476 millones", *El Pais* (Madrid, 24 April 1994, https://elpais.com/diario/1994/04/26/economia/767311228_850215.html. Accessed 16 July 2023. In 2012, Santander absorbed, Banesto. Eduardo Segovia "Santander se come Banesto tras no encontrar socios al precio exigido por Botín", *El Confidencial* (Madrid 18 December 2012). https://www.elconfidencial.com/economia/2012-12-18/santander-se-come-banesto-tras-no-encontrar-socios-al-precio-exigido-por-botin_374757/. Accessed 16 July 2023.

[124] Carlta Vitzthum and Christopher Rhoads "Hispanoamericano, Banco Santander Agree to Merge in $11.35 Billion Deal", *The Wall Street Journal* (New York 18 January 1999), https://www.wsj.com/articles/SB916407621616738500. Accessed 16 July 2020.

[125] Elisabeth Nash "Spanish Banks in Pounds 20bn Merger", *Independent* (London, 16 January 1999), https://www.independent.co.uk/news/business/spanish-banks-in-pounds-20bn-merger-1074255.html. Accessed 16 July 2023.

[126] Santander "Our History".

[127] Jonathan Karp and Keith Johnson "Banco Santander Wins Banespa Sale, Topping Rivals With $3.6 Billion Bid" *Wall Street Journal* (New York, 21 November 2000), https://www.wsj.com/articles/SB974737464734107847. Accessed 16 July 2023.

[128] Pamela Druckerman "Santander Buys Serfin for $1.56 Billion, Taking Lead in Mexican Banking Market", *Wall Street Journal* (New York 9 May 2000), https://www.wsj.com/articles/SB957822014671100477, Accessed 16 July 2023.

[129] Santander "Our History".

[130] Santander "Our History". "Banco Santander's European Dreams", Wharton (8 September 2004) https://knowledge.wharton.upenn.edu/article/banco-santanders-european-dreams/. Accessed 16 July 2023; Mark Mulligan and Paul J Davies "Santander Profits Driven by Abbey Acquisition", *Financial Times* (London 27 July, 2005). https://www.ft.com/content/b0eae68c-fe85-11d9-94b4-00000e2511c8. Accessed 16 July 2023.

border acquisition.[131] Santander integrated Abbey to IT and training activities and was efficient in terms of cost reduction (25% by 2008). Botin reported that the "new Abbey" showed "proportionately more deposits than the English Banking System, lower costs, more provisions, a better credit portfolio and higher profits, and all while increasing market share".[132]

In 2007, Santander was recognized as "the twelfth largest bank in the world by market capitalisation and the seventh by profit and we boasted the largest retail network in the Western world: 10,852 branches".[133] That same year Sir Fred Goodwin, RBS CEO invited Santander to join RBS and Fortis in the bid of Dutch ABN AMRO bank. This was the first time three banks joined to make a hostile takeover bid (ABN AMRO was in negotiations with Barclays at the time). The deal was closed, Fortis took the Dutch business, RBS the Asian division and Santander took Banco Real in Brazil and Antonveneta in Italy.[134]

Next year Santander acquired Alliance & Leicester and Bradford & Bingley in the UK, therefore reaching 1,300 branches in the country positioning as third-largest bank by deposits.[135]

In 2010, another phase of Santander internationalization process took place with the acquisition of Sovereign Bankcorp for USD 1.9 billion.[136] In 2011, Santander acquihired a Polish bank, Bank Zachodni WBK.[137]

In 2012, Santander floated 25% of the shares of Santander Mexico, which was the third largest in the world that year. In 2014 Ana Botin succeeded his father Emilio Botin III, and became the family member of the third generation to lead the bank, even though they do not have a majority stake in Santander.

[131] Pedro Parada, Luisa Alemany and Marcel. Planellas "The Internationalization of Retail Banking: Banco Santander's Journey Towards Globalisation", *Long Range Planning*, Vol. 42 (2009), 654–677.

[132] Parada et al. "The Internationalization of Retail Banking", 654–677.

[133] Santander "Our History".

[134] Parada et al. "The Internationalization of Retail Banking", 654–677.

[135] Santander "Our History".

[136] "Spain's Santander Buys Sovereign for $1.9 Billion," *New York Times* (New York, 3 October 2018), https://dealbook.nytimes.com/2008/10/13/spains-santander-buys-sovereign-for-19-billion/. Accessed 20 July, 2023.

[137] Santander "Our History".

In 2017, Santander acquired Banco Popular Español, S.A. after the ECB announced it to be "failing of likely to fail". The ECB then informed the Single Resolution Board (SRB), which adopted a resolution scheme entailing the sale of Banco Popular Español S.A. to Banco Santander S.A.[138] The final price was a symbolic €1.[139]

A Retail Bank "Subsidiary Governance Model"
According to Santander's 2022 Annual Report

> "Santander is a retail bank operating in 3 regions (Europe, North America and South America) and in 10 main markets. Furthermore, we have two global businesses: like Santander Corporate & Investment Banking; Wealth Management & Insurance Our business model is based on three pillars: • Customer focus: Deepening the relationships with our customers through a simpler value proposition, superior customer experience and our digital proposition • Our scale: Local scale and leadership. • Diversification. Our geographic and business diversification allow us to overcome regional challenges in our footprint and business lines".[140]

"Grupo Santander is structured into legally independent subsidiaries whose parent company is Banco Santander, S.A. Its registered office is in Santander (Cantabria, Spain), while its corporate centre is located in Boadilla del Monte (Madrid, Spain). It has a Group-Subsidiary Governance Model (GSGM) and good governance practices in place for its core subsidiaries".[141]

The main features that underpin this model are: (1) each subsidiary is governed prudently to ensure its economic solvency; (2) management of subsidiaries is led by local management with local experience; (3) subsidiaries are subject to local regulation and supervision, under global supervision of ECB; (3) customer funds are secured by local deposit insurance; (4) "Subsidiaries finance themselves autonomously when it

[138] ECB "ECB Determined Banco Popular Español S.A. Was Failing or Likely to Fail", https://www.bankingsupervision.europa.eu/press/pr/date/2017/html/ssm.pr170607.en.html. Accessed 20 July, 2023.

[139] "Banco Popular Fails and Is Bought by Santander", *The Economist*, https://www.economist.com/finance-and-economics/2017/06/10/banco-popular-fails-and-is-bought-by-santander (10 June 2017).

[140] Santander 2022 Annual Report, 111.

[141] Santander 2022 Annual Report, 256.

comes to both capital and liquidity; (5) "Intra-group risk transactions are limited, transparent and carried out under market conditions."; (6) Each subsidiary has its own recovery plan.[142]

Santander believes this subsidiarity model best fits their retail business model. First because retail banking requires proximity to customer. Second, because it provides the "right incentives" for local management, since they are hold accountable for the performance in their respective unit. Third, because the structure provides "greater transparency" to the market, particularly when the stock is partially listed and subject to local stock exchange disclosure requirements.[143]

The Spanish BBFC also considers it structure has "considerable benefits" from a supervisory perspective since in "peace time" locally managed subsidiaries are easy to supervise by the local authorities and in crisis times the subsidiaries act as a "firewall" to reduce contagion and hence systemic risk. It is also possible to cut off a subsidiary if necessary.[144]

Santander main markets are Europe −47% weight of profit/operating areas—(Spain, Portugal, United Kingdom, Poland), Latin America −37% weight of profit/operating areas—(Brazil, Chile, Argentina, Uruguay, Colombia and Peru) and North America −16% weight of profit/operating areas—(USA and Mexico) (Fig. A.10).

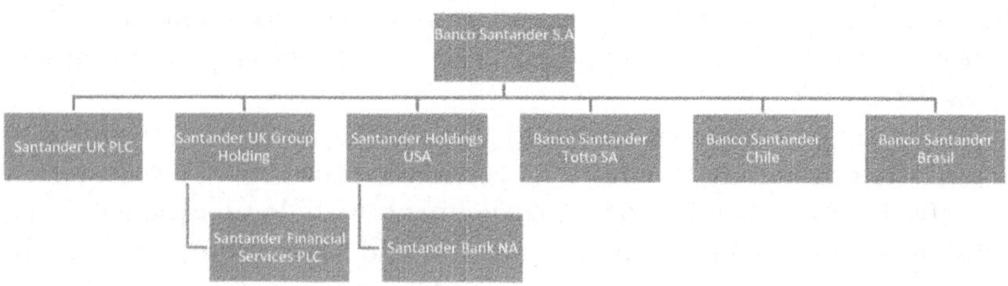

Fig. A.10 Simplified Santander Group Corporate Chart (*Source* Santander Annual Report 2023)

[142] Santander 2019 Annual Report, 256.

[143] UK Parliament "Supplementary Written Evidence Submitted by Santander." Santander's response to the Treasury Select Committee's request (dated 18 January 2011) for supplementary evidence on the Santander Group's subsidiary's structure. https://publications.parliament.uk/pa/cm201011/cmselect/cmtreasy/writev/banking/m42.pdf.

[144] UK Parliament "Supplementary Written Evidence Submitted by Santander".

Banco Santander Resolution Strategy
Santander reassures that "The Single Resolution Board's preferred resolution strategy for the Group contemplates multiple points of entry for the resolution of the entire Santander Group. Given the potential adverse effects the liquidation of the Group's European-based banks could have on the real economies in which it operates, a bail-in resolution is expected, thus allowing operating entities to continue business activities. Outside of Europe, the SRB defers identification of an appropriate resolution strategy to each of the relevant resolution authorities in their respective jurisdictions. This includes Santander's US operations which would be resolved under U.S Bankruptcy Code (SHUSA and SC) and by the FDIC (SBNA)".[145]

Regarding the points of entry, "The Single Resolution Board identified nine different points of entry for the Santander group, which will be subject to a separate resolution process from that of the parent. Those separate points of entry are: Spain (which is the largest as it also includes the European operations of Santander Consumer Finance as well as all equity holdings in subsidiaries abroad), Portugal, the U.K., Poland, the U.S., Mexico, Brazil, Chile, and Argentina. Each point of entry would be required to build up its own cushions of bail-in-able instruments to face a potential resolution scenario, provided that it is required to do so by host authorities".[146]

The application of the four-indicator matrix pointed out in Chapter 6 show Santander is a typical case where MPOE strategy would apply swiftly. As examined above, Santander is a Retail focused institution, structured mainly through subsidiaries, and described as a decentralized bank. All these would suffice for regulators to choose the MPOE strategy. Almost all the advantages of MPOE pointed out by the doctrine are present in the Santander structure.

First, Santander has proven in the Argentine financial crisis of 2001 that the subsidiary model did not foster contagion to other subsidiaries of the group. The same may be said from the Eurozone financial crisis of 2007–2009, which did not gravely affect Latin American subsidiaries.

[145] FDIC "Banco Santander, S.A. Resolution Plan for U.S. Operations Public Section December 31, 2018", https://www.fdic.gov/regulations/reform/resplans/plans/santander-165-1812.pdf. Accessed 20 April 2023.

[146] S&P Global Ratings, September 2019.

Second, MPOE's outcome would not probably become "non-cooperative", since the resolution is ring fenced in a territory and cross-border cooperation is not as essential as in SPOE resolution scenario. In most jurisdictions where Santander operates, the bank leads in national rankings. Hence, a failure of any of such subsidiaries would have a huge impact in the national financial system, and the need of local authorities' intervention would be much needed.[147]

Third, the corporate structure based in subsidiaries and a decentralized model make the group less complex, and hence easier to resolve for resolution authorities. Additionally, this resolution strategy may foster the development of capital markets in the territories where the subsidiary operates.

Finally, the fourth indicator (territorial approach to resolution) would not be a problem since feasible and efficient cross border resolution would be possible even if the different jurisdictions apply different legal resolution regimes. Contrary to a SPOE resolution-strategy where a home authority will have to carry and coordinate the whole resolution process, in MPOE each authority will apply resolution tools under local law.[148]

As in the case of the German Model and British Model, a hybrid model would be feasible, applying a SPOE resolution strategy for the Eurozone and a MPOE for the other subsidiaries. In the Eurozone BBRD and SRM simplify the process and blur national banking barriers. In the rest, a MPOE would be feasible and will determine a swift resolution process.

As the doctrine recognizes, MPOE strategy has its own costs in terms of using more loss absorbing capacity, in terms of a possible splitting of the group after the resolution process is done, and in terms of organizing independent critical shared services that would assist subsidiaries of the group.

[147] Sonsoles Eirea Álvarez and Manuel Ordás Fernández "A Multiple Resolution Scheme for Spanish Global Systemically Important Banking Groups", Estabilidad Financiera No. 27, Banco de España, (2014), 82.

[148] Fernandez de Liz, Pardo, Santillana, Martin "Regulation Outlook", 28.

Advantages of MPOE as a preferred resolution strategy for Santander	*Challenges of the MPOE strategy*
Firewalls to contagion: Argentine 2001 Crisis and Eurozone 2007–2009 financial crisis	Need of independent critical share services
Smooth resolution with no problems of "non-cooperative" resolution outcomes	Need of more loss absorbing capacities
Less complex structure, easy to resolve	A possible outcome is a splitting group
Foster local capital markets	
Feasible and efficient cross border resolution would be possible even if different jurisdictions apply different legal resolution regimes	

Bibliography

Abramovsky A., Mason I., Tischner R. and Bessman S. "Enforcement: A Survey of Three Approaches to Insurance Regulatory Enforcement: The USA, the UK and Sweden" in J. Burling and K. Lazarus *Research Handbook on International insurance law and regulation* (Edward Elgar 2012).

Abrams B. and Settle R. "Pressure-Group Influence and Institutional Change: Branch—Banking Legislation During the Great Depression" (1993) Public Choice.

Adalet M. "The Effect of Financial Structure on Crises: Universal Banking in Interwar Europe" (2009) Working Paper, No. 0910, TÜSİAD-Koç University Economic Research Forum.

Adams J. *The Big Fix: Inside the S&L Scandal: How an Unholy Alliance of Politics and Money Destroyed America's Banking System* (Wiley Publishers 1990).

Adrian T. and Shin H. "Financial Intermediaries, Financial Instability and Monetary Policy." (2008) Proceedings of the Federal Reserve Bank of Kansas City Conference at Jackson Hole.

Al Mamun A., Kabir Hassan M. and Van Lai S. "The impact of the Gramm-Leach-Bliley act on the financial services industry" (2004) *Journal of Economics and Finance*, Vol. 28, No. 3.

Alexander K. "Regulating the Structure of the EU Banking Sector" (2015) *European Business Law Review*.

Allen, F., Capie F., Fohlin C., Miyajima H., Sylla R., Wood G. and Yafeh Y. "How Important Historically Were Financial Systems for Growth in the UK, US and Japan? World Bank Project on Financial Structure, 2010.

Allen, F. and Gale D. *Comparing Financial Systems* (MIT Press 2001).

M. J. Sheppard Gelsi, *Corporate Structure and Banking Resolution*, Palgrave Macmillan Studies in Banking and Financial Institutions, https://doi.org/10.1007/978-3-031-59948-4

Allen K. "UK Finance Industry Dominates European Scene" *Financial Times*, September 5, 2018.

Allianz 2017 Annual Report.

Alter, D. "The "Business of Banking" in New York—An Historical Impediment to the OCC's Proposed National "Fintech Charter" (2017) *Yale J. on Reg. Notice & Comment*, Vol. 36.

Amel D. and Liang N. "The Relationship Between Entry into Banking Markets and Changes in Legal Restrictions on Entry" (1992) Antitrust Bulletin.

Anheier H., Kauffman S. and Ziaja S. "Ten Years After the Global Financial and Economic Crisis" (2018) The Governance Report 2018, Hertie School of Governance.

Annual Survey Issue "Financial Institutions and Regulations, the S&L Crisis: Death and Transfiguration" (1991) *Fordham Law Review*, Vol. 59.

Arcand J. L., Berkes E. and Painzza U. "Too Much Finance?" (2012) IMF Working Paper WP/12/161.

Areeda P. and Turner D. F. "Predatory Pricing and Related Practices Under Section 2 of the Sherman Act" (1975) *Harv. L. Rev.*, Vol. 88, 697.

Aristotle *The Nicomachean Ethics of Aristotle* Sir D. Ross (Translator) (OUP 1963).

Armour J., Awrey D., Davies P., Enriques L., Gordon J., Mayer C. and Peyne J. *Principles of Financial Regulation* (OUP 2016).

Arner D. *Financial Stability, Economic Growth, and the Role of Law* (Cambridge University Press 2009).

Artikis P., Mutenga S. and Staikouras S. "A Practical Approach to Blend Insurance in the Banking Network" (2008) *The Journal of Risk Insurance*, Vol. 9, No. 2.

Ashcraft A. "Are Bank Holding Companies a Source of Strength to Their Banking Subsidiaries?" (2008) *Journal of Money, Credit and Banking*.

Automotive News "German Cross-Shareholding System Unwinds as Deutsche Bank Exits" http://www.autonews.com/article/20091101/ANE02/311019997/german-cross-shareholding-system-unwinds-as-deutsche-bank-exits. *Autonews* (2009).

Avery H. "The Numbers That Prove Lehman Was Deal of the Century for Barclays" *Euromoney* (London, 18 September 2013).

Avgouleas E. and Goodhart C. "Critical Reflections on Bank Bail-ins" (2015) *Journal of Financial Regulation*.

Avraham D., Selvaggi P. and Vickery J. "A Structural View of U.S. Bank Holding Companies" (2012) *FRBNY Economic Policy Review*.

Ayadi R., Llewellyn D. T. Schmidt R. H., Arbak E. and Pieter De Groen W. "Investigating Diversity in The Banking Sector in Europe Key Developments, Performance and Role of Cooperative Banks" (2010) Centre for European Policy Studies.

Ayadi R., Schmidt R. H. and Carbó Valverde S. *Investigating Diversity in the Banking Sector in Europe: The Performance and Role of Savings Banks* (CEPS 2009).

Bae K.-H., Koo Kang J. and Mo Kim J. "Tunneling or Value Added? Evidence from Mergers by Korean Business Groups" (2002) *The Journal of Finance*, Vol. 56, No. 6.

Bailey A. "Promoting a Prudent and Stable Financial System" (2011) Future of the Retail Banking Conference, London, Bank of England.

Bairoch P. "International Industrialization Levels from 1750 to 1980" (1982) *The Journal of European Economic History*.

Baker M. and Collins M. "London as an International Banking Centre, 1950–1980" in Y. Cassis and E. Bussiere, *London and Paris as International Financial Centres in the Twentieth Century* (OUP 2007).

Baliga S. and Polak B. "Banks Versus Bonds: A Simple Theory of Comparative Financial Institutions" (1995) Cowles Foundation Discussion Paper, Yale.

Ballet M. "Saint-Simonism and Utilitarianism: The History of a Paradox. Bentham's Defense of Usury Under Saint-Amand Bazard's Interpretation" (2011) Working Paper GATE.

Balls E., Howat J. and Stansbury A. "Central Bank Independence Revisited: After the Financial Crisis, What Should a Model Central Bank Look Like?" (2016) M-RCBG Associate Working Paper Series, No. 67, Mossavar-Rahmani Center for Business & Government or of Harvard University.

Balluk K. "Investment Banking: Linkages to The Real Economy and the Financial System" (2015) Bank of England Quarterly Bulletin, 55.

Baluch F, Mutenga S. and Parsons C. "Insurance, Systemic Risk and Financial Crisis" (2011) Geneva Papers on Risk and Insurance-Issues and Practice, 36(1).

"Banco Santander's European Dreams" Wharton, 8 September 2004, https://knowledge.wharton.upenn.edu/article/banco-santanders-european-dreams/.

Bank of England "The Bank of England's approach to resolution" (2017).

——— "Credit Union Quarterly Statistics" (2018) Q3.

Bank of Financial Settlements "The Supervision of Financial Conglomerates" (1995). A Report by the Tripartite Group of Bank, Securities and Insurance Regulators.

Barclays Annual Report 2020, https://home.barclays/content/dam/home-barclays/documents/investor-relations/reports-and-events/annual-reports/2020/Barclays-PLC-Annual-Report-2020.pdf.

———. Annual Report 2023.

———. "Important Information About Barclays Insurance Services", https://www.barclays.co.uk/content/dam/documents/premier/BAR_9914957_Cropped.pdf.

——— "Our History", https://home.barclays/who-we-are/our-history/.

Bardoscia M. and Ka-Kay Pang R. "Ring-Fencing in Financial Networks" Bank of England (2023) https://www.bankofengland.co.uk/-/media/boe/files/working-paper/2023/ring-fencing-in-financial-networks.pdf.

Baron D. and Besanko D. "Strategy, Organization and Incentives: Global Corporate.

Banking at Citibank" (2001) *Journal of Industrial and Corporate Change.*

Barr M., Jackson H. and Tahyar M. *Financial Regulation: Law and Policy* (Foundation Press 2018).

Barth J. and Sun Y. "A New Look at the Performance of Industrial Loan Corporations" (2018) Utah Center for Financial Services, The University of Utah.

Basel Consultive document. Global Systemically Important Banks-Revised Assessment Framework. March 2017.

Basel Committee on Banking Supervision (BCBS) "Global Systemically Important Banks: Updated Assessment Methodology and the Higher Loss Absorbency Requirement" (2013).

Baum T. and Gruson M. "The German Banking System-System of the Future? Brooklyn *Journal of International Law* (1993).

Baxter P. and Jack S. "Qualitative Case Study Methodology: Study Design and Implementation for Novice Researchers" (2008) The Qualitative Report, Vol. 13 No. 4.

Becalli, E. Anolli M. and Borello G. "Are European Banks Too Big? Evidence on Economies of Scale" (2015) LSE Research Online, LSE.

Beck T., Demirgüç-Kunt A. and Levine R., (2000) "A New Database on Financial Development and Structure" (2000) *World Bank Economic Review*, Vol. 14.

Beck T., Coyle D., Dewatripont M., Freixas X. and Seabright P. "Bailing Out of the Banks: Reconciling Stability and Competition—An Analysis of State-Supported Schemes for Financial Institutions" (2010) CERP.

Beck T. and Demirgüç-Kunt A. and Levine R. "Financial Institutions and Markets across Countries and Over Time: Data and Analysis" (May 2009) World Bank Policy Research Working Paper 4943.

Beck H. N. "Opportunities for Nonbanking Companies to Acquire Depository Institutions in the Wake of the Competitive Equality Banking Act of 1987" (1988) *Bus. Law.*, Vol. 44, 1053.

Becker C. *The Declaration of Independence. A Study in the History of Political Ideas* (Harcourt, Brace and Co. 1922).

Beckett P. "Citigroup to Split Off Travelers Unit in an IPO Expected Early Next Year", *Wall Street Journal* (New York 20 December 2001).

Bednar J., Eskridge W. and Ferejohn J. Jr. "A Political Theory of Federalism" (1999) Word Bank.

Behr P. and Schmidt R. "The German Banking System: Characteristics and Challenges" (2015) White Paper No.32 SAFE.

Benston G. J. "Universal Banking" (1994) *Journal of Economic Perspectives*, Vol. 8, No. 3.

Berger A., Kashyap A., Scalise J., Gertler M. and Friedman B. M. "The Transformation of the U.S. Banking Industry: What a Long Strange Trip It's Been" (1995) Brooking Papers on Economic Activity.

Bermann G. "Taking Subsidiarity Seriously: Federalism in the European Community and in the United States" (1994) *Columbia Law Review*.

Binder J.-H. "Concepts, Requirements and Tools" in J.-H. Binder and D. Singh *Bank Resolution: The European Regime* (OUP 2016).

——— "Banking Union and the Governance of Credit Institutions—A Legal Perspective" (2015) Working Paper No. 96, Leibniz Institute for Financial Research SAFE.

——— "Cross-Border Coordination of Bank Resolution in the EU: AL Problems Resolved?" in M. Haentjens, *Research Hanbook on Cross-Border Bank Resolution* (Edward Elgar, 2019).

——— "Resolution Planning and Structural Bank Reform Within the Banking Union" in J. Castaneda *European banking Union. Prospects and Challenges* (Routledge 2015).

——— "Resolution Regimes in the Financial Sector. In Need of Cross-sectoral Regulation? In V. Colaert, D. Busch and T. Incalza *European Financial Regulation: levelling the cross-sectoral playing field* (Bloomsbury, 2019).

——— "Ring-Fencing: An Integrated Approach with Many Unknowns" *European Business Organization Law Review* (2015).

——— "Financial Services Groups Under EU Law" in Okutan Nilsson G. *Comparative Corporate Group Law. Conference in Honour of Prof. Dr. Unal Tekinalp's 80th Birthday* (Twelve Plates Publishing, 2018).

Binder J.-J. and Brown A. "Bank rates of Return and Entry Restrictions, 1869–1914" (1991) *Journal of Economic History*.

Bernanke B. "Implementing a Macroprudential Approach to Supervision and Regulation", Speech at the 47th Annual Conference on Bank Structure and Competition, Chicago, Illinois, May 5, 2011.

——— "On Milton Friedman's Ninetieth Birthday", Remarks by Governor Ben S. Bernanke at the Conference to Honour Milton Friedman, University of Chicago, Chicago, IL, November 8, 2002.

——— *The Federal Reserve and the Financial Crisis* (Princeton University Press 2013).

Bernanke B. and James H. "The Gold Standard, Deflation, and Financial Crisis in the Great Depression: An International comparison" in R.G. Hubbard, *Financial Markets and Financial Crisis* (Chicago University Press 1991).

Binham C. "FSB to Dust Off Plan for Designating "Systemically Important" Asset Managers" *Financial Times* (London 12 January 2017).

Blackrock "Comments on the Consultative Document of Assessment Methodologies for Identifying Non-Bank, Non-Insurer Global Systemically Important Financial Institutions" (2014).

——— "Who Owns the Assets? Developing a Better Understanding of the Flow of Assets and the Implications for Financial Regulation" (2014).

Blanche D. "The Regulation of French Financial Co-operatives: From Local Co-operatives to Global Banking Groups Subject to the Post-Crisis Regime for Banking Resolution" (2016) 11th Strasbourg European Meeting—European Parliament.

Block C. D. "A Continuum Approach to Systemic Risk and Too Big to Fail" (2012) *Brook J. Corp Fin &Com L.*, 289.

Blumstein J. "Federalism and Civil Rights: Complementary and Competing Paradigms" (1994) *Vand. L. Rev.*, Vol. 47, 1251.

Bodenhorn H. "Bank Chartering and Political Corruption in Antebellum New York" in E. Glaeser and C. Goldin (eds) *Corruption and Reform: Lessons from America's Economic History* (University of Chicago Press 2006).

——— "Double Liability at Early American Banks" (2015) NBER Working Paper No. 21494.

——— "Entry, Rivalry and Free Banking in Antebellum America" (1990) *The Review of Economics and Statistics*, Vol. 72.

——— *State banking in Early America: A New Economic History* (OUP 2002).

Bolton J. E. *Small Firms: Report of the Committee of Inquiry on Small Firms* (London Her Majesty's Stationery Office 1978).

Bolton P. and Oehmke M. "Bank Resolution and the Structure of Global Banks" (2018) Discussion Paper No. 778. Paul Woolley Centre Working Paper No. 59.

Bordo M. "The Impact and International Transmission of Financial Crisis: Some Historical Evidence: 1870–1933" (1985) *Revista di Storia Economica*, 2.

Boyd J H. and Prescot E. C. "Financial Intermediary-Coalitions" (1986) *Journal of Economic Theory*, 38.

Bradley C. M. and Jones K. D. "Loss Sharing Rules for Bank Holding Companies: An Assessment of the Federal Reserve's Source-of-Strength Policy and the FDIC's Cross Guarantee Authority" (2008) *Financial Markets, Institutions & Instruments*, Vol. 17 Issue: 4.

Braithwaite T. and Guerrera F. "US Treasury Sells Remaining Citi Share" *Financial Times* (London 7 December 2010).

Brämer P. and Gischer H. "An Assessment Methodology for Domestic Systemically Important Banks in Australia" (2013) The Australian Economic Review, vol. 46, no. 2.

Briault C. "D-SIB Designation and Capital Surcharges" (2016) KPMG.

Broadbent B. "Central Banks and Digital Currencies" (2016) Bank of England.

Broom L. and Markham J., *Regulation of Bank Financial Service Activities* (4th Edition, West 2011).

Brouthers L. E. Gao Y. and Napshin S. "Keiretsu Centrality—Profits and Profit Stability: A Power Dependence Perspective" (2014) *Journal of Business Research*, Vol. 67, No. 12.

Brown E. "The New Laws and Regulations for Financial Conglomerates: Will They Better Manage the Risks than the Previous Ones?" (2011) *American University Law Review*, Vol. 60, No. 5, Article 2.

Bryant W. C. *The Legislative History of Banking in the State of New York, During the Period of Fifty Years, from A.D. 1791 to A.D. 1841* (1855).

Buerstetta G. "Riegle-Neal Interstate Banking and Branching Efficiency Act of 1994" (1995) *Annual Review of Banking Law*.

Bûlbul D., Reinhard R., Schmidt H. and Schuwer U. "Saving Banks and Cooperative Banks in Europe" (2013) White Paper Series No. 5 Center of Excellence Sustainable Architecture for Finance in Europe.

Burns A. F. "The Independence of the Federal Reserve System" (1976) Challenge.

Buschgen H. E. "The Universal Banking System in the Federal Republic of Germany" (1979) *Journal of Comparative Corporate Law and Securities Regulation*, 2.

Cable J "Capital Market Information and Industrial Performace: The Role of West German Banks" (1985) *The Economic Journal*, 95.

Cacho J. "Metropolitan Life y Banco de Santander crean una compañía de seguros con un capital inicial de 5.000 millones de pesetas" *El Pais* (Madrid 7 July 1987).

Calem P. "The Impact of Geographic Deregulation on Small Banks" (1994) *Federal Reserve Bank of Philadelphia*, 17.

Calomiris C. W. "Corporate-Finance Benefits from Universal Banking: Germany and the United States 1870–1914" (1993) NBER Working Paper Series.

——— "Regulation, Industrial Structure and Instability in U.S. Banking" in M. Klasner and L. White (EDS) *Structural Change in banking* (Business One-Irwin 1993).

——— "The Costs of rejecting Universal Banking: American Finance in the German Mirror, 1970–1914" in N. Lamoreaux and D. Raff *Coordination and Information: Historical Perspectives on the Organization of Enterprise* (University of Chicago Press 1995).

——— "The Political lessons of Depression-Era Banking Reform" (2010) *Oxford Overview of Economic Policy*, Vol. 26.

Calomiris C. W. and Haber S. *Fragile by Design: The Political Origins of Banking Crisis and Scarce Credit* (Princeton University Press 2014).

Calomiris C. W. and C. Ramirez "Financing the American Corporation: The changing menu of Financial relationships" (1996) NBER Working Papers Series on Historical Factors in Long Run Growth.

Calomiris C. W. and Ramirez C. "The Political Economy of Bank Entry Restrictions: Theory and Evidence from the U.S. in the 1920's" (2004) Working Paper, Columbia University.

Calomiris C. W. and Schweikart L. "Was the South Backward? North-South Differences in Antebellum Banking" (1988) Colombia University working paper.

Cameron R. "Founding the Bank of Darmstadt" (1956) Explorations in Entrepreneurial History.

——— "Banking in the Early Stages of Industrialization. A Preliminary Survey" (1963) *Scandinavian Economic History Review*.

——— "The Credit Mobilier and the Economic Development of Europe" (1953) *The Journal of Political Economy*.

Cámara del Tribunal de Justicia de São Paulo, *TELENOVA COMUNICAÇÕES LTDA vs TELMEX DO BRASIL LTDA*; J. Garcez, *Elementos Básicos de Direito Internacional Privado*. Porto Alegre: Síntese (1999).

Campbell S. "Usury and Annuities of the Eighteenth Century" (1928). *L. Q. Rev.*, Vol. 44, 47.

Canals J. *Universal Banking: International Comparison and Theoretical Perspectives "Universal Banks Versus Specialized Banks"* (OUP 1997).

Capie F. "British Financial Crisis in the Nineteenth and Twentieth Centuries" in N. Dimsdale and A. Hotson *British Financial Crisis Since 1825* (2014 OUP).

——— *The Bank of England: 1950s to 1979* (CUP 2010).

Capie F. and Collins M. "Have the Banks failed British Industry? (1991) IEA.

Carlin W. and Mayer C. "How Do Financial Systems Affect Economic Performance? (1999) University College London and Said Business School, University of Oxford.

Carlson M. and Mitchener K. "Branch Banking as a Device for Discipline: Competition and Bank Survivorship During the Great Depression" (2007) NBER Working Paper Series.

Carmassi J. and Herrig R. J. "Complexity and Systemic Risk: What's Changed Since the Crisis" in A. Berger, P. Molyneux and J. O. S. Wilson *The Oxford Handbook of Banking* (OUP 2015).

——— "The Corporate Complexity of Global Systemically Important Banks" (2016) *J. Financ Serv Res*.

Carmel R. "Glass-Steagall: Some Critical Reflections" (1980) *Banking Law Journal*.

Carosso V. P. *The Morgans: Private International Bankers, 1854–1913* (1987).

Carow K. A., Cox S. R. and Roden D. M. "The Role of Insider Influence in Mutual-to-Stock Conversions" (2007) *Journal of Money, Credit and Banking*, Vol. 39, No. 6.

Carr J. Jr. and Pax T. J. "Forms of Entry, Operation, Expansion and Supervision of Foreign banks in the United States" in M. Gruson and R. Reisner *Regulation of Foreign Banks. United States and International* (Michie Butterworth 1995).

Cartinhour G. *Branch, Group and Chain Banking* (The Macmillan Company 1931).

Cassis Y. "Crises and Opportunities" (OUP 2011).

Catterall R. *Second Bank of the U.S.* (The University of Chicago Press 1903).

Cebenoyan S. A., Cooperman E. and Register C. A. "Ownership Structure, Charter Value, and Risk-Taking Behavior for Thrifts" (1999) *Financial Management*, Vol. 28, No. 1.

Cebula R. "Bank Failures in Light of the Gramm-Leach-Bliley Act" (2010) *Atlantic Economic Journal.*

Cecchetti S. and Kharroubi E. "Why Does Financial Sector Growth Crowd Out Real Economic Growth? (2015) BIS Working Papers No. 490.

——— "Reassesing the Impact of Finance and Growth" (2012) BIS Working Papers No. 381 BIS.

Cerrutti E., Dell' Ariccia G. and Martinez Peria M. "How Banks Go Abroad: Branches or Subsidiaries? (2005) Policy Research Working Paper No. 3753, Washington DC. World Bank.

Chaddad F. R. and Cook M. L. "The Economics of Organization Structure Changes: A US Perspective on Demutualization" (2004) *Annals of Public and Cooperative Economics*, Vol. 75, No. 4, 12.

Charlety S. *Historia del Sansimonismo* (Alianza Editorial 1969).

Chen H., Cummins J. D., Viswanathan K. and Weiss M. A. "Systemic Risk Measures in the Insurance Industry: A Copula Approach" (2013) Working Paper, Template University.

Chester N. "The Nationalization of the British Industry 1945–51" (1975) HMSO.

Chew J. "Multiple Point of Entry. The Forgotten Alternative" The Clearing House.

Chinard G. *Thomas Jefferson, the Apostle of Americanism* (The Floating Press 2011).

Čihák M., Demirgüç-Kunt A., Feyen E. and Levine R. "Benchmarking Financial Development Around the World" (2012) World Bank Policy Research Working Paper 6175 Financial Development and Structure Dataset (updated July 2018).

Čihák M. and Nier E. "The Need for Special Resolution Regimes for Financial Institutions—The Case of the European Union" IMF Working Paper No. 2009/200.

Citigroup 2020 Annual Report.

——— 2018 Annual Report. www.citi.com/annualreport.

——— 2019 Resolution Plan Public Section July 1, 2019.

——— Second Quarter 2019 Results and Key Metrics.

——— Form 8-K, "Current Report" U.S. Securities and Exchange Commission.

——— Resolution Plan Public Section July 1, 2023.

Claessens S., Herring R. J., Schoenmaker D., Summe K. A. "A Safer World Financial System: Improving the Resolution of Systemic Institutions" (2010) Geneva Reports on the World Economy 12.

Claire Clarke M. St. and Hall D. A. *Legislative & Documentary History of the Bank of the United States, Reprints of Economic Classics* (Routledge 1996).

Clapham J. *The Bank of England—A History, Vol I 1694–1797* (CUP 1944).

——— *The Economic Development of France and Germany 1815–1914* (CUP 1936).

Cline W. "Further Statistical Debate 'Too Much Finance'" (2015) Working Paper Series WP 15–16 Peterson Institute for International Economies.

——— "Too Much Finance or Statistical Illusion? (2015) Policy Brief PB 15–9 Peterson Institute for International Economies.

Clipici E. and Bolovan C. "Bancassurance-Main Insurance Distribution and Sale Channel in Europe" (2012) *Scientific Bulletin—Economic Sciences*, Vol. 11.

Clozel L. "SoFi Withdraws Bank Application in Wake of Scandal" *American Banker* (New York 13 October 2017).

Collins M. *Banks and Industrial Finance in Britain 1800–1939* (Palgrave Macmillan 1990).

Commercial Banking (Practical Law Note 2–5070807) (Thomson Reuters 2019).

Committee on Payments and Securities Settlement (January 2001).

Core Principles for Systemically Important Payment Systems. BIS (2001) https://www.bis.org/cpmi/publ/d34e.pdf.

Comptroller's Handbook, Safety and Soundness (OCC 2013).

Conti Brown P. *The Power and Independence of the Federal Reserve* (Princeton University Press 2016).

——— "The Institution of Federal Reserve Independence" (2015) *Yale Journal on Regulation*, Vol. 32, No. 2.

Cordell L. R., Mac Donald G. and Wohar M. "Corporate Ownership and the Thrift Crisis" (1993) *The Journal of Law & Economics*, Vol. 36, No. 2, 10.

Corrigan E. "Are Banks Special?" (1982) Federal Reserve of Minneapolis.

Cottrell P. "Established Connections and New Opportunities. London as an International Financial Centre 1914–1958 in Y. Cassis and E. Bussiere *London and Paris as International Financial Centres in the Twentieth Century* (OUP 2007).

Council of Australian Law Deans, CALD Statement on the Nature of Research (May and October 2005).

Cournede B. and Denk O. "Finance and Economic Growth in OECD and G20 Countries" (2015) OECD Economics Department Working Papers No. 1223.

Crawford J. "Single Point of Entry: The Promise and Limits of the Latest Cure for Bailouts" (2014), University of California Hastings College of the Law. Legal Studies Reaserch Paper Series No. 132, 109 Northwestern University Law Review Online 103.

Credit Agricole.

——— 2020–2021 Integrated Report.

——— 2022–2023 Integrated Report.

——— Annual Financial Report Registration Document 2017.

CUNA "Credit Unions Trend Report" (2020) CUNA.

Crotty J. "Structural Causes of the Global Financial Crisis: A Critical Assessment of the 'New Financial Architecture" (2009) *Cambridge Journal of Economics*.

Crow D. and Morris S. "Investment Banking: The Battle for Barclays" *Financial Times* (London 20 January 2019).

Cuaresma J. "The Gramm-Leach-Bliley Act" (2002) *Berkeley Technology Law Journal*.

Cull R., Haber S. and Imai M. "Related Lending and Banking Development" (2011) *Journal of International Business Studies*, Vol. 42, No. 3.

Cull R. and Martinez Peria M. "Bank Ownership and Lending Patterns During the 2008–2009 Financial Crisis" (2012) The World Bank Development Research Group Finance and Private Sector Development Team.

Cummins J. D. and Weiss M. A. "Systemic Risk and the US Insurance Sector" (2014) *Journal of Risk and Insurance*, Vol. 81, No. 3.

D'Alvia D. "Law and the Market: Private Actors and Self-Regulation, Towards a New Role of Public International Law" (2018) *European Business Law Review*.

Da Rin M. "Understanding the Development of the German Kreditbanken, 1850–1914: an Approach from Economics on Information" (1996) *Financial History Review*.

Danielsson J. and Zigrand J. P. "Are Asset Managers Systemically Important" (2015) *Vox*.

Daunton M. "Gentlemanly Capitalism" and British industry 1820–1914. *Past and Present n 122* (OUP 1989).

Davies, R. Richardson P., Katinaite V. and Manning M. "Evolution of the UK Banking System" (2010) Bank of England Quarterly Bulletin (Q4).

Davis L. "The Investment Market 1870–1914; The Evolution of a National Market" (1965) *Journal of Economic History*, 26.

Day K. *S&L Hell: The People and the Politics Behind the $1 Trillion Savings and Loan Scandal* (W. W. Norton & Co. 1993).

De Franssu J.-B., de Manuel Aramendia M. and Lanoo K. "Rethinking Asset Management from Financial Stability to Investor Protection and Economic Growth" (2012) Report of CEPS-ECMI Task Force.

De Larosière J., Balcerowicz L., Issing O., Masera R., McCarthy C., Nyberg L., Pérez J. and Ruding O. "Report by the High-Level Group on Financial Supervision in the EU", 25 February 2009. Available at http://ec.europa.eu/internal_market/finance.

De Meester B. "The Global Financial Crisis and Government Support for Banks: What Role for the GATS? (2010) *J. Int Economic Law*, Vol. 13, No. 1.

De Tocqueville A. *Democracy in America*, Vol I and II (The Floating Press 2009).

De Young R. "Scale Economies Are a Distraction" (2010) The Real Issue for Policy Is Credible Resolution of Failing Financial Firms, Not Bank Size. Scale Economies in Banking Symposium.

Deeg R. "On the Development of Universal Banking in Germany" in D. J. Forsyth and D. Verdier *The Origins of National Financial Systems Alexander Gerschenkron Reconsidered* (Routledge 2002).

Del Angel G. A "The nexus between business groups and banks: Mexico, 1932–1982" (2016) Business History.

Delamaide D., Osman Y. and Schnell C. "Deutsche Bank Partners with Tech Firm to Offer Online Insurance Product" (2018) Handelsblatt *Global* (Berlin, 16 January 2018).

Dell'Ariccia G. Martinez Peria M. S, Igan D., Addo Awadzi E., Dobler M. and Sandri D. "Trade-offs in Bank Resolution" (2018) IMF Technical Note.

Dermine J. "European Banking Integration: Don't Put the Cart before the Horse" (2006) New York University Salomon Center, Financial Markets, Institutions & Instruments, Vol 15, No. 2.

DeSoto R. and Bascom L. *Bailout: The Bankrupting of America* (Futura Press 1992).

Detzer D., Dodig N, Evans T. and Herr H. "The German Financial System" (2013) FESSUD.

Deutsche Bank Adherence to ISDA, November 2015.

——— Annual Report 1989.

——— Annual Report 1992.

——— Annual Report 1995.

——— Annual Report 1996.

——— Annual Report 2016.

——— Annual Report 2017.

——— Annual Report 2020.

——— Annual Report 2023.

——— History. Chronicle 1870 Until Today. Available at https://www.db.com/company/en/media/Deutsche-Bank-History--Chronicle-from-1870-until-today.pdf.

——— Ratings. Available at https://www.db.com/ir/en/current-ratings.htm, 2018. For 2021, ratings see https://www.db.com/ir/en/current-ratings.htm.

——— Media Release (March 5, 2017). Available at https://www.db.com/newsroom_news/2017/medien/deutsche-bank-refines-strategy-and-announces-capital-increase-en-11483.htm.

——— Media Release "Deutsche Bank Strengthens Its Insurance Business" (16 January 2018). Available at https://www.db.com/newsroom_news/2017/deutsche-bank-strengthens-its-insurance-business-en-11763.htm.

Deutsche Bundesbank Monthly Report April 2015 "Structural Developments in the German Banking Sector" (2015).

——— Monthly Report as of July 30, 2018 (2018).

——— "The Shadow Banking System: Small but Internationally Connected" (2012) *Financial Stability Review*.

Deyoug R. "Banking in the United States" in A. Berger, P. Molyneux and J. Wilson *The Oxford Handbook of Banking* (OUP 2012).

Diamond D. W. and Dybvig P. H. "Bank Runs, Deposit Insurance, and Liquidity" (1983) *Journal of Political Economy*, Vol. 91, No. 3.

Diamond D. W. "Financial Intermediation and Delegated Monitoring" (1984) *Review of Economic Studies*, 51.

Dierick F. "The Supervision of Mixed Financial Services Groups in Europe (2004) Occasional Paper Series No. 20 (ECB).

Dietrich D. and Vollmer U. "Are Universal Banks Bad for Financial Stability? Germany During the World Financial Crisis" (2012) The Quarterly Review of Economics and Finance.

Dixon A. *The New Geography of Capitalism: Firms, Finance and Society* (Oxford Scholarship Online 2014).

Dixon L., Clancy N. and Kumar K. B. *Hedge Funds and Systemic Risk* (Rand Corporation 2012).

Dombret A. and Kenadjian P. *Resolution in Europe: The Unresolved Questions* (De Gruyter 2019).

Downin A. "Ambidexterity Drives Credit Union Success, CUSOs Make it a Reality" (2017) *Credit union Times* (Washington D.C. 12 April 2017).

Drake P. and Neale F. R. "Financial Guarantee Insurance and Failures in Risk Management" (2011) *Journal of Insurance Regulation*, Vol. 30, No. 2.

Druckerman P. "Santander Buys Serfin for $1.56 Billion, Taking Lead in Mexican Banking Market" *Wall Street Journal* (New York 9 May 2000).

Dwyer G. Jr. "Wildcat Banking, Banking Panics and Free Banking in the United States" (1996) Economic Review Federal Reserve Bank of Atlanta.

DZ Bank Annual Report 2017.
Easterbrook F. H. and Fischel D. R. "Limited Liability and the Corporation" (1985) *The University of Chicago Law Review*.
EBA "EBA discloses first list of O-SIIs in the EU" (EBA 2016).
——— "Guide on Banking Resolution (2022).
——— "Guidelines on Disclosure of Indicators of Global Systemic Importance" (2022).
Eberle E. "The Methodology of Comparative Law" (2011) *Roger Williams University Law Review*, Vol. 16, No. 1, Article 2.
EC "Commission Requests Germany to Bring State Guarantees for Public Banks into Line with EC Law" (2001) 8 May 2001.
ECB "ECB Determined Banco Popular Español S.A. Was Failing or Likely to Fail". Available at https://www.bankingsupervision.europa.eu/press/pr/date/2017/html/ssm.pr170607.en.html.
Edmonds T. "Credit Unions" Briefing Paper Number 01034 (2015) House of Commons.
——— "List of Supervised Banks" (2023).
Edwards F. "Banks and Securities Activities: Legal and Economic Perspectives on the Glass-Steagall Act" in L. G. Goldbergand, L. J. White *The Deregulation of Banking and Securities Activities* (Lexington, MA, Lexington Books 1979).
——— "Banks and Securities Activities: Legal and Economic Perspectives on the Glass-Steagall Act" in L. G. Goldberg and L. J. White *The Deregulation of Banking and Securities Activities* (Lexington Books 1979).
Edwards F. and Fischer K. *Banks, Finance and Investment in Germany* (CUP 1994).
Edwards F. and Ogilvie S. "Universal Banks and German Industrialization: A Reappraisal" (1996) *Economic History Review*.
Effros R. *Current Legal Issues affecting Central Banks*, Vol. I (IMF 1992).
——— "Addendum to Central Banks in an Age of Standardization" (Effros 2004).
——— "Central Bank in the Age off Standardization" Manuscript (Effros 1999).
——— *Current Legal Issues Affecting Central Banks*, Vol. II (IMF 1994).
Eichhorst M. "The Insurance and Reinsurance Law Review—Germany" (2017) Edition 5 the Law Reviews.
Eichler N. *The Thrift Debacle* (University of California Press 1989).
Eijffinger S. "Single Resolution Mechanism" in Banking Union: The Single Resolution mechanism" (2013) Monetary Dialogue, European Parliament.
EIOPA "Opinion to Institutions of the European Union on the Harmonisation of Recovery And Resolution Frameworks for (Re)insurers Across The Member States" (July 2017).

Eirea S. Álvarez and Ordás Fernández M. "A Multiple Resolution Scheme for Spanish Global Systemically Important Banking Groups" (2014) Estabilidad Financiera No. 27, Banco de España.

Elazar D. *Exploring Federalism* (University of Alabama Press 1991).

Elbaum B. and Lazonick W. (eds) *The Decline of the British Economy* (OUP 1986).

Electronic submission by The Clearing House, SIFMA, ABA, FSR, GFMA to the FDIC Re. FDIC's Notice and Request for Comments on the Resolution of Systemically Important Financial Institutions: The Single Point of Entry Strategy (2014) FR Docket No. 2013–30057.

Eling M. and Pankoke D. "Systemic Risk in the Insurance Sector: A Review and Directions for Future Research" (2016) *Risk Management and Insurance Review.*

Elkington W. *Bancassurance* (1993) *Chartered Building Societies Institutions Journal.*

Elliot D. "Designating Systemically Important Financial Institutions: Balancing Costs and Benefits" (2012) Testimony Before the House Financial Services Subcommittee on Financial Institutions and Consumer Credit.

——— "Systemic Risk and the Asset Management Industry" (2014) The Brookings Institution.

Elliot D. and Litan R. E. "Identifying and Regulating Systemically Important Financial Institutions: The Risks of Under and Over Identification and Regulation" (2011) Brookings Institutions Policy Brief.

Elsas R. and Krahnen J. P. "Is Relationship Lending Special? Evidence from Credit-File Data in Germany" (1998) *Journal of Banking and Finance*, 22.

——— "Universal Banks and Relationships with Firms" in J. P. Krahnen and R. Schmidt *The German Financial System* (OUP 2004).

European Association of Co-Operative Banks "Consultative Document "Effective Resolution of Systemically Important Financial Institutions. Recommendations and Timelines" (2011).

European Commission "Towards an EU Directive on the Prudential Supervision of Financial Conglomerates" MARKT/3021/2000 (2000).

——— Proposal for the Regulation of the European Parliament and the Council on structural measures improving the resilience of EU Credit institutions (Liikanen Report) (2014).

European Systemic Risk Board. "Recovery and Resolution for the EU Insurance Sector: a Macroprudential Perspective" (2017) Report by the ATC Expert Group on Insurance.

Faia E. and Weder di Mauro B. "Cross-Border Resolution of Global Banks" (2015) Federal Reserve Bank of Dallas Globalization and Monetary Policy Institute Working Paper No. 236.

Falsenfeld C. "The Bank Holding Company Act: Has It Lived Its Life" (1993) *Villanova Law Review*.

Faltermeier R. "The German Banking System-Types of Banks and Experience from the crisis" (2013) Universitätsverlag Potsdam.

——— "The German Banking System-Types of Banks and Experience in the Crisis" (2013) U. Potsdam.

Fama E. "What's Different About Banks?" (1985) *Journal of Monetary Economics*, 15.

Fanto J. "Breaking Up Is Hard to Do": Should Financial Conglomerates be dismantled? (2010) Brooklyn Law School.

FDIC "Banco Santander, S.A. Resolution Plan for U.S. Operations Public Section (31 December 2018) https://www.fdic.gov/regulations/reform/resplans/plans/santander-165-1812.pdf.

——— "Resolution of Systemically Important Financial Institutions: The Single Point of Entry Strategy" Federal Register/Vol. 78, No. 243/Wednesday, December 18, 2013.

——— Quarterly Banking Profile (2019).

——— "The S&L Crisis: A Chrono-Bibliography" (2002).

FDIC and Bank of England "Resolving Globally Active, Systemically Important, Financial Institutions" (2012) A Joint Paper by Federal Deposit Insurance Corporation and the Bank of England.

Federal Reserve Bank of Minneapolis "A History of Central Banking in the United States" (2019).

Federal Reserve Board "Banking, Groups and Chains" (1930).

Federal Reserve History "Riegle-Neal Interstate Banking and Branching Efficiency Act of 1994" (1994).

——— "Financial Services Modernization Act of 1999, Commonly Called Gramm-Leach-Bliley".

Federation Bancaire Francaise "The French Banking System" (2008).

Feeley M. and Rubin E. *Federalism: Political Identity and Tragic Compromise* (University of Michigan Press 2011).

——— *Federalism: Political Identity and Tragic Compromise* (University of Michigan Press 2008).

Feldenkirchen W. "Banking and Economic Growth: Banks and Industry in Germany in R. Lee *The Nineteenth Century and Their Changing Relationship During Industrialization" in German Industry and German Industrialization. Essays in German Economic and Business History in the Nineteenth and Twentieth Centuries* (Routledge 1991).

Fell J. and Schinasi G "Assessing Financial Stability: Exploring the Boundaries of Analysis" (2005) National Institute Economic Review No. 192 April.

Fernandez de Liz S. "The Multiple-Point-of-Entry Resolution Strategy for Global Banks" (2015) BBVA Press Article.

Fernandez de Liz S., Pardo J. C., Santillana V. and Martin G. "Compendium on Resolution Strategies: A Multiple Point of Entry View" (2014) BBVA Regulation Outlook.

Fernandez de Liz S., Pardo J., Santillana V. and Martin G. "Regulation Outlook: Compendium on Resolution Strategies: A Multiple-Point-of-Entry View" (2014) BBVA Research.

Fiechter J., Okter Robe I., Ilyina A., Hsu M., Santos A. and Surti J. "Subsidiaries or Branches, Does one Size Fit All? (2011) IMF Staff Discussion Note.

Financial Holding Companies: Business Activities and Regulation ID 1–526–1845 (Practical Law, Thomson Reuters, 2019).

Financial Times Lexicon. http://lexicon.ft.com/Term?term=bancassurance.

FINMA "Resolution of Global Systemically Important Banks FINMA Position Paper on Resolution of G-SIBs" (2013).

Fiordelisi F. and Ricci O. *Bancassurance in Europe. Past, Present and Future* (Palgrave Macmillan 2012).

Fischer K. and Pfeil C. "Regulation and Competition in German Banking: An Assessment in J. P. Krahnen and R. Schmidt *The German Financial System* (OUP 2004).

Fisher R. W. "Ending 'Too Big to Fail': A Proposal for Reform Before It's Too Late" (2013) Federal Reserve Bank of Dallas.

Fletcher I. *Cross-Border Insolvency: National and Comparative Studies: Reports* (Tubingen 1992).

Fohlin C. "Banking Systems and Economic Growth: Lessons from Britain and Germany in the Pre-World War I Era" (1998) Review, Federal Reserve Bank of Saint Louis.

——— "Economic, Political and Legal Factors in Financial System Development: International Patterns in Historical Perspective" (2000) California Institute of Technology, Social Science Working Paper 1098.

——— "Regulation, Taxation and the Development of the German Universal Banking System 1884–1913" (2002) European Review of Economic History.

——— "Universal Banking Networks in Pre-War Germany: New Evidence from Company Financial Data" (1997) Research in Economics.

——— "Universal Banking in Pre-World War I Germany: Model or Myth? (1999) Explorations in Economic History 36.

Foxwell H. "A History of Barclays Bank" (1927) *The Economic Journal*, Vol. 37, No. 147.

Foxwell H. "The Financing of Industry and Trade" (1917) *The Economic Journal*, Vol. 27, No. 108.

Franks J., Mayer C., Hardie J. and Malinvaud E. "Capital Markets and Corporate Control: A Study of France, Germany and the UK" (1990) *Economic Policy*, Vol. 5, No. 10, Europe.

Freedman C. and Goodlet C. "Large-Value Clearing and Settlement Systems and Systemic Risk (1996) 7(2) North American Journal of Economics and Finance.

Freis J. H. Jr. "An Outsider's Look into the Regulation of Insider Trading in Germany: A Guide to Securities, Banking, and Market Reform in Finanzplatz Deutschland (1996) *B. C. Int'l & Comp. L. Rev.*, Vol. 19, 1.

Freixas X., Loranth G. and Morrison A. "Regulating Financial Conglomerates" (2007) *Journal of Financial Intermediation*, 16.

Friedman B. M. and Kuttner K. N. "Implementation of Monetary Policy: How Do Central Banks Set Interest Rates?" (2010) NBER Working Paper No. 16165, JEL No. E43, E52, E58.

Friedman M. and Schwartz A. *A Monetary History of the United States, 1867–1960* (Princeton University Press 1963).

——— *The Great Contraction 1929–1933* (Princeton University Press 1965).

FSB "Consultative Document Effective Resolution of Systemically Important Financial Institutions Recommendations and Timelines" (2011).

——— "Developing Effective Resolution Strategies and Plans for Systemically Important Insurers" (2016).

——— "Global Systemically Important Insurers (G-SIIs) and the Policy Measures That Will Apply to Them" (July 2013).

——— "FSB Statement on Identification of Global Systemically Important Insurers" (2017).

——— "Next Steps on the NBNI G-SIFI Assessment Methodologies" (2015).

——— "Policy Recommendations to Address Structural Vulnerabilities from Asset Management Activities" (2017).

——— "Principles on Loss-Absorbing Capacity of G-SIBS in Resolution Total Loss-Absorbing Capacity (TLAC) Term Sheet (2015).

——— "Principles for Cross-Border Effectiveness of Resolution Actions" (2015).

——— "Recovery and Resolution Planning for Systemically Important Financial Institutions: Guidance on Developing Effective Resolution Strategies" (2013).

——— "Recovery and Resolution Planning: Making the Key Attributes Requirements Operational Consultative Document (2012).

——— "Reducing the Moral Hazard Posed by Systemically Important Financial Institutions. FSB Recommendations and Time Lines" (2010).

——— Recovery and Resolution Planning for Systemically Important Financial Institutions: Guidance on identification of Critical Functions and Critical Shared services" (2013).

——— Resolution Report: "Keeping the Pressure Up" (2018).

——— "Review of the Techncial Implementation of the TLAC Standard (2019).

——— "Thematic Review on Bank Resolution Planning. Peer Review Report" (2019).

——— "The FSA's Approach to Introduce the TLAC Framework" (2018).

——— "The FSB Endorses and Imporved Network" (2022).
——— "2013 Update of Group of Global Systemically Important Banks (G-SIBs)" (2013).
——— "2014 Update of List of Global Systemically Important Banks (G-SIBs)" (2014).
——— "2015 Update of List of Global Systemically Important Banks (G-SIBs)" (2015).
——— "2016 List of Global Systemically Important Insurers (G-SIIs)" (2016).
——— "2017 List of Global Systemically Important Banks (G-SIBs)" (2017).
——— "2018 List of Global Systemically Important Banks (G-SIBs)" (2018).
——— "2019 List of Global Systemically Important Banks (G-SIBs)" (2019).
——— "2020 List of Global Systemically Important Banks (G-SIBs)" (2020).
——— "2021 List of Global Systemically Important Banks (G-SIBs)" (2021).
——— "2022 List of Global Systemically Important Banks (G-SIBs)" (2022).
——— "2017 List of Global Systemically Important Insurers (G-SIIs)" (2017).
——— "2018 Resolution Report: "Keeping the Pressure Up" (2018) Seventh Report on the Implementation of Resolution Reforms.
——— 2020 Resolution Report: Be Prepared" (2020).
FBS, IMF and BIS "Report to G-20 Finance Ministers and Governors Guidance to Assess the Systemic Importance of Financial Institutions, Markets and Instruments: Initial Considerations" (2009).
FBS and IOSCO "Consultative Document (2nd) Assessment Methodologies for Identifying Non-Bank Non-Insurer Global Systemically Important Financial Institutions Proposed High-Level Framework and Specific Methodologies" (2015).
FSOC "Authority to Require Supervision and Regulation of Certain Nonbank Financial Companies," Second Notice of Proposed Rulemaking and Proposed Interpretive Guidance, Federal Register, Vol. 76, No. 201 (18 October) (2011).
——— "Study and Recommendations on Prohibitions on Proprietary Trading and Certain Relationships with Hedge Funds and Private Equity Funds, (Volker Rule)" (2011).
Fulton M. and Girard J. "Co-operatives and Mutual Canada, Demutualization of Co-operatives and Mutuals" (2015) COOP.
Furlong F. "The Gramm–Leach–Bliley Act and Financial Integration" (2000) FRBSF Economic Letter, 2000–10.
Furse D. "Taking the Long View: How Market Based Finance Can support Stability" (2014) Bank of England Quarterly Bulletin 54.
Gallaguer D. M. "Comment Letter on OFR Study on Asset Management" (2014) Issues 2.
Gambacorta L. and Van Rixtel A. "Structural Bank Regulation Initiatives: Approaches and Implications" (2013) BIS.

Gande A. and Saunders A. "Are Banks Still Special When There Is a Secondary Market for Loans?" (2012) *Journal of Finance*, 67.

Gande A., Puri M., Sanders A. and Walter I. "Bank Underwriting of Debt Securities: Modern Evidence" (1997) *The Review of Financial Studies*, Vol. 10, No. 4.

Geneva Association "Systemic Risk in Insurance—An analysis of Insurance and Financial Stability" (2010).

Gerschenkron A. *Economic Backwardness in Historical Perspective* (Harvard University Press 1962).

Gerston L. *American Federalism: A Concise Introduction* (Routledge 2015).

Ghosh P. and Reosti J. "PenFed Deal Feeds Bankers' Fears of Unlimited Credit Union Membership" (2019) American Banker.

Giedeman D. "Branch Banking Restrictions and Finance Constrains in Early—Twentieth-Century America" (2005) *The Journal of Economic History*, Vol. 65, No. 1.

——— "The Riegle-Neal Act and Local Banking Market Concentration" (2004) *International Advances in Economic Research.*

Gleeson S. and Guynn R. *Bank Resolution and Crisis Management: Law and Practice* (OUP 2016).

Goldsmith R. *Comparative National Balance Sheets: A Study of Twenty Countries, 1688–1978* (University of Chicago Press 1985).

——— *Financial Intermediaries in the American Economy since 1900* (Princeton University Press 1958).

Golembe C. H. "One-Bank Holding Companies" in H. Prochnow *The One-Bank Holding Company* (Rand McNally 1969).

Gonulal, S. Goulder N. and Lester R. "Bancassurance—A Valuable Tool for Developing Insurance in emerging Markets" (2012) Policy Research Working Paper 6196, The World Bank.

Goodhart C. *Money, Information and Uncertainty* (MacMillan 1989).

——— "Myths of the Lender of Last Resort" (1999) International Finance 2:3.

——— "The Bank of England 1970–2000" in R. Michie and P. Williamson (eds) *The British Government and the City of London in the Twentieth Century* (CUP 2009).

——— *The Business of Banking, 1891–1914* (LSE 1972).

——— *The Evolution of Central Banks*, (MIT Press 1988).

——— "The Vickers Report: An Assessment" (2012) *Law and Financial Markets Review.*

Goodhart C. and Hartmann, P. Llewellyn D., Rojas-Suarez L. and Wesibrod S. *Financial Regulation: Why, How and Where Now?* (Routledge 1997).

Goodhart C. and Lastra R. "Equity Finance: Matching Liability to Power" (2019) *Journal of Financial Regulation.*

——— "Populism and Central Bank Independence" (2018) *Open Econ. Rev.*

Goodhart C. "If Banks Should Act as Utilities, Why Not Treat Them as Such?" (Vox 2011) https://voxeu.org/article/if-banks-should-act-utilities-why-not-treat-them-such.

Gordon J. "The Empty Call for Benefit-Cost Analysis in Financial Regulation" (2014) *The Journal of Legal Studies*, Vol. 43, No. S2, Benefit-Cost Analysis of Financial Regulation: A Conference Funded by the Alfred P. Sloan Foundation and Supported by the Coase-Sandor Institute for Law and Economics.

Gordon J. and Judge K. "The Origins of a Capital Market Union in the United States" (2018) Working Paper No. 584 (The Center for Law and Economic Studies Columbia University School of Law).

Gordon J. and Ringe W. "Bank Resolution in Europe: The Unfinished Agenda of Structural Reform" (2015) ECGI Law Working Paper No. 282.

Gortsos, Christos "The European Banking Regulation Handbook", Vol. I (Palgrave Macmillan 2023).

——— "The Single Resolution Mechanism (SRM) and the Single Resolution Fund (SRF): Legal Aspects of the Second Main Pillar of the European Banking Union (Fifth-Extended and Fully Updated-Edition)", Available at SSRN 2668653 (2019).

Gouge W. *A Short Story of Paper Money and Banking in the United States, including an account of Provincial and Continental Paper Money* (T.W. Ustick 1833).

Government Accountability Office "Industrial Loan Corporations Recent Asset Growth and Commercial Interest Highlight Differences in Regulatory Authority" (2005).

Green E.H. "Rentiers Versus Producers the Political Economy of the Bimetallic Controversy" (1988) *English Historical Review*.

Gros D. "Too Interconnected to Fail = Too Big to Fail: What Is in a Leverage Ratio?" *Vox.org* (January 2010). http://voxeu.org/article/too-interconnected-fail-too-big-fail .

Grossman R. *Unsettled Account: The evolution of Banking in the Industrialised World Since 1800* (Princeton University Press 2010).

Grossman R. "Fear and Greed: The Evolution of Double Liability in American Banking, 1865–1930" (2007) *Explorations in Economic History*, Vol. 44, No. 1, Elsevier.

Gruenberg M. J. Chairman FDIC "Volcker Alliance Program" (2013).

Gruson M. "Supervision of Financial Conglomerates in the European Union" (2008) *Current Developments in Monetary and Financial Law*, Vol. 4, IMF.

Gruson M. and Nikowitz W. "The Second Banking Directive of the European Economic Community and Its Importance for Non-EEC Banks" (1988) *Fordham International Law Journal*.

Gruson M. and Schneider U. H. "The German Landesbanken" (1995) *Colum. Bus. L. Rev.*

Gruson M. and Reisner R. *Regulation of Foreign Banks, United States and International* (Second Edition, Michie 1995).

Guerber H. A. *Myths of Greece and Rome Narrated with Special Reference to Literature and Art* (American Book Company 1893).

Guine C. "Global Systemically Important Insurers" (2014) Financial Stability Report.

Guinnane T. "Delegated Monitors, Large and Small: Germany's Banking System, 1800–1914" (2002) *Journal of Economic Literature*, Vol. 40, No. 1.

Guynn D. "Framing the TBTF Problem: The Path to a Solution" in Martin Neil Baily and John B. Taylor *Across the Divide: New Perspectives on the Financial Crisis* (Hoover Institution 2014).

H. Rockoff "The Free banking Era. A Re-examination" (1974) *Journal of Money, Credit and Banking*, Vol. 6, No. 2.

Haag H., Steffen J. L. and Mueller H. "Banking Regulations in Germany: Overview" (2018) *Practical Law*.

Habib M. A. Johnsen D. B. and Nail N. Y. "Spinoffs and Information" (1997) *Journal of Financial Intermediation*, Vol. 6, No. 2.

Hackethal A. "German Banks and Banking Structure" in J. P. Krahnen and R. Schmidt *German Financial System* (OUP 2004).

Haldane A. "The Age of Asset Management" (2014) BIS Central Bank Speech LSE.

Hall P. A. and Soskice D. *Varieties of Capitalism: The Institutional Foundations of Comparative Advantage* (Oxford Scholarship Online 2003).

Hamilton A. "Final Version of the Second Report on the Further Provision Necessary for Establishing Public Credit (1790) Report on a National Bank.

Hammond B. "Jackson, Biddle and the Bank of the United States" (1947) *The Journal of Economic History*, Vol. VII, No. I.

Harrington S. "The Dodd Frank Act, Solvency II, and the US Insurance regulation". (2013) The Journal of Financial Perspectives, EY.

Harrington S. "The Financial Crisis, Systemic Risk, and the Future of Insurance Regulation" (2009) *The Journal of Risk and Insurance*, Vol. 76 No. 4.

Harvard Law Review Association "Branch, Chain and Group Banking" (1935) *Harvard Law Review*, Vol. 48, No. 4.

Hartz L. *The Liberal Tradition in America* (Harvest 1991).

Hebb G. "Conflicts of Interest in Commercial Bank Security Underwritings: United Kingdom Evidence" (2003) *Quarterly Journal of Business and Economics*, Vol. 42, No. 1/2.

Herring R. "The Challenge of Resolving Cross-Border Financial Institutions" (2014) *Yale Journal of Regulation*, Vol. 31.

Herring R. and Santomero A. M. "The Corporate Structure of Financial Conglomeartes" (1990) *Journal of Financial Services Research*, 471–497.

Heyde F. and Neyer U. "Credit Default Swaps and the Stability of the Banking Sector" (2010) *International Review of Finance.*

Hikino H. and Chandler A. *Scale and Scope: The Dynamics of Industrial Capitalism* (Harvard University Press 2009).

Hill J. and Ligere E. "Insurance and Reinsurance in the UK (England and Wales): Overview" (Thomson 2018).

Histoire Du Groupe Crédit Agricole (Crédit Agricole, 2018). https://www.Crédit-agricole.com/le-groupe/histoire-du-groupe-Crédit-agricole.

Hoschka T. *Bancassurance in Europe* (St. Martin's Press 1994).

HSBC Holdings plc's Annual Report and Accounts 2023.

Hubert O. and Pince A. D. *Banking Regulation in France: Overview* (Practical Law 2020).

Huertas T "Are Banks Still Special?" (2017) LSE.

——— "A Resolvable Bank" in K. E. Scott, T. H. Jackson and J. Taylor *Making Failure Feasible: How Bankruptcy Reform Can End Too Big to Fail* (Hoover Institution Press 2015).

——— "The Rise of the Modern Business Enterprise: The Case of Citibank" (1985) *Business and Economic History.*

Hüfner F. "The German Banking System: Lessons from the Financial Crisis" (2010) OECD Economics Department Working Papers, No. 788, OECD Publishing.

Humphrey D. "Why Do Estimates of Bank Scale Economies Differ? (1990) Economic Review, Federal Reserve Bank of Richmond.

Hupkes E. "Form Follows Function—A New Architecture for Regulating and Resolving Global Financial Institutions" (2009) *European Business Organization Law Review.*

IADI Resolution Issues for Financial Cooperatives-Overview of Distinctive Features And Current Resolution Tools" (2017).

IAIS "Basic Capital Requirements for Global Systemically Important Insurers" October 2014.

——— Country Report 18/207 "United States: 2018 Article IV Consultation—Press Release; Staff Report and Statement by the Executive Director for United States" (2018).

——— Country Report No. 16/194: "Germany. Crisis Preparedness, Bank Resolution and Crisis Management Frameworks-Technical Note" (2016).

——— Insurance and Financial Stability "The Characteristics of the Insurance Business Model Including Insurance Techniques Make It Very Unlikely for Traditional Insurance to Be Systemically Relevant" p. 18 (IAIS, 2011) https://www.iaisweb.org/page/supervisory-material/other-supervisory-papers and-reports//file/34379/insurance-and-financial-stability-november-2011.

——— "Global Financial stability Report, Statistical Appendix" (2012).

——— "Global Systemically Important Insurers: Initial Assessment Methodology" (2013).
ICA "Statement on the Co-operative Identity" (2007) International Cooperative Alliance.
IIF "Achieving Bank Resolution in Practice Are We Nearly There Yet? (2014) A report of the IIF Cross-Border Resolution Working Group September.
IMF "Cross-Cutting Themes in Economies with Large Banking Systems" (2010).
——— Country Report No. 16/191, Germany (2016).
——— "France: Financial Sector Assessment Program—Detailed Assessment of Observance of Insurance Core Principles" (2013).
IMF/World Bank "An Overview of the Legal, institutional and regulatory Framework for Bank Insolvency" (17 April 2009).
Inham G. *Capitalism divided: the City and Industry in British social development* (Macmillan 1984).
Institute of International Bankers "Global Survey 2014".
International Cooperative Alliance the "Co-operative Principles (2018).
ISDA 2015 Universal Protocol.
Jackson H. E. and Half C. "Background Paper on Evolving Tends in the Supervision of Financial Conglomerates" (2002) Harvard Law School.
Jackson H. E. and Massman S. "The Resolution of Distressed Financial Conglomerates" (2017) *RSF: The Russell Sage Foundation Journal of the Social Sciences*, Vol. 3, No. 1, 48–72.
Jackson T. H. "Bankruptcy Code Chapter 14: A Proposal" in Kenneth E. Scott and John B. Taylor *Bankruptcy Not Bailout: A Special Chapter 14* (Hoover Institution Press 2012).
James C. and Wier P "Borrowing Relationships, Intermediation and the Cost of Issuing Pubic Securities" (1990) *Journal of Financial Economics*, 28.
Jaremski M. "National Banking's role in US Industrialization, 1850–1900" (2013) Working Paper 18789, National Bureau of Economic Research.
Jay Choi, J. Hiraki T. and J. Landi "The Value of Multinationality and Business Group for Japanese Firms" (2014) *Journal of Corporate Finance*, Vol. 29.
Jay J. Federalist Paper No. 2 (1787).
Jayaratne J. and Strahan P. "The Finance-Growth Nexus: Evidence from Bank Branch Deregulation" (1996) *The Quarterly Journal of economics*.
Jeffreys J. *Trends in Business Organisations in Great Britain Since 1856, with Special Reference to the Financial Structure of Companies, the Mechanism of Investment and the Relations Between the Shareholder and the Company* (University of London 1938).
Jeng-Yan T. "The Gramm--Leach--Bliley Act: Optimal Interest Margin Effects of Commercial Bank Expansion into Insurance Underwriting" (2012) Applied Economics Letters.

Jin K.-Y. "How to Eat an Elephant: Corporate Group Structure of Systemically Important Financial Institutions, Orderly Liquidation Authority, and Single Point of Entry Resolution" (2015) *The Yale Law Journal*.

Jobst A. "Systemic Risk in the Insurance Sector. A Review of Current Assessment Approaches in the Geneva Papers on Risk and Insurance" (2014) *Issues and Practice*, Vol. 39, No. 3.

Johnson S., La Porta R., Lopez-de-Silanes F. and Shleifer A. "Tunneling" (2000) *The American Economic Review*, Vol. 90, No. 2.

Joint Committee "List of Financial Conglomerates 2017 Financial Conglomerates with Head of Group in the EU/EEA" (October 2017).

Joint Forum "Core Principles: Cross-Sectorial Comparison" (2001).

Jones G. *British Multinational Banking, 1830–1990* (OUP 1995).

JPMorgan "The History of JPMorgan Chase & Co. 200 Years of Leadership in Banking" (2018).

Kamil H. and Rai's K. "The Global Credit Crunch and the Foreign Bank's Lending to Emerging Markets, Why Did Latin America Fare Better?" (2010) IMF Working Paper No. 10/102.

Karp J. and Johnson K. "Banco Santander Wins Banespa Sale, Topping Rivals with $3.6 Billion Bid" *Wall Street Journal* (New York, 21 November 2000).

Kaufman G. G. and Scott K. "What Is Systemic Risk and Do Financial Regulators Retard or Contribute to It? (2003) *Independent Review*, Vol. 7, No. 3, 371.

Keller E. A. "Introductory Comment: A Historical Introduction to the Securities Act of 1933 and the Securities Exchange Act of 1934" (1988) *Ohio State Law Journal*, 49.

Kelley E. W. Jr. "Are Banks Still Special?" (1997) Federal Reserve.

Kennedy W. *Industrial Structure, Capital Markets and the Origins of British Decline* (CUP 1987).

Key Attributes of Effective Resolution Regimes for Financial Institutions (2011).

Keynes J. M. "The Prospectus of Money, November 1914" (1914) *Economic Journal*, 24.

——— *Proposals for an International Currency (Clearing) Union* (1942).

——— *The General Theory of Employment, Interest and Money* (London: Macmillan 1936).

Kimball S. L. "The Purpose of Insurance Regulation: A Preliminary Inquiry in the Theory of Insurance Law" (1960) *Minn. L. Rev.*, Vol. 45, 471.

King M "Twenty Years of Inflation Targeting" (2012) Stamp Memorial Lecture London School of Economics.

Klein R. W. "Insurance Market Regulation: Catastrophe Risk, Competition and Systemic Risk" in G. Dionne *Handbook of Insurance* (Springer 2013).

Klein P., Wuebker R. and Zoeller K. "Relationship Banking and Conflicts of Interest: Evidence from German Initial Public Offerings" (2016) *Journal of Corporate Finance*.

Knox J. *A History of banking in the United Sates* (Rhodes 1903).

Koguchi K. and Forestieri G. *Financial Conglomeartes* (Organization for Economic Co-operation and Development 1993).

Kokkoris I. and Olivares-Caminal R. *Antitrust Law Amidst Financial Crisis* (CUP 2010).

Konczal M. "Sheila Bair: Dodd-Frank Really Did End Taxpayer Bailouts" *WSJ* (18 May 2013).

Konzelmann S., Fovargue-Davies M. and Schnyder G. "Varieties of Liberalism: Anglo-Saxon Capitalism in Crisis?" (2010) Centre for Business Research, University of Cambridge, Working Paper No. 403.

——— "The Faces of Liberal Capitalism: Anglo-Saxon Banking in Crisis? (2012) *Cambridge Journal of Economics.*

Kroszner R. and Rajan R. "Is the Glass-Steagal Act Justified? A study of the U.S. Experience with Universal Banking Before 1933." (1994) The American economic Review, vol 84, No. 4.

Krummel H. J. "German Universal Banking Scrutinized. Some Remarks Concerning the Gessler Report" (1980) *Journal of Banking and Finance*, 4.

Kumar R., *Strategies of Banks and Other Financial Institutions: Theories and Cases* (Elsevier 2014).

Kupiec P. and Wallison P. "Can the Single Point of Entry Strategy Be Used to Recapitalize a Systemically Important Failing Bank?" (2015) *Journal of Financial Stability*, 20.

La Porta R., López-de-Silanes F. and Zamarripa G. "Related Lending" (2003) *The Quarterly Journal of Economics*, Vol. 118, No. 1.

La Porta R., Lopez-De-Silanes F., Shleifer A. and Vishny R. W. "Legal Determinants of External Finance, (1997) The Journal of Finance, Vol. 52, No. 3.

Labonte M. Who Regulates Whom? An Overview of the U.S. Financial Regulatory Framework (2017) Congressional Research Service.

Laeven E. "Insider Lending and Bank Ownership: The Case of Russia" (2001) *Journal of Comparative Economics*, Vol. 29, No. 2.

Lamoreaux, N. R. "Banks, Kinship, and Economic Development: The New England Case" (1986) *Journal of Economic History*, Vol. 46, No. 3, 647.

Lamoreaux N. *Insider Lending, Banks, Personal Connections, and Economic Development in Industrial New England* (CUP 1994).

Langston E. and Brandt S. *Understanding the S&L Crisis: A Guide for Beginners and Congressmen* (Squeaky Wheel Press 1990).

Larson M., Schnyder G. Westerhuis G. and Wilson J. "Strategic Responses to Global Challenges: The Case of European Banking, 1973–2000" (2011) *Business History*, Vol. 53, No. 1.

Lastra R. *Central Banking and Banking Regulation* (Financial Markets Group of the London School of Economics and Political Science 1996).

——— "Cross-Border Resolution of Banking Crisis" (2006) Paper Presented at the Conference on "International Financial Instability. Cross-border Banking and National Regulation" Sponsored by the Federal Reserve Bank of Chicago and International Association of Deposit Insurers.

——— "Northern Rock and Banking Law Reform in the UK" in F. Bruni and D. T. Llewellyn *The Failure of Northern Rock: A Multi-dimensional Case Study* (SUERF—The European Money and Finance Forum 2009).

——— *International Financial and Monetary Law* (2nd Edition, Oxford 2015).

Lastra R., Ayadi R., Olivares-Caminal R. and Russo C. "The Different and Operational Structures of Banking Groups in the Euro Area, and Their Impact on Banks' Resolvability" (2016) European Parliament.

Lastra R. and Olivares-Caminal R. "Cross Border Insolvency: The Case of Financial Conglomeartes in J. Raymon Laborsse, R. Olivares-Caminal and D. Singh *Financial Crisis Management and Bank Resolution* (Informa 2009).

Lastra R. and Olivares Caminal R. and Russo C. (2017) "The Provision of Critical Functions at Global, National and Regional Level—Is There a Need for Further Legal/Regulatory Clarification if Liquidation Is the Default Option for Failing Banks? European Parliament.

Lastra R. and Sheppard M. "Ethical Foundations of Financial Law" in C. Russo, R. Lastra and W. Blair *Research Handbook on Law and Ethics in Banking and Finance* (Elgar 2019).

Lastra R. and Wood G. "The Crisis of 2007–09: Nature, Causes, and Reactions" (2010) *Journal of International Economic Law*, Vol. 13, No. 3.

Law S., Kutan A. and Naseem N. "The Role of Institutions in Finance Curse: Evidence from International Data" (2018). *Journal of Comparative Economics*.

Lazen, V. Eguiluz C "Conflictos De Interés En Servicios Financieros: Taxonomía y Mecanismos De Control Regulatorio" (2006) Superintendencia de Valores y Seguros – Chile.

Lee P. "The Source-of-Strength Doctrine: Revered and Revisited—Part I" (2012) *The Banking Law Journal*.

Leroux E. "Trade in Financial Services under the World Trade Organization" (2002) *Journal of World Trade*, Vol. 36, No. 3.

Levy-Leboyer, M. and Lescure M. "France" in R. Sylla and G. Toniollo *Patterns of European Industrialization*, Chapter 8 (Routledge, Chapman, and Hall 1991).

Lex "Commerzbank: waiting for Deutsche Bank" *Financial Times*, (London, August 7, 2018).

Lloyds 2023 Annual Report.

Lloyds Banking Group Annual Report and Accounts 2018.

Lopez C. "The Asset Management Industry, Systemic Risk, and Macroprudential Policy" (2017) *Journal of Financial Transformation*, Vol. 45.

Loriaux M. France *After Hegemony: International Change and Financial Reform* (Cornell University Press 1991).

Lovett W. and Mallow M. *Banking and Financial Institutions Law in a Nutshell* (8th Edition, West Academic Publishing, 2014).

Lowenstein L. "Financial Transparency and Corporate Governance: You Manage What You Measure" (1996) *Columbia Law Review*.

Lowy M., *High Rollers: Inside the Savings and Loan Debacle* (Praeger Publishers 1991).

Lubben S. and Wilmarth A. "Too Big and Unable to Fail" (2016) GW Law School Public Law and Legal Theory Paper No. 2016–44.

Macey J. and Miller G. "Double Liability of Bank Shareholders: History and Implications" (1992) *Wake Forest L. Rev.*, Vol. 27, 31.

Macey J. and Miller G. "The McCarran-Ferguson Act of 1945: Reconceiving the Federal Role in Insurance Regulation" (1993) *N.Y.U. L. Rev.*, Vol. 68, 13.

Madison J. *The Federalist No 45* (B. Wright Ed. 1961).

Malone D. *Jefferson and His Time*, Vol. I (Little, Brown & Co. 1948).

Manvell Jeannot J. "An International Perspective on Domestic Banking Reform: Could the European Union's Second Banking Directive Revolutionize the Way the United States Regulates its Own Financial Services Industry? (1999) *American University International Law Review*, Vol. 14, No. 6.

Massman S. "The Orderly Liquidation Authority: Fanatical or Familiar? Idealistic or Unrealistic? (2014) DASH Harvard University.

Maurer N. and Haber S. "Related Lending and Economic Performance" (2007) *The Journal of Economic History*, Vol. 67.

Maycock J., *Financial Conglomeartes: The New Phenomenon* (Gower Publishing Company 1986).

Mayer C "New Issues in Corporate Finance" (1988) *European Economic Review*, 32.

Mayer M. *The Greatest-Ever Bank Robbery: The Collapse of the Savings and Loan Industry* (Charles Scribner's Sons 1990).

McGuire J. and Dow S. "Japanese Keiretsu: Past, Present, Future" (2009) *Asia Pac J. Manag.*, 26.

McIntyre C. L. "The Nonbank Bank Loophole to the Bank Holding Company Act of 1956—The Need for Congressional Action" (1986) *Alabama Law Review*, Vol. 37, 713.

McKillop D., Glass J. and Ferguson C. "Investigating the Growth Performance of UK Credit Unions Using Radial and Non-Radial Efficiency Measures" (2002) *Journal of Banking and Finance*, Vol. 26 No. 8.

Mcvea H., *Financial Conglomeartes and the Chinese Wall: Regulating Conflicts of Interest* (OUP 1993).

Meeting Between Federal Reserve Board Staff and Representatives of Foreign Banking Organizations (9 July 2012).

Meltzer A. *A History of the Federal Reserve*, volume 1: 1913–1951 (University of Chicago Press 2003).

Merck Martel M., Van Rixtel A. and Gonzalez Mota E. "Business Models of International Banks in the Wake of the 2007–2009 Global Financial Crisis" (2012) Estabilidad Financiera Num. 22 (Banco de España).

Messik G. *Credit Union Service Organizations* (NACUSO 2018).

Meyerqwitz S. "The Source-of-Strength Doctrine" (2012) *The Banking Law Journal*.

Meyerqwitz S. "The Source-of-Strength Doctrine—Part II" (2012) *The Banking Law Journal*.

Michie R. *British Banking: Continuity and Change from 1694 to the Present* (2016 OUP).

——— "'The Emergence and Survival of a Financial Cluster in Britain' in Learning from Some of Britain's Successful Sectors: An Historical Analysis of the Role of Government" (2010) BIS Economics Paper No. 6, Department of Business Innovation and Skills.

——— *The Global Securities Market: A History* (OUP 2006).

Michie R. and Mollan S. "British and American Banking in Historical Perspective: Beware of False Precedents" (2011) *History and Policy*.

Miller J. *The Origins of the American Revolution* (Standford University Press 1943).

Minsky H. P. "The Modelling of Financial Instability. an Introduction in Modelling and Simulation" (1974) Vol 5. Proceedings of the Fifth Annual Pittsburgh Conference, Instruments Society of America.

——— *The Economics of Money, Banking, and Financial Markets* (Pearson Education Limited 2016).

Mishkin F. "Evaluating FDICIA" (1996) Federal Reserve Bank of New York Graduate School of Business, Columbia University and National Bureau of Economic Research.

Mitchell M. "Citicorp and Travelers Plan to Merge in Record $70 billion Deal". *The New York Times* (New York 7 April 1998).

Moody J. and Fite G. *The Credit Union Movement: Origins and Development, 1850–1980* (Kendall/Hunt, 1984).

Morentz Markeley D. "The Impact of Financial Deregulation on Rural Capital Markets in Virgina. An Analysis of Bank Decision Making" (1984) Virginia Polytechnic Institute and State University.

Morgan G., Sturdy A., Daniel J. and Knights D. "Bancassurance in Britain and France: Innovating Strategies in the Financial Services" (1994) The Geneva Papers on Risks and Insurance.

Morris C. *The Law of Financial Services Groups* (OUP 2019).

Morris M. and Anicich E. "Bank of America and Merrill Lynch Merger" (2015) Columbia Business School Case Works.

Morris S., Smith R. and Storbeck O. "Deutsche Bank Struggles with Rising Funding Costs" *Financial Times* (London 10 September 2018).

Morrison A. "Universal Banking" in A. Berger, P. Molyneux and J. O. S. Wilson *The Oxford Handbook of Banking* (OUP 2010).

Morrison A. and Wilhelm W. *Investment Banking, Institutions, Politics and the Law* (OUP 2008).

Morton G. "Banking Regulation and Treatment of Foreign Banks in the United Kingdom" in M. Gruson and R. Reisner *Regulation of Foreign Banks. United States and International* (Michie 1995).

Moysich A. "Federal Deposit Insurance Corporation" in *(FDIC) History of the Eighties: Lessons for the Future*. Vol. 1, *An Examination of the Banking Crises of the 1980s and Early 1990s* (FDIC 1997).

Mulligan M. and Davies P. J. "Santander Profits Driven by Abbey Acquisition" *Financial Times* (London 27 July, 2005).

Mulloy P. and Lasker C., The Riegle-Neal Interstate Banking and Branching Efficiency Act of 1994: Responding to Global Competition" (1995) *J. Legis.*, Vol. 21, 255.

Muñoz D "Restructuring, Resolution and Insolvency: Shift of Tasks from Judicial to Administrative Authorities" ECB Legal Conference on "Restructuring, Resolution and Insolvency: Shift of Tasks from Judicial to Administrative Authorities" (2017).

Murphy N. B. "European Union Financial Developments: The Single Market, the Single Currency, and Banking" (2000) *FDIC Banking Review*, 13.

NAIC "Global Systemically Important Insurers" (2021).

Nadler P. "The One-Bank Holding Company" (1968) Banking New York.

Nasel "A Framework for Dealing with Domestic Systemically Important Banks" (2012) BIS.

Nasel "Regulatory Consistency Assessment Programme (RCAP) Assessment of Basel III G-SIB Framework and Review of D-SIB Frameworks-United States" (2016) BIS.

Nasel "Global Systemically Important Banks: Assessment Methodology and the Additional Loss Absorbency Requirement" (2011) Consultative Document.

Nash E. "Spanish Banks in Pounds 20bn Merger" *Independent* (London 16 January 1999).

National Commission on Financial Institution Reform, Recovery and Enforcement, *Origins and Causes of the S&L Debacle a Blueprint for Reform* (1993).

NatWest Annual Report (2023).

Nazareth A. L. "Speech by SEC Staff: 'Come with Me to the SEC' Remarks Before the Brown University Commencement Forum" (2003).

Neale F. and Peterson P. "The Effect of the Gramm-Leach-Bliley Act on the Insurance Industry" (2005) *Journal of Economics and Business*, Vol. 57, No. 4.

Neuberger H. and Stokes H. "German Banks and German Growth 1883–1913: An Empirical View" (1974) *The Journal of Economic History*, Vol. 34, No. 3.

Ng K. "Free Banking Laws and Barriers to Entry in Banking, 1838–1860" (1988) *The Journal of Economic History*, Vol. XLVIII, No. 4.

Nieto M. and Wall M. "Breaking Down Geographic Barriers on Banks: U.S. and EU Recent Experiences" (2015) Federal Reserve Bank of Atlanta.

Nippania S. and Green K. W. Jr. "The Banking Industry After the Riegle–Neal Act: Re-structure and Overall Performance" (2002) *The Quarterly Review of Economics and Finance*.

Nivoix S. "Specificities of the French Cooperative Banking Groups Facing the 2007–2012 Crisis" (2016) *China-USA Business Review*, Vol 15.

Noked N. "Separate Entity Doctrine for U.S. Branches of Foreign Banks" (2012) *Harvard Law School Forum on Corporate Governance*.

Nolle D.E. "US Domestic and International Financial Reform Policy: Are G20 Commitments and the Dodd Frank Cat in Sync?" (2011) 2 No. 4 (Board of the Federal reserve Sys.; International Finance Discussion Papers No. 1024.

Noodt Taquela M. "Concursos y Quiebras" in Fernández Arroyo and P. Diego (ed) *Derecho Internacional Privado de los Estados del Mercosur: Argentina, Brasil, Paraguay y Uruguay* (Zavalia 2003).

Nurullah M. and Staikouras S. "The Separation of Banking from Insurance: Evidence from Europe" (2008) *Multinational Finance Journal*, Vol. 12.

Nussle J. BankThink "Banker Concerns About Credit Union Mergers Are Overblown" (2019) American Banker.

Nyberg L. "How Do Conflicts of Interest in Universal Banking Emerge and What Are the Arguments for a Separation of Commercial and Investment Banking?" (2004) *BIS Review*, 47.

O'Sullivan M. "Acting Out Institutional Change: Understanding the Recent Transformation of the French Financial System" (2017) *Socio-Economic Review*.

O'Brien Sir L. "Key Issues in Monetary and Credit Policy. Text of an Address by the Governor to the International Banking Conference in Munich on 28th May 1971" (1971) Bank of England Quarterly Bulletin.

OCC—Interpretive Letter No. 684 (4 August 1995).

——— "Activities Permissible for National Banks and Federal Savings Associations, Cumulative, 2017 Edition" (2017).

Offer A. "Narrow Banking, Real Estate and Financial Stability in the UK c.1870–2010" in N. Dimsdale and A. Hotson *British Financial Crisis since 1825* (OUP 2014).

Office of Financial Research (OFR) "Asset Management and Financial Stability" (2013).

Omarova S. and Tahyar M. That which we Call a Bank: Revisiting the History of Bank Holding Company Regulation in the United States" (2011). Review of Banking and Financial Law, Vol 31.

Oney C. "Fintech Industrial Banks and Beyond: How banking innovations affect the Federal Safety Net" (2018) 23 Gordham J. Corp & Fin.

Orhangazi Ö. "Financial deregulation and the 2007–08 US financial crisis" (2014) FESSUD, Working Paper Series No. 49.

Ory J. and Lemezeri Y "The French Co-operative Banking Group Model: Too Good to be True? (2010) XIXème Conférence de l'AIMS.

Ory J., Gurtner E. and Jaeger M. "The Challenges of Recent Changes in French Cooperative Banking Groups" (2006) RECMA Revue Internationale de L'Economie Sociale" No. 301.

Oura H. "The Asset Management Industry and Financial Stability" (2015) IMF.

Owen Smith E. *The German Economy* (Taylor & Francis Group 2002).

Padoa Scioppa T. "The Transformation of the European Financial System" (2002) ECB.

Panizza U. "Non-linearities in the Relationship Between Finance and Growth" (2017) The Graduate Institute Geneva and CEPR.

Parada P., Alemany L. and Planellas M. "The Internationalization of Retail Banking: Banco Santander's Journey Towards Globalisation" (2009) Long Range Planning, 42.

Pardo J., Mirat P., Fernandez de Lis S. and Santillana V. "Multiple Point of entry resolution strategy: a natural approach for descentralised retail banking groups" (2014) BBVA Research.

Park H. "The Consevatism of British Banks in the Interwar Period, Re-examined" (2012) Mineo.

Park S. C. and Xie X. "Reinsurance and Systemic Risk: The Impact of Reinsurer Downgrading on Property-Casualty Insurers" (2011) Working Paper, California State University.

Pavlovich A. "Banking Group Companies: Which Entities Are Caught by the Special Resolution Regime?" (2015) *Journal of International Banking & Financial Law*, Vol. 30, No. 2, 2 JIBFL.

Peleckiene, V. Peleckies K., Dudzeviciute G. "New Challenges of Supervising Financial Conglomeartes" (2011) *Intellectual Economics*, Vol. 5 No. 2 (10).

Penn B. "Banking Regulation in the UK: Overview (Practical Law, Thomson Reuters, 2018).

"Permissible Securities Activities of Commercial Banks Under the Glass-Steagall Act" (GSA) and the Gramm-Leach-Bliley Act (GLBA) (2010). Congressional Research Service.

Petersen, B. and Rajan R. "The Benefits of Lending Relationships: Evidence from Small Business Data" (1994) *Journal of Finance*, Vol. 49.

Philipon T. and Reshef A. "Wages and Human Capital in the US Finance Industry (2012) *Quarterly Jorunal of Economics*, Vol. 127, No. 4.

Pilzer P., *Other People's Money: The Inside Story of the S&L Mess* (Simon and Schuster 1989).

PIMCO Submission to the Consultative Document (2nd), Assessment Methodologies for Identifying Non-Bank Non-Insurer Global Systemically Important Financial Institutions (2015).

Plessis A. *The History of banks in France* (Elgar 2003).

Powell J. "Ending "Too Big to Fail" (2013) Remarks at the Institute of International Bankers 2013 Washington Conference Washington, D.C.

PRA "Statement of Policy Designation of Investment Firms for Prudential Supervision by the Prudential Regulation Authority" (2013) PRA.

——— PRA Rulebook Glossary (2023).

——— "The PRA Approach to Banking Resolution (2023).

——— "Which Firms Do We Regulate? (2018).

Practical Law Note 7–521–7963 "Finance Fundamentals: Bank Holding Company v Financial Holding Company" (Practical Law, Thomson Reuters, 2019).

Preston H. "Branch Banking with Special Reference to California Conditions" (1922) *Journal of Political Economy*, Vol. 30, No. 4.

Price M., Henry D. "Deutsche Bank Fails Fed Stress Test While Three U.S. Lenders Stumble" *Reuters* (28 June 2018).

Private Equity Investments" ID 2–506–0525 (Practical Law, Thomson Reuters, 2019).

Proctor C. *The Law and Practice of International Banking* (OUP 2015).

Rajan R. "The Entry of Commercial Banks into the Securities Business: A Selective Survey of Theories and Evidence" (1995) NYU.

Ramakrishnan R. and Thakor A. V. "Information Reliability and a Theory of Financial Intermediation" (1984) *Review of Economic Studies*, 51.

Randall C. "The FSB's 'Key Attributes': The Road to Cross-Border Resolution of Financial Institutions" (2012) Scoping Paper Prepared for the Cross-Border Resolution Symposium Bingham Centre for the Rule of Law.

Randall S. "Insurance Regulation in the United States: Regulatory Federalism and the National Association of Insurance Commissioners" (1999) *Florida State University Law Review*, Vol. 26 625.

RBS Annual Report and Accounts 2018.

Reitz J. "How to Do Comparative Law" (1998). *The American Journal of Comparative Law*, Vol. 46, No. 4.

Reosti J. "Do Credit Unions Still Warrant a Tax Exemption?" (2018) American Banker.

Restreppo M. "The Convergence of Commercial and Investment Banking Under the Gramm-Leach-Bliley Act: Revisiting Old Risks and Facing New Problems" (2005) Law and Business Review of the Americas.

Rex S. "The Building Societies Act 1986—A BSA Summary Sixth Edition" (2013) Building Society Association.

Rhodes C. "Financial Services: Contribution to the UK Economy" (2018) Briefing Paper, Number 6193, House of Commons Library.

Richardson G. "The Great Depression" (2019) Federal Reserve History.

Richardson G., Komai A. and Gou M. "Banking Act of 1935" (2013) Federal Reserve History.

Riefler D. "Branch Banking and Chain Banking" (1930) Editorial Research Reports (Vol. 1).

Riesser J. *The German Great Banks and Their Concentration in connection with The Economic Development of Germany* (National Monetary Commission, Washington 1911).

Riker W. "The Senate and American Federalism" (1955) *The American Political Science Association*, Vol. 49, No. 2.

Risk Management of Financial Derivatives, Comptroller's Handbook (OCC 1997).

Roberts R. "London as an International Financial centre, 1980–2000: Global Powerhouse or Wimbledon EC2?" in Y. Cassis and E. Bussiere *London and Paris as International Financial Centres in the Twentieth Century* (OUP 2007).

——— "What's in a Name? Merchants, Merchant Bankers, Accepting Houses, Issuing Houses, Industrial Bankers and Investment Bankers" (1993). *Business History*, Vol. 35, No. 3.

Robinson E. "Jes Staley Stakes Barclays's Future on Investment Banking" *Bloomberg*, (New York 26 September 2018).

Rockoff H. "Prodigals and Projecture: An Economic History of Usury Laws in the United States from Colonial Times to 1900" (2003) NBER Working Paper 9742.

Romer C. D. "The Nation in Depression" (1993) *The Journal of Economic Perspectives*, Vol. 7, No. 2 American Economic Association.

Rothbard M. *A History of Money and Banking in the United Sates. The Colonial Era to World War II* (Ludwig Von Mises Institute 2002).

Roy S. and M. Kemmeb D. "The Run-Up to the Global Financial Crisis: A Longer Historical View of Financial Liberalization, Capital Inflows, and Asset Bubbles" (2019) International Review of Financial Analysis.

Rubin E. "Puppy Federalism and the Blessings of America" (2001) *The Annals of the American Academy of Political and Social Science*, Vol. 574;.

Ryder N. "The Regulation of Credit Unions: A Comparative Analysis Between the USA and Great Britain" (2005) *Journal of Banking Regulation*, Vol. 6, No. 3.

Ryder N. and Chambers C. "The Credit Crunch-Are Credit Unions Able to Ride Out the Storm?" (2009) *Journal of Banking Regulation*, Vol. 11, No. 1, 76-86.

S&P "31 European Banking Groups Assigned Resolution Counterparty Ratings; Four Collateralized Notes Upgraded; UCO Removed" (S&P Global, 12 June 2018).

——— Global Ratings, September 2019.

——— Report "Cooperative Banking Sector Germany" (2018).

Saapar I. and Soussa F. "Financial Consolidation and Conglomeration: Implications for the Financial Safety Net", in L. Halme, C. Hawkesby, J Healey, I. Saapar and F. Soussa *Financial Stability and Central Banks, Selected Issues for Financial Safety Nets and Markets*, (Bank of England 2000).

Saint Simon H. de *Catecismo Político de los Industriales* (Aguilar, 1960).

——— de *L'Industrie* (1966).

Sandbu M. "Brexit and the Future of UK Capitalism" (2019) *The Political Quarterly*.

Santander.

——— Annual Report 2019.

——— Annual Report 2022.

——— Archivo Histórico Santnder (2023).

——— Our History (2023).

Santos J. "Commercial Banks in the Securities Business: A review" (1998) *Journal of Financial Services Research*, Vol. 14, No. 1, Klewer Academic Publishers, Boston.

Saunders A. and Walker I *Universal Banking in the United States. What Could We Gain? What Could We Lose?* (OUP 1994).

Sax C. A. and Sloan III M. "The Bank Holding Company Amendments of 1970" (1970), 39 George Washington Law Review.

Scalia A. "The Two Faces of Federalism" (1982) *Harvard Journal of Law and Public Policy*, Vol. 6.

Scherer, P. Zeller S. *Banking Regulation in Germany* (German Law Publishers 2009).

Schildbach J. "Universal Banks: Optimal for Clients and Financial Stability. Why It Would Be Wrong to Split Them Up" (2012) Deutsche Bank DB Research.

Schillig M. "Bank Resolution Regimes in Europe-Part I: Recovery and Resolution Planning, Early Intervention" (2013) *European Business Law Review*, Vol. 24, No. 6, N/A.

Schinasi G. et al "Modern Banking and OTC Derivatives Markets—The Transformation of Global Finance and its implications for Systemic Risk" (2000) IMF Occasional Paper No. 203.

Schoenmaker D. "The Different Legal and Operational Structures of Banking Groups in the Euro Area and the Impact on Banks' Resolvability" (2016) European Parliament.

Schooner H. and Taylor M *Global Bank Regulation: Principles and Policies* (Elsevier, 2010).

Schroeders Annual Report 2017.

Schuler M. "Integrated Financial Supervisor in Germany" (2004) Discussion paper No. 04–35 ZEW.

Schull B. "The Separation of Banking and Commerce in the United States: An Examination of Principal Issues" (1999) OCC Economics Working Paper.

Schwarcz S. "Beyond Bankrupcty: Resolution as a Macroprudential Regulatory Tool. (2018) *Notredame Law Review*.

Schweitzer P. "Banks and Banking—A Review of a Definition" (1977) *Banking L. J.*, Vol. 94, 6, 7.

Segovia E. "Santander se come Banesto tras no encontrar socios al precio exigido por Botín" *El Confidencial* (Madrid 18 December 2012).

Shan Y. G. "Can Internal Governance Mechanisms Prevent Asset Appropriation? Examination of Type I Tunneling in China" (2013) *Corporate Governance: An International Review*, Vol. 21, No. 3.

Sheppard Gelsi M. "Desvío de oportunidades de negocios de la Sociedad Anónima: Un supuesto de responsabilidad de los directores" (2007) Revista de Derecho, Universidad de Montevideo.

Sherman M. "A Short History of Financial Deregulation in the United States" (Center for Economic and Policy Research 2009).

Shiwakoti R. K., Iqbal A. and Funnell W. "Organizational form, Business Strategies and the Demise of Demutualized Building Societies in the UK" (2018) *Journal of Banking and Finance*, 94.

Shull B. "Banking, Commerce and Competition Under the Gramm-Leach-Bliley Act" (2002) Antitrust bulletin.

——— "The Separation of Banking and Commerce in the United States: An Examination of Principal Issues" (1999) OCC Economics Working Paper.

Shull B. and White L. "Of Firewalls and Subsidiaries: The Right Stuff for Expanded Bank Activities" (1998) New York University Center for Law and Business Working Paper #CLB-98–017.

Shull B. and White L. J. "The Right Corporate Structure for Expanded Bank Activities" (1998) *Banking L. J.*, Vol. 115, 446.

Simpson A. "Wells Fargo Closing Down Its Personal Insurance Business" (28 November 2017) *Insurance Journal*.

Skeel D. Jr. "Single Point of Entry and the Bankruptcy Alternative" (2014) University of Pennsylvania Law School. Penn Law: Legal Scholarship Repository.

Skinner C. P. "Regulating Nonbanks: A Plan for SIFI Lite" (2017) *Geo. L. J.*, Vol. 105.

Skipper H. "Financial Services Integration Worldwide: Promises and Pitfalls" (2001) Insurance Regulation, Liberalisation and Financial Convergence, OECD.

Smethurst J. and Rudin S. "Confining Insurers to Insurance Business" (Lexology 2018).

Smith A. *An Enquiry into the Nature and Causes of the Wealth of Nations* (1982 [1776]).

Smithonian.com M. Jancer "How Eight Conglomerates Dominate Japanese Industry" (7 September 2016).

Snowden K. "Mortgage rates and American Capital Market Development in the Late Nineteenth Century" (1987) *Journal of Economic History*.

——— "Historical Returns and Security Market Development, 1872–1925 (1990) *Explorations in Economic* History, Vol. 27.

Sommer J. "Why Bail in? And How!" (2014) *Economic Policy Review*.

Spong K. and Robbins E. "Industrial Loan Companies: A Growing Industry Sparks a Public Policy Debate" (2007) Federal Reserve of Kansas City Economic Review, 41.

Sprague O.M. "Branch Banking in the United States" (1903) *The Quarterly Journal of Economics*, Vol. 17.

Spruill C. R., *Conglomerates and the Evolution of Capitalism* (Southern Illinois University Press 1982).

Sraffa P. "The Bank Crisis in Italy" (1922) *Economical Journal*, Vol. 32, No. 126.

Staikouras S. "Business Opportunities and Market Realities in Financial Conglomerates" (2006) The Geneva Papers, 31.

Standard Chartered Annual Report and Account 2023.

Steinherr A. and Huveneers C. "On the performance of differently regulated financial institutions: Some empirical evidence" (1994) Journal of Banking and Finance 18.

Stiroh K. J. and Rumble A. "The Dark Side of Diversification: The Case of US Financial Holding Companies" (2006) *Journal of Banking & Finance*, Vol. 30, No. 8.

Stone T. "The Past, Present and Future of the ILC Bank (2019) De Banked.

Story J. "Finanzplatz deutschland: National or European response to internationalisation?" (1996) German Politics, 5:3.

Stritzel S., The Riegle-Neal Interstate Banking and Branching Efficiency Act of 1994: Progress Toward a New Era in Financial Services Regulation" (1995) *Syracuse Law Review*, Vol. 46.

Suetorsak R. "Keiretsu and Risk: An Examination of the Risk Exposure of Keiretsu Banks in Japan" (2007) *J. Econ. Finan.*

Summers B. "Clearing and Payments Systems: The Role of the Central Bank"(1991) Federal Reserve Bulletin.

Sylla R. "Federal Policy, Banking Market Structure, and Capital Mobilization in the United States, 1863–1913" (1969) Journal of Economic History 29.

Sylla R. "US Securities Markets and the Banking System, 1790–1840" (1998) Federal Reserve Bank of Saint Louis.

Symons E. Jr. and White J. *Banking Law: Teaching Materials* (West Group 1991).

Talbourdet P., Gumpelson J. and Brocas D. Maffei "Restructuring and Insolvency in France: Overview" (Thomsen Reuters 2018).

Tart C. "Expansion of the Banking Industry Under the Riegle-Neal Interstate Banking and Branching Efficiency Act of 1994: Is the banking Industry Headed in the Right Direction?" (1995) *Wake Forest Law Review.*

Tarullo D. "Regulating Systemically Important Financial Firms" (Speech 3 June 2011).

——— "Toward Building a More effective Resolution Regime: Progress and Challenges" (18 October 2003).

Temin P. "The Economic Consequences of the Bank War" (1968) *Journal of Political Economy*, Vol. 76.

Temin P. and Voth H. J. *Prometheus Shackled: Goldsmith Banks and England's Financial Revolution After 1700* (OUP 2013).

Temin P. "Lessons for the Present from the Great Depression" (1976) The American Economic Review, Vol. 66, No. 2, Papers and Proceedings of the Eighty-eighth Annual Meeting of the American Economic Association.

Teunissen M. "Bancassurance: Tapping into the Banking Strength" (2008) The Geneva Papers 33.

The Bank of England's Approach to Resolution October 2017.

The Financial Crisis Inquiry Commission "The Financial Crisis Inquiry Report. Final Report of the National Commission on the Causes of the Financial and Economic Crisis in the United States" (2011) Official Government Edition.

The House of the Lords, European Union Committee "The Future of EU Financial Regulation and Supervision" (2008).

Theodore S. and Sondergaard T. "Total Loss-Absorption Capacity (TLAC): Does It Matter? (2014) Scope Bank Ratings.

Thomas M. "Allianz and Its Fateful Acquisition of Dresdner Bank" (2016) *Strategic Direction*, Vol. 32, No. 6.

Thompson J. H. "A Global Comparison of Insider Trading Regulations" (2013) International Journal of Accounting and Financial Reporting.

Thomson J. B. "On Systemically Important Institutions and Progressive Systemic Mitigation" (2009) *DePaul Business and Commercial Law Journal*, 135.

Tilly R. "German Banking, 1850–1914: Development Assistance for the Strong" (1986) *The Journal of European Economic History*.

———. "Universal Banking in Historical Perspective" (Mohr Siebeck, 1998) *Journal of Institutional and Theoretical Economics*, Vol. 154, No.1.

Tobin J. "On the Efficiency of the Financial System" (1984) *Lloyds Bank Review*, 153.

Tombini A. "Universal Banking: The View of Brazil" (2012) *The Quarterly Review of Economics and Finance*, 52.

Trainar P. "La Bancassurance: Generalization ou déclin du modèle? (2008) Revue déconomie financière.

Trichet J.C. "Financial Stability and Insurance Sector" (2010) Geneva Papers on Risk and Insurance-Issues and Practice, 30.

Tschoegl A. and Guillen M. F. *Building a Global Bank: The Transformation of Banco Santander* (Princeton University Press 2008).

Tucker P. "Solving Too Big to Fail-Where Do Things Stand on Resolution? Speech at the Institute of International Finance (October 2013).

U.S. Dept. of Justice, Competition and Monopoly: "Single-Firm Conduct Under Section 2 of the Sherman Act" (2008).

UK Parliament "Supplementary Written Evidence Submitted by Santander" (2011) Santander's Response to the Treasury Select Committee's Request for Supplementary Evidence on the Santander Group's Subsidiary's Structure.

US Department of the Treasury "Blueprint for a Modernized Financial Regulatory Structure" (2008).

——— "Modernizing the Financial System. Recommendations of safer, more competitive banks" (1991).

US SEC, Office of the Inspector General, Office of Audits "SEC's Oversight of Bear Stearns and Related Entities: The Consolidated Supervised Entity Program" (2008) Report No. 446-A.

Van Aaken A. "Prudence or Discrimination? Emergency Measures, the Global Financial Crisis and International Economic Law" (2009) *J. Int. Economic Law*.

Van den Berghe L. *Financial Conglomeartes. New Rules for New Players?* (Klewer Academic Publishers 1995).

Van den Berghe L. and and Verweire K. "Convergence in the Financial Services Industry" (2001) *The Geneva Papers on Risk and Insurance*, Vol. 26 No. 2.

Vander Vennet R. "Cost Efficiency of Financial Conglomerates and Universal Banks in Europe". (2002) *Journal of Money, Credit and Banking*. Vol. 34, No. 1.

Verdier D. "Explaining Cross-National Variations in Universal Banking in Nineteenth-Century Europe, North America and Australasia" in D. Forsyth and D. Verdier *The Origins of National Financial Systems: Alexander Gerschenkron Reconsidered* (Routledge 2002).

Verdier D. *Moving Money: Banking and Finance in the industrialized World* (CUP 2003).

Verweire K. and Van den Berghe L. *Creating the Future with All Finance and Financial Conglomeartes* (Klewer Academics Publishers 1998).

Vir Bhatia A. "Consolidated Regulation and Supervision in the United States" (2011) IMF Working Paper Monetary and Capital Markets Department Strategy, Policy, and Review Department.

Vitols S. "Changes in Germany's Bank-Based Financial System: A Varieties of Capitalism Perspective" (2004) WZB Discussion Paper, No. SP II-03.

Vitzthum C. and C. Rhoads "Hispanoamericano, Banco Santander Agree to Merge in $11.35 Billion Deal" *The Wall Street Journal*, (New York 18 January 1999).

Vives X. "Competition and Stability in Banking" (2010) IESE Business School, University of Navarre, Working Paper WP 852.

Von Beescwitz B. and Foos D. "Banks' Equity Stakes and Lending: Evidence from a Tax Reform" (2018) Discussion Paper Deutsche Bundesbank No. 06.

W. Sombart *Volkswirtschaft im neunzehnten Jahrhundert* (Georg Bondi 1909).

Waldman A.R. "OTC Derivatives and Systemic Risk; Innovative Finance or the Dance into the Abyss? (1994) *American Law Review*, Vol. 42, 1023.

Walker G. "The Law of Financial Conglomeartes: The Next Generation" (1996) *Int'l L.*, Vol. 57, 96.

Wallis J., Sylla R. and Legler J. "The Interaction of Taxation and Regulation in Nineteenth-Century U.S. Banking" in C. Goldin and G. Libecap *The Regulated Economy: A Historical Approach to Political economy* (University of Chicago Press 2001).

Walter I. "Universal Banking: A Shareholder Value Perspective" (1997) *European Management Journal*, Vol. 15, No. 4.

——— Universal Banking: A Shareholder Value Perspective" (1996) New York University Stern School of Business, Working Paper Series.

Walter J. "Not Your Father's Credit" (2006) Federal Reserve Bank of Richmond Economic Quarterly 92/4.

Wan J. "Systemically Important Asset Managers: perspectives on Dodd-Frank's Systemic Designation Mechanism" (2016) *Columbia Law Review*, Vol. 116, No. 3.

Ward A. and Mckillop D. "An Investigation into the Link Between UK Credit Union: Characteristics, Location and Their Success" (2005) *Annals of Public and Cooperative Economics*, Vol. 76, No. 3.

Ward A. and Mckillop D. and Willson J. "The Development of Credit Unions and Their Role in Tackling Financial Exclusion" *Public Money & Management* (2007) Vol. 27, No. 1, 2.

Waters D. "Financial Stability and Regulated Funds" (2014) ICI Global.

Weschler H. "The Political Safeguards of Federalism: The Role of the States in the Composition and Selection of the National Government" (1954) *Columbia Law Review*, 54.

West M. "The FDIC's Supervision of Industrial Loan Companies: A Historical Perspective" (Supervisory Insights 2004).

Wettereau J. "The Branches of the First Bank of the United States" (1942) *The Journal of Economic History*, Vol. 2, Supplement: The Tasks of Economic History.

White B. and Dash E. "Barclays Reaches $1.75 Billion Deal for a Lehman Unit" *New York Times* (New York 17 September 2008).

White E. "A Reinterpretation of the Banking Crisis of 1930" (1984) *The Journal of Economic History*, Vol. 44, No. 1.

——— "Voting for Costly Regulation: Evidence from Banking Referenda in Illinois, 1924" (1985) *Southern Economic Journal*, Vol. 51, No. 4.

White M. *The Philosophy of American Revolution* (OUP 1978).

Wilcox J. and Dopico L. "Credit Union Mergers: Efficiencies and Benefits" (FRBSF Economic Letter 2011).

Williams J. L. & Zesch S. *Savings Institutions: Mergers, Acquisitions and Conversions* (Law Journal Press ed. 2010).

Wilmarth A. "Controlling Systemic Risk in an Era of Financial Consolidation" in Current Developments in Monetary and Financial Law (2005) IMF, Vol. 3.

——— "The Dark Side of Universal Banking: Financial conglomerates and the Origins of the Subprime Financial Crisis" (2009) *Connecticut Law Review*.

——— "The Dodd Frank Act: A Flawed and Inadequate Response to the Too-Big-to Fail Problem" (2011) *Or. L. Rev*, Vol. 89, 951.

——— *Taming the Megabanks: Why we need a New Glass-Stegal Act* (OUP 2020).

Wiltse C. *The Jeffersonian Tradition in American Democracy* (1960).

Winkler A. "Primer: FSOC's SIFI Designation Process for Nonbank Financial Companies" (2014) AAF.

Wojcik K. P. "Bail-in in the Banking Union" (2016) *Common Market Law Review*, Vol. 53, No. 1.

Wymerersch E. "Financial Institutions as Members of Company Groups in the Law of the European Union" (2001) *European Business Organization Law Review*.

Xie L. "Universal Banking, Conflicts of Interest and Firm Growth" (2007) *Journal of Financial Services Research*.

Yellen J. "Hearing Before the Committee on Banking, Housing, and Urban Affairs, United States Senate, One Hundred Thirteenth Congress, First Session on Nomination of Janet L. Yellen, of California, to Be Chairman of the Board of Governors of the Federal Reserve November 14, 2013" (2013).

Yin R. *Case Study Research. Design and Methods*, Fifth Edition (Sage Publications 2013).

Yokoi-Arai M. "GATS's Prudential Carve Out in Financial Services and Its Relation with Prudential Regulation" (2008) *The International and Comparative Law Quarterly*, Vol 57, No. 3.

Yonnet F. "Claude-Henri de Saint Simon, L'Industrialisme et les banquiers" (2004) Cahiers d' économie Politique.

Z/Yen Group "The Global Financial Services Index" (Corporation of London 2018).

Zarutskie R. "Evidence on the Effects of Bank Competition on Firm Borrowing and Investment" (2006) *Journal of Financial Economics*, Vol. 81, No. 3.

Zavodnyik P. *The Rise of Federal Colossus: The Growth of Federal Power from Lincoln to F.D.R* (Praeger Series on American Political Cultures 1st Edition 2011).

Zavvos G. S. "Banking Integration and 1992: Legal Issues and Policy Implications" (1990) *Harv. Int'l. L. J.*, Vol. 31, 463.

Index

M. J. Sheppard Gelsi, *Corporate Structure and Banking Resolution*, Palgrave Macmillan Studies in Banking and Financial Institutions, https://doi.org/10.1007/978-3-031-59948-4

D

G

V

W

Z

SPRINGER NATURE

GPSR Compliance

The European Union's (EU) General Product Safety Regulation (GPSR) is a set of rules that requires consumer products to be safe and our obligations to ensure this.

If you have any concerns about our products, you can contact us on ProductSafety@springernature.com

In case Publisher is established outside the EU, the EU authorized representative is:

Springer Nature Customer Service Center GmbH
Europaplatz 3
69115 Heidelberg, Germany

The manufacturer's authorised representative in the EU is Springer Nature Customer Service Centre GmbH, Europaplatz 3, 69115 Heidelberg, Germany. If you have any concerns regarding our products, please contact ProductSafety@springernature.com

Printed and bound by CPI Group (UK) Ltd, Croydon, CR0 4YY

28/09/2026

02224060-0008